COMMENTARY ON THE DOCUMENTS OF VATICAN II

COMMENTARY
ON THE DOCUMENTS OF VATICAN II

GENERAL EDITOR:

Herbert Vorgrimler

EDITORIAL COMMITTEE:

Heinrich Suso Brechter
Bernhard Häring
Josef Höfer
Hubert Jedin
Josef Andreas Jungmann
Klaus Mörsdorf
Karl Rahner
Joseph Ratzinger
Karlheinz Schmidthüs
Johannes Wagner

COMMENTARY
ON THE DOCUMENTS
OF
VATICAN II

Volume IV

DECLARATION ON CHRISTIAN EDUCATION
DECLARATION ON RELIGIOUS FREEDOM
DECREE ON THE CHURCH'S MISSIONARY ACTIVITY
DECREE ON THE MINISTRY AND LIFE OF PRIESTS

BURNS & OATES/HERDER AND HERDER

1969
HERDER AND HERDER NEW YORK
232 Madison Avenue, New York, N. Y. 10016

BURNS & OATES LIMITED
25 Ashley Place, London S. W. 1

Original Edition:
"Das Zweite Vatikanische Konzil, Dokumente und Kommentare",
Herder, Freiburg, Part II, 1967 (pp. 357—404 and 703—748), and Part III, 1968 (pp. 9—239)

Translated by
Hilda Graef, W. J. O'Hara and Ronald Walls

Nihil Obstat: John M. T. Barton, S. T. D., L. S. S., Censor
Imprimatur: † Patrick Casey, Vic. Gen.
Westminster, 15th January 1969

First published in West Germany, © 1969, Herder KG
Printed in West Germany by Herder
SBN: 223 29431 4

CONTENTS

Abbreviations VII

Declaration on Christian Education
  by Johannes Pohlschneider 1

Declaration on Religious Freedom
  by Pietro Pavan 49

Decree on the Church's Missionary Activity
  by Suso Brechter 87

Decree on the Ministry and Life of Priests
  History of the Decree by Joseph Lécuyer 183
  Commentary on the Decree by Friedrich Wulf, Paul-J. Cordes and
  Michael Schmaus 210

Subject Index 299

Index of Names 303

PUBLISHER'S NOTE

The publishers have not given the text of the Council documents in this book, as separate text editions, both in Latin and English, are easily available. All quotations from the English translation of the Council texts in this volume have been taken from *The Documents of Vatican II* (Walter M. Abbott, S. J., General Editor; Joseph Gallagher, Translation Editor), © America Press, published in New York, 1966, by Guild Press, Herder and Herder, and Association Press, and in London, 1966, by Geoffrey Chapman Ltd. Grateful acknowledgment is made herewith for permission to quote from these texts.

ABBREVIATIONS

AAS	*Acta Apostolicae Sedis*
AKK	*Archiv für Katholisches Kirchenrecht*
CIC	*Codex Iuris Canonici*
D	H. Denzinger, *Enchiridion Symbolorum* (32nd edition, 1963)
DC	*Documentation Catholique*
GL	*Geist und Leben*
HK	*Herder-Korrespondenz*
HTG	H. Fries, ed., *Handbuch theologischer Grundbegriffe,* 2 vols. (1962—63)
LTK	J. Höfer and Karl Rahner, eds., *Lexikon für Theologie und Kirche,* 10 vols. and an index vol. (2nd edition, 1957—67)
MTZ	*Münchner Theologische Zeitschrift*
NRT	*Nouvelle Revue Théologique*
NZM	*Neue Zeitschrift für Missionswissenschaft*
PG	J.-P. Migne, ed., *Patrologia Graeca,* 161 vols. (1857—66)
PL	J.-P. Migne, ed., *Patrologia Latina,* 217 vols. and 4 index vols. (1878—90)
TWNT	G. Kittel, ed., *Theologisches Wörterbuch zum Neuen Testament,* continued by G. Friedrich (1933 ff.); E. T.: *Theological Dictionary of the New Testament* (1964 ff.)
ZKT	*Zeitschrift für Katholische Theologie*
ZMR	*Zeitschrift für Missionswissenschaft und Religionswissenschaft*

Declaration on Christian Education

by
Johannes Pohlschneider

in collaboration with

Jules Victor Daem, Marie van Waeyenbergh, Paolo Dezza, Augustin Mayer, Josef Auda, Josef Dreissen, Franz Heckenbach, Elisabeth Mleinek, Franz Pöggeler, Heribert Schauf, Heinrich Selhorst *

Introduction

I. HISTORY OF THE DECLARATION

In the fascicle containing the questions presented on 2 July 1960 by Pope John XXIII to the commission entrusted with preparing the Second Vatican Council ("Quaestiones Commissionibus Praeparatoriis Concilii Oecumenici Vaticani II positae"[1]), in the material apportioned to the commission "De studiis et seminariis" ("Concerning studies and seminaries") we find a special chapter devoted to "De scholis catholicis" ("On Catholic schools"). This topic was to be treated *ex integro,* that is, in its totality, in respect of the rights of the Church and of parents, and also in respect of the duty of the State to support these schools financially.

It is not difficult to find the motive for including the topic of Catholic schools in the programme of the Council in the letters which bishops and heads of religious orders had sent to the Pope after they had been invited to inform him of the topics they wanted to see on the agenda of the Council. The *Acta et Documenta Concilio Vaticano II apparando* (Series I, Appendix, vol. II, part II, pp. 508–19) shows how many bishops had requested a discussion of

---

* *Translated by Ronald Walls*
[1] This fascicle and all other documents have appeared in the *Typis Polyglottis Vaticanis* of the Vatican Press. The references in this essay are to these publications — unless otherwise stated.

1

these problems. This interest was stimulated, no doubt, by the threat to Catholic schools in many countries from State monopoly of education, from which results a lack of financial support for Catholic schools, so that, because of the large fees, only the well-to-do are able to send their children to Catholic schools. In addition, concern has arisen over the mentality that has grown up even in fairly wide Catholic circles in recent decades, which doubts the apostolic value and hence the necessity or usefulness of Catholic schools.

There is yet another fact which throws light on the importance of this topic for the Council. As we know, Pius XI and Pius XII both thought about continuing the Vatican Council; and these two Popes even went so far as to produce preliminary catalogues of topics to be discussed in such an assembly. It has recently become known that both catalogues included the school question (cf. *La Civiltà Cattolica* III [1966], pp. 27 and 209).

A. The schemata *De scholis catholicis* ("On Catholic schools")

The Preparatory Commission on Studies and Seminaries, to which was entrusted the topic of Catholic schools, was composed of bishops, priests, religious and one layman. The president was Cardinal Joseph Pizzardo, the secretary Augustin Mayer, O.S.B., now Abbot of Metten and at that time rector of the St. Anselm's Benedictine philosophical and theological university in Rome. This commission concluded its work in March 1962 when it produced the first version of the schema for a constitution *De scholis catholicis*. This ran to 36 pages of text and notes, and was divided into a Preface and seven chapters: "General principles of education"; "The importance and requirements of a Catholic school"; "The rights of the family and the Church"; "The training, rights and duties of teachers"; "The necessity of preserving and developing the Catholic school"; "The means required to maintain Catholic schools"; "Central organization and co-operation". To the schema of the constitution on Catholic schools, two were added concerning decrees. The first was entitled: "De studiis academicis ab universitatibus tum catholicis tum ecclesiasticis provehendis" ("On academic studies at Catholic and Church universities"); and it contained two chapters: 1) "De universitatibus catholicis" — "On Catholic universities" (8 pages); and 2) "De studiorum ecclesiasticorum universitatibus" — "On universities for ecclesiastical studies" (24 pages). The second schema was entitled: "De obsequio erga Ecclesiae Magisterium in tradendis disciplinis sacris" ("On obedience to the magisterium of the Church in respect of theological science"), and it contained three chapters: 1) "Notiones fundamentales" — "General principles" (12 pages); 2) "De ratione docendi sacram scripturam" — "On the manner of teaching holy Scripture" (12 pages); 3) "De doctrina S. Thomae servanda" — "On preserving the doctrine of St. Thomas" (20 pages).

On 12 and 13 June 1962 the Central Commission examined the schema put before them and passed on their comments to the Commission for Studies and Seminaries. On 7 July 1962 the secretariat of the commission responded by producing an improved text which incorporated many of the comments made. This revision principally concerned the Preface and the arguments about the duties and rights of teachers and those concerning the freedom of schools. The central sub-commission "De schematibus emendandis" ("On improving the schemata") informed the Commission for Studies and Seminaries that the second version of the schema was approved as a constitution "De scholis catholicis". To this were added the two decrees we have mentioned, dealing with academic studies, and the obedience due to the Church's magisterium in respect of theological disciplines. The report of the approval expressed by the sub-commission to the Preparatory Commission was conveyed on 15 December 1962 to the Conciliar Commission, which meantime had been formed to supersede the Preparatory Commission. We will speak about this new commission shortly. The schema itself is to be found in the collection *Schemata Constitutionum et Decretorum ex quibus argumenta in Concilio disceptanda eligentur,* series IV (1963), pp. 279–343, comprising three parts: I) "De scholis catholicis" ("On Catholic schools"); II) "De studiis academicis" ("On academic studies"); III) "De obsequio erga Ecclesiae Magisterium in tradendis disciplinis sacris" ("On obedience to the magisterium of the Church in respect of theological disciplines").

This second version of the schema of the constitution *"De scholis catholicis"* was placed before the Conciliar Commission "De seminariis, de studiis et de educatione catholica" ("On seminaries, studies and Catholic education"), which had been constituted after the opening of the Council, and had superseded the Preparatory Commission. Both the president and the secretary were transferred to the new commission, as were several collaborators and experts from the Preparatory Commission. As early as their session on 3 December 1962, the commission was unanimous in suggesting that the third part of the schema — that concerning obedience due to the magisterium — would be better worked into a dogmatic constitution. They had in mind either the *De Ecclesia* or the *De fontibus revelationis* (as this schema was still entitled at that time). In the sessions which followed the commission examined the first two parts of the schema and revised them along the lines laid down by a Co-ordinating Commission in a letter dated 30 January 1963. Thus it came about that the third part of the schema was dropped and the first two became more closely knit and were shortened by a concentration on fundamental principles and on pastoral norms. The rest was left to post-conciliar instructions and the projected revision of the Code of Canon Law.

3

On 2 March 1963 the Conciliar Commission finished the third draft of the schema *De scholis catholicis,* and this version was examined on 25 March 1963 by the Co-ordinating Commission. As soon as the comments of this commission were made, work on a fourth draft was begun, the result being a few alterations in the Preface, and further abbreviations in some paragraphs. On the instructions of Pope John XXIII, this fourth draft, contained in a 32-page booklet, dated 22 April 1963, was sent to all of the Council fathers. There were three parts in this schema: I) "De educatione" — "On education"; II) "De scholis catholicis in genere" — "On Catholic schools in general"; III) "De universitatibus catholicis" — "On Catholic universities". To these three chapters were attached three appendices containing particular topics to be dealt with in post-conciliar instructions or incorporated in the new legal code.

During the session of the Council in the autumn of 1963, the Conciliar Commission met to study the comments made by the Council fathers and by episcopal conferences. Thus emerged the fifth draft of the schema, which comprised a Preface and three sections: I) "De educatione"; II) "De scholis in genere" (1: "Fundamentalia de omnibus scholis principia" — "Fundamental principles for all schools"; 2: "Peculiares de scholis catholicis normae" — "Special norms governing Catholic schools"); III) "De universitatibus catholicis". Although the new version showed a notable improvement on the earlier drafts, it did not contain any significant changes, either in respect of structure or of content.

Scarcely was the new schema ready — it had not even been put before the Council fathers — when the Co-ordinating Commission, pressing at this particular stage of the Council, for a restriction of the material to be dealt with by the assembly of bishops, on 23 January 1964 asked the Conciliar Commission to reduce the schema *"De scholis catholicis"* to a simple *votum.* This *votum* was to underline the importance of education and of Catholic schools, to state the chief principles which must inspire education and culture, and herald worthy legislation within the framework of the coming revision of the Code of Canon Law.

In several sessions between 3 and 10 March, the commission turned its attention to the redaction of this *votum,* the Co-ordinating Commission meanwhile, however, intimating its hesitation, and drawing attention to the difficulties that had come to light. On 17 April 1964 the Co-ordinating Commission decided that instead of a *votum, propositiones* would simply be compiled, as had been done with some of the other *schemata.* These propositions were to contain the essential points upon which the Council fathers had to vote. All else was to be settled either in the revision of the Code of Canon Law, or become the subject-matter of special instructions on the part of the Holy See.

And so the Conciliar Commission set about dividing the material contained in the fifth draft into seventeen *Propositiones de scholis catholicis* ("Propositions concerning Catholic schools"). This resulted in the sixth draft of the schema. This sought to satisfy the demands of the Co-ordinating Commission, but clearly it did not correspond to the ideas of the Conciliar Commission itself. For this reason it appended a long explanatory note and the text of the fifth draft of the prepared schema to the *Schema propositionum de scholis catholicis*. The result was a 32-page booklet which was presented to the Council fathers in May 1964. The propositions, worked out in accordance with the instructions received, had not satisfied the members of the commission; now they failed to harmonize with the ideas and wishes of the Council fathers, many of whom complained that such an important schema, instead of being expanded, had been reduced to an inadequate form. Indeed, the Council fathers, and one episcopal conference especially, following the suggestion of an expert on the commission, demanded a radical alteration of the schema. This was produced during the third session of the Council.

B. From *De scholis catholicis* to *De educatione christiana*

At the beginning of the third session of the Council in September 1964, the Conciliar Commission met to examine the comments of the Council fathers and the episcopal conferences. In view of the contradictory opinions being expressed, the proposal was put forward to transform the *Propositiones de scholis catholicis* into a *Declaratio de educatione christiana* ("Declaration on Christian Education"), which would be content to describe and stress the importance of education in its whole extent, and point out the many and difficult problems involved, while the proper treatment of the problem — now impossible in the Council itself — should be referred to a post-conciliar commission. This proposal was accepted, and in great haste a schema of the Declaration on Christian Education was prepared, discussed, accepted and presented to the Co-ordinating Commission in October. When this commission had approved the new version, it was circulated to the Council fathers to facilitate a discussion of the new draft during the third session of the Council. This was a seventh redaction of the schema dealing with topics concerning education and schools. It was printed and appeared in a 14-page booklet entitled: *Relatio super schema declarationis de educatione christiana (olim schema propositionum de scholis catholicis) Textus declarationis*. This time the schema had undergone radical alteration, as is evident from the new title. We shall now explain the reasons for this.

From the discussions of the commission and the comments of the fathers it became clear that the topic "De scholis catholicis" had been too narrowly conceived, and that the Council had to face the much wider problem: "De educatione christiana".

With the spread of education throughout the world, encouraged by all governments and by great international organizations, notably by UNESCO, the number of schools of every sort is increasing everywhere. Even so, these schools are still not enough to cope with the ever-increasing number of pupils. It should be noted that the number of pupils has greatly increased during these years, not simply in proportion to the growth rate of the population, but also as a result of the ever-increasing percentage of children who attend school. The number of these children has begun to grow, partly as a result of the campaign against illiteracy, but also because of the raising of the compulsory school-leaving age, which in many places takes children well beyond the primary school, extending the period of education to ensure that the young receive a more complete technical and occupational training.

The Church can but rejoice at this progressive reduction of ignorance and the wider dissemination of culture. At the same time she is aware that in many regions the multiplication of schools in general is not matched by an equivalent increase in the number of Catholic schools, which are often staffed and supported by priests and by religious, both men and women. Indeed, Catholic schools, instead of increasing, are showing a numerical decline in several countries. Thus, many Catholic pupils are being compelled, in increasing numbers, to attend non-Catholic schools. The number of such pupils is increasing more and more even in those countries — like the U.S.A., for example — where Catholics had made amazing sacrifices to enable all Catholic children to attend Catholic schools. Today this is impossible, at least in the many countries where Catholic schools are not assisted by the State — as they are in Holland, and in many States of West Germany, where Catholic schools are in fact State schools. The Church, assembled in the Council, could not ignore the situation as it is in most countries. Thus the Council fathers could not rest content to deal only with Catholic schools and forget all about those children (the majority in most countries) who cannot attend a Catholic school. And so the picture had to include all schools.

There is another aspect which must not be ignored either, for it is no less important for our problem. There can be no doubt that even today the school is still a most important instrument in the education of youth. On the other hand, it cannot be denied that its importance is waning, in consequence of the rising influence of other educational forces outside the school — e.g. the social means of communication and various youth organizations. Whereas formerly the child spent a great part of his life with his family or in school, where it spent much of its free time as well as the periods of instruction, today this is not so to the same degree. Holidays are now longer, and holiday travel is much easier in this age of tourism. The impressions gained by children through these things profoundly affect their education. Even during the school session the child of today spends much of his time outside school. In addition, the child's education is being moulded all the time by his exposure to the influence of sport, glossy magazines, films and television. Anyone who wants to form youth according to the spirit of Christianity has to devote interest and attention not only to the school, but also to all of these other factors affecting education.

For these reasons the Conciliar Commission found itself facing a much wider problem, whereas the Co-ordinating Commission kept on pressing for a more restricted approach. The only possible solution was to limit the aim to the production of a simple declaration which, while foregoing a worthy treatment of this far-reaching topic, would show that the Council was aware of the importance and seriousness of the problem, and would solemnly explain its significance, referring the exhaustive treatment of the subject, which had proved too vast for treatment within the Council, to a post-conciliar commission.

On 17 November 1964 the *relator*, Mgr. Jules Daem, Bishop of Antwerp, presented the Declaration to the Council, and discussion began. On account of lack of time this was limited to two days. On 19 November it was over. Twenty-one of the Council fathers had an opportunity of making verbal intervention. Then the motion to end the debate was put and carried by the plenary session. Thus 13 speakers who had given notice of their intention to speak were prevented from doing so. They sent in their comments in writing, and in the course of the following months other Council fathers and episcopal conferences sent in contributions also. As well as those who approved the substance of the schema there were others, who disliked both the alteration of the title and also the new structure of the schema. They were worried about Catholic schools which they saw being threatened or neglected in many parts of the world, and were afraid that the new text would precipitate even greater difficulties. Others complained of the brevity with which such important issues had been handled.

At the conclusion of the discussion the *relator* observed that the Declaration was in no way intended to minimize the importance of Catholic schools. It had been necessary, however, to look beyond this particular topic; moreover, a post-conciliar commission would properly examine this topic from every angle, enlisting the collaboration of lay men and women possessing wide experience of school and educational systems. Meanwhile, the Conciliar Commission was to explain, revise and improve the text, taking account of the numerous comments, if the Council approved of the substance of the text. In the 26th general congregation, on 19 November 1964, an overwhelming majority of the Council fathers voted for the acceptance of the text. These were the results of the voting:

a. The schema in general

Votes cast:	1879
Placet	1457
Non placet	419
Invalid	3

b. Preface and sections 1–3

Votes cast:	1891
Placet	1592
Non placet	157
Placet juxta modum	140
Invalid	2

c. Sections 4–6

Votes cast:	1906
Placet	1465
Non placet	159
Placet juxta modum	280
Invalid	2

d. Sections 7–8

Votes cast:	1891
Placet	1592
Non placet	155
Placet juxta modum	141
Invalid	3

e. Sections 9–11 and Conclusion

Votes cast:	1873
Placet	1588
Non placet	173
Placet juxta modum	110
Invalid	2

Following this universal approval the Conciliar Commission reassembled at the end of April 1965 to examine carefully the numerous suggestions for improvement, in order that the most perfect text be produced — one that would be best adapted to the needs of our times. The result was the eighth redaction of the schema, contained in a 54-page booklet, and circulated to the Council fathers on 6 October 1965. It contained the *Textus emendatus et modi (emended text with proposed alterations) a Patribus Conciliaribus propositi, a Commissione de seminariis, de studiis et de educatione catholica examinati;* in addition it contained the *Quaesita,* and six particular questions and one general question, for the Council fathers to settle.

Although in lay-out and substance the new schema did not depart from its predecessors, it had been considerably expanded. Indeed, it was twice as large, and had been improved and completed in many points. The fact that the schema had undergone a notable change — not in substance but in form — provoked a group of bishops who were opponents of the Declaration to press for a fresh discussion of the schema in the Council hall; they wanted at least to have the opportunity of approving with *juxta modum.* The moderators would not concede to this request, for they did not want the precise work-schedule of the Council to be held up. Finally, the *relator* appointed 13 October 1965 as the date when a definitive vote would be taken on the text. On 12 October, however, it was announced that the vote would be still further subdivided. A leaflet was circulated with a list of 13 questions in place of the 6 particular questions and one general question, which the commission had proposed. The fathers were now asked to vote on these 13. On 13 October the *relator,* Bishop Daem, officially presented the schema in its new, improved text, with the *expensio modorum,* and on 13 and 14 October the voting took place. Despite a final attempt by a few of the Council fathers to destroy the Declaration by circulating several hundred copies of an appeal to vote against it, opinion was very much in favour of the Declaration, so that it became possible to put the Declaration as a whole to the definitive vote of the general congregation. Of the total 2096 votes cast, 1912 of the Council fathers voted *Placet,* 183 *non placet,* and one vote was spoiled. In the seventh public session of the Council on 28 October 1965, of the 2325 Council fathers, 2290 voted *placet* and 35 *non placet.* Thereupon the Declaration on Christian Education was solemnly promulgated by the Pope.

II. THE CONTENTS OF THE DECLARATION

The Declaration comprises an Introduction, twelve articles (1–4 on education; 5–7 on schools; 8–9 on Catholic schools; 10–11 on faculties and universities; 12 on co-operation) and a Conclusion.

The Introduction states the reality and importance of the problem of education in the world, and stresses the deep involvement of the Church in the solution of this problem. The principles enumerated in the "Declaration" are to be deepened and elaborated after the Council by a special commission, and adapted to the special needs of the various nations by the appropriate episcopal conferences.

§ 1 expounds the universal right to education. Total education includes moral and religious education; none may rob the young of this sacred right to a proper education.

§ 2 describes the nature of Christian education upon which all Christians have a claim and which elevates and perfects natural education, not merely for the benefit of the faithful, but for the benefit of the whole of society.

§ 3 describes the educators — parents, State, Church — and their duties and rights.

§ 4 indicates the various instruments of education used by the Church: those that are peculiar to the Church (catechesis, the liturgy, etc.); those that are universal (social means of communication, associations, etc.), and which the Church seeks to permeate with her spirit.

§ 5 stresses the importance of the school and distinguishes it from the other instruments of education. This illumines the importance of the vocation to teach.

§ 6 expounds the right of parents to choose a school for their children, and the duty of the State to provide the necessary means to guarantee the exercise of this right; any monopoly of schools is illegitimate.

§ 7 demonstrates the necessity of the Church to keep close to youth who attend schools of the most diverse kinds: through the testimony of her teaching, the apostolic activity of co-pupils, through the ministry of those who preach the gospel of salvation.

§ 8 confirms the right of the Church to establish and direct Catholic schools of every type and grade; the importance and characteristic marks of such schools are expounded. Of the teachers in such schools is demanded thorough preparation and genuine apostolic action; necessary likewise is the co-operation of parents.

§ 9 lists the various types of Catholic schools and reminds us of the necessity of encouraging above all the types demanded by modern conditions (e.g. occupational, technical, special schools, and academies).

§ 10 underlines the importance of Catholic faculties and universities which make real the public, perpetual and universal presence of Christian thought in advanced culture. Specially mentioned are the encouragement of Catholic universities or colleges, and the necessity of keeping in close touch with young Catholics who attend the other universities.

§ 11 emphasizes the special importance of theological faculties; then it stresses the necessity of a revision of canon law as it affects these faculties, so that these institutions can receive greater encouragement.

§ 12 stresses the necessity of closer collaboration between separate scholastic institutions (as between faculties in a university), and also between Catholic schools, likewise between Catholic and non-Catholic schools, to the advancement of the good of the whole of human society.

The Conclusion calls for generosity on the part of the young who want to take up the excellent task of education. There follow moving words of gratitude to all — priests, religious, and laity — who are at present engaged in this work, and finally words of encouragement to all who serve the work of pedagogy, to persevere in their chosen task and carry on with their important apostolic work.

III. THE DECLARATION AND THE OTHER COUNCIL DOCUMENTS

In the "Declaration" before us the Council explicitly deals with Christian education, stating principles and fundamental norms. But because there is a close relationship between the problem of education and various other sets of problems dealt with by the Council, it is obvious that we shall find the problem of education discussed in other Council documents as well. And so, anyone who wants to find out the complete view of Vatican II on the subject of education must not limit his attention to this one declaration. At this point we must, therefore, refer to those conciliar texts which complement the "Declaration".

In the Dogmatic Constitution on the Church, we find elements connected with Christian education, in the description of the Church as the mystical body of Christ (art. 7), in the exposition of the universality of the people of God (art. 13), in the treatment of the missionary character of the Church (art. 17), in the demonstration of the universal vocation to holiness (art. 46) and in the explanations about how to achieve this (art. 42).

In the Constitution on the Sacred Liturgy those norms which concern liturgical education and active participation in the liturgy (arts. 14–20) as well as those concerning musical and artistic training (art. 127) have a special value in respect of education.

The Decree on Ecumenism recommends getting to know each other (art. 9), a better ecumenical education (art. 10) and a proper exposition of the faith (art. 11). In addition this whole decree throws light on the importance of co-operation inspired by the ecumenical spirit, most of all where the problem of schools is concerned, and in the cause of the maintenance of public morality and, in particular, the protection of youth.

In the Declaration on Religious Freedom we find important elements with an educational aspect: the stressing of the rights of the individual and of the community in the religious sphere (art. 1), as well as arguments about the purpose and the basis of this freedom (art. 2) and about the Church's mission in the search for truth (art. 14).

In the Decree on the Church's Missionary Activity the Council specially insists on the education of the indigenous clergy (art. 16), of the catechists (art. 17) and of the Christian people in general (art. 18), while in its treatment of the co-operation of all in missionary activity it recommends the missionary education of all the members of the Church (arts. 35–41).

In a special way, in the Decree on the Apostolate of the Laity, besides various references scattered throughout the document, in Chapter VI, which treats of education for the apostolate (arts. 28–32), we find a short summary of the Christian theory of education. Its necessity, its principles and its criteria are demonstrated, and the specific instruments, which are of special importance in training for the apostolate, are enumerated.

The Decree on Priestly Formation, too, is important from the educational point of view, for although devoted primarily to those who desire to become priests, it contains norms and principles which are of interest throughout the whole field of education.

We ought to mention also the interesting pointers given in the Decree on the Appropriate Renewal of the Religious Life, where it discusses the education of religious (art. 18).

The Decree on the Instruments of Social Communication deals with media that are of vast importance in the education of youth as well as in the formation of the adult mind; and Christian education must pay heed to these things. We mention specially articles 15–16. These discuss the Christian-inspired formation of the minds of the experts whose work lies in the fields of the press, films, radio and television, and also the formation of the judgment of the consumers of all of these forms of journalism and entertainment.

Finally, the Pastoral Constitution on the Church in the Modern World demonstrates the importance of education in world responsibility and in human solidarity (art. 32). Here we find important norms of education within the family (arts. 48–50), of cultural education (art. 61), of education for the undertaking of various tasks in economic and social life (art. 66) and, finally, of international education aimed at the peaceful coexistence of nations (art. 89).

IV. TRENDS IN THE DECLARATION

If we compare the Declaration on Christian Education with earlier documents of the Church's magisterium, in particular with the encyclical *Divini illius Magistri* of Pius XI, dated 31 December 1929, two characteristic marks of the Declaration become obvious: continuity and progress.

Continuity is immediately established in the title itself. The Declaration deals with *Christian education,* and the encyclical with *the Christian education of the young* (*AAS* 22 [1930], p. 49). This fact must be stressed in order to exclude any interpretation which would suggest that the change from the title *De scholis catholicis* to that of *De educatione christiana* implied a departure from the fundamental principles of the encyclical. Any such assumption would be totally unjustified.

The close connection with the encyclical is further made plain by the renewed insistence on the rights and duties of parents, of the State and of the Church in respect of education. In particular, the right of parents freely to choose a school for their children is stressed, and from this is deduced the duty of the State to provide the necessary financial aid. Likewise the importance of Catholic schools is again stressed, whether these schools are controlled directly by the Church or by some other body able to ensure that a truly Catholic education is provided in these schools.

Finally, this continuity is established by the fact that, besides agreement in title, the encyclical *Divini illius Magistri* is quoted ten times in the notes to the Declaration.

Progress beyond the standpoint of the encyclical is obvious in the new attitude of openness to the world, which is characteristic of Vatican II. Begun by Pope John XXIII and continued by Pope Paul VI — especially in his encyclical *Ecclesiam Suam* — this openness has been solemnly proclaimed in several documents of Vatican II, principally in the Pastoral Constitution on the Church in the Modern World.

The Declaration reveals this openness first of all in its attitude to non-Catholic schools. While it reiterates the importance of Catholic schools, it turns its attention to non-Catholic schools also, not with suspicion, but with goodwill and an avowed readiness to co-operate, motivated by the desire to provide real service through the education of truly Christian teachers, through religious instruction and other pastoral efforts on behalf of pupils.

This openness is not restricted to the sphere of schools, but extends to all other instruments of education like, for example, the instruments of social communication, which, it is true, had not been overlooked by the encyclical *Divini illius Magistri* either. But these media are presented by the Declaration in a fresh way, just as they are when examined in their total extent in the Decree on the Instruments of Social Communication, to which the Declaration refers.

Finally, this openness of the Declaration becomes truly universal by facing every problem of human education, even when these are concerned with non-believers. The Church recognizes the enormous importance of education for the material and spiritual well-being of nations, and confirms her intention of helping all nations, especially those undergoing a process of evolution. She means to co-operate with every international organization which advances education in the world, and all the members of the people of God are invited and encouraged to join willingly in giving effective support to this aim.

Commentary

The Declaration on Christian Education begins with an Introduction, in which a few programmatic ideas are formulated. These are of fundamental importance to the understanding of the articles which follow. These ideas merit, therefore, thorough examination.

At the very start of the Introduction one such thesis is adumbrated. It affirms that the Council has thoroughly examined the decisive importance of education for the individual and for society. In the course of their labours the Conciliar Commission had become aware of this decisive importance of all that concerns education in the present day.[1] The first schema *De scholis catholicis* of 22 April 1963 contained, indeed, a section "De educatione"; but it was essentially restricted to education in schools. As time went by, the awareness grew that the whole complex of education today extends far beyond the sphere of the institutional school, and that it presents a many-sided problem. By reason of this awareness the seventh draft was entitled *De educatione christiana*. This alteration of the overall conception and of the title greatly enhanced the value of what the Declaration was saying. Now it possessed a leading thought, a *leitmotif*, which plainly gave first place to pedagogy in all forms of the imparting of knowledge. This perspective amounted to taking a stand in an age of widespread positivism in scientific outlook, in which learning, fact-finding and instruction are all too easily confused with the whole of human education.

Another significant thought is to be found in the notion of education in the service of society. In the very first sentence it speaks of the "ever-mounting influence (of education) on the social progress of this age". Appropriately this appeared in the first draft *De scholis catholicis* and is mentioned in nine out of the twelve articles of the Declaration. It may, therefore, be regarded as another fundamental idea of the Introduction.

---

[1] Cf. *Relatio super schema declarationis de educatione christiana* (1965), pp. 55 ff.

The formulation clearly shows what the Council thought about the relationship between education and social progress. Current tendencies aim at discovering the requirements of social progress through sociological categories and to make social progress the sole yard-stick of the educational system. In contrast, the phrase "the influence of education on the social progress of this age" moves in the opposite direction, and expresses an understanding of the priority of pedagogic and moral values over the "requirements" of society. By reason of this order of values, social phenomena are not the formative principles of education, but on the contrary, education and discipline are the principles governing the formation of social life. This does not prejudge the question of the legitimate significance of these things in the sphere of education.

This interpretation is supported by other passages in the Declaration dealing with social life, which see education and discipline as forces of social reform. The notion that education is a function of society is totally foreign to these passages. All the more vigorous, therefore, is the thought that education is the servant of the true well-being and progress of society. They see education as God's call, addressed to the pedagogic and creative urge in man, to build up religious and moral social structures, which alone make possible a responsible and free social life that is worthy of man.

Among the chief ideas of the Introduction must be included the allusion to "the circumstances of our times". This reappears repeatedly in the subsequent articles. In the Introduction it is expressed in the enumeration of various practical questions that are relevant to education today. The first part of the Introduction mentions the individual's change of attitude and his desire for education, the education of adults, *education permanente,* education and the division of social roles, education and democratization, educational opportunities through leisure and the technical means of communication, population development and educational economy, learning machines and the perfecting of methods, literacy and *education base* and, finally, the weightier pronouncements of international, political bodies concerning human rights in respect of education.

The notion of "the circumstances of our times" produced a series of particular topics, which first appeared in the eighth draft, the so-called *Textus emendatus,*[2] and which provide the Declaration with a valuable actualization and widening of horizon. But the first part of the Introduction also shows that the Council did not understand "the circumstances of our time" in the sense of a collection of facts relevant to education, from which guiding principles for the educational system could immediately be deduced. The idea of "the circumstances" has, however, another important leading

[2] *Schema declarationis de educatione christiana, Textus emendatus et modi* (1965), p. 55.

thought for consequence. This, too, emerges in the Introduction, and dictates the method of the following twelve articles. It expresses the intention to keep to basic statements. These "circumstances" provided the Council with some idea of the complexity of the problem of education today, and caused the fathers to reformulate the theme and redefine its limits. And so, the Council contented itself with affirming "certain basic principles", as the Introduction states in its second last sentence. Further elaboration was left to a post-conciliar commission, and adaptation to local conditions referred to regional episcopal conferences.

A special status among the "circumstances of our times" is given to the "public documents" declaring the "primary rights of men with respect to education, especially those of children and of parents", so that here, too, we may see a fundamental thought of the Declaration. By "public documents" the Declaration means the declaration of the United Nations of 10 December 1948 on human rights, and that of 20 November 1959 on the rights of children. The Council noted these declarations with a certain satisfaction, because they recognize those notions of natural law which are characteristic of Catholic educational theory,[3] and to which full appeal is made in Articles 1, 3 and 6. Standing upon the ground of natural law the Council felt itself to be an active collaborator in the activities of international educational organizations.[4]

In view of the overall intentions of the Council the question arises, however, whether the arguments from natural law in the Declaration do not have another aspect. Against the background of the theology of the Council, insofar as it becomes evident from the Pastoral Constitution on the Church in the Modern World, statements on education made from the standpoint of natural law take on a special character. In strong words, this theology stresses the obligation of Christians to take part in public life. The basis for this task is seen in the more general obligation to co-operate in perfecting the order of creation, of which the educational system is a part. In the process, in terms of this theology, the Church declares her solidarity, in a certain respect, with the world, and expresses her part in responsibility for its well-being.[5] Even in the text of a conciliar document, statements of natural law remain objectively and formally bound to the natural law that is founded upon the metaphysics of human nature. Nonetheless, within the framework of the ecclesiological view of creation proper to the theology of the Council, natural law is assumed into the enduring order that is

---

[3] *Gaudium et spes*, Articles 84, 85 and 89.
[4] Cf. the message of Pope Paul VI to the Secretary General of UNESCO, dated 26 August 1965.
[5] *Gaudium et spes*, Article 40.

characterized by the incarnation of Christ. Hence there must be an appropriate interpretation of the rights of parents and children in respect of education in terms of this larger context that emerges from the theology of the Council.

The last and central thought of the Introduction contains the notion of the Church's redemptive mission in the world of education. This thought plays a fundamental part in the whole Declaration, especially in Articles 2, 3, 4, 7 and 8. We may correctly describe it as the dominant *leitmotif* of the Declaration. It appears in the eighth draft, occasioned by the refashioning of the whole conception of the chema on education, in the so-called *Textus emendatus,* and, through the decisive theological viewpoint of responsibility for salvation, links the Declaration with the other conciliar documents. This dominant thought is based upon the affirmation that "in fulfilling the mandate she has received from her divine Founder to proclaim the mystery of salvation to all men, and to restore all things in Christ, Holy Mother the Church must be concerned with the whole of man's life..." The following part of the sentence proves that the Church does not conceive her mission as narrowly spiritual, but, as befits her essence, as an incarnational process. On this view all of the elements in the educational system are potential media of redemptive encounter. The Church emerged from the devine-human incarnational event of her Founder, Jesus Christ. In terms of this foundation she conceives herself as the embodiment in time and space of the redemptive will of God. Hence she is so closely bound up with the thought of the incarnation of the redemptive will of God that concern over palpable mediators might be regarded as *the* characteristic of her theology. The interdependence of nature and grace is the law of her thinking and the axiom of her action. Against the background of her incarnational self-exposition, the Church develops a sense for the redemptive potentialities in economic, social and cultural circumstances. In the language of the Council: "Holy Mother the Church must be concerned with the whole of man's life, even the earthly part of it insofar as that has a bearing on his heavenly calling. Therefore she has her role to play in the progress and spread of education." This concern arises from the incarnational understanding of the Church's redemptive mission. This ist the "cure of souls" in the original sense of a concern for the whole sphere of human life in the light of the coming kingdom of God. This, then, is the pastoral viewpoint, which dictated the treatment of the problems of education by the Council. It supplies a perspective that emerges directly from the essence and mandate of the Church. It is this perspective, more than the systematic treatment of particular points, which assures the Declaration of positive significance in the years to come.

Article 1. Because the Declaration recognizes the universal and unrestricted

right of men to education, and because it sees this right as founded upon the personal dignity of man, the Declaration is an outstanding testimony to human dignity in general. Through it the Church expresses her concern both for man's eternal end and also for his equipment for life in this world. Without becoming lost in details, the Declaration has some basic things to say about the harmony between natural realities and supernatural goals. With complete realism it desires to erect education upon an anthropological foundation, alluding as it does to the endowments of man, including among these his total psychological structure. This embraces a complete educational programme, for it has in mind the most advanced and specific education of the most highly gifted as well as the elevation of those who are physically and intellectually less well-endowed.

In the very first article the difference between the sexes is brought out as a principle of differentiation in education. The importance of this for the Church is seen again in a later passage (Article 8), where the independent education of the sexes is discussed in detail.[6]

There is a social aspect, too, in the basic notion of education. The Declaration, however, passes over the topic of man in his family, for this is to be discussed in detail in later articles (3, 5 and 6). In Article 1 it is more concerned with the social and cultural conditioning of man; every man grows up within a specific cultural environment, which he accepts. Cultural tradition is not seen, however, as a static entity, a cultural inheritance handed solidly down from the past, to which the individual must adapt himself, but as containing, rather, the highly dynamic capacity to co-operate, in the measure of his own potentialities, with his own historical progress. The fact that his "ancestral heritage" must not be understood as national cultural parochialism is proved by the following demand that "this education should pave the way to brotherly association with other peoples, so that genuine unity and peace on earth may be promoted".

The Declaration strongly insists that no man lives for himself alone, but must, by reason of his nature, fulfil a social function. This arises not simply from the exigencies of co-existence but, more deeply, from the obligations of social justice. This social function relates to his whole environment, close and remote, and even to the relationship between peoples and their peaceful co-operation.

By reason of its examination of the social and cultural function of man, the Declaration demands the utilization in education of the results of modern science, especially where these illumine the nature of man. Hence it expressly demands that Catholic pedagogy constantly strives for a scientific basis, and

---

[6] The encyclical *Divini illius Magistri;* Pohlschneider, "Bildungsprobleme auf dem Konzil" in *Katholische Frauenbildung* 67, no. 2 (1966), pp. 65—71.

19

thus assists the healthy development of the principles of Catholic educational theory, as well as their timely application to our own age.

It would seem to be important that in this context the Declaration grants considerable space in education to pedagogic, didactic and psychological knowledge. This applies to the intellectual and moral development of the young as well as to the properly phased, positive and prudent sex-education, which receives special mention. The demand, in the very first article, for pedagogically sound sex-education, is a clear indication that the Council desired to take account of the changed circumstances of life of children and youth, making use of proper pedagogical instruments. It is significant that sex-education is integrated into the sphere of pedagogic and psychological educational work.

In all of its arguments the second part of Article 1 turns a new light upon the sublime goal as well as the special tasks of education. Every word speaks for itself, and the whole passage makes clear how deep a concern the Church has for the education of the young, and how deeply involved the Church wants to be in the problems and tasks of education. This solicitude turns the conclusion into a fervent plea to all to make a reality of this right of men to a religiously based education.

Article 2 discusses the goal of Christian education. In the first draft *(Textus prior)* of the Declaration (1964), this theme had already appeared in the first article. The present final version, however, devotes the first article to the right of all men to a thorough education. In Article 2 the discussion of the goal of Christian education develops organically from the theme of Article 1. This change in arrangement is significant in that Christian education is set in a more organic context and approached from a more comprehensive angle.[7]

This article concludes by reminding the bishops of "their acutely serious duty to make every effort to see that all the faithful enjoy a Christian education of this sort, especially young people, who are the hope of the Church". In order to substantiate this exhortation, the article expands the biblical and theological arguments to cover the whole field of Christian education.

Examining the biblical-theological basis of Christian education we are struck by the absence in the Declaration, as in the encyclical *Divini illius Magistri* of Pope Pius XI (31 December 1929), of a definition of the concept of Christian education.[8] This expresses the intention of the Declaration to

[7] "Ampliore visione": the *relatio* of the *relator*, Bishop Daem of Antwerp.

[8] Hitherto the relevant literature has confined itself to definitions of the concept of education or of Christian education. Cf. K. Erlinghagen, *Grundlagen katholischer Erziehung. Die prinzipiellen Erziehungslehren der Enzyklika Pius' XI. "Divini illius Magistri"*, p. 29; O. Betz, "Erziehung" in *HTG*, I, pp. 319 ff.; G. Fischer in *LTK*, II, cols. 1136—9.

be descriptive rather than definitive. There is another comparison that is significant for our understanding of this second article. In the first draft of 1964 the goal of Christian education was defined as "the human and at the same time religious perfection of men". Our present text, like *Divini illius Magistri*, speaks more correctly of the true goal of Christian education and its constitutive elements. To obviate any misunderstanding which would fail to identify the religious with the Christian, the final text has explicitly chosen the word "Christian". This greater precision is exhibited in the reference to the right of the baptized to a Christian education, in place of the "perfectio humana simul et religiosa" of the original text. The context explains what this education means in the concrete. Similarly the emended text shows how a moralistic-humanist conception of Christian education has been replaced by an ontic-existential foundation of Christian education in the biblical-theological understanding of human nature.

Following the lines of this new foundation Article 2 establishes the right of all Christians to a Christian education. Consequently, the Declaration cites the sacrament of baptism as the appropriate foundation. The dedication of the baptized to God implies the right to an education in accordance with the redemptive will of God. On the other hand there is the corresponding duty of instructing the baptized in the whole breadth and depth of the reality of baptism and of leading him "to a personally perfected faith". [9]

A further goal of Christian education is said to be teaching the baptized to adore God. Those who have been reborn of the Spirit (Jn 3:3 ff.) and sanctified by the truth, i.e. by the word of God revealed in Jesus Christ, are destined "to adore God the Father in spirit and in truth". Sanctification in baptism is aimed at the participation of the baptized in the liturgy. Accordingly the function of Christian education is to prepare young Christians for participation in the celebration of the mysteries of salvation. [10]

Yet another aim of Christian education is described as the moral and religious formation of men "in righteousness and in the sanctity of truth". Through baptism the "old man" of sin has died and a new life in Christ has begun. In his new being "he ought now to step forth as the new man he is in Christ, he must become what he is". [11] With this statement of aims the Declaration proclaims Christian education as the self-realization of the "righteousness and holiness" that rests upon baptism, in the sense expressed in the Letter to the Ephesians.

In addition, Christian education should help the baptized to become more conscious of his *being in Christ*, so that the eschatological virtue of hope

[9] O. Betz, *loc. cit.*, II, p 629.
[10] "Constitution on the Sacred Liturgy", art. 10; cf. also "Constitution on the Church", art. 34.
[11] H. Schlier, *Der Brief an die Epheser*, p. 28.

becomes a reality (cf. 1 Pet 3:15). On the other hand, in the power of this hope the baptized ought to become able to contribute to the formation of this world according to a Christian pattern. The alteration of the *Textus prior* of 1964 reveals what is to be understood by this. In that text we find the phrase "consecratio mundi". On account of the controversy around this the concept was changed by one of the fathers to "christiana mundi conformatio".[12] This final formula expresses the idea that Christian education is aimed at hope, and presses towards the Christian formation of the world, thus possessing a certain ambivalence. It must make clear to the baptized that, on the one hand, he remains obligated to this world, as was the Son whom the Father sent into the world, while, on the other hand, he must draw the world into the transformation effected in baptism. This must be brought about by his walking in the steps of the Lord, imbuing all that is human with the life received in baptism, and seeing everything in the light of the coming of the Lord. The impulse towards this eschatological existence contains within itself the natural values that are to be integrated in the being of the redeemed man.

This integrating power of Christian education in association with the eschatological and Christian mastery of the world in the last analysis serves the well-being of the whole human family. The eschatological orientation of Christian education towards hope and with a view to building up the mystical body of Christ and of human society reminds us at once of the ideas underlying the "Constitution on the Church". The foundation of Christian education upon biblical theology explains the above-mentioned admonition of the Council to the bishops to pay great heed to Christian education. Article 2 is, moreover, of fundamental importance for the articles which follow, for these are intelligible only as logical developments from this article and when seen in their organic connection with it.

Article 3. This article is addressed to most important formative influences which, in virtue of their nature, have a duty to educate children, and which accordingly have the right to carry out the function of education. Legitimate educational agencies are: parents, the State and the Church. Their mutual relationship is one of co-ordination and collaboration. Parents come first in rank. Their right as educators is based upon the law of nature. Their partnership in the society of the Christian family has a special educational power, insofar as they live by the grace of the sacrament.

The educational power of parents and of the family rests upon the fact that the child spends the first years of his life within the family circle, and there receives a stamp that never leaves him all the rest of his life; there, too, he forms the foundation of his future social behaviour. Upon the

---

[12] Cf. *Modus 7* in *Textus emendatus*, p. 30.

parents' position and also upon the importance of education within the family the Declaration bases the right and the duty of parents to educate their children; they are also stewards of the child's own right to an education. This right of the child to education is related not merely to education in general, but to an education in harmony with his individuality, with his style and degree of talent. For this reason neither the parents nor the State nor any other legitimate educational agency may control the child as they please. In the exercise of their rights they are bound to consider the natural endowment of the child as well as his supernatural end.

The Declaration strongly stresses the educational right of parents, but it recognizes no less clearly the rights in this field of other agencies. These are based upon the fact that the parents transfer part of their obligations and rights to other educational institutions — the school and the State. This thought presents an essential insight in the Christian view of education. The genuine educational rights and functions of the State are here recognized, for in advancing the common good the State has a disciplinary function to perform. One of the tasks of the State is to protect the rights of the primary agents of education, to give them assistance, and to promote all of their initiatives. Here, however, the principle of subsidiarity must be respected; and this means that any monopoly of education is excluded. The State must take over educational functions which others cannot perform. The State's claims and measures must never be allowed to run counter to the educational rights of parents. The Declaration thus lays great weight upon concord between the rights of the parents on the one hand and the claims and policy of the State on the other.

In this article the Church expounds also her own educational rights, duties and task. This task she sees primarily as carrying out her redemptive work. We must stress specially that the Church sees her educational mandate in the light of the basic theological ideas of the other decrees; and her effort to make redemption a reality is directed not merely to her own members, but to the whole of society, to all mankind. At the end of the article the goal of the Church's educational effort is declared to be to make the world a more human place. This is an expression of the self-interpreting spirit of the Church of Vatican II.

Article 4 describes the appropriate instruments by which the Church seeks to accomplish, in the most complete way possible, the aims of Christian education (Article 2). The list includes only the most important instruments. First mentioned is catechetical instruction. This ought to present the doctrine of redemption, clarify it, expound it and, finally, put it into practice. Thus the depth and the riches of the mysteries of salvation will be unfolded and seen in their critical significance for the life of the individual Christian as for the community, and made to bear fruit.

The faith becomes embodied in the life of the growing Christian. Faith is the first element in salvation (Rom 10:9; Eph 2:8) and makes possible the new life in Christ as the realization of the truths of redemption. Accordingly, the aim of catechetical instruction is not just to produce faith in the sense of theological assent, but to produce a realization of truth in the sense of "making the Christian truths present as motive forces, as, indeed, the supreme motives of evaluation, of judgment and choice in every area of human life".[13] According to the Declaration the whole thing turns on imparting a grasp of the Christian mysteries of faith that will be "the soil for rich growth and the ripening of countless acts of faith which are, in the full sense, 'works of repentance', deeds arising from a constant turning towards Christ".[14] In this way life in the Spirit of Christ is nourished. Catechetical instruction reaches its climax in leading the baptized to "a knowing and active participation in the liturgical mystery" and in inspiring them to apostolic action. At this point the Declaration refers to the Constitution on the Sacred Liturgy (Article 14). Our most intense confrontation with redemptive reality comes in the celebration of the Christian mystery. Through the liturgical celebration the believer is put in a position where he can experience "the presence of the divine act of redemption under the veil of symbols",[15] and by faith appropriate for himself the redemptive work of Christ, progressively becoming more like Christ. By its own logic the liturgical celebration of the mystery overflows into apostolic action in everyday life. "The liturgy in its turn inspires the faithful to become 'of one heart in love' when they have tasted to their full of the paschal mysteries; it prays that 'they may grasp in deed what they hold by creed'. The renewal, in the Eucharist, of the covenant between the Lord and man draws the faithful into the compelling love of Christ and sets them afire."[16]

Article 4 mentions other instruments of Christian education "which contribute mightily to the refinement of spirit and the moulding of men". These are not part of the inner circle of Christian education, but are vital for the success of Christian education. Among these instruments the article strongly stresses the forces that mould public opinion. It is striking to see the media of social communication linked with catechetical instruction. Their mention in this context is a significant indication of the importance attached by the fathers to technical means of communication as instruments of Christian education.

The Declaration also mentions the many groups and associations devoted

[13] G. C. Negri, "Die Glaubenshaltung als Ziel der Katechese" in G. Stachel-Zeuner, ed., *Einübung des Glaubens. Klemens Tilmann zum 60. Geburtstag* (1965), p. 151.
[14] *Ibid.*
[15] T. Kampmann, *Jugendkunde und Jugendführung*, I, p. 232.
[16] Constitution on the Sacred Liturgy, art. 10.

to the intellectual and physical development of the young, but chiefly the schools. These last mentioned institutions give the cue for the next article. The Council fathers, with all their insight into the importance of scholastic education, saw quite clearly, however, that Christian education is given not only in school but in extra-scholastic institutions as well. This represents a realistic assessment of the modern educational situation, which has been described thus from the proper quarter: "A great part of life, including recreation, social activity, and sport, is carried on outside school, in various associations, in summer and winter camps, in reading newspapers, listening to records, at the films or watching television; and all the imagery to which people are subjected teaches them to think, feel and act according to the language of that imagery." [17]

This article reflects the image of modern society and draws the appropriate conclusions. All of the forces of education must be harnessed in the service of the goals of Christian education. This attitude represents a notable advance from the standpoint of earlier statements by the Church. For the first time things such as the media of social communication, associations for physical and intellectual development and youth groups are enlisted in the service of education. "It was precisely the recognition of the importance of these instruments which motivated the Council not to restrict their interest to schools, but to extend their view to the whole field of education." [18]

Article 5. Of all the educational agencies apart from the family, the school enjoys a special importance. The imparting of the treasures of education — the school's most obvious function — has, according to the Declaration, a most diverse and far-reaching effect. The Declaration sees great value in wide knowledge and a many-sided formal schooling, but first place is given to character formation. Hence the article demands proper co-ordination of comprehensive personal education with the ability to master life's practical problems, which involves preparation for an occupation and for life within society.

In what follows the article provides a guiding idea for the school problems of our times, by demanding that legitimate educational agencies should work together in mutual trust, within the school. Among the associations which ought to take part in an effort to advance the schools, there are, on the one hand, all those that work together in a particular school. On the other hand there are those social forces which have an interest based upon the nature and function of the school system as a whole. In this case co-

---

[17] P. Dezza, "L'Educazione cristiana nella Dichiarazione Conciliare" in *La Civiltà Cattolica* 117 (1966) I, p. 112.
[18] *Ibid.*

operation at some central point is envisaged, at the critical points, it might be, of legislation and administration. In substance all co-operation can relate to the organization of the school system or even to its inward structure. Thus, concern for education can in fact become a concern devoted to the whole human family, bringing, through an interplay of all the forces at work, encouragement and progress to the community.

In conclusion the article turns its attention to teachers, observing that they take up their task as helpers of the parents (see Article 8 for details) and representatives of human society in need of education.

The vocation of the teacher demands, according to the Declaration, not only intellectual gifts, but gifts of heart also — a special kind of sense of vocation, for to form human beings is a task that goes far beyond the scope of any other profession.

Close heed must therefore be paid to the training of teachers. The demand for a constant readiness for renewal and adaptation is one that merits much thought. This means first of all that the teacher, in imparting knowledge, must always be abreast of the newest advances in science, and, at a deeper level, that he must be aware of his own need of progressive religious self-formation.

Article 6. Once again the Declaration stresses the inalienable rights of parents in education, and does so in respect of one of the most important of all the questions touching practice. The Church emphatically demands that parents have a real and not just theoretical freedom to choose schools for their children. It is not enough to give official recognition to this right: the inclusion of this in the positive law of the State is a basic demand of democracy; there must be no practical administrative measures which make this right ineffective. Such undermining of the right occurs frequently, no doubt, as a result of the uneven distribution of State funds, and as a result of other deliberate measures which obstruct the free exercise of parental rights. The Declaration recommends alertness, therefore, to all regional dangers, and new methods, as they emerge, whereby opponents of the rights of parents seek to restrict these rights. Of the State the Church demands distributive justice and practical goodwill in the exposition and application of this right. Only so can freedom and the common good be simultaneously advanced.

In concise and telling remarks, the second part of the article sketches the extent of the State's concern for schools. This makes clear how great is the importance of schools and schooling for the State itself. But the school cannot be the sole normative force in the realm of schools and pedagogy. Above all it must protect the freedom of conscience of those entitled to education. And so reference is again made to the fact that the State ought to work according to the principle of subsidiarity. Consequently, there is an uncompromising rejection of any kind of State monopoly of schools. This holds good universally for all time. The school legislation of every State must be tested against this principle. This would show that in many States, which boast of democracy, there is in fact a school monopoly, not always extending to the entire system, but covering very large areas.

The confessional State schools that exist in some parts of Germany are to be found in scarcely any other country. For this reason no mention is made of them in the Declaration. This does not imply disapproval: on the contrary, the Council regarded it as self-evident that general Catholic principles of education apply to Catholic confessional schools administered by public officials (cf. Article 9). Concerning the ownership of schools in general, the Declaration enunciates no principles. It explicitly affirms, however, that the State may be an owner of schools (Article 3, section 2).

This article concludes by stressing the duty of all the faithful to take a deep personal interest in Catholic schools, to speak up for them and to advance their cause. This exhortation is addressed not only to experts and pedagogues, but to all the faithful. From this we are not to conclude that a general discussion by all is desired or the direct personal participation of all in the affairs of the schools is advocated. A means of mutual exchange and inward strength, as also of effective influence outside, would be a formation of associations. Such associations are commended to parents in particular, because it is they who most need information, a clear purpose and mutual support, to help them make the weighty decisions demanded from them.

Article 7 does not make any material statement on the "scholae non catholicae". In place of the critical reserve that characterized earlier ecclesiastical pronouncements, we find sympathetic solicitude.

The Council fathers were not only aware, in formulating this article, that all over the earth many Catholic children have to attend non-Catholic schools, but they wished also to make their pastoral care available to the teachers and pupils.

Although the primary support for Catholic pupils in non-Catholic schools is the doctrine of salvation, "doctrina salutis", the Church shoulders a heavy responsibility ("officium gravissimum") not merely in respect of religious, but also in respect of moral, education.[19] For both aspects of education the

---

[19] Can. 1113. "Parentes gravissima obligatione tenentur prolis educationem *tum religiosam et moralem*, tum physicam et civilem pro viribus curandi, et etiam temporali eorum bono providendi." M. Conte a Coronata (*Institutiones Iuris Canonici*, III: *De Sacramentis* [1948], pp. 842 f.) speaks of the "educatio religiosa et moralis": "a. Educatio *religiosa* ... b. Educatio *moralis* ..."; F. X. Wernz and P. Vidal (*Ius Canonicum*, V; *Ius Matrimoniale* [1946], pp. 762 f.) comments on the canon cited: "Circa animam. Parentes tenentur prolem educare educatione *civili, morali et religiosa* ... Quae educatio civilis debet esse coniuncta cum

"testimonium vitae" of the Catholic teacher in such schools is of utmost importance. The Church's claim to be competent to impart moral education in non-Catholic schools is to be distinguished from the view of many non-Catholic politicians and pedagogues, who concede no more than the Church's right to co-operate in religious education.

Moral education is not to be understood as something independent of, or antithetical to, the Christian faith. Just as the doctrina salutis embraces the whole of the faith and includes active Christian life, so moral education of a Christian kind must appear as an imparting of Christian doctrine, and, at the same time, be an introduction to Christian life, translating religious education in the narrower sense into practical life.

The Church's deep interest in non-Catholic schools is expressed in the deliberately superlative phrase "officium gravissimum".

The noun "help" and the verb "to help" dictate the tenor of the measures the Church proposes, in this article, to apply to Catholic pupils in non-Catholic schools. "Help" may be understood in a subsidiary sense: the supplementary support of what is supplied by the schools or the families by way of the education of children.

In all schools the "principia moralia et religiosa familiarum" ought to be the yard-stick of education that is given to Catholic children. In the Church's view the school ought to educate instructively and instruct educatively. (The first sentence of the article speaks not of "educantur" but of "instituuntur".)

Above all, Catholic children attending non-Catholic schools must receive personal and apostolic help from Catholic teachers and from their fellow-pupils, who are capable of giving that help.

This help must compensate for the absence of the institutional influence

educatione *morali et religiosa*, est enim educatio hominis moralitatis capacis nec separari proinde possunt evolutio et cultus intellectus et voluntatis; porro cuiuslibet moralis obligationis principium efficax et vindex Deus est, ideoque nulla voluntatis ad moralitatem informatio vera fieri potest, nisi habita ratione principiorum religiosorum elevato, petenda sunt ab unica vera religione revelata seu ab Ecclesia catholica." F. M. Cappello, *De Sacramentis*, V: *De Matrimonio* (1947), pp. 724 ff.: "Educatio alia est physica et civilis, alia *moralis et religiosa* ... Educatio spiritualis: Debit esse *moralis, religiosa*, catholica. *Moralis* quatenus adolescentes instituantur iuxta firmissima et sanctissima moralitatis principia, quae per naturalem legem innotescunt, quaeque bonum agere et malum devitare certo itinere praecipiunt. *Religiosa*, quatenus huismodi principia non aliunde desumantur firma cum certitudine atque inconcusso robore nisi ex religione. Sane educatio importat rectam institutionem voluntatis: iamvero forma rectitudinis est ipsa moralitas: ergo necessario requiritur puerorum educationem. *Moralitatis autem inhaeret, tamquam fundamento, religioni.* Sola enim religio docet quaenam sunt officia quibus homo adstringitur Deo, quomoda ipse ad Deum tamquam ad supremum finem naturae ordinatur, quomodo in Deo tantum perfecta undequaque habetur sanctio pro morali ordine servando, ita ut, Dei conceptu sublato *atque vinculo religioso remoto, vera moralitas neque dari neque concipi possit.*"

of the Church. This "actio apostolica" which the Church expects these "condiscipuli" to perform, is not regarded as a violation of the neutrality of the non-Catholic school.

The text leaves open the possibility of "auxilium spirituale" for Catholic children in such schools being provided either in these schools or elsewhere. The statement that this assistance may be provided by institutions which are able to take account of prevailing circumstances, may be interpreted as a sign of special adaptability and as the invitation to develop new forms.

The attendance of Catholic children at non-Catholic schools puts a burden upon parental responsibility in that care must be taken to ensure that the "formatio christiana" keeps pace with the "formatio profana". The separation of profane from Christian education, apparently unheard of in early ecclesiastical pronouncements, may yield good results in the future. It is not, however, to be interpreted as the Church giving up the attempt to permeate all departments of instruction and all forms of school life with the Christian spirit; it is, rather, a recognition of the autonomy of the separate departments of instruction.

The article does not imply the Church's approval of the lay or Christian community school. We cannot deduce from this article that the Church thinks the so-called "school of the Christian confessions" to be desirable.

The teacher must take up the task of *docere* as well as of *moderari*. In the context the latter phrase signifies that mere imparting of knowledge is not enough in Christian education. The teacher must be both educator and moulder of character. The phrase suggests that the teacher ought to impart knowledge and give direction, and also arouse and direct the pupil's own initiative.

In the concluding sentence the Council points out that the "auctoritates et societates civiles" must take the pluralism of modern society seriously, and hence create the preconditions for allowing the formation and education of children in all schools according to the moral and religious convictions of their parents.

Article 8. The *modi* of the fathers caused this article, "De scholis catholicis", to be expanded both in the *Textus emendatus* and in the final agreed version, to almost four times its original length in the *Textus prior*. Now it appears as the longest of all the articles. This fact indicates its importance. Most of the *modi* applied to this article. It is the heart of the Declaration. Because the precursors of the *Declaratio de educatione christiana*, i. e. the *Schema propositionum de scholis catholicis* (1964) and the *Schema constitutionis de scholis catholicis* (1963), had dealt in detail with the Catholic school, now that the theme had been changed to include the whole wide field of Christian education, a drastic curtailment of what had been said about Catholic schools was unacceptable. The fathers still regarded the topic of the Catholic school as important enough to merit essential expansion, and they made use of ideas which had already been put forward in the earlier drafts.

The name "schola catholica" was deliberately retained in spite of contrary proposals which would have preferred, in a decree on *Christian* education, to have spoken of the *Christian* school. Here, as in the title of the Declaration, the somewhat ambiguous word "Christian" is identical with the unambiguous word "Catholic". By "Catholic school" (also called "private school" or "independent school") the Council understood a school established and managed by the institutional Church (diocese, parish, religious congregation, etc.) and also, quite generally, a school run according to the Catholic faith.

In non-Christian missionary countries the Catholic school stands for something quite different from what it does in fully Christianized countries. In missionary countries Catholic schools are frequently the first seed-beds of divine love, the vehicles also of human culture, and they make a strongly apostolic impact. The presence of the Church in the class-room may precede her presence in the surrounding culture.

The name "Catholic school" implies a programme.[20] The Catholic school as an instrument of education ought to actualize the principles of Christian education with its goal as the *consecratio mundi*, and so make the Church present. The guaranteed real and institutional presence of the Church in the school may be regarded as a model for the presence of the Church in the modern world as demanded in the Pastoral Constitution on the Church in the Modern World. The Church becomes present in the school.

As an attitude towards God, religion implies a positive attitude to the world and to reality, because God is the creator of this world and, in Jesus Christ, its redeemer. The Catholic school must, because of its nature, be true to its cultural mandate to the world and to the task of forming men. The cultural goal is mentioned first, and while this implies no precedence over the formation of men, it counters the reproach that the Catholic school does not give sufficient place to cultural education in comparison with religious training.

The word "proprium" ("distinctive purposes") introduces the specific characterization of the Catholic school, which had been repeatedly demanded in the *animadversiones*. The community of the Catholic school must be a fellowship in the freedom of the children of God. This freedom, as a ped-

[20] G. Schulz-Benesch, *Zum Stil katholischer Schule heute* (1964); F. Pöggeler, *Das Wagnis der Schule* (1962); A. Heuser, *Die katholische Schule* (1961); J. Dreissen, *Die Schule in ekklesiologischer Sicht* (1960); W. Sacher, *Die katholische Schule* (1954); T. Soiron, *Das Geheimnis der christlichen Schule* (1935).

agogical principle, postulates an inward inspiration; but freedom is not caprice (cf. *Dignitatis humanae*, Articles 1 and 2). This inspiration, therefore, excludes neither genuine authority nor genuine obedience. On the contrary, by effective guidance the young person must be led to a truly religious and moral life that pleases God. By stressing fellowship all exaggerated individualism in pedagogy is renounced and the social dimension of the human person underlined (cf. Pastoral Constitution on the Church in the Modern World", Article 25). A man develops his own personality only in community. The *una simul* takes an incarnational pedagogy orientated towards Christ seriously, and opposes the dualism of man and Christ. The man is perfected in the Christian.

The message of salvation is the organic principle of all human culture. We are concerned at this point with the aim of education. All knowledge imparted to pupils through properly phased instruction — this idea possesses "gradation" also — must be viewed and evaluated from the valid perspectives of Christian faith. Here the primacy of character formation over education is stressed as plainly as one could wish.

"Aperit" ("it opens itself up"): with due regard to the age of the pupil, the Catholic school is a school open to every dimension of education. Because the Church is a world-Church, and not a Church in a backwater, the school dare not lead an insular life, must never become a ghetto, a "hortus conclusus", a hot-house with specially warmed air *(sic patres)*. The Church in the world demands a school that is in the world. Christian education ought thoroughly to immunize young people against the manifest dangers of our modern world, and make them capable of a Christian mastery of the world. A positive understanding of and relationship to the world lays the obligation upon the Christian to become involved in civic life. Hence every form of world-avoiding, world-negating and world-rejecting pedagogy is excluded, as are all kinds of indifference to, and disengagement from, social and political life. To opt out of the world is incompatible with responsible Catholic faith. A school that maintains a Catholic breadth and openness can do much to repair the present deficiency in education, forming leaders, who will exercise an excellent apostolate by acting as a leaven in Church and State. This apostolate is the principle and crown of Christian education. By this apostolic principle, which is demanded for schools in other conciliar documents also (e.g. the Decree on the Apostolate of the Laity, Article 30, sec. 4), everyone is diverted from an in-turned concern about his individual salvation and made aware of his responsibility for the salvation of all.

According to the view of the Declaration, the Catholic school ought, in virtue of its most characteristic essence, to fulfil the following functions: it forms a fellowship in the freedom of the children of God; it helps the young to develop the reality of his baptism in a spirit of imitation of Christ, until he has formed a truly human and Christian personality; in its education it proclaims and realizes the salvation of the individual and of the world as the supreme organizing principle of that education; it enters into a positive and open relationship with the world that was created by God, redeemed through Christ, and is called to become a new heaven and a new earth.

The crux of the whole article is the central passage. The first section describes the nature, function and goal of the Catholic school in such detail as to place the importance of the Catholic school for the people of God and for the people of the State in their human community in a true light. Against this background once again it solemnly proclaims the Church's right "freely to establish and to run schools of every kind and at every level". This passage is central to the sense of the article. In the *modi* the fathers laid great store upon the affirmation that this right arises from the Church's right to education (cf. Article 3, sec. 3) and is of natural and divine origin. It extends to the establishment and management of schools of every kind, including special schools (cf. Article 9), as well as schools of every grade: nursery schools, primary schools, technical schools, types of secondary schools, and all forms of colleges and universities. By proclaiming this right the Declaration counters the trend towards State monopoly of schools (but cf. also Article 3). This right has for a corollary the obligation of the State to support Catholic schools as it does its own, for these schools serve the State as well as the Church. Parents, whose children attend such schools, are citizens of the State with corresponding rights and duties. One of these obligations is to pay taxes, which contribute to the support of State schools. Only where the governments of the various States fulfil their obligations, can the Church be adequately present in the school. If their staffing and material support are not subsidized by the State, there easily arises the danger of these schools becoming schools for the rich, who alone are able to pay the fees. Ceasing to be truly public, these schools then fail to make the Church fully present.

The last section deals with the importance of the teacher. In view of the programme of the Catholic school and the initiation of that programme, they are called "auctore". If the teacher is to be true to the functions of the Catholic school, as an "auctor", he must be properly equipped. It is worth noting that the *ars educandi* is specially emphasized. In the light of this function the institutions for training teachers acquire their importance. What the Dogmatic Constitution on the Church says of the laity in Article 36 applies perfectly to teachers in Catholic schools: "Therefore, by their competence in secular fields and by their personal activity, elevated from within by the grace of Christ, let them labour vigorously, so that by human labour, technical skill, and civic culture created goods may be perfected for the benefit of every last man, according to the design of the Creator and the light of his Word. Let them work to see that created goods are more fittingly distributed among men, and that such goods in their own way lead to general progress in human and Christian liberty."

To fulfil these requirements the teacher must possess a thorough scientific education and approach his pupils armed with an all-embracing, personal and open-minded pedagogy. Pedagogic methods in our schools, especially in residential schools, undoubtedly require constant examination and renewal in line with the circumstances of the times. Education for the kingdom of God in the world is education for heaven.

Education becomes informed by character formation. Where the formation of the pupil is concerned, the primary thing in his attachment to the teacher is neither word nor example, but Christian personality. A teacher's pedagogic effectiveness is always dependent on the Christian reality which rules and permeates him. This reality is the only thing that produces an effect. Because the teacher-pupil relationship is always a two-sided, indeed a many-sided give and take, the inward riches of the teacher's faith and knowledge, as it reaches out to the pupils, very largely determines the quality of the class or of the school.

By his teaching and his life every master must bear witness to the Master, Jesus Christ. This witness consists above all in mutual love and an apostolic spirit. The love of the Holy Spirit loosens the tongue and reveals himself in dialogue. This dialogue should take place within the school between the teachers, and between teachers and pupils and vice versa. This intra-school dialogue ought to be a form of the ecclesial dialogue. It is carried out on a basis of common faith, in an atmosphere of love, truth, trust and the fundamental equality and fraternity which is found among the people of God.

This dialogue must not evaporate when school is over, for it has an ecclesial nature. In this dialogue the pupil, as a partner in the conversation, must be taken seriously according to his phase of development. The teacher must adjust himself to his partner and try to understand what is in his mind. Hence this section demands that attention be paid to the difference of the sexes and to the divinely ordained goals specially set before each. This observation (cf. Article 1) is no doubt directed against co-education in schools insofar as it ignores the difference between the sexes. This distinction is to be observed, however, in all education — "in universa educatione" —. Education differentiated according to sex is demanded quite simply by the objective difference between the sexes. How this is to be worked out is not specified in detail.

The pedagogic dialogue must not degenerate into a mere leading by the nose. In the process of education and formation the young are fully entitled to a "participatio actuosa". The goal of education by another is education by oneself.

Outside school dialogue should be carried on between teachers and parents and between all of those engaged in education. Thus the dialogue reaches out to become dialogue with the world, and the school can be regarded as a providential instrument in the revival of this dialogue as described in the encyclical *Ecclesiam Suam*.

Such dialogue as this actualizes simultaneously the presence of the Church and the specific scope of Christian education: formation of personal faith, the exercise of Christian fraternity and the awaking of a missionary and ecumenical spirit.

The function of the teacher in the Catholic school is not a *dominium* but a *ministerium*, which must always take its bearings from the *ministerium* of Christ and his Church. This ministry is, in the last analysis, a service to faith and to salvation. As such it is an apostolate. The ecclesial ministry of the teacher as a vocational multiplicator is always a service to the community. From the solemn language of the Council one may conclude that they set great store by the establishment of the apostolic ministry of the teacher in the best sense of the word.

Article 8 is concerned with the legitimate claim of the Church to have schools of her own and with the great importance of these for the good of earthly society and the spread of the kingdom of God. Pupils and teachers have an important apostolate to fulfil. The importance of the Catholic school is matched by the corresponding responsibility of Catholic parents to send their children to Catholic schools "when and where this is possible", thus continuing the education begun within the Catholic family circle; and they must support such schools to the best of their ability (cf. *CIC*, can. 1374). This earnest admonition is set against the background of the negligence of many Catholic parents in this regard. But there is also the fear that at any time governments might refuse to provide the required assistance. At the same time the Council fathers gratefully acknowledged that in many countries such as England, Scotland, Holland, Belgium and in several West German *Länder* (states within the Federal Republic), Catholic schools receive substantial subsidies from public funds.

Article 9. The first sentence makes evident that there are several connotations of the phrase "Catholic school". The most obvious and most common has in mind a school run by the Church or by a Catholic institution, and therefore assumed to bear the stamp of a Catholic Christian spirit. But it is made clear by the drafts of *De scholis catholicis* and by various memoranda from the bishops and comments of the fathers that it is not those who run the school but the spirit inspiring it that represents the formal and decisive factor distinguishing the Catholic school from others (cf. *De* *scholis catholicis* [1963], n. 11; [1964], n. 8; *De educatione christiana* [1965]; *Textus emendatus*, nn. 7–8; and the final text, nn. 8–9). One suggested clarificatory supplement ran: "inter scholas catholicas iure merito censentur et commendantur eae scholae quae quibusdam in regionibus ab auctoritate civili pro discipulis catholicis eriguntur, dummodo universa instructio spiritu catholici sit imbuta." The reason why this supplement was not accepted was probably because it applied to the schema *De scholis catholicis*, and after its expansion into the *De educatione christiana* and into a more general framework, such a specification was scarcely relevant. But there can be no doubt that the essence of the definitive statements includes the said form under the concept of the *schola catholica*. Likewise the much repeated demand that the State provide the funds for these schools, points in the same direction.

The proper and legitimate form of a Catholic school must manifest the power to stimulate and encourage the formation of Christian personality. Its form of being and acting provides a model in the wide area of the *servitium scholasticum* of the Catholic Church not least in the sphere of newly erected dioceses. Its spiritual and intellectual form can be manifested in a multitude of internal and external school structures. In schools attended by non-Catholic pupils a special missionary and apostolic responsibility is laid upon the specifically Christian elements in instruction and education. Here, above all, it must become apparent that the school is a ferment of Christian life — even for the surrounding district. Teachers in such schools take the lead in the apostolate of the faithful. Their formative efforts, undertaken in a spirit of tolerance and consideration, add up to the creating of a human, brotherly and righteous world according to the spirit of the gospel.

The second part of this article draws attention to the fundamental importance of primary and secondary schools. These schools provide a valuable foundation for education. Religious and moral knowledge and attitudes, at this stage imparted in collaboration with the child's home, as a rule make a deep and lasting impression. These primary and secondary schools, along with a good Catholic home, have a special pedagogic power. Their preservation and improvement are of critical importance for the Church, and the Church owes a debt of gratitude to Catholic families. With their irreplaceable educational effort, these schools are all the more necessary today, because they provide the normative foundation for the multiplicity of types of school that present needs demand.

When reviewing Christian education and the Catholic school system, the importance of these additional types of educational institution must not be overlooked. Those mentioned are: professional and technical schools, institutes for adult-education, for promoting social services and for training teachers. These institutions extend beyond the main edifice of the school system. In them the industrial society of our own day makes its special demands of the Church. The Declaration replies with an earnest appeal for help. On its view, Christian education is an inseparable factor in professional and adult education — its basis indeed. In this the Church lays hold upon her great tradition. She sees work and worship, in terms of the example of the Lord and his apostles, as an obligatory unity. The mightier the advance of technology and man's control of energy, the more urgent is the call for conscientious, responsible and God-fearing men. Technology is the logical application and exploitation of the laws of creation. A technical civilization lacking transcendent direction is a danger to body and soul. Professional education must, therefore, be a vehicle of a more comprehensive education. Profession ought to become human self-realization, which must prove itself in humanity and fellowship, in religion and Christlikeness. Men, Christians, must not be mere technicians, but technicians must be men and Christians. The whole man must become an image of the model that is recognized as the man and the Christian. We are not surprised, therefore, when religious formation is specially mentioned as well as specialist education, in connection with the training of teachers. Special schools are included in the list of educational institutions. Even more than other educational institutions, these can appeal to the redemptive mandate for the ministrations of redemptive pedagogy.

The document exhorts us never to shrink from constant sacrifice so that the task of the Catholic school may be perfectly fulfilled. Having in mind different countries and specific conditions the Declaration exhorts us to show special concern for the economically oppressed, the victims of social injustice, the heterodox and the unbelievers. It is not enough that well cared for children from well-off and religious homes should enjoy the advantages of a Catholic school. The object is to make this kind of school available to the greatest possible number. Above all it must be available to those who most need it, to those who in the past may have been excluded for economic reasons. To these the Catholic school owes above all else the testimony of the truth of faith and the ministry of the love of Christ. The *admonitio vehemens* which the Declaration addresses to the bishops and to all who believe in Christ is intended to silence the complaint that the gospel is not abundantly preached to the poor. Through children and through poor children in particular the Lord gives a special sign of his presence to the Catholic school. The Catholic school should see this sign, for it becomes visible only to faith. It should observe it, because in the end of the day the Lord will confirm it. And so the ministry of the school, performed in faith, like the celebration of the Eucharist, exists in a state of fruitful tension between the presence and the return of the Lord.

Article 10. The Declaration gives close and thorough attention to universities. This accords with the nature and the essential task of the Church. She must devote the greatest interest to those places of higher education in which the minds of our future leaders are being formed, where scientific research is carried on *ex professo,* and where men are constantly looking for solution to the problems which oppress mankind. "Indeed, if hunger exists in the world, then it is the job of the universities to study means of increasing production and improving the distribution of products, so that all may enjoy them. If we are oppressed by disease, then it is the job of the universities to discover their cause and the remedies, and to train competent physicians to apply them. If ignorance is still prevalent, then it is the job of the universities to work out suitable programmes, and scientifically and pedagogically to train tutors who will give basic education and prepare suitable candidates for special professions. If so many nations are poor, then it is the job of the universities to teach us how to foster economic advance by the application of new techniques. For this reason all nations look with special interest to the universities, and new states make every effort to erect at least one university of their own."[21] In a message to the Fédération Internationale des Universités Catholiques, meeting in Tokyo from 27 to 30 August 1965, Pope Paul VI said: "More than ever before, the university is called upon today to develop directive energies, which have as their aim to lead their people to an appropriate level of development, which alone can enable them to enjoy the benefits of God's creation."

Before speaking of the Catholic university in particular, the Declaration stresses that the Church is concerned quite generally with the discovery of truth. Here we are reminded of Pope Paul VI's message to intellectuals, which he handed over to the philosopher, Jacques Maritain on 8 December 1965 at the solemn conclusion of the Council in St. Peter's Square in Rome. This message concluded with the words of St. Augustine: "Seeking, let us desire to find; and finding, let us desire to seek further."

Scientific research is explicitly granted its proper freedom. This counters the reproach that a Christian, bound as he is to a philosophy of life, cannot be scientific in outlook. In reality there can be no contradiction between faith and science. The First Vatican Council had already declared: "Science, because it proceeds from God, the Lord of all knowledge, by the help of his grace leads back to him, if it is pursued in the correct manner."[22] Vatican II as well, in the Pastoral Constitution on the Church in the Modern World, took up this thought when it declared: "This sacred Synod, therefore, recalling the teaching of the First Vatican Council, declares that there

---

[21] P. Dezza in *La Civiltà Cattolica* 117 (1966), I, p. 119.
[22] D 1799.

37

are 'two orders of knowledge' which are distinct, namely, faith and reason. It declares that the Church does not indeed forbid that 'when the human arts and sciences are practised they use their own principles and their proper method, each in its own domain'. Hence, 'acknowledging this just liberty', this sacred Synod affirms the legitimate autonomy of human culture and especially of the sciences."[23] Mundane science is not sufficient by itself. It appeals immediately for supplementation by metaphysics, for a synthesis and spiritual foundation, for an explanation of the riddle of our being. As St. Augustine said, "Our heart is restless, until it repose in thee." Any dehumanizing or absolutized objectification of science in this sense is a self-deception. The concept of a dehumanized science "was suddenly shattered, when the majority of atomic scientists began to face problems of conscience, asking questions about the human significance of their discoveries. They began to see that their so-called purely scientific approach was nothing but a component in a military project."[24] Academic freedom and being bound by a dogma of faith are not contradictory concepts. "No man has ever asserted that dogma can teach us all truth. As a rule faith reveals to us those truths which we could never have discovered by our own reflection."[25] On the other hand, faith (as a rule) says nothing about such things as we examine in the secular sciences. Therefore the Christian has no fear of true freedom, which indeed "knows no other bond except to the truth that makes free and opens the mind to a philosophy of life without which man cannot be at ease in this world".[26] The Declaration is magnanimous and free from all timidity and fear of the results of research. It believes that in the last analysis men can find their way to God along all roads, because God is the origin and centre of all truth. "Truth is a deep well; the deeper one digs, the more abundantly the water flows, whereas error is but a broken cistern" (Lacordaire). Faith and reason are bound to converge in a single truth, although at times each must conscientiously respect the proper laws and autonomy of the other. The labours of the doctors of the Church, especially those of St. Thomas Aquinas, are shining examples of this harmony between faith and knowledge.

The Church's great concern is to ensure that within the universities students grow up, who will be fully equipped with the intellectual apparatus of our modern age, and who at the same time, as witnesses to the faith, will carry out fruitful apostolic activity in the world.

The Declaration puts great store upon the effectual presence of the Church

[23] Pastoral Constitution on the Church in the Modern World, art. 59.
[24] E. Schillebeeckx, in N. A. Luyten, ed., *Forschung u. Bildung, Aufgaben einer katholischen Universität* (1965), pp. 35 f.
[25] N. A. Luyten, *op. cit.*, p. 33.
[26] E. Schillebeeckx, loc. cit., p. 40.

in all universities, whether Catholic or not, through a theological faculty or, where that is impossible, through a religious-scientific institute or a chair of theology. As Schillebeeckx says, the inexpressible given reality underlying every science requires "the scientific explication we call theology. The presupposition of every science proves, therefore, that theology, as reflection upon faith and upon supra-mundane reality in the light of faith, can assume a reasonable and central position in the *universitas scientiarum;* that, indeed — for the faithful — along with philosophy, theology too can appropriately be called the 'central inter-faculty', because it seeks to penetrate the deepest ground of every reality and humanity, and it does this by scientific reflection upon faith. For its part, theology demands the right of coexistence alongside the other faculties, from which it receives an essential contribution to its problems." [27]

The full significance of what the Council has said about the Catholic university and its importance will be understood only by those who know something about the universality of the Church and her presence in almost every country, and who know the influence Catholic universities exert upon the culture of the most diverse peoples. [28]

There can be no doubt that the Catholic universities of the world are a factor that cannot be ignored. But what of their international constitution? Academic freedom and religious faith are not mutually exclusive, as has been explained already.

It has been said that a Catholic university is a foreign body in our

---

[27] *Ibid.*, p. 45.

[28] The international bulletin *Pro mundi vita*, published in Brussels and Amsterdam, lists, in no. 12 (1966), 72 Catholic universities affiliated to the Fédération Internationale des Universités Catholiques, or at least associated with that federation. In reality the number is greater. This same bulletin names 22 Catholic universities in the U.S.A. We know of at least 32 Catholic universities in that country — in addition to numerous Catholic colleges — and these are attended by between 3000 and 12 000 students. In Latin America the FIUC includes 21 Catholic universities. In reality there are 32, of which, however, only the Universidad Catolica of Chile has more than 5000 students. Between 1964 and 1966 four new Catholic universities were established in Latin America. In Canada there are 6 Catholic universities, including the University of Montreal with 24 000 students. In time to come the University of Lovanium, founded in 1954 by Louvain, will assume great importance for Africa. In Asiatic countries, Indonesia, Japan, the Philippines, South Korea, Taiwan and Lebanon, there are 15 Catholic universities in all. Besides the institutions designed chiefly for theological education, in Europe there are only 12 Catholic universities, none of them in Germany. The French Catholic universities of Paris, Lille, Angers, Lyons and Toulouse can count a total of just over 17 000 students. Most important of all are the Catholic Universities of Navarre in Pamplona (founded in 1960 by Opus Dei), of Nimeguen (founded in 1923, with 5000–6000 students), of Milan (founded in 1920, about 20 000 students), and of Louvain, the most important of them all (founded in 1425, over 20 000 students — about 50 % of all the students in Belgium).

pluralistic society. But is it not a contradiction in terms when "in the name of such pluralism, which guarantees the right of existence to all religious and philosophical views, all institutions, no matter how different their ideologies, the right of existence is denied to Catholic universities"?[29]

It has been said that the idea of a Catholic university has its origin in a narrow ghetto mentality. In the Christian view, it would seem to be more accurate to say that those who have their senses and thoughts imprisoned within this world are the people who inhabit an intellectual ghetto. He who by contrast expands his soul towards God, embracing in his mind heaven and earth, time and eternity, is neither narrow nor one-sided. Nor do the intellectual dons of the Catholic university intend for one moment to insulate their students from the culture and the intellectual movements of the modern age. Of them is true, rather, what the Church in her liturgy says of Don Bosco, the charismatic pedagogue of modern times: "Cor eius sicut latitudo maris" ("God gave him wisdom and knowledge in abundance and a breadth of heart like the expanse of the ocean").

It has been said that the Catholic university suits our age least of all, because it contradicts the ecumenical spirit of Vatican II. To affirm that the Council believed that the Catholic mind must surrender itself in order to establish dialogue with the separated brethren, is to mistake the deepest aim of the Council. "True ecumenical dialogue presupposes full partners, who know what they are talking about and are also convinced of the importance of the whole business. The more Catholic universities are able to imbue their professors and students with the Catholic spirit, the better partners will they turn out for ecumenical conversations."[30]

In summary we might say that the existence of Catholic universities not only serves the true well-being of peoples, but also upholds the authentic idea of what a university is. From its origin in the Middle Ages until today the university has never been a mere reservoir of knowledge, the mere spatial juxtaposition of the most diverse faculties, but has always aimed at being a genuine *universitas scientiarum*, i.e. a co-ordinating spirit ought to permeate all faculties and create a synthesis, so that knowledge acquired at a university will provide a man with an answer to the question about the meaning of his own existence. St. Augustine's words ought never to apply to a university: "For Thou hast commanded, and so it is, that every inordinate affection should be its own punishment."[31]

Strongly as the Declaration stresses the influence of the Catholic university upon the cultural development of peoples, it by no means devotes its atten-

[29] N. A. Luyten, *op. cit.*, p. 25.
[30] *Ibid.*
[31] Augustine, *Confessions*, I, 12, 13.

tion exclusively to the university when dealing with centres of higher education. The university is but one of several possibilities. The Council issued a special warning about the thoughtless multiplication of the number of Catholic universities; for it seemed quite clear to them that in the world of the mind, quality, not quantity, is the decisive thing, and that the Church's effort, therefore, must primarily be directed to attaining a high intellectual standard in her universities. Nor could the Council fathers fail to see the size of the economic problems involved in establishing a university with its libraries, laboratories and other equipment to which it would be entitled, and also the difficulty of obtaining professors of high scientific calibre and genuine Christian spirituality.[32] Thus, sensible, worldwide planning is necessary in order to erect a limited number of Catholic universities of a high intellectual and religious standard in those places all over the world where their scientific and apostolic impact will be most effective. The Church's universal interest in culture and the intellectual progress of human society must naturally turn her attention to the non-Catholic universities.

Bishop H. van Waeyenbergh, for many years Rector of the University of Louvain, made a significant intervention at the Council on 19 November 1964, appealing to Pope Paul VI and vehemently calling for magnanimous and serious co-operation of Catholics with non-Catholics in all scientific institutes. He drew attention likewise to the possibility of establishing Catholic institutes for theological, philosophical and social sciences in the vicinity of public universities, and linked with them. This would create the preconditions for mutual intellectual stimulus.

The Council very properly demanded careful spiritual care of students in all universities. In the past this has been neglected in many places.[33] In this connection the desirability becomes very obvious of having hostels for students everywhere, and of *Catholic university centres,* where students and professors have an opportunity of meeting and receiving advice on the problems of science, faith and morals, which they encounter in their studies, and of taking part in discussion on these things.[34]

In conclusion it must be said, that Article 10, on universities, breathes a

---

[32] Cf. P. Dezza, *op. cit.,* p. 121, and Bishop H. van Waeyenbergh's intervention in the Council on 19 November 1964.

[33] Until 1963 there was, for example, an official chaplain at only three of the State universities in the whole of Latin America. Only two had their own university or students' chaplaincy. Four leading Venezuelan laymen sent a memorandum on university pastoral problems to the episcopal conference in August 1966. Of 45 000 students in the country, they said, scarcely 350 were involved in any organized apostolate. Cf. *Pro mundi vita,* 12 (1966), p. 34.

[34] Cf. P. Dezza, *op. cit.,* p. 122.

broadminded, global spirit of tolerance, all-embracing love and apostolic Eros.

Article 11. This article deals chiefly with theological faculties. What it means by these faculties is best understood from the Latin text. In this, two different terms are used to describe theological faculties. The first section of the article uses the term "scientiarum sacrarum facultates", the second section, "ecclesiasticae facultates". Both concepts come from the Apostolic Constitution *Deus scientiarum Dominus* of Pius XI, dated 24 May 1931.[35] In this constitution on theological faculties the term "scientiarum sacrarum facultates" denotes university faculties in which theological disciplines are studied, whereas the term "ecclesiasticae facultates" denotes various independent faculties. These might be theological faculties, but they might also be faculties of sciences allied to theology — of philosophy, for example.[36] Consequently, Article 11 of the Declaration deals with theological faculties in the strict sense. It has in mind those university institutions which, in their teaching and research, treat of theological disciplines. As such they are dealt with in the second section of the article also under the more comprehensive title "ecclesiastical faculties".

The contents of Article 11 are characterized by a special viewpoint. It is clearly differentiated from the perspectives of the Apostolic Constitution. This constitution views the faculties from the angle of the history of education and the organization of studies, and also from the juridical angle. The viewpoint of Article 11, by contrast, is pastoral. It sees the theological faculties and those of allied sciences in the context of the present redemptive operation of the Church. Clearly this presence tends to orientate thought and life towards the principles of science. Viewed from the pastoral angle the theological faculties, therefore, as places where the faith permeates science, are specially suited to serve the redemption of the present day. It is from this viewpoint that the Council formulated Article 11, which is essentially an enumeration of the contributions it expects to receive from the theological and allied faculties. There are practical tasks, for the accomplishment of which a structural reform and a scientifically more intense and extensive orientation of these faculties to the present day is demanded at the conclusion of the article.

The faculties perform their scientific activity through teaching and research. The first group of functions expounded in the article belong to the sphere of teaching. This activity is of direct service to the Church's redemptive work. It has to do in detail with the training of priests, the education

---

[35] Pius XI's Apostolic Constitution *Deus scientiarum Dominus,* dated 24 May 1931: *AAS* 23 (1931), pp. 241–61.
[36] *Ibid.,* pp. 247 and 253.

of theological lecturers and scholars as well as preparation for the more difficult tasks in the intellectual apostolate. Although this enumeration keeps to the traditional framework of the catalogue of theological faculties, in the second group of functions new viewpoints and accents become apparent. The tasks of the second group lie in the field of research. A more fundamental exploration of the various theological departments should lead to a deeper understanding of revelation, to a better unfolding of tradition, to dialogue with non-Christians and with separated Christians, as well as to an answer to the problems associated with the advance of science. In thus stating the nature of the task, theological research is directed to the acutely problematic area, in which today's theological questions are posed. Also to be raised are problems connected with the development of scientific exegesis and the history of dogma, which in turn are connected, in various respects, with problems arising in the ecumenical field, and out of the ever-changing situation in the field of advancing secular science.[37]

The post-conciliar commission will have to develop Article 11 in detail. In so doing it cannot rest content with a list of traditional functions within the sphere of doctrine, for preaching the word and giving instruction, catechesis and pastoral care make too heavy and too specific demands upon the teaching activity of the theological faculties. In the field of research, and for the discussion of present-day theological and scientific problems, the commission will have to provide a pastorally inspired orientation; for the problem of faith and the capacity to believe is acutely emerging in a new form on account of the increasing infiltration of scientism into every area of life.

In the second part of the article the Council turns its attention to "ecclesiastical faculties". From the constitution *Deus scientiarum Dominus* we know that the phrase denotes faculties of theology and other faculties connected with theology. Of these faculties the document demands further active development of their sphere of scientific work and a lead in deeper study, using modern methods and aids. This permanently relevant demand is given precise point by the statement which follows, that the ecclesiastical faculties should undertake further scientific development by "revision of their own bylaws". In this reform the Council sees the precondition of scientific advance. The Council did not propose any law for internal faculty structure, but felt obliged, by reason of their pastoral responsibility for science and its role in the redemptive work of the Church, to call upon the faculties of theology and its allied sciences to reform their internal structure along the lines of university self-administration.

Article 12. In this article the Council ends its practical pronouncements

[37] Cf. Vatican II, Decree on Priestly Formation, arts. 13–18.

on the topic of Christian education with an appeal for co-operation within the school and university systems. It does not go into the reason for this co-operation, but simply underlines its necessity, drawing attention to the daily increasing necessity of co-operation at every level of ecclesiastical, national and international life.

In the relevant literature the necessity of such co-operation is frequently said to lie in the phenomenon of socialization. The argument runs: the phenomenon of the formation of progressively closer bonds and dependencies between men and in social structure must be given an organizational, technical, psychological and economic expression in the field of education. In contrast to this the context shows that the Council was not proceeding from sociological categories of collectivization, but from the pastoral idea of their responsibility for the educational system. The criterion of the necessity for co-operation is pastoral responsibility, not the phenomenon of socialization. This fact appears from the *modi* of the fathers. These demanded that the pastoral perspective be stressed in this question of co-operation, by, for example, the addition of the adjective "pastoralis" — "in order to lay more stress upon the pastoral point of view and less upon the technical and administrative aspect".[38] The *relator* left this out, not because the idea was wrong, but because it was already included in the word "cooperatio". "The term 'cooperatio' must retain its conceptual fullness, which embraces both the pastoral and technical aspects."[39] Intervention and reply showed that for the fathers the "scopus pastoralis" was the dominant viewpoint, from which the organizational, planning and economic aspects were to receive their order and meaningful realization.

Moreover, this idea of co-operation is closest to the meaning of the Latin word "cooperatio". It denotes voluntary unity of action by autonomous partners. In this sense it functions as the dominant idea in many forms of co-operation. But in all forms the marks of freedom and independent partnership are present. On this level of rational co-operation there is no room for organizational identity or uniformity in policy.

The text distinguishes between co-operation among Catholic schools, and co-operation between Catholic and non-Catholic schools. The kind of co-operation envisaged among Catholic schools is not described more precisely. The Latin text does, perhaps, suggest something. This text uses the word "co-operation", which suggests a close and binding relationship between the partners. It denotes a unity of action reaching down into the core of the scholastic institution. It denotes a co-ordination of teaching power, of teaching methods and learning methods, of school-rooms and of geographical and

[38] *Textus emendatus et modi* (1965), p. 51, art. 12, 1.
[39] *Ibid.*, p. 51, art. 12, 1 R.

economic educational circumstances; in short, it denotes a certain planning of education. Although the word is not explicitly used in the text (it is interchanged with "collaboration" and "co-ordination"), what is meant is quite clear. At all events the notion of co-operation excludes planning education in isolation; "suitable co-ordination" is what is required. What is envisaged is the planning of education according to the yardstick of pastoral responsibility, so that limits will be set to the dangers of arbitrary administrative power and false policy.

Co-operation between Catholic and non-Catholic schools is described by the word "collaboration". This implies a looser and less close relation between the partners. Alluding to *Pacem in Terris* the criterion of this collaboration is said to be "the well-being of the whole human family".[40] This remark is significant in that it demonstrates the Council's approval of an open attitude towards non-Catholic schools, and it understands this openness as co-ordination between scholastic bodies, basing this collaboration upon common responsibility for the common good. Details and more precise information about various forms of collaboration may be lacking, but within the framework of aims the appeal for collaboration represents a decided advance, manifested by the fact that for the first time in an important official Church document Catholic schools are called to public co-operation with each other, by reason of the interdependence of salvation, and to public collaboration with non-Catholic schools, by reason of shared responsibility for the common good.

The fathers saw even greater opportunities for co-operation at the university level. By this the text understands mutual assistance through a co-ordination of scientific personnel and through intercommunication and agreement in scientific work. Thus the question again arises as to how far this co-ordination in the university system is to go in respect of organization, administration, scientific programming and the economics of education. By asserting that there are greater opportunities of co-ordination at university than at school level, and by deeming it necessary to expound co-ordination in the Catholic school system as the planning of education, the document must mean this exposition to apply even more to the university system. To this, too, the affirmation applies that the planning of science and the concepts used therein, given correct pastoral co-ordination, might provide fruitful viewpoints for modern Catholic educational theory. That the Council did not see co-ordination among universities simply as a matter of planning, is demonstrated by the fact that it demands not only mutual assistance among universities, but also among the faculties in each university. Such a demand can scarcely be said to interest those concerned with planning policy and

---

[40] Pope John XXIII's *Pacem in terris*, 11 April 1963: *AAS* 55 (1963), p. 284.

studying the economics of education. Obviously the authors of the document were not thinking here of policy and economics, but of the attempt to overcome the isolation of the learned faculties through inter-faculty co-ordination, and within this framework to foster the unity of culture and knowledge.

In conclusion the document lists a few forms of co-operation, which have been partially realized already. Exchange of lecturers, visiting professors and scientific conferences are common forms of co-operation among universities. A system of agreement on the erection of basic faculties within individual universities and of focal departments within separate faculties is going on now, and in this way scientific division of labour is progressing.[41] In this connection it is worth mentioning the attempts that are being made in new universities to encourage co-operation in the form of working groups.

A last form of co-operation within the educational system concerns the associations and administration that govern school and university institutions. This is not mentioned explicitly in Article 12; but it is implied in the formula "cooperatio in re scholastica". This has to do with the co-operation of educational associations and of ecclesiastical school departments.

The appropriate scene of co-operation at the level of universities and ecclesiastical faculties is the Roman administrative department known as the Congregation for Seminaries and Universities. At the school level it is the diocesan, regional and national educational departments which are the points of contact for Catholic educational institutions. These provide the area of co-operation in the sphere of the Church's school and educational responsibilities.[42] As well as these school departments in many cases there are also co-operative committees and associations for parents and teachers. These apply themselves to problems of the school system, with the intention of representing Catholic educational ideas in a pluralist society.

At the international plane these associations and institutions again actively co-operate in two important scholastic and educational co-ordinating centres. At Brussels there is the *Office International de l'Enseignement Catholique* (OIEC) which co-ordinates the work of these national school departments and the above-mentioned associations. The OIEC, just like the national co-ordinating bodies, does not limit its activity to fostering co-operation within the Catholic educational system, but operates also with and within the

---

[41] On the recommendation of their scientific advisers, the theological faculties of West Germany have an agreement on the formation of basic departments at the separate theological faculties.

[42] The competence of national school departments differs greatly and is quite independent of their juridical status at any particular time. Their chief work is to co-ordinate activity in school administration, to advise on school law, to deal with problems affecting teachers and parents, and to represent the school system in public life.

school and educational organizations of the national and international economic and political unions. [43]

The second important co-operative body for Catholic ideas concerning schools and education is specially concerned with co-operation with the United Nations Organization for Education, Science and Culture (UNESCO). This body is the Centre Catholique International de Coordination auprès de l'UNESCO (CCIC). Its headquarters are in Paris. This co-ordinating centre collects the ideas and suggestions on schools and education which come in from the various associations including the OIEC in Brussels, for the purpose of co-operating in the worldwide tasks of UNESCO.

In addition to the CCIC in Paris and the OIEC in Brussels, we must note also the co-ordinating work of international Catholic unions concerned with schools and education. Above all, there is at university level the Fédération Internationale des Universités Catholiques (FIUC) in Rome, at the level of adult and intellectual education, the organization known as Pax Romana (MIIC and MIEC) in Freiburg, Switzerland, and within the framework of teachers' unions there is the Union Mondiale des Enseignants Catholiques (UMEC) in Rome.

Conclusion. Bearing in mind the vastness of the educational problem, and the variety of regions within the worldwide Church, each with a different historical heritage, the Council has deliberately refrained from treating the problems of Christian education in greater detail. Instead of a comprehensive decree they produced a declaration. The full significance of this declaration can only be made clear by a post-conciliar commission, whose task will be to apply the document to differing circumstances, thus achieving relevance and a more profound actualization of principles. Nonetheless, the document has made the importance of Christian education perfectly clear, and also pointed out the relevant problems on a worldwide scale, as well as the responsibility of fulfilling the office of Christian education. The closing exhortation to youth shows a realistic judgment of the situation: "This sacred Synod urgently implores young people themselves to be aware of the excellence of the teaching vocation, and to be ready to undertake it with a generous spirit..." This reveals a healthy confidence in the rising generation, who are asked to obey the call of God and help especially in places where there is a shortage of teachers.

The Council has a word of recognition for priests, religious and laymen who are devoting themselves to the sacrificial and self-denying service of

---

[43] We must mention specially: co-operation with UNESCO in Paris, with the United Nations' Organization for Food and Agriculture (UNFAO) in Rome, with the United Nations' International Labour Organization (UNILO) in Geneva, with its children's work (UNICEF) in Paris, and also with the European unions like the cultural department of OEEC in Paris and with the cultural committee of the European Council in Strasbourg.

this unique work of education. This explicit acknowledgment of the high dignity of the work of Catholic pedagogues is most unusual and has no parallel in any other conciliar texts. It is, therefore, to be regarded as a deliberate token of the high esteem in which the Council holds the work of the Catholic educator. The appeal to men to persevere in this work is supported by the belief that through forming pupils according to the Spirit of Christ, by the art of true education, and by scientific labours to produce good results, the renewal of the Church desired by the Council will be advanced, and the Church made present to the modern world, especially among educated people.

Declaration on Religious Freedom

by
*Pietro Pavan**

Introduction

1. Chapter IX of the Schema of the Constitution *"De Ecclesia"*

During the preparatory phase of the Council, while working out the schema on the Church, the Theological Commission had only considered the problem of the relations between Church and State. Hence it had also examined the subject of religious freedom from this point of view, insofar as it is one aspect of the problem. In 1962 the Council fathers were presented with two draft texts on the Church, during the preparatory phase and the first session of the Council respectively. Both treated the problem in the ninth chapter, the first draft at greater length, the second more concisely. But the doctrine contained in both documents was fundamentally the same and may be summed up as follows:

"Deus est auctor Societatis civilis et fons omnium bonorum quae per ipsam in omnia membra profluunt. Societas civilis ergo Deum honorare et colere debet. Modus autem quo Deus colendus sit nullus alius esse potest in praesenti oeconomia quam ille quem Ipse sibi exhibendum determinavit in vera Christi Ecclesia. Cultui ergo publico ab Ecclesia praestito Civitas sese associare debet non tantum per cives, sed etiam per illos qui auctoritate praediti Societatem civilem repraesentant" (*Schema Constitutionis de Ecclesia* [Rome, 1962], Cap. IX: "De Relationibus inter Ecclesiam et Statum necnon de Tolerantia Religiosa", n. 3, § 2).

"Sicut autem nullus homo Deum modo a Christo statuto colere potest, nisi ipsi constet Deum per Iesum Christum esse locutum, immo nisi cognoscat missionem salutiferam Ecclesiae, sic etiam Communitas civilis ad id faciendum non obligatur, nisi prius factum revelationis a civibus acceptum sit, itemque a Potestate civili, quatenus populum repraesentat. Pro ratione igitur, qua Potestas civilis personam agens populi, Christum cognoscit et ab Eo

---

* *Translated by Hilda Graef*

conditam Ecclesiam, aliter ac aliter ad invicem se habere utramque pote-
statem ad profectum utriusque civitatis, Ecclesia semper agnovit. Civibus
autem in bonum ipsius communitatis plena libertas concedatur eligendi, ut
vita civilis secundum principia catholica informetur, adeoque secundum
verba Sancti Gregorii Magni, 'coelorum via largius pateat' (S. Gregorius M.,
Epist. 65, ad Mauricium: *PL,* LXXVII, 663)" (*Schemata Constitutionum et
Decretorum, Secunda Series, De Ecclesia et de B. Maria Virgine* [Rome, 1962],
Cap. IX, De Relationibus inter Ecclesiam et Statum, n. 43).

Hence, if almost all members of a society or the majority profess the true,
that is to say the Catholic, religion, the State, too, has the duty to profess
it. Those citizens who belong to other religions *do not have the right not to
be prevented from professing these religions;* however, for the sake of the
common good the State may tolerate their profession, both for the sake of
the common good of the relevant community and for that of all mankind.

If, on the other hand, almost the whole of a community or its majority
is non-Catholic, it is the duty of the State to follow the natural law in every
respect. Hence it must leave Catholics completely free to profess their own
religion and it must leave the Church free to accomplish her mission.

During the preparatory phase of the Council as well as at its start both
the Council theologians and the fathers were distinctly opposed to this view
of religious freedom. Later, however, the section on the relations between
Church and State was removed from the schema on the Church; hence the
subject of religious freedom was no more discussed in this connection.

2. The Process of Maturation

The final version of the Declaration on Religious Freedom was perfected
only in a long and varied process of evolution.

Even during the preparatory phase of the Council the Secretariat for the
Promotion of Christian Unity had produced a text on religious freedom. It
contained nineteen paragraphs, divided into an introduction and three
chapters:

a) De bonis fidei in caritate promovendis
b) De catholicorum cooperatione cum eis qui non sunt catholici
c) De relatione inter Ecclesiam et societatem civilem

On 18 June 1962, Cardinal A. Bea submitted this text to the Preparatory
Central Commission. But the text was rejected on the grounds that the
Secretariat was not competent to draw up the schemata which were to be
proposed for discussion.

Indeed, at that time the competence of the Secretariat in this question had
not yet been clarified. This problem was solved on 22 October 1962. On that
day John XXIII raised the Secretariat to the same rank as the Council

Commissions, empowering it to submit the drafts it had drawn up to the Council. Hence the Secretariat continued its examination of religious freedom.

3. The First Schema
(Chapter V of the Decree on Ecumenism)

The first version of the document on religious freedom proposed in the aula formed chapter five of the schema of the Decree on Ecumenism, which was handed to the fathers on 19 November 1963. A series of five *relationes* was added to it, the fifth, read by E. J. M. de Smedt, Bishop of Bruges, treating of religious freedom.

The reason why the theme of religious freedom was proposed to the Council on the initiative of the Secretariat for Unity is mentioned in this *relatio*. It is said there that many non-Catholics are opposed to the Church or at least suspect it of Machiavellianism, because it demands freedom for itself in those political communities where Catholics are in the minority, while refusing the same freedom to non-Catholics in political communities where Catholics are in the majority. Hence it was essential for the Church to state its view on religious freedom unequivocally. Unless this was done, a larger and deeper development of the ecumenical movement would be difficult, perhaps even impossible.

Several fathers spoke on chapter V during the general discussion on the schema, which took place from 19 to 21 November 1963. The Council decided, however, to leave the special examination of religious freedom to the next session. Hence there was no voting on this chapter in the second session.

4. The Second Schema *(Declaratio prior)*

During the second and the third sessions of the Council the fathers were able to examine the schema on religious freedom in detail. Within this period the Secretariat for Christian Unity received nearly four hundred suggestions and emendations which were collected in a volume of 280 pages. The new elements in these proposals were taken into account when the second schema was drawn up.

Among these new elements was the conviction of many fathers that the Council ought to produce a special document on religious freedom. The reason given for it was that religious freedom was a subject transcending in importance and extent the limits of ecumenism; for it was absolutely essential also for the relations of the Church to all mankind.

The Co-ordinating Commission shared this view. On 18 April 1964 it suggested that the text on religious liberty should be presented to the Council as a special Declaration, apart from the schema on ecumenism. During this phase, however, the document still appeared as a continuation of the schema on ecumenism; it comprised nos. 25 to 31 of this schema and was entitled: "Declaratio *prior* de libertate religiosa seu de iure personae et communitatum ad libertatem in re religiosa." It is here called *Declaratio prior* to distinguish it from *Declaratio altera* which dealt with Jews and non-Christians.

The basic and unifying idea of the schema was that every man is a person, and that this highest dignity derives from his divine vocation.

"Vocatio enim divina, quae homini iter ad Deum et ad salutem in Deo aperit atque praescribit, maximam revera personae humanae dignitatem constituit. Quapropter in sociali convictu libertas sequendi hanc vocationem sine ulla imposita vel impediente coactione cum maximum et unicuique proprium bonum tum aliarum libertatum fundamentum ac tutelam constituit, atque ideo ab unoquoque tanquam verum strictumque ius erga eos quibusdam vitam degit habenda et observanda est" (n. 29).

The second schema was sent to the Council fathers on 2 April 1964. It contained five pages of annotations, a *relatio* and a short summary. A second *relatio* on the schema, drawn up by Bishop E. J. M. de Smedt of Bruges, was distributed on 22 September, after the beginning of the third session.

The discussion in the Council hall took place from 25 to 28 September (86th to 89th general congregation). Forty-three fathers spoke, the last four in the name of more than seventy fathers. Several different opinions were voiced, some of them radically contradicting others. Nevertheless, there was increasing agreement on the need for the Council to pronounce on this delicate and complicated subject.

There was no voting on the second schema either.

5. The Third Schema *(Textus emendatus)*

After the discussion of the second schema in the aula the fathers raised the question of competence: "Which organ of the Council is responsible for improving the document on religious freedom?" The question was decided in favour of the Secretariat for Unity. It was decided, however, to refer the improved text to five members of the Theological Commission for examination; it was then to be given back to this commission. On 9 November 1964 it was approved by the Commission with a large majority, though certain further alterations were proposed.

As has been said before, 43 fathers had taken part in the discussion of the second schema in the aula. After the discussion about a hundred further suggestions were submitted to the Secretariat. The third schema took account of the wishes of the fathers. It was entitled *Textus emendatus* and was placed before the Council as an *independent document* with the same title as the second schema: Declaration on Religious Freedom or on the Right of the Person and of Communities to Freedom in Matters Religious.

The plan was now quite different from that of the preceding drafts; and this difference became even more pronounced in all following draft texts. Besides, the theme of religious freedom is far more developed in this third schema. It begins with the statement that modern men are becoming ever more conscious of their own personal dignitiy. In the new schema this dignity is the basic motif, but it is understood above all as responsibility of action.

The increased consciousness of their own dignity led men to want greater freedom in all spheres, especially in religious matters, and hence to demand that this freedom should be guaranteed by setting well-defined limits to the authority of the state. Thus the constitutional state came into being.

Consequently religious freedom, too, was seen in a new context. This is why the Council considered it right to think about it and produce a Declaration on the subject. Religious freedom is proclaimed to be a right of the person; it consists in freedom from coercion, whether on the part of individuals or of public authority. This freedom is twofold: in matters of religion no one may be compelled to act against his conscience, and no one may be prevented from acting according to his conscience.

This freedom is based on rational grounds. The schema lays down the duties of the State with regard to this right of the person and the criteria according to which its exercise may be limited. It is, moreover, a right that extends also to religious communities and to families. Religious freedom is then considered in the light of revelation: it is a freedom which agrees perfectly with the liberty that belongs to the Church when it accomplishes its divine mission. It also agrees with the liberty of the act of faith; it is confirmed by the actions of the Lord and the apostles; it is a standard for the apostolate of the Church both of the hierarchy and the laity. The summing up resumes and develops a motif of the two preceding drafts: in our present pluralistic society religious freedom is essential for preserving the peace both within the individual political communities and in the whole world.

On 17 November the third schema was presented to the fathers together with a *relatio* by Bishop de Smedt and a second *relatio* of the Secretariat for Christian Unity, answering the doubts and difficulties stated by some of the fathers. The following are the most important: the doctrine as exposed by the schema was an implicit profession of religious indifferentism or at least favoured it; the neutralistic view of the State was contradicting the Church's teaching on this matter.

On the same day the Secretary General of the Council announced that the voting on the new version would take place on 19 November.

In the meantime, however, an important group of fathers demanded that, according to article 30, § 2, of the *Ordinamento* of the Council, the voting should be delayed, so that there would be sufficient time for a thorough examination of the text. For, the fathers suggested, this was a theme of the utmost importance; besides, the new text contained substantial alterations.

In view of this petition the Secretary General announced on the following day (18 November) that, before the voting on the schema on religious freedom, the question whether this voting should take place would itself be put to the vote on 19 November.

But on 19 November (126th general congregation) this voting, too, was cancelled; instead, Cardinal E. Tisserant read the following communication in the aula in the name of the presidial council:

"Quoad suffragationem schematis declarationis de libertate religiosa, plures Patres exceptionem fecerunt quod congruum tempus datum non fuerit ad maturanda consilia, ad deliberationes capiendas, attento praesertim, quod novus textus, iudicio quoque Secretariatus ad unitatem Christianorum fovendam in relatione expresso, novam structuram exhibeat et nova enuntiet. Re maturius perpensa, visum est Consilio Praesidentiae negotium, quod Ordinem Concilii Celebrandi tangit, non posse a Congregatione generali per suffragationem decerni. Idcirco, idem Consilium Praesidentiae statuit, post auditam relationem non esse procedendum ad suffragationem in hac Concilii sessione. Patres autem qui volunt suas animadversiones proponere, id faciant scriptis intra diem 31 ianuarii anni 1965."

This communication caused great excitement among most fathers. On the same day an express letter containing 441 signatures was sent to the Pope with the following words:

"Beatissime Pater
reverenter sed instanter, instantius, instantissime petimus ut suffragatio circa declarationem de libertate religiosa ante finem huius sessionis Concilii concedatur, ne fiducia mundi et christianorum et non christianorum amittatur..."

In the same general congregation Bishop de Smedt read his *relatio*, repeatedly interrupted by long applause.

Because of the heated atmosphere of the Council the Pope referred the case to the special court that had been created for the purpose of deciding such controversial cases. The court declared that the decision of the presidial council corresponded exactly to the *ordinamento* of the Council both in letter and in spirit.

The Pope, too, agreed to this decision with the following words, which Cardinal Tisserant read out in his name in the aula on 20 November:

"Nomine Summi Pontificis haec communico:
Noverint Patres dilationem in suffragando fuisse a Consilio Praesidentiae concessam, quia ad normam Ordinis Concilii celebrandi concedenda erat.

Eam insuper postulabat reverentia quaedam erga libertatem Patrum Conciliarum, quibus maxime cordi est rite et profunde schema tanti momenti examinare atque perpendere. Itaque schema declarationis 'De libertate religiosa' in proxima Concilii Sessione tractabitur et, si possibile sit, antequam alia schemata tractentur."

Thus this exciting affair was finished without the Council having been able to vote on the third schema on religious freedom.

6. The Fourth Schema (*Textus reemendatus*)

On 19 November 1964 Cardinal Tisserant had informed the fathers in his communication read in the Council hall that they could submit their views on the third schema to the general secretariat of the Council till 31 January 1965; the period was then extended to 17 February. The general secretariat received 218 suggestions, twelve of which were made in the name of several fathers, which were then transmitted to the Secretariat for Christian Unity.

From 18 to 28 February a group of Council theologians and advisers examined the individual suggestions very carefully and then began to work out proposals for a new schema.

In their plenary session from 28 February to 6 March the members of the Secretariat thoroughly discussed the third schema, the relevant suggestions of the fathers, their examination by advisers and *periti* and their proposals for a new text. The latter was edited at the end of the session under the heading *Textus reemendatus*.

At the beginning of April the *once more amended text* was transmitted to Cardinal Ottaviani as the president of the Commission for the Doctrine of Faith and Morals, who communicated it to the members of the Commission. The latter sent seventeen written suggestions to the Secretariat for Unity.

During the session of the members of the Secretariat which began on 2 May the text was once more altered according to these suggestions and thus received its final form as the fourth schema.

On 11 May the Co-ordinating Commission approved the schema, and on 27 May Paul VI gave permission to send it to all the Council fathers. In a fascicle of 54 pages both the amended and the re-amended texts were published side by side. The fascicle also contained a *relatio* of the Secretariat, in which the suggestions of the fathers on the third schema were summarized and which described the leading ideas that had guided the development of the fourth schema. The *Textus reemendatus* is divided into four parts:

1. The present historical situation and the Declaration of the Council on Religious Freedom
2. This freedom in the light of reason

55

3. In the light of revelation

4. In the historical situation of the present.

A special number (n. 9) on *salvation history* was inserted in the third part in order to show that religious freedom was based on this; in the final number (n. 14) two paragraphs had been added which stated that at the present time it was necessary to educate people, especially young people, for the right use of freedom in all departments of life, hence also in the religious sphere. The structure of the fourth schema is basically the same as that of the third, the essential elements of which are taken over. They are, however, presented in a shorter, clearer and more orderly form, the sequence of thought being less complicated and more evident. Hence not a few fathers considered it providential that the third schema had been neither discussed nor voted on in the aula, though of course not as regards the motives nor the manner in which the final decision had been arrived at.

According to the communication read by Cardinal Tisserant in the aula on 20 November 1964, the fourth schema was the first document to be discussed in the fourth session of the Council which began on 14 September 1965.

The discussion was opened on 15 September, continued on the 16th and 17th, and was resumed on 20 September. The next day, following the proposal of the Moderator, the fathers declared the discussion closed by an almost unanimous vote. Sixty-two suggestions had been made orally, about a hundred more had been made in writing to the Secretariat of the Council. Three basic attitudes emerged in the discussion:

a) A group of fathers agreed completely with the schema and demanded its publication without any alterations.

b) A second group declared the doctrine laid down in the text unacceptable and demanded that it should either be rejected or drawn up according to different principles.

c) A third group agreed substantially with the schema, but suggested more or less important alterations either regarding its structure, or its doctrine, or its style.

Hence there was an oppressive atmosphere of uncertainty both inside and outside the Council hall. How many fathers would accept at least the substance of the schema? How many would reject it altogether? And if it would have to be amended, what doctrinal trend would have to be followed?

The Secretariat for Christian Unity, which was responsible for the schema, asked the Council authorities to arrange for a decision in the aula, also because the fathers had never yet made known their view on religious freedom through a vote. In the evening of 20 September after a lively discussion, the plenary assembly of the Council authorities declared that there was to be no voting. But on the next day the Pope intervened and decided that the fathers were to be invited to make known their opinion on the following question on the same morning:

"Utrum textus reemendatus de Libertate Religiosa, placeat Patribus tamquam basis definitivae Declarationis ulterius perficiendae iuxta doctrinam catholicam de vera religione et emendationes a Patribus in disceptatione propositas et approbandas ad normam Ordinis Concilii."

Result of the voting: 2222 fathers present, 1997 *placet*, 224 *non placet*, 1 invalid vote.

On 22 September three fathers wished to speak once more on the same schema, each in the name of seventy or more fathers. According to the *regolamento* of the Council they were allowed to do so, and thus ended a debate that was perhaps the most violent ever to have taken place in the aula. It had been rich in dramatic moments, reflecting the love of truth and pastoral concerns as well as the interests of the various milieus in which the fathers have to exercise their apostolate.

7. The Fifth Schema *(Textus recognitus)*

After the discussion of the fourth schema in the Council hall the Secretariat for Christian Unity at once appointed a subcommission which was to draw up the fifth schema. It consisted of several members of the Secretariat and three other members, assisted by several theologians of the Council and advisers of the Secretariat. The subcommission began its work on 27 September by examining more than two hundred suggestions, some of which contained the demands of several, in certain cases of more than a hundred, fathers.

The proposals of the subcommission were extensively discussed in three plenary sessions of the members of the Secretariat. Thus the fifth schema, entitled *Textus recognitus*, was completed on 22 October, exactly a month after the discussion of the newly amended text had finished. The *revised* text was sent to the fathers in their living quarters. It was contained in a fascicle of 86 pages, in which both texts, the newly corrected and the revised one, were printed side by side. It also contained two *relationes*, one by Bishop E. J. M. de Smedt of Bruges, which emphasized some principles on which the Declaration was based; the other by the Secretariat, in which the wishes of the fathers were summarized and the reasons and contents of the alterations due to these wishes were explained.

The *relatio* of the Secretariat states at the beginning of part 2 that the principles of the doctrine of the fourth schema had been approved by a large majority of the Council fathers. For this reason only those proposals needed to be included in the fifth schema which, though numerous, did not substantially modify these principles, but could improve the structure and clarity of the document.

Besides, the *relatio* emphasized that the present form of the document corresponded better to the special character of the Declaration.

Above all, the subtitle qualifies the freedom with which the document is concerned by the two terms *socialis* and *civilis*. This is done for two reasons: a) to point out that there is no question of the relations between the person and truth or between the person and God, but of the interpersonal relations in human and political society; b) to suggest further that the document does not deal with the freedom with which the relations between Catholics are ordered within the Church itself, but with that freedom according to which the relations of men with one another as well as with social groups and public authority are ordered within the sphere of religion.

The fifth schema consists of fifteen articles divided into a Preface (Article 1) a centre piece (Articles 2–14) and a conclusion (Article 15). The Preface consists of two parts. The first part takes over number one of the preceding schema, but with certain changes emphasizing the responsibility of the person in the exercise of freedom, especially with relation to spiritual matters and to religion. The second part repeats and develops some elements which had already been present in the earlier schema, but differently formulated and in different contexts. According to the schema under consideration God has revealed that the way to salvation is to be found in the only true religion which is the Catholic Church, which Christ has commissioned to announce his message to all men (cf. Mt 27:19 f.). It follows from this that just as there is an obligation to seek for truth and to accept it according to one's certainty, so there is also the obligation to accept and profess the Catholic religion as soon as, and in so far as, it is known. *Hence it is an obligation which concerns and binds the conscience, because truth binds only in virtue of its own light.* But, as has been said before, religious freedom, with which the Declaration deals, concerns only the relations between persons in human society, and it consists in freedom from external coercion. Hence it does not touch the Catholic doctrine of the one true religion, the only Church of Jesus Christ and men's moral obligations towards it. This, of course, does not mean that religious freedom as a right of every individual in his relation to others can be completely divorced from the exercise of his freedom as an obligation to truth. The first is a function of the second, since it is based on this that men may not be prevented from following the truth in the measure as it appears to them.

Over and above this, the end of part two of the Preface reads: "In taking up the matter of religious freedom this sacred Synod intends to develop the doctrine of the Popes on the inviolable rights of the person and on the constitutional order of society" (*Textus recognitus*, p. 4, lines 12–18).

It is clear that this passage was added to the Preface in order to alleviate some doubts in the minds of some fathers with regard to the danger of religious indifferentism and of disagreement with earlier doctrinal statements.

The main part of the revised text is also divided into two sections, the first of which comprises Articles 2 to 8. Here the essential elements or the more important aspects of religious freedom are presented, such as it is taught in the Declaration.

1. Its essence: it is a right of the person, or, in other words, a natural right.

2. Its content: it is freedom from external compulsion.

3. Its basis: the dignity of the human person.

4. Its subject: every physical person and the moral persons of the religious communities.

5. The duties of the public authorities with regard to religious freedom: recognition, respect, protection, promotion, limitation.

6. Education for the exercise of freedom, especially of religious freedom.

The major changes in the fifth schema as compared with the fourth concern the basis of religious freedom and the duties of the public authorities with regard to it. As to its basis, the dignity of the human person in its relation to truth — *regarded as a value* — is especially emphasized. As regards the public authorities, these have the particular duty to be actively concerned to assure that the members of society have sufficient possibilities to exercise their rights and to fulfill their religious duties. Section 2 of the main part comprises Articles 9–14. There religious freedom is presented in the light of revelation. This section is substantially identical with the previous text. Article 9 on salvation history is left out, however, because it had raised too many difficulties and is also not an essential part of the document. The order of the subjects is slightly changed; some biblical proof texts are replaced by others, which seemed better suited to show that the actions of Christ and the apostles favoured religious freedom.

The conclusion of the fifth schema resumes that of the fourth, but here the sections on education for the exercise of freedom are left out because they had been taken over into the main part as Article 8.

Voting on the fifth schema took place on 26 and 27 October 1965. The two customary methods were used. The first used the two forms: 1) *Placet,* that is Yes; 2) *non placet,* that is No. This was designed to show whether the principal elements and the doctrinal trend of a document were accepted or rejected. Thus the fifth schema was voted on according to the following division:

First voting: Article 1
Second voting: Articles 2–3
Third voting: Articles 4–5
Fourth voting: Articles 6–8
Fifth voting: Articles 9–10

Sixth voting: Articles 11–12

Seventh voting: Articles 13–15.

On 27 October the highest number of fathers took part in the voting; it amounted to 2239; on the same day the highest number, 254 out of 2238, voted *non placet* at the sixth voting. Thus a large majority approved of the essentials of the definitive schema.

The second method of voting, on the other hand, comprises three possibilities: *placet, non placet,* and *placet juxta modum.* The last formula means agreement with the substance of the document, but asking for a change according to a *modus* suggested by the voter. The voting according to this second method took place as follows:

First voting: Articles 1–5

Second voting: Articles 6–8

Third voting: Articles 9–12

Fourth voting: Articles 13–15.

The highest number of voting fathers was reached at the third voting, on 27 October; it amounted to 2236. The highest number of votes *placet juxta modum* was cast at the first voting, on 26 October, 534 out of 2161 votes. Thus one of the most important stages in the evolution of the document on religious freedom had been reached; for now it had received almost its final form.

8. The Sixth Schema *(Textus denuo recognitus)*

Thus the fifth schema had been accepted with a large majority. When the fathers had voted according to the second method, however, it became evident that a considerable number intended to propose alterations. Actually the Secretariat of the Council transmitted more than six hundred *modi* to the Secretariat for Christian Unity, some of which were very important and not a few were proposed in the name of several fathers. Hence three working groups were formed, consisting of fathers who were members of the Secretariat, and they were assisted by Council theologians and advisers. All the *modi* were examined. But it was obvious that those rejecting the essential elements of the document or the main trend of its doctrine could not be considered or accepted, since the document had already been accepted with a much larger majority than the two thirds demanded by the *ordinamento* of the Council. Thus it was the task of the members of the Secretariat to consider which proposals were to be discussed, because they could contribute to an improved form and clarity of the text or to a clarification of an important statement.

On 8 and 9 November the members of the Secretariat examined the proposals of the three working groups in a plenary session and decided on the alterations which were once more to be made in the document. Thus the sixth schema came into being which was entitled "Textus *denuo* recognitus".

Fifty-nine changes were made in all. The majority were merely literary or had only formal importance. Nevertheless, within the framework mentioned above there were also several more important alterations; for example, the following sentence was inserted in the first part of the Preface: "The demand is also made that constitutional limits should be set to the powers of government, in order that there may be no encroachment on the rightful freedom of the person and of associations." This was meant to emphasize that the legal authorities of the political communities must show more consideration for modern man's increasing consciousness of the special dignity of the person. Because of this greater consciousness the problem of religious freedom had become more urgent and determined the global historical situation; hence the demand that the Council should produce a declaration on it. The importance of this consciousness showed itself also in the fact that the dignity of the person, understood as the claim to exercise responsibility, became the motive of the whole document. Furthermore, in the last paragraph of the Preface the word "recent" was added to "Popes". This was done because some fathers asserted again and again that the doctrine of the document contradicted the doctrine of the Popes on religious freedom. This addition was meant to suggest to these fathers that they should consider not only the doctrine of Leo XIII and his immediate predecessors, but also that of his successors, especially Pius XI, Pius XII, John XXIII and Paul VI. Such a sober and objective consideration could not but result in the certainty that there had, of course, been a doctrinal development, but that its last phase tended towards what was said in the Council document, if it did not actually agree with it. Another important insertion is that on the nature of the common welfare in Article 6 and on the duties of government in this respect. As is noted in the text of the document, this was already contained in the encyclical *Pacem in terris* (n. 59). This addition was meant to remove the doubts of some fathers who still believed that the neutralistic character of the State was implicitly asserted in the document. Hence it was thought useful to take up the proposal of some *modi* and to emphasize the positive duty of the State with regard to religion. This duty, however, must be exercised within the limits of its competence, which does not include pronouncing judgment on the value of a religious faith, but must create the conditions within which the members of a society can exercise their rights and fulfill their religious duties.

The sixth schema was sent to the fathers in a fascicle of 88 pages. It contained the *expensio modorum* and two *relationes,* one by Bishop de Smedt of Bruges, the other by the Secretariat for Christian Unity. The first explains the principles on which the fathers had worked in the final phase of the document; in the second the *expensio modorum,* that is, the examination of the *modi,* is summarized. The alterations are enumerated and the way in which the fathers were going to vote on the sixth schema is stated. The voting took place on 19 November. Of 2216 fathers 1954 voted positively, 249 negatively, and 13 votes were invalid. In the ninth public session on 7 December 1965, the Declaration on Religious Freedom, which begins with the words *Dignitatis humanae,* received 2308 positive and 70 negative votes, 8 votes being invalid. In this Session the Declaration was promulgated. Thus ended the evolution of a Council document which is of historical importance both for the Church and for humanity. It was worked out in a dramatic struggle, during which one of the most important doctrines was further deepened and clarified. In an important article in *La Stampa* (Turin, 9 December 1965), V. Gorresio welcomed it with these words: "The schema which deals with religious freedom constitutes by itself a genuine development of doctrine, perhaps the greatest and most characteristic progress achieved by the Council."

Commentary

Article 1 is divided into two parts. The first part emphasizes a characteristic phenomenon of modern times. Men are becoming increasingly conscious of their own personal dignity, which shows itself as a claim to greater freedom, regarded as an exercise of responsibility. Such a claim is particularly evident in the sphere of intellectual and spiritual values, especially also in the religious sphere. This is, moreover, also a claim concerning the function and organization of public authorities, which may legitimately be exercised only within legally defined limits. Hence these must be laid down as clearly as possible in order to guarantee the necessary space for the freedom of the citizens.

In such a historical situation there will be a new conception of religious freedom: in social relations it appears as a mutual right. It must, therefore, be understood as an expression of personal dignity and as an exercise of responsibility. Hence freedom is both duty and love, especially as regards spiritual values and above all with regard to God. This is why the Council has dealt with religious freedom and has issued a Declaration on it.

The second part contains some clarifications destined to remove existing doubts among the Council fathers. For many were afraid that the Declaration on Religious Freedom as a right of the person might lead to religious indifferentism or could at least be interpreted in this way by Christians, whether Catholic or Protestant, as well as by unbelievers. Hence the text deals with the following doctrines: 1. God has revealed a way in which men's salvation can be realized in Jesus Christ. 2. Such a way exists in the only true religion which "subsists in the Catholic and apostolic Church". 3. Men are bound to seek the truth, "especially in what concerns God and his Church", and also to embrace the truth and obey it insofar as it is apprehended. 4. The truth imposes itself and binds the conscience by virtue of itself, of the light that goes forth from it. 5. Religious freedom, however, does not concern the relation of the person to truth, but the mutual relationships between physical as well as moral persons. Hence the "traditional Catholic doctrine on the moral duty of men and societies toward the true religion and toward the one Church of Christ" is left untouched.

Another difficulty of the Council fathers has already been mentioned in the Introduction. This concerned the question whether the doctrine of the Declaration contradicted the teaching of the Popes, especially of Leo XIII. The Council text, however, does not regard this teaching as having been defined by a Pope in its final form once and for all, but sees it as gradually developing through new papal contributions, especially in our own century. This doctrine develops, as it were, like a seed, which first germinates and then beomes an ever more vigorous plant. As is emphasized in the text, under the influence of the evolving historical situation the Popes have increasingly emphasized the dignity of the human person and pronounced this to possess inviolable rights in the economic, social, political, cultural, moral and religious spheres.

The encyclical *Pacem in terris* may be regarded as a synthesis of this teaching, which the present Council document developed still further.

A third difficulty concerned the question whether the Declaration did not imply a laicistic and neutralistic conception of the State, which would also contradict the Christian social doctrine that had already been accepted. Hence the last sentence of Article 1 mentions the teaching of recent Popes on the constitutional order of society.

This was done in order to suggest that the doctrine of the Declaration agrees with the basic tendency of the modern view of the State such as it emerges in the cultural and legal spheres of the political communities. This is the democratic constitutional State, the essential elements of which have been discussed by recent Popes from Pius XI to John XXIII. This State can certainly not be confused with the laicistic or neutralistic State which had always been condemned by the Popes and which the Council, too, could only reject.

Article 2 is undoubtedly the most important article of this Declaration. The first part gives the main content of the document:

1. Every man has a right to religious freedom because he is a person.

2. The object or content of this right is freedom from coercion on the part of individuals or of social groups or any human power.

3. This freedom from coercion has a double meaning: "in matters religious no one is to be forced to act in a manner contrary to his own beliefs"; within due limits no one is "to be restrained from acting in accordance with his own beliefs, whether privately or publicly, whether alone or in association with others".

4. This right has its foundation in the dignity of the human person, such as it is known in the light of revelation and by reason.

5. It is a right of the person which is to be recognized as a civil right in the constitutional law of the political society.

Some of these points need to be explained more fully; on others we shall comment in the following pages.

1. "Haec Vaticana Synodus declarat personam humanam ius habere ad libertatem religiosam" is a solemn statement which characterizes the document and gives it its historical importance.

In the last phase of the discussion on religious freedom the Council fathers were unanimous on the principle that every man has the right to freedom in the religious sphere. Nevertheless, there continued to be a difference of opinion as to the basis of this right. A militant minority insisted that it must be regarded as a positive civil right and be based on the relation to the common good with regard to the present historical situation. These reasons, mentioned in Article 15 of the document, are above all: a) religious pluralism which exists in all political communities even though in different degrees; b) the increasingly close relation between the political communities within the individual continents as well as on the global plane, so that an event in one society immediately reacts on all others; c) men's greater consciousness of their personal dignity which does not tolerate interference from others, be they individuals, social groups or public authorities.

An ever increasing majority of the fathers became convinced that the motives mentioned had certainly contributed to the new views on the problem of religious freedom; thus these motives caused the Council to take an interest in the subject. Nevertheless, the right to religious freedom must be regarded as *a fundamental right of the person* or as a *natural right, that is, one grounded in the very nature of man,* as the Declaration itself repeats several times. Hence there can be no doubt that the majority of the fathers shared the point of view of the Declaration. This emerges also from the last sentence of this section: "Hoc ius personae humanae ad libertatem religiosam in iuridica societatis ordinatione ita est agnoscendum, ut ius civile evadat."

2. As has been said, the object of the right is freedom from coercion. Hence the object is essentially negative: it consists in not acting, that is to say, in the religious sphere compulsion is excluded or not used. It is important to be clear about the negative nature of the object, so as to avoid the idea that the object of the right to religious liberty is connected with the content of religious faith. If the content is error, this happens if it is implicitly demanded that a man should have the right to profess and spread error. Now these are evils, and of course no one can have the right to evil actions, thus the following statement of Pius XII must be interpreted in this sense: "What does not correspond to truth and moral norms has objectively no right to exist, to be propagated and to act" (Allocution of 6 December 1953). This results quite clearly from the nature of the right.

Since a right exists in a person, this means that all other persons are in duty bound to recognize and respect this right. The subject of the right has the duty to actualize its content; but no one can have the duty to actualize an immoral object. Hence it is easy to understand that those fathers who continued to base the content of the right to religious freedom on the elements of religious faith could not but express their opinion that such a right belongs only to those who professed the true faith. Hence they failed to understand how such a right could be conceded also to those professing religions that are not true.

But the deepest reason why the contents of religious faith are not and cannot be the object of religious freedom is that the relation between the persons and these contents is not a legal but rather a metaphysical or logical or moral one. Since the legal relationship is essentially an inter-subjective relation, it can only exist between physical and moral subjects or persons. For the reasons given above it is useful to remember also that the object of a right must be good or at least be capable of being directed towards a good. Now freedom from coercion as a principle by which to order inter-human relationships is something good: it is actually a condition as well as a guarantee that men can act according to their nature, that is, responsibly, as will be explained more fully later on. Certainly, freedom from coercion in the religious sphere can be realized badly, if errors are professed and propagated, whether in good or in bad faith. But the abuse of a right does not destroy it; at most it may make it advisable to prevent the exercise of this right according to appropriate criteria. But this subject will be more fully discussed later.

3. As has been seen, the expression "freedom from coercion" in the text has two meanings: in the religious sphere no man may be compelled to act against his conscience; and no one may be prevented from acting according to his conscience.

It must first be stated that here the term "conscience" means above all responsibility, so that the statement must be understood thus: In the religious sphere no one may be compelled to act in a way different from that in which he himself has *decided* to act, and no man may be prevented from acting according to this way.

In the second place "conscience" means moral rectitude, so that the statement means this: In the religious sphere no one may be compelled to act in a way different from that in which he knows himself *obliged* to act; and he may not be prevented from acting according to this way. Thus it is clear that the problems of the true or the erroneous conscience are not touched on at all in the document. The reason for it is that the problems discussed are moral, not legal. They belong directly and formally to the relation between person and truth, not to the relation between person and person. Besides, as we shall see, the right of men to religious freedom results from the objective demands based on their nature of free and intelligent beings who are therefore destined to responsible action. Hence this right is not conditioned by the fact that they may or may not have a true and right, or a right but erroneous conscience. But this does not exclude that one of the most profound reasons for such a right is that men may be able faithfully and without hindrance to follow the light of truth, according to its presence in their mind.

Thirdly, the doctrine of the Church has always acknowledged, at least implicitly, and frequently also explicitly, that men have the right not to be compelled to act against their own conscience in religious matters; indeed this doctrine was demanded in the theological teaching on the freedom of the act of faith.

For several centuries, however, this right was not acknowledged by Christian society; this was the case if men's religion was not the true one or if they refused to accept the true religion. This attitude will be discussed in the commentary on Article 12.

4. As the document explains, the right to religious freedom is based on the dignity of the human person, such as it is recognized in the light of revelation and through human reason itself.

The dignity of the human person is the motive that marks and unifies the whole document. It is realized in three ways.

First of all historically, as has already been stated in the Introduction and in the commentary on Article 1. The Council wanted to make a statement on the subject because modern men had become more acutely conscious of their personal dignity, and hence the problem of religious freedom had taken on a new aspect.

Secondly, the freedom of the person is approached from the point of view of man's duty to assume responsibility for his relation to God in personal decisions. When the person has reached the point at which he can distinguish between true and false, between good and evil, he shares in deciding his own eternal destiny. True, this remains always a gift of God, but it is at the same time the result of a personal decision; therein lies its highest dignity. Thus Article 11 reads: "God calls men to serve him in spirit and in truth. Hence they are bound in conscience but they stand under no compulsion. God has regard for the dignity of the human person whom he himself created; man is to be guided by his own judgment and he is to enjoy freedom." It goes without saying that man's unalterable personal responsibility for his relation to God demands freedom from social religious pressure; indeed, this inescapable responsibility is itself the ontological root of the right of the person to religious freedom.

Thirdly, the dignity of the person resulting from his relation to truth is examined in the document in a threefold way: a) a relation between man and truth as a value (Article 2, paragraph 2); b) a relation between man and self-existing truth, which is the true, transcendent and personal God himself (Article 3); c) a relation between man and revealed truth, which is the supernatural order itself (Article 10) at the centre of which is the Word made man. The consideration of each of these three relations leads to the same result: the dignity of the human person demands freedom from compulsion regarding the religious sphere of social life.

The second part of Article 2 treats of the relation between man and truth as a value in order to clarify how the right to religious freedom is based on the dignity of the person resulting from this relation. In fact, there is a certain divergence between the first and the second part of this article in doctrine as well as in content. This is shown by the form of the presentation: the first part is a sequence of statements, each sentence being, as it were, a solemn declaration in which the Council is profoundly involved; the second part, on the other hand, is concerned with arguments in which the "engagement" of the Council is less evident. This explains why several of the fathers and theologians of the Council regarded the following article as the more suitable place for the subject developed in the second part. But those favouring the insertion in Article 2 prevailed, because this was the most important article of the whole document; hence it seemed fitting that it should be reasonably complete.

The second part of Article 2 states that men are endowed by nature with reason and free will and hence are personally responsible for their actions. They must therefore realize the need and the duty to seek the truth, especially in the religious sphere. They must also adhere to this truth in the measure in which they find it and order their life in accordance with it. Thus there are three factors, knowledge, love and action, through which men develop and perfect their personalities. But truth can be known only in the light of truth. Its inner evidence can never be replaced by external force; it can, on the other hand, be an element of confusion. Adhering to truth is an act of love which must be free. Though all expressions of life may conform to the truth that has been grasped, they are not humanly valid if they are produced not through personal decision but under pressure from the surrounding world. This demand is rooted in the very essence of this relation, regardless of subjective disposition. According to the Declaration, therefore, the right to immunity from coercion remains, even if it is abused. Its exercise, however, may be prevented if the abuse leads to the overthrow of the public order, as is shown in the following.

Article 3. Here the dignity of the human person is considered as based on man's relation to self-existing truth.

Once men have opened their hearts to the knowledge of the true God, they will also realize that he is the principal source of their own existence as well as the last end towards which it is moving. They will realize further that their relation to God is ordered according to his eternal, objective and universal law, which they must seek to know in order to obey it.

With regard to this law the text considers the two ways in which men come to accept it: a) its knowledge; b) its application to concrete cases.

As to the first, the Declaration states that the knowledge of the divine law results from personal inquiry into truth, carried on with the aid of instruction and dialogue. But what is the criterion that governs the mutual relations of men seeking the truth? It is honesty, in the sense of having the duty to communicate to others the truth as seen by oneself, and also in the sense of assenting to the thought of others in as far as this is believed to be true. But this presupposes an atmosphere of freedom in society and the absence of any coercion that would force men into particular lines of thought. For such compulsion would inevitably lead to lies, double talk, and in the religious sphere especially to mere formalism.

As regards the application of the divine law to concrete cases, this is demanded by the judgment of man's conscience, which he must faithfully follow throughout his life in order to reach his last end, which is God. Now this presupposes that he is not forced to act against his conscience nor prevented from acting in accordance with it. True, religious faith is concerned above all with interior acts which are free and voluntary; but man is by his nature a social being and hence intended to bear social witness to his faith. Thus the right to religious freedom is rooted in the profound claim of man to be honest with himself also in this delicate sphere. This claim is one of the most obvious aspects of his dignity. To neglect this right would mean to violate his dignity and to reject the order established by God, who has created men as free social beings.

The last paragraph of Article 3 emphasizes one of the reasons why the public authorities are obliged to acknowledge and esteem religious freedom: namely that by their very nature the religious acts transcend the order of terrestrial and temporal affairs, while the competence of governments is restricted to this sphere.

Article 4. This article considers the subjects of the right to religious freedom.

It must first be repeated that the subjects of this right are human beings considered as persons. Hence it is a right that belongs to all, believers as well as unbelievers. When speaking about the sphere in which this right is valid the fathers used the expression *in re religiosa:* "in religious matters". It was certainly chosen because it was very comprehensive.

The atheist solves the religious problem in a negative way. Yet it cannot be denied that this solution, too, belongs to the sphere of religious matters.

69

The religious communities, too, are subjects of the right to freedom. According to the text, "the freedom or immunity from coercion in matters religious which is the endowment of persons as individuals is also to be recognized as their right when they act in community".

It must be admitted that this sentence is not very clear. Hence some notes will help to arrive at a correct interpretation. The Council wants here to emphasize once more that men are by nature social beings and hence have the natural right to profess their individual religious faith also externally and in a communal form (cf. Article 3, para. 3). It also expresses the legitimacy of religious communities, since they are based on the fact that men are essentially social beings, and they result from this very fact. Hence the second sentence of this paragraph runs: "Religious bodies are a requirement of the social nature both of men and of religion itself." It was also the intention of the Council to stress that the Catholic Church differs in origin from all other religious communities. The social nature of men is the basis of these religions, and even with regard to the Catholic Church this basis retains its value and may therefore be important for the encounter with non-Catholics. Nevertheless the Catholic Church is a divine foundation: it was established by Christ and is the only true religion (cf. Article 13). It would nevertheless be wrong to interpret the sentence just quoted as meaning that, apart from the Catholic Church, all other religious communities are merely the sum of their members. They are rather regarded as sociological and juridical units, hence as true moral persons and direct subjects of rights and duties.

The same article circumscribes the extent of the community's right to religious freedom. Such communities may not be prevented by force from fashioning their own life through the activities enumerated in Articles 2 and 3, nor from publicly teaching and professing their faith by word of mouth and in writing (para. 4). They must, however, avoid unworthy means, "especially when dealing with poor or uneducated people" *(ibid.)*, and also any methods "considered an abuse of one's own right and a violation of the right of others" *(ibid.).* The last sentence is rather unfortunate, for it might suggest the idea that the abuse of one's own right *always* implies the violation of the right of others, which is not true. It is even less true in the present context. Even though it is true that the communities abuse their right if they try to propagate their own religion by wrong methods, this does not imply that by doing so they *always* violate the right of others. If this were affirmed, it would justify an intervention of the State limiting religious freedom, so that there would be a risk of its complete suppression. Hence the sentence under discussion must be interpreted in the spirit of the whole document with special reference to Article 7, para. 2. It may therefore be interpreted in this way: such an action is regarded as an abuse of one's own right; *sometimes* it may also involve violating the right of another. The right mentioned implies particularly that religious bodies should not be prohibited from showing the special value of their doctrine for the organization and inspiration of the activities and institutions of the temporal order (Article 4, para. 5).

It is particularly important that, while the extent of the communities' right to religious freedom is circumscribed in Article 4, the document nowhere defines this right with regard to individuals. It can, however, be ascertained by analogical reasoning, in complete accord with the complex content of the document. Hence in the case of individual persons, too, the right to religious freedom means, first, that they should not be prevented from religious acts by which God is duly worshipped; secondly, that they must not be hindered from communicating and spreading their own religious faith, using suitable means for doing so; and it means, finally, that they may not be prevented from influencing temporal institutions according to the spirit of their own religious principles. According to one Council father this claim derives directly from the objective moral order, which is that all human activity is ultimately judged by the relation between a man and God, whatever its particular content or sphere. This is at least implied also in the last sentence of the article.

Article 5. Apart from human persons and religious bodies, individual families, too, must be regarded as subjects of the right to religious freedom. Here the parents have the duty to order the religious life. They have the right to determine the religious education of their children in accordance with their own religious beliefs; hence they have the right to choose schools and other educational institutions with this end in view. Governments, in consequence, must acknowledge and respect this right. This duty concerns especially two cases: a) if the government prescribes a form of education in which the religious formation is ruled out, as is the case in totalitarian States; b) if it forces the children to attend religious instruction which is not in agreement with the religious beliefs of the parents, which is or may be the case in so-called denominational States. These rights of the parents — which are also their duties — are also violated if they are formally recognized by law but are prevented from being exercised in fact. This is the case if all members of a society without distinction are forced to contribute to an educational system designed for all, without being given the opportunity to educate their children according to their particular religious beliefs. Hence the text says: "Government, in consequence, must acknowledge the right of parents to make a genuinely free choice of schools and of other means of education. The use of this freedom of choice is not to be made a reason for imposing unjust burdens on parents, whether directly or indirectly" (Article 5).

Article 6. According to this article all have the duty to realize the right to religious freedom, whether individuals, social groups, the Church and other religious communities, "in virtue of the duty of all toward the common welfare, and in the manner proper to each" (Article 6, para. 1).

The encyclical *Pacem in terris* declares that in modern times, however, the common welfare consists above all in preserving the rights and duties of the human person: "Therefore the State must be especially concerned on the one hand that these rights should be acknowledged, protected and furthered, and on the other that everyone can fulfill his duties more easily" (n. 59).

Hence it is the principal duty of the government to acknowledge and respect the right to religious freedom. The document states this implicitly in the last paragraph of Article 3: "Government, therefore, ought indeed to take account of the religious life of the people and show it favour . . . however, it would clearly transgress the limits set to its power were it to presume to direct or inhibit acts that are religious." This is why governments must refrain from such actions to which the last paragraph of this article alludes.

Secondly, the governments must guarantee and protect the right to religious freedom. Hence, according to the text of the Declaration, "government is to assume the safeguard of the religious freedom of all its citizens, in an effective manner, by just laws and by other appropriate means" (Article 6, para. 2).

Thirdly, government has the duty to foster religious freedom, that is, "to help create conditions favourable to the fostering of religious life, in order that the people may be truly enabled to exercise their religious rights and to fulfill their religious duties" *(ibid.)*.

Now it may happen that a political community finds itself in a situation where it is considered useful that a certain religion should be granted "special legal recognition". If this should be the case, the text declares that "it is at the same time imperative that the right of all citizens and religious bodies to religious freedom should be recognized and made effective in practice" (Article 6, para. 3). On this subject the opinions of the fathers were very divided. A minority asserted that whenever the Catholics were in a majority, the State had the duty to favour a Catholic State for the sake of the truth. Other fathers held a diametrically opposed view and wanted that this subject should not be mentioned at all. There were also those who said that there were religiously qualified States. This is a fact that cannot be denied. This provided an opportunity to declare that in such cases every man and every religious body must be granted the right to religious freedom and to its exercise.

It was finally also suggested that this case should be considered in hypothetical form. This view gained acceptance and was therefore expressed in the text.

Article 7. In the life of human society all rights are exercised together with others; and the same applies to the right of freedom in religious matters.

This concerns especially individual men and women, who are bound to exercise their rights responsibly, that is, according to the moral order, in other words with respect for the rights of others and the demands of the common good (Article 7, para. 1).

But it is possible and has actually happened more than once in human history that men abuse their religious freedom, using it as a pretext for actions that are harmful to individuals or communities, or in order to justify these actions once they have been committed. In such cases it goes without saying that individuals as well as society have the right to defend themselves. In principle this defence is reserved to government, though not in arbitrary fashion, but according to the objective criterion of justice or, as the text has it, "controlled by juridical norms which are in conformity with the objective moral order" (Article 7, para. 3). In this context we would point out the laborious process by which the Council fathers gradually arrived at the view expressed in the Declaration.

As has been said before, we must realize above all that the abuse of a right does not lead to its being abolished. Otherwise there could be no rights at all, because there is none that cannot be abused, and that men actually have abused (cf. Article 2, para. 2). Secondly, the abuse of a right does not empower the government to prevent its exercise. This had already been stated by Pius XII with special reference to religious matters. "Can God", the Pope asked, "who could easily suppress error and moral aberrations, nevertheless choose in some cases the *non impedire* without prejudice to his infinite perfection? May he, in certain circumstances, give no command, impose no duty, indeed give no right to men to hinder and suppress what is erroneous and false? One glance at reality compels an affirmative answer. It shows that there is a great deal of error and sin in the world. God rejects them, nevertheless he allows them to continue. Hence the thesis that religious and moral aberration must be hindered whenever possible because its toleration is in itself immoral, is not absolutely and unconditionally valid. On the other hand, God has not given human authority such an absolute and universal commandment, neither in the sphere of faith nor in the sphere of morals. Neither general human conviction nor Christian consciousness nor the sources of revelation or the practice of the Church are aware of such a command" (Allocution of 6 December 1953).

Therefore not every abuse of the right to religious freedom is sufficient to warrant the exercise of the right to suppression by the government. Hence the problem: What is the criterion to be used by the government for determining when it is bound to prevent the abuse of religious freedom? The first criterion proposed by the fathers during the evolution of the document was the common good: The government can and may consider itself authorized to limit the exercise of the right to religious freedom if the common good demands it. But many Council fathers objected at once that this criterion was too vague; it left many possibilities for an arbitrary or generally insufficiently justified limitation of the right. So it was proposed that the objective goal of a society should be accepted as a criterion. But the same and also other fathers said that this was equally vague, and the right to religious freedom was in this case, too, exposed to the arbitrary decisions of the government. Moreover, while looking for a suitable criterion the fathers were seeking to avoid two pitfalls: on the one hand individuals and communities must be prevented from violating the rights of others and harming society under pretext of religious freedom, on the other hand governments must not be allowed arbitrarily to limit the right to religious freedom in the name of justice. Pius XII had been confronted with substantially the same problem, and he had suggested that the limitations of religious faith and practice of the citizens should be governed by the criminal law of the State. "... in each territory of a political community the citizens of each member State are allowed to practise their religious faith ... *in so far as this does not violate the criminal law of the State in which they reside*" (*ibid.*, our italics). In the constitutions of many modern States — especially of those that have come into existence after the disappearance of the colonial powers — the public order is the criterion of the limitation of the right to religious freedom. This criterion had already been stated in Article 10 of the French Declaration of the Rights of Man, 1789; it is also to be found in other documents of a universal or regional character such as the Convention of the members of the Council of Europe for the Protection of the Rights of Man and Fundamental Liberties (Article 9, para. 2) which was signed in Rome on 5 November 1950. There is only a formal rather than a substantial difference between the criminal law mentioned by Pius XII and the public order named by the constitutions of the modern States. Both state the elements which the moral consciousness of men regards as essential for a decent communal life.

The fathers finally agreed on the criterion of the public order, while adding some important precisions.

Above all the document describes what is involved in the public order by declaring that it consists of the basic elements of the common good, namely: a) the effective safeguard of the rights of all citizens and the peaceful settlement of conflicts of rights; b) sufficient protection of public peace; the proper guardianship of public morality (Article 7, para. 3).

It is further said more exactly that public order does not mean just any actual situation, but an order of common life conforming to the objective demands of justice. This presupposes that the essential conditions for a decent social life are present.

The document declares further that the public peace, which is one of these conditions, does not only consist in the absence of social unrest, but is a "genuine public peace, which comes about when men live together in good order and in true justice" (Article 7, para. 3). The last two additions were made at the request of a great many fathers who had said that public order might be made a pretext for a government to justify the limitation of religious freedom. This is the case especially when the existing public order is the product of an erroneous ideology and is used by the State as a means for preserving and advancing this ideology.

It must, however, be said that despite these additions the criterion of public order, too, is open to abuse, for the simple reason that there simply is no criterion which governments might not abuse to violate religious freedom. The fathers were well aware of this; nevertheless they decided to include this criterion in the text because they considered it the most suitable to solve this difficult problem. Moreover, it was the least difficult for modern men to understand, because it has been widely accepted in the spheres of law and politics. Besides, it confirms, even though only implicitly, the doctrine that unites all the parts of the Declaration.

This criterion means, therefore, that the lawful limitation of religious freedom must be based on the necessity to protect the basic elements of the common good that have been mentioned before. Hence it must not be governed by religious motives, as if the State were obliged to permit and advance this freedom if the religion is, or is supposed to be, the true one, but to prevent its exercise if the religion professed by the citizens is, or is supposed to be, a false one. As has been said before, governments are not competent to judge the content of a religion. Men's right to religious freedom, understood as freedom from coercion, is not based on the real or supposed truth of their religion, but on the indestructible responsibility of the individual to solve the religious problem by a personal decision.

Finally, the limitation of religious freedom should always be governed by the principle according to which "the freedom of man (must) be respected as far as possible, and curtailed only when and in so far as necessary" (Article 7, para. 4).

Article 8. This article deals with the necessity to educate men to the right use of freedom in all spheres, hence also in the sphere of religion. There are many factors in our society which make it more difficult for men to exercise their freedom and to act responsibly.

The ever increasing emphasis on the natural sciences in the curricula of every kind, scientific research itself, the technical inventions, the constant assimilation of the processes of production to the results of scientific and technological progress, all these lead men to concentrate on these spheres, to investigate the world ever more thoroughly in order to discover the forces it contains and the laws by which it is governed. Further, men seek to create instruments corresponding to the laws with which to use and dominate these elements and powers, to rationalize the economy and to increase productivity. Thus they are ever more deeply involved in mathematical and scientific knowledge, in technological creations as well as in the highly complex world of economics. All this contributes to creating a mentality which makes it difficult for them to follow their deepest personal instincts and to open themselves to the universal spiritual values, to the moral good and to justice.

Further, the senses, the imagination and the emotions are increasingly influenced by the intensity of traffic and by the ever more refined methods of propaganda and advertising on radio and television, in the cinema, the illustrated press, daily and weekly papers. All this makes it almost impossible to arrive at an inner peace and recollection necessary for personal judgment and decision. Thus the conduct of men is influenced by a continuous succession of situations, becoming increasingly the product of immediate explosive reactions in the sensual sphere instead of being the result of free and conscious decisions.

This socialization also intensifies the relations between individuals and produces a growing number of associations for the pursuit of collective interests. Besides, by enlarging the activities of government even in such delicate social sectors as health, education, professional training, communications and culture itself, this socialization tends increasingly to reduce the sphere in which men can make personal decisions and act on their own initiative and responsibility (cf. the encyclical *Mater et Magistra*, n. 67).

With regard to these phenomena Article 8 of the Declaration says that "many pressures are brought to bear upon men of our day, to the point where the danger arises lest they lose the possibility of acting on their own judgment" (para. 1). It is not difficult to show that these phenomena also prevent men from finding the true reason why the social life implies a relation between those who have to govern and those whose duty it is to obey. Because no valid reason for obedience is forthcoming, individual liberty is emphasized. Hence the order and discipline that exist in society are produced by the pressure of the milieu or by self-interest rather than by a free decision which is both a right and a duty: "On the other hand, not a few can be found who seem inclined to use the name of freedom as the pretext for refusing to submit to authority and for making light of the duty of obedience" *(ibid.).*

But there is also another side to it. The phenomena we have mentioned have also a positive influence on the social life. Scientific progress applied to the economy enormously increases production. Hence an increasing number of people can satisfy their elementary needs and raise their standard of living: there are new possibilities for work; elementary education is enlarged and improved; there is more time for recreation and access to all kinds of cultural pursuits becomes less difficult. Moreover, through the modern means of communication, the press, the cinema, radio and television individuals take part in the human destiny on a worldwide basis (cf. *Mater et Magistra*, n. 66).

Thus men are living a richer and more varied life which encourages the individual to realize his own personal dignity. This realization tends to express itself in legal terms. But legal concepts imply rights as well as duties. When men become conscious of both they already communicate with a sphere of values such as truth, goodness, justice, that is to say, with universal values which are, as it were, reflections of God. Then they will desire to live in union with him and thus receive guidance for their whole life (cf. *Pacem in terris*, n. 42 f.).

Hence the characteristic features of our time may have positive as well as negative effects. For this reason it is right and even necessary to educate men so that they may learn to use these features for their own perfection. They must be helped above all to discover the deeper aspects of reality, particularly human beings themselves. For self-knowledge is the knowledge of one's own mind and spirit, of its demands, its laws, its workings and its destiny. It is further the knowledge of one's own thought processes, the feeling for beauty and artistic values, the consciousness of duty and of the moral order; social sense and the objective demands of justice; response to the call of the Infinite and of the light of self-existing truth which is God.

Secondly, education must aim at enabling man to judge according to moral principles and thus to exercise responsibility. It must foster the conviction that one's own basic rights are best guaranteed by acknowledging and respecting the rights of others; that we also have the duty to realize the contents of these rights. For example, we cannot demand that others should not bring unjustified pressure to bear in the religious sphere unless we are prepared not to do the same to them.

Finally, this education serves to develop the team spirit in pursuing mutually profitable ends. Thus men begin to understand and esteem one another, and there develops an atmosphere of confidence, of mutual benevolence and reconciliation, because those who are in the truth can confess it openly, and those who are in error can find the truth. This is true in every sphere, hence also in religion.

"Therefore the Vatican Synod urges everyone, especially those who are charged with the task of educating others, to do their utmost to form men who will respect the moral order and be obedient to lawful authority. Let them form men too who will be lovers of true freedom — men, in other words, who will come to decisions on their own judgment and in the light of truth, govern their activities with a sense of responsibility, and strive after what is true and right, willing always to join with others in co-operative effort" (Article 8, para. 2).

Article 9. This article contains essentially three statements:

a) Religious freedom, understood as the right of the person to immunity from external coercion, is not formally affirmed by revelation.

b) Nevertheless, religious freedom is deeply rooted in revelation.

c) The reason for it is that, as has been said before, religious freedom is based on the dignity of the person. This dignity is fully known only in the light of revelation. In this light, therefore, men recognized more clearly the constitutive elements of their own nature and hence also their personal dignity. Their elevation to the supernatural order can be known only in the light of revelation. This elevation raises their dignity almost to infinity. In this light, and above all in the knowledge of Christ, the incarnate Word, men realize much more clearly, and as it were experience, that man's relation to God is conscious, free and responsible. And for this reason freedom in social relations must be a right.

Article 10. This considers the dignity of the human person which springs from its relation to revealed truth, which is the same as the supernatural order that is centred in the Word made man.

It is a basic element of Catholic doctrine that the act of faith through which a man is introduced to the spiritual order must be a free act. Free not in the sense of its being indifferent whether this act is made or not, but in the sense that, once a man has come to a sufficient knowledge of revealed truth and has realized his duty to consent to it, he can do so only by a free personal decision, even though this decision is valid only through a special assistance of God which is called grace. Hence by its very essence the act of faith excludes any form of coercion. "Ad fidem quidem nullus est cogendus invitus" (Augustine: *PL*, XLIII, 315).

It is evident that the act of faith can most easily be made in a milieu where religious freedom is recognized as a right, that is to say, where coercion in this sphere is prohibited.

Article 11. Here should be remembered what Paul VI says in his encyclical *Ecclesiam suam:* "No one was forced to take up this dialogue of salvation. It was an unheard-of invitation to love. It meant a frightening responsibility for those to whom it was addressed (cf. Mt 11:21) — it left them free to respond to or to reject it; but through the multitude of signs and miracles (cf. Mt 12:38 ff.) it was adapted to the needs and capacities of the hearers according to the credibility of the signs themselves (cf. Mt 13:13), in order to make it easier for the hearers to give their free consent to the divine revelation without depriving them of merit" (n. 77).

The Council fathers were deeply divided in their views of scriptural arguments in favour of religious freedom. Some thought it useless to quote texts for the simple reason that religious freedom in the sense of the Declaration was never mentioned in Scripture. Moreover, it was considered irreverent to press relevant passages so as to draw out a content which they did not actually possess. Other fathers, on the contrary, said that religious freedom could and must be proved only by arguments taken from revelation: hence it was their duty carefully to look for scriptural texts with this end in view. And, these fathers added, if this was not possible, the Council ought not to deal with this subject, let alone issue a Declaration on it, for a Council could only make doctrinal decisions in the light of revelation. During the debate, however, the line taken by the document emerged ever more clearly and was finally accepted almost unanimously. Undoubtedly the relation between God and man is revealed unmistakably in Christ, in words truly expressing an inner and direct transcendental relation in truth and love, which is therefore free and absolutely responsible.

The Lord has never used compulsion in order to move his hearers to accept his teaching. "He wrought miracles to shed light on his teaching and to establish its truth. But his intention was to rouse faith in his hearers, not to exert coercion upon them (Cf. Mt 8:28 f.; Mk 9:23 f.)." In solemn words he clearly emphasized the relation between men's eternal destiny and their moral and religious life in time, but he never brought pressure to bear and never forced them to walk or continue in the good way or leave evil (cf. Mt 11:20–24; Mk 16:16). Nor did he ever suggest to use compulsion; on the contrary, he taught exactly the opposite (cf. Mt 13:30, 40 ff.). In his continuous dialogue with men of all sorts he never used the method of oppressive repetition, but always showed tact and understanding, presenting the truth in a way suited to the capacities of his hearers: "He refused to be a political Messiah, ruling by force (cf. Mt 4:8 ff.; Jn 6:15) ... He showed himself the perfect Servant of God (cf. Is 42:1–4); 'a bruised reed he will not break, and a smoking wick he will not quench' (Mt 12:20)" (Article 11, para. 4).

When the dispute about the messianic kingdom between the Lord and the leaders of his people had reached its height, Christ ordered Peter to put away his sword (Mt 26:51–54; Jn 18:36) and chose the Cross in order to complete his saving work (cf. Jn 12:32).

It may therefore be said that religious freedom as a right of the person has not actually and formally been stated in the teaching and the example of Christ; nevertheless they show unequivocally that "God calls men to serve him in spirit and in truth. Hence they are bound in conscience but they stand under no compulsion. God has regard for the dignity of the human person whom he himself created; man is to be guided by his own judgment and he is to enjoy freedom. This truth appears at its height in Christ Jesus, in whom God perfectly manifested himself and his ways with men" (Article 11, para. 1 f.). It is certain that through this teaching and example or rather through the whole work of Christ a new way has appeared in the social relations of men, and when the time was ripe this way led to the declaration of the right of the person to religious freedom.

The apostles continued the work of the Master by following his teaching and example. Hence they did not use compulsion or other means unworthy of the gospel. "With a firm faith they held that the gospel is indeed the power of God unto salvation for all who believe" (Article 11, para. 8). "And they preached the Word of God in the full confidence that there was resident in this Word itself a divine power able to destroy all the forces arrayed against God (cf. Eph 6:11–17) and to bring men to faith in Christ and to his service (2 Cor 10:3 ff.)." Besides, like their Master, so the apostles, too, taught that the civil authority has its origin in God: "For there exists no authority except from God" (Rom 13:1), hence it must be respected and obeyed, when it is exercised legitimately within its own sphere, that is, in the sphere of earthly and temporal ends: "Let everyone be subject to the higher authorities . . .; he who resists the authority resists the ordinance of God" (Rom 13:1 f.). At the same time, however, they steadfastly resisted the governing power when this was opposed to the will of God. They then said: "We must obey God rather than men" (Acts 5:29). One new and typical fact of Christian society became ever more evident in their doctrine as well as in their work, namely that according to the order of salvation there are two powers in the family of men, "the ecclesiastical and the civil, the one being set over divine, the other over human things. Each in its kind is supreme, each has fixed limits within which it is contained, limits which are defined by the nature and special object of the province of each, so that there is, we may say, an orbit traced out within which the action of each is brought into play by its own native right" (Leo XIII, encyclical *Immortale Dei*, n. 6; cf. encyclical *Sapientiae Christianae*, n. 12). Here it is stated that there are two authorities within the family of men, established by divine ordinance; however, the civil authority is not competent in the religious sphere; not a few theologians believe that this incompetence is one of the deepest roots of the right of the person to religious freedom.

Article 12. It is true that the Church follows "the way of Christ and the apostles" when she recognizes the right of the person to religious freedom. Yet the last sentence of the same paragraph states: "In the life of the People of God as it has made its pilgrim way through the vicissitudes of human history, there have at times appeared ways of acting which were less in accord with the spirit of the gospel and even opposed to it" (Article 12, para. 1). This complex theme requires some explanation.

In Christ human beings are invited and encouraged to realize in themselves a genuine balance. For they should not only be conscious of belonging, as it were, horizontally to human and political society, but they should also realize their vertical dimension by opening their hearts to the knowledge and love of the true, infinite God.

Once men are fully conscious of being unable to develop their own religious dimension except by responsibly exercising their freedom in the duty and love towards God, they will also realize that this freedom may not be curtailed but must rather be fostered in the social sphere. This means that all compulsion must be removed from the religious sphere.

When Christianity entered history, it came into collision with the Roman Empire. Many documents, among them especially a letter from the proconsul of Bithynia, Pliny the Younger, to the Emperor Trajan (c. 111/112), make it clear that one of the deepest reasons for the long drawn-out conflict between Christianity and the Roman Empire was the latter's claim to divinity. For it sought to absorb men into itself by reducing them to instruments of its own greatness, while Christianity taught them to see themselves in the light of Christ. It unmasked the wonders of the world that fascinate the human spirit and caused men to experience their original freedom most clearly in themselves by opening their hearts to the knowledge and love of the true, infinite God. Hence Christianity demanded a new social structure so that men might fully exercise this freedom without any hindrance.

The opposition between the two institutions representing contrary philosophies was solved by the Edict of Milan (313): all subjects of the empire, both Christians and those professing other religions, were accorded freedom to profess their faith.

The Church has always at least theoretically recognized the right of men not to be forced to embrace Christianity, for the reason stated above, namely because the act of faith, though binding, can only be made freely.

Nevertheless, as has also been said before, throughout the centuries men living within the Christian society were not accorded the right to profess their religion if this was not held to be the true one. This practice was very widespread, in terms of both space and time, and the factors which had led to it are manifold and complex. A detailed exposition would be beyond the scope of this commentary. To explain why this line of conduct survived so many historical periods we must mention several elements of this doctrine which were not questioned for a long time and indeed were held to be indisputable. Among these elements we must mention especially one, according to which rights are based directly on spiritual values, that is to say, on truth and goodness; hence the so often repeated, seemingly self-evident principle: truth has all the rights, error has no right.

According to this view only he who is in the truth has the right to profess it, because only truth can communicate this right; on the other hand the man who is in error has no right to profess it, for error cannot communicate any right.

It follows with the same stringent logic that the man who follows the true religion has the right to confess it, for only the true religion communicates this right. On the other hand, a man who adheres to an erroneous religion, cannot have the right to confess it, because an erroneous religion cannot communicate this right. However, the confession of an erroneous religion may be tolerated so as to avoid greater evils, according to the example of God, who, though he does not will error and evil, yet permits or tolerates both in view of a greater good, as is taught in the parables of the tares among the wheat (Mt 13:30–42).

A second element of this doctrine is a particular view of the common good and a corresponding view of the duties of the State towards it. According to this view the true religion is the most important element of the common good, both because religious truth is a factor making for political unity and because this truth is the source of morality, which must react positively on all sectors of the community, especially on those of the temporal order.

Religious error, on the other hand, can only be an element of social disintegration on which the moral consciousness cannot be nourished. Since the *raison d'être* of the State is the common good, the State has the duty to acknowledge, protect and favour the true religion. It has also the duty — at least in principle — to prevent the confession and propagation of religions which are not true, because, for the reasons mentioned, the spread of error, especially in religious matters, can only be detrimental to the common good.

True, in order to avoid greater evils or in view of a greater good the State may tolerate that such religions are confessed and propagated, but it can never give its citizens the right to confess and propagate them, since this is an evil, and no one can have the right to commit an evil act. If, therefore, the aforementioned elements of the doctrine are considered immutable, it follows that only Catholics can be granted the right to religious freedom, because Catholicism is the only true religion.

In order to arrive at the doctrine of the Declaration, according to which all men are granted religious freedom as a basic personal right, it was necessary for people to become more conscious of their own dignity, defined as personal responsibility. Another necessity was the general conviction that the rights are not directly and formally based on spiritual values such as truth, moral goodness and justice, but that the subjects of these rights are persons, indeed only physical or moral persons. It was also necessary to understand that the relations involving rights are always inter-personal relations, not relations between persons and spiritual values. Finally, it was necessary to understand that the basic rights of the person with regard to spiritual values are freedom from external coercion or the secure practice of worship and freedom to accept such values. Since this greater consciousness of the dignity of the person was understood as the claim to inner freedom and freedom from coercion in the exercise of responsibility, it reacted necessarily on the legal organization and the exercise of public authority. This means that the concept of the constitutional State came into existence and was realized, at least to a certain degree and in a certain form. It had gradually to free itself from the rationalistic, positivist, agnostic, liberalist and other trends to which it owed its origin. It also had to become clear that its essential elements were perfectly compatible with the Christian view of life. Thus it developed into the democratic constitutional State dedicated to the common good. This included the creation of a social milieu which not only acknowledged and defended the basic rights of the person, but also provided the necessary means (or at least honestly tried to provide them) needed to exercise these rights and to fulfill the corresponding duties.

Now all these doctrinal changes came to be made only in modern times after a painful and complex evolution characterized by profound contradictions, but also undoubtedly guided by the light of the gospel which showed the infinite value of the human person. "Thus the leaven of the gospel has long been about its quiet work in the minds of men. To it is due in great measure the fact that in the course of time men have come more widely to recognize their dignity as persons, and the conviction has grown stronger that in religious matters the person in society is to be kept free from all manner of human coercion" (Article 12, para. 2).

Article 13. This deals with the relation between religious freedom as a right of the person and the Catholic Church. In the Declaration this relation is discussed under a fourfold aspect.

There is first the historical aspect (Article 12). When the Church entered the history of mankind and penetrated society with its spirit, men were accorded the right to foster their relation with God freely and responsibly. This is undoubtedly the meaning of the Edict of Milan (313) which pinpoints one of the most important stages of civilization. Secondly, the relation between the Catholic Church and religious freedom is considered under the doctrinal aspect, which may be described thus:

a) The Church has always acknowledged religious freedom as a principle, that is, the right of men not to be forced to accept the true religion, especially because of the special freedom of the act of faith.

b) The Church has always defended religious freedom as the right of men not to be prevented by force from confessing the true, that is, the Catholic religion. The recognition of this right by human society was furthered by the blood of innumerable martyrs.

But as regards religious freedom as a right of the person not to be prevented from practising one's religion whatever it may be, the Church began to recognize this only in modern times and teaches it definitively in the present document. Doctrinal reasons for this have been briefly explained in the preceding article.

The relation between the Church and religious freedom is, thirdly, regarded in view of her own mission. This aspect is touched upon in the present article. The Church demands complete freedom to accomplish her mission for two reasons:

a) Because of her divine mission to "go into all the world and preach the gospel to the whole creation" (cf. Mk 16:15; Mt 28:18 ff.) (Article 13, para. 2).

b) "The Church also claims freedom for herself in her character as a society of men who have the right to live in society in accordance with the precepts of Christian faith" *(ibid.)*.

Now it was soon said that, if the Church demanded religious freedom for herself for these two reasons, it did not follow that this freedom differed from that which she conceded to all men and all other religious communities. Since every right is defined by its object, it must be said that the freedom the Church demands as her own right is the same as that which she asks for all others, that is, freedom from coercion in the sense explained above.

Some Council fathers thought that the declaration of religious freedom would have "negative effects in the life of the Church". But the Council declared this freedom to be a right of the person because this was a truth. It is due to the dignity of man and fully corresponds to God's plan in the present order of salvation.

But even with regard to its effects on the life of the Church we ought not to fear that these might be negative; they may rather be positive, for only "where the principle of religious freedom is not only proclaimed in words or simply incorporated in law but also given sincere and practical application, there the Church succeeds in achieving a stable situation of right as well as of fact and the independence which is necessary for the fulfilment of her divine mission ... At the same time, the Christian faithful, in common with all other men, possess the civil right not to be hindered in leading their lives in accordance with their conscience" (Article 13, para. 3 f.).

The last sentence of Article 13 states that "a harmony exists between the freedom of the Church and the religious freedom which is to be recognized as the right of all men and communities and sanctioned by constitutional law" (para. 4). The expressions are not quite clear. At first glance it would seem that two different freedoms are mentioned, whereas the one — freedom from coercion — that is, the freedom of the Church, equals the other, which is due to all men and all communities in matters religious.

True, there is a difference between the two freedoms, but only with regard to the sources, since the Church claims this freedom also and above all because of the divine command to fulfill her saving mission for the benefit of all mankind (see above).

Fourthly, the relation between the Church and religious freedom is considered with regard to her apostolic method, and this is the subject of the next article. Now, if the right to religious freedom is accorded to all men and communities because of their dignity as persons, and if this right is highly regarded and effectively protected, the general climate of opinion will be more favourable to the mission of the Church. Such a climate will make it easier for men to follow the light of truth also in religious matters as soon as they perceive it. Thus the obstacles produced by the social environment which so often make it difficult to follow this light are removed or at least diminished.

While thus proclaiming religious freedom the Council fathers also reminded the faithful that the Church must be "faithful to the divine command, 'Make disciples of all nations' (Mt 28:19)" and therefore "must work with all urgency and concern 'that the Word of God may run and be glorified' (2 Thess 3:1)" (Article 14, para. 1). They therefore admonish all Catholics to take part with confidence in spreading the light of life (cf. Acts 4:29) and to work with apostolic vigour, even to the shedding of their blood "in the Holy Spirit, in unaffected love, in the word of truth" (2 Cor 6:6f.) (Article 14, para. 2).

At the same time they demand that they should exercise their apostolate "never — be it understood — having recourse to means that are incompatible with the spirit of the gospel" (Article 14, para. 3), and this includes undoubtedly the use of force. On the other hand, they are to collaborate in the mission of the Church a) by prayer, sacrifice, the Christian witness of their life; b) by understanding others, respecting their personal dignity, in patient and persistent love; c) especially in the power of the Word of God and the efficacy of the Holy Spirit in souls: according to God's saving plan such activity will always be an expression of God's infinite love; the deepest mystery, however, will remain hidden. While exercising one's apostolate "all is to be taken into account — the Christian duty to Christ, the life-giving Word which must be proclaimed, the rights of the human person, and the measure of grace granted by God through Christ to men, who are invited freely to accept and profess the faith" (Article 14, para. 3).

Article 15. This resumes the basic motive of the whole document, the dignity of the human person, which is now considered historically. It states particularly that the desire of men to be able freely to practise their religion both in private and in public has been declared in most constitutions and is reflected in civil law. The same right has solemnly been recognized in international documents. This sentence refers especially to the Human Rights Declaration which had been accepted by the General Assembly of the United Nations on 10 December 1948.

The present document, however, also states that religious freedom is not equally guaranteed by all modern constitutions. There are those that restrict it to acts of worship alone, as is the case in the totalitarian States. There are others that guarantee the right to worship and also freely to propagate one's religious faith by the modern means of communication; this is the case in the constitutions of many authoritarian States. Finally, there are constitutions which guarantee freedom of worship and religious propaganda as well as freedom to found movements and institutions with temporal aims for this purpose, and which may belong to the economic, social, political and cultural spheres. This is the case in the constitutions of most democratic States. It is obvious that full religious freedom is guaranteed only by the last group of constitutions.

It says further that "forms of government still exist under which, even though freedom of religious worship receives constitutional recognition, the powers of government are engaged in the effort to deter citizens from the profession of religion and to make life difficult and dangerous for religious communities" (Article 15, para. 1). This refers undoubtedly to totalitarian governments of Marxist character. It was stated, however, that there are similar situations in strictly denominational States; in them, too, the religious life of individuals and communities not belonging to the official religion of the State is made difficult and sometimes even impossible.

The Council fathers express their satisfaction with the first state of affairs, but deplore the second (Article 15, para. 2).

The later paragraphs of the final article deal with other aspects of the present historical situation. There is a constant progress towards the unity of the human race which is due to the factors of our modern civilization, especially to the enormous technological advances and their effects in the economic, social, political, cultural, moral and religious spheres.

This progress towards unity results in the fact that "men of different cultures and religions are being brought together in closer relationships" (Article 15, para. 3). Hence religious pluralism is on the increase within the existing political communities and even more in the developing ones. In such a situation the document declares, "in order that relationships of peace and harmony may be established and maintained within the whole of mankind, it is necessary that religious freedom be everywhere provided with an effective constitutional guarantee, and that respect be shown for the high duty and right of man freely to lead his religious life in society" (Article 15, para. 4).

These historical facts have certainly contributed to the decision of the Council fathers to proclaim religious freedom as a right of the person *today;* but this right is based, as has been said before, not on historical facts but on the claim due to the dignity of the human person.

Decree on the Church's Missionary Activity

by
Suso Brechter *

Origin and History of the Decree

No Council has ever so consciously emphasized and so insistently expounded the Church's pastoral work of salvation and its worldwide missionary function as Vatican II. On 25 January 1959, to the great surprise of everyone, in the Basilica of St. Paul, Pope John XXIII announced the holding of an Ecumenical Council, and by Whitsunday 17 May 1959 he had already appointed the *Commissio Antepraeparatoria* as its first executive administrative organ. This was to receive the wishes and advice of the bishops throughout the world and the suggestions of the Curial congregations, consider and study the topics which would probably be dealt with and, finally, set about forming the agencies and organs responsible for the preparation of the Council.[1] The president of this commission for the first preparatory phase was Cardinal Tardini; it succeeded in completing its work by 1 May 1960.[2]

The motu proprio *Supremo Dei nutu* of 5 June 1960 set up ten preparatory commissions and two secretariats.[3] The Secretariat of State on 6 June announced the appointment of the Prefect of the Congregation for the Propagation of the Faith, Cardinal G. P. Agagianian, as president, and titular Archbishop D. Mathew, former Apostolic Delegate for British East Africa in Mombasa, as secretary of the Preparatory Commission for the Missions. When fully constituted, this commission had 22 members (4 archbishops, 4 bishops, 14 priests from religious orders) and 32 consultors (4 archbishops, 4 bishops, 4 secular priests, 20 priests from religious orders). The strong proportion of members of religious orders and congregations is not surprising because right down to the present day they have almost exclusively under-

---

* *Translated by W. J. O'Hara.*
[1] *Acta et Documenta Concilio Oecumenico Vaticano II apparando*, Series I (*Antepraeparatoria*), Vol. I: *Acta Summi Pontificis Joannis XXIII* (1960), 22 pages.
[2] Vol. III (1960), pp. IX–XIII.
[3] *AAS* 52 (1960), pp. 433–7.

taken the entire missionary work of the Church. Analysed by nationalities, Germany had nine members, Italy eight, Spain six, Belgium, Holland and France four each, U.S.A. three, Canada and China two each, Austria, Ireland, Portugal, U.S.S.R., Honduras, Venezuela, Philippines, Australia, India and Ghana one each. The coloured clergy were unfortunately very poorly represented, with one African, two Chinese and one Indian; of these, moreover, two lived in Rome and only one was directly occupied in missionary work. On the other hand, eleven overseas bishops and working missionaries from the Philippines, Honduras, Venezuela, Australia, Pakistan, India, Korea, Japan, Tanzania, and Oceania were appointed to the Preparatory Commission for the Missions. But even this selection was not really satisfactory. Some surprise was caused by the relatively large number (39) drawn from missionary headquarters: retired missionary bishops and former apostolic delegates. Among them, it is true, were many personalities with long and rich missionary experience, superiors of missionary orders and congregations or their assistants, missiologists and ethnologists, administrators and publicists, professors of the papal universities and clerics serving in Curial offices.[4] In addition, two officials from *Propaganda Fide*, S. Paventi, a "minutant", and Fr. Nicolas Kovalsky, an archivist, were appointed secretaries of the Preparatory Commission for the Missions.

1. THE DRAFT OF THE PREPARATORY COMMISSION

The commission set to work full of optimism, but its task soon proved extremely hard and thankless.[5] The opening meeting took place on 24 October 1960 in the Church of Propaganda. The cardinal president gave an address, and Mgr. Paventi made some announcements on questions of procedure. Five sub-commissions were set up, each with its own secretary. For administrative reasons it was decided not to distinguish between members and consultors in these bodies. The programme of work was divided into the following sections: administration of the sacraments and liturgy; organization of the missions and reform of the Code of Canon Law; the life of the clergy and of the Christian people; reform of the training of clergy and religious; support for the missions from the faithful.

The chief task of the Preparatory Commission for the Missions was to

---

[4] S. Brechter, "Konzil und Mission", *Die katholischen Missionen* 81 (1962), p. 144.
[5] A very precise and detailed account of the work is given by S. Paventi, "Entstehungsgeschichte des Schemas *De activitate missionali Ecclesiae*", in J. Schütte, ed., *Mission nach dem Konzil* (1967), pp. 48–81. J. Glazik has written a brief report: "Die Mission im II. Vatikanischen Konzil", *ZMR* 50 (1966), pp. 3–10, and "Das Konzilsdekret Ad Gentes", *ibid.*, pp. 66–71.

inquire what solutions were possible and what reforms necessary in order to provide suitable training of missionaries, promote missionary work and give all the faithful a larger share in it. The secretaries of the sub-commissions were given a list of topics and problems falling within their scope, but no particular questions were laid down. In fact they were expressly authorized to make alterations and additions. Those members of the sub-commissions who were in Rome met as a rule every fortnight for a working session, in two groups, alternating from week to week. The secretaries met eight times in all, once a month on the average, to tighten up and co-ordinate the work. Between 26 October 1960 and the end of April 1961, 63 meetings were held.[6] Finally a small mixed commission was also formed with a few members of the Preparatory Commission for the Liturgy, and, after three special conferences, met in two sessions on 17 and 18 February.[7] Some liturgical principles which were to be incorporated in the missionary schema had to be harmonized with the guidelines accepted or under discussion in the Liturgical Commission.

When the work of the sub-commission had been more or less completed, and questions of procedure for the plenary sessions of the commission had been carefully checked by the secretaries, all the members and consultors of the Preparatory Commission were called to Rome for its first full meeting on 17 April 1961. This plenary session lasted from 19 to 26 April. Thirty-five members and consultors took part in the College of Propaganda on the Janiculum under the presidency of Cardinal Agagianian and, in his absence, of Archbishop Mathew. In eight whole-day sessions the relevant problems were candidly and thoroughly discussed. Many questions could be settled and dismissed, but a considerable residue had to be referred back to the sub-commissions for further consideration. These bodies set to work again indefatigably. Subsequently a special editorial sub-commission was set up to draft the schemata already approved in plenary session. This consisted of the secretaries of the sub-commissions, Bishops Sartre and Van Valenberg and Fathers Caulfield, Cauwe, Cho, Eldarov, Moya, Rubio and A. Seumois. The heavy task was completed in nine meetings[8] between 30 September and 9 November, and so was the preparatory work for the second and in fact final working session of the plenary commission.

The second plenary session of the Preparatory Commission, 20–30 November, approved all the schemata submitted, with the exception of the hotly

---

[6] The precise dates are in Schütte, *op. cit.*, p. 52. The special number of *L'Osservatore Romano della Domenica:* "Il Concilio Ecumenico Vaticano II" speaks (p. 34) of 96 sessions (297 hours).

[7] *Ibid.*, p. 52.

[8] *L'Osservatore Romano* mentions 12 meetings from 30 September to 16 November 1961.

contested preface; a special commission was set up to recast this. After the departure of the foreign and oversea members of the commission, the Roman members, in particular the secretaries of the sub-commissions, completed the editorial work on the draft schemata, meeting on 5, 12, 15, 19 December 1961 and 2 January 1962. At a final meeting on 2 February 1962, agreement was also reached on the new version of the preface.

The draft produced by the Preparatory Commission for the Missions was the result of earnest endeavours and valuable argument, but also of much sterile controversy. It proposed the following topics for presentation to the Council:

Caput   I: De regimine Missionum
Caput   II: De disciplina cleri
Caput III: De religiosis
Caput IV: De sacramentis et de S. Liturgia
Caput   V: De disciplina populi christiani
Caput VI: De studiis clericorum
Caput VII: De cooperatione missionali

These amounted in fact to seven schemata elaborated in the preparatory period; they were printed in seven separate fascicules of 28, 14, 10, 20, 16, 16 and 7 pages respectively. The chief complaint about them was the excessively theoretical and juridical form of the decree, which took far too little account of the sometimes very concrete suggestions and proposals sent from the missions themselves.[9] By the very nature of the case the work had had to be done for the most part by professors, Curial officials and members of religious orders permanently resident in Rome. Co-ordination with other commissions was faulty, but at this preparatory stage of the Council it could hardly have been otherwise.

2. THE DRAFT OF THE CONCILIAR COMMISSION

With the opening of the Council on 11 October 1962, the work and competence of the preparatory commissions ceased. The appointment of the conciliar commissions immediately produced the first surprises and tensions. In each instance 16 members were chosen by the Council and nine were nominated by the Pope, who also appointed the cardinal-president. The latter in turn appointed two vice-presidents and a secretary from the members of the commission. Cardinal Agagianian was again president of the

---

[9] The *vota* and *propositiones* of the Council fathers from Asia and Africa amounted to 1242 printed folio pages.

conciliar Missionary Commission. Its members, at first 24 in number, were almost exclusively missionary bishops belonging for the most part to the native hierarchy. Another welcome feature was the stronger representation of the Latin-American Church. In the course of the Council it was found desirable and necessary to widen the commission, which in the end consisted of 4 cardinals, 12 archbishops, 12 bishops and 3 heads of religious orders.[10] As auxiliaries there were also a secretary, a vice-secretary and a relatively large number of *periti*. This body inherited the work of the Preparatory Commission.

The missionary schemata had already been submitted at the end of January and the beginning of February to the Central Preparatory Commission,[11] which considered them at its meetings of 28–31 March.[12] Cardinal Confalonieri, the president of this commission, returned the documents on 12 May 1962 with observations and criticisms and the express request for a prompt reply and comment.[13] On 5 June 1962, Cardinal Agagianian transmitted the requested information.[14] The central sub-commission *De schematibus emendandis* expressed the view that in cases where the content of the missionary schemata coincided or overlapped, they could be incorporated in the working programme of other commissions, so that the interests of the missions would be fully guaranteed. Five of the schemata were accordingly removed (II, III, IV, V, VI). What was left, with some slight alterations and a few adaptations, was Schema I: *De regimine Missionum,* and Schema VII: *De cooperatione missionali,* plus the preface which had been framed with such difficulty and dispute, and which proved a particularly valuable basis for the subsequent elaboration of the conciliar schema. On the other hand the section on the lay apostolate was removed from the Schema *De apostolatu laicorum* and was made available for incorporation in the missionary schema. Cardinal Agagianian wrote on 9 June 1962 to inform all the members of the Preparatory Commission how things stood and thanked them for the work done.[15]

The conciliar Missionary Commission was therefore faced with a large task. The fact that only two out of seven schemata had survived was more to be welcomed than regretted. It was a real gain generally and from the missionary point of view that the Liturgical Commission had taken over the fundamental questions of the liturgical adaptation of the universal Church. This brought those burning questions from the periphery as it were into the centre of the Church's life. In order to avoid unnecessary overlapping, fruit-

[10] The list of names is given in Schütte, *op. cit.,* pp. 79–81.
[11] *Archiv. Comm. Praeparat.,* Rubr. 8/8, Prot. N. 343/62, 346/62.
[12] Rubr. 1 Prot. N. 363/62.
[13] Rubr. 8/8, Prot. N. 372/62, 373/62, 374/62, 375/62, 376/62, 377/62, 378/62, 379/62.
[14] Prot. N. 386/62.
[15] Rubr. 3, Prot. N. 4/62.

ful and forward-looking solutions had to be sought in several other domains, e.g., clerical education, renewal of the religious orders, the pastoral work of bishops, mobilization of the laity, ecumenical work, Christian education, mass-media, etc., if for no other reason than to co-ordinate more closely the great variety of subjects involved. Many percipient and well-informed Council fathers even considered dispensing with a special separate missionary schema; everything concerning missionary activity, they thought, should on principle be incorporated into the Constitution on the Church.

It is all the more surprising that in fact the Missionary Commission did not once meet during the first session of the Council, apart from an invitation to the College of *Propaganda Fide* on 28 November 1962, for the purpose of personal contact and friendly exchange of ideas.[16] During the first session of the Council, in fact, the general attitude of the fathers to the missions was not entirely favourable. Some bishops from ancient Christian countries appeared to have realized for the first time at the Council that the missions are a vital function of the Church. From the very first day the great assembly of the Church received a markedly missionary stamp from the presence of numerous bishops from every country and race in the world. Almost a quarter of the fathers represented a tenth of the faithful in the "younger Churches". Almost a third of these missionary bishops belonged to the native clergy. And how they let fly in their conciliar speeches! In the subsequent course of the Council, their interventions became much less frequent. Some spoke with a good deal of emotion and sometimes with a certain naiveté, unconscious of the full extent and depth of the problems involved. Particularly sharp tones were noticeable in criticism of the organization and methods of the Congregation of *Propaganda Fide*. Demands were made for its abolition; for all authority and jurisdiction over the missionary territories to be taken from it; for it to be reduced to an administrative body charged with collecting and distributing funds for the missions. Unrealistic ideas of this sort were also clandestinely circulated by publicity methods.

Since all the schemata discussed in the aula, with the exception of the schema on the Liturgy, were rejected (those on Revelation, the Church, the Blessed Virgin) and the continuation of the Council was assured,[17] it was wise and appropriate to allow time for people's minds to calm.

Directly after the close of the first session, the vice-president of the Missionary Commission, Bishop V. Sartre, and the secretary, Mgr. Paventi, together with a number of *periti* present in Rome, set to work to prepare

---

[16] *Archiv. Comm. Conc.*, Prot. N. 4/62.
[17] Towards the end of the first session, Pope John had announced the future programme of work: *Ordo agendarum tempore quod inter conclusionem primae periodi Concilii Oecumenici et initium secundae intercedit* (1962).

a new draft schema. A further seven sittings followed in January and February, but no agreement was reached on a new version. There were irreconcilable differences of opinion on matters of principle. Cardinal Agagianian took the chair at the meeting on 22 January 1963, and gave important instructions for future work. In view of the importance of the missionary schema, missionary problems in other conciliar texts must not be neglected or ignored; they were not a monopoly of the Missionary Commission. Constant contact must in particular be maintained with the Co-ordinating Commission. A special letter should be addressed to the president of that commission, Cardinal Cicognani, requesting that since the original missionary schema had been so curtailed, two or three *periti* from the Missionary Commission might be called in when missionary problems were under discussion in other conciliar commissions. All members of the Missionary Commission should receive the texts drawn up by the Preparatory Commission but with the proviso that only fascicules I and VII were to be subjected to further study.[18] Finally he announced that the full commission would be called to Rome for its first plenary session on 20 March.

The working period lasted from 20 to 29 March, with nine full sessions; the discussions were unprofitable and uninspiring. The chairman was usually Cardinal Agagianian. As head of the official body responsible for the missions, he was continually asked for official declarations of principle about the traditional idea of the missions and the methods of *Propaganda Fide*. Opinions and standpoints were so divergent that the conciliar Missionary Commission never in any phase of its existence formed a unity or became an effective working team. The composition and form of the schema continued to be disputed, proposal was followed by counter-proposal, the whole material was repeatedly rearranged and recast. Before the plenary commission broke up, agreement was at least ultimately achieved on the arrangement of the material. This was an extremely meagre achievement for the first plenary session of this commission, from which so much had been hoped. The carrying out of its decision had to be entrusted to a small editorial commission.

The proposed text entitled *De Missionibus* consisted of two parts and a preface:

Prooemium
Pars I: De ipsis Missionibus
      Caput   I: De principiis generalibus missionum

---

[18] *Archiv. Comm. Conc.*, Prot. N. 3/63. Cardinal Cicognani communicated to Cardinal Agagianian, under the date of 30 January, the decision of the Co-ordinating Commission that the material prepared by the Preparatory Commission for the Missions and passed by the Preparatory Central Commission was to be used in the new version of the schema.

Caput II: De sacro ministerio in missionibus
          Art. 1: De apostolatu cleri
          Art. 2: De apostolatu laicorum
Caput III: De regimine missionum
Pars II: De cooperatione missionali
    Caput   I: De debito missionali
    Caput II: De cooperatione episcopatus et cleri
    Caput III: De cooperatione laicorum exhortatio

The new text was submitted at the beginning of June to the Co-ordinating Commission, which examined it, passed very unfavourable judgment on it and returned it with corresponding comments and criticisms. Finally it was issued to all the Council fathers for discussion.

With the beginning of the second session, the Missionary Commission at once went into action again and held ten plenary sessions between 23 October and 3 December, to discuss the judgment expressed by the Co-ordinating Commission and the opinions sent in by the Council fathers. Criticism of the text had been unusually severe. In the commission itself the unbridged and unbridgeable differences flared up again. A few members put forward new drafts drawn up individually or by common effort. A complete recasting of the schema was inevitable. Moreover, the Theological Commission had decided in the meantime to incorporate a chapter on the missionary character of the Church's work into the Constitution on the Church (Article 17) and had asked the Missionary Commission for an appropriate text. This was accordingly drafted by a group of *periti*.[19] After detailed discussion and thorough rewriting, this received the approval of the full commission and was handed over to the Theological Commission. It was now possible to omit from the schema any fuller treatment of the theological basis of the missions. The tug-of-war began once more over the division and arrangement of the materials. Finally agreement was reached on 3 December 1963, with only one dissentient voice out of 24, on a schema *De Missionibus*. This consisted of a preface and four chapters, amounting to 23 printed pages.[20]

Prooemium
Caput   I: De principiis doctrinalibus
Caput II: Rationes generales apostolatus missionalis
Caput III: De formatione missionali
          A. De missionariis exteris
          B. De missionariis localibus
Caput IV: De cooperatione missionaria

[19] The Commission for Studies also submitted to the Missionary Commission for approval a text which was to be incorporated in the schema on Priestly Formation.
[20] Conciliar printed matter: *Schema de Missionibus (sub secreto)* (1964).

The schema passed through the usual official stages. In January it was approved by the Co-ordinating Commission and sent to all the Council fathers for comment, with the proviso that critical remarks must be handed in by 3 March 1964. Despite the shortness of time, suggested emendations were sent in by 67 fathers, 17 from Europe, 13 from America, 16 from Africa and 21 from Asia, amounting to 283 pages of typescript. Five fathers wrote in the name of bishops' conferences, seven on behalf of groups. On 4 May 1964 the members of the commission were again invited to Rome for a plenary session. However, before they could start to consider the proposed amendments, decisions were taken by higher authority which made it necessary to shelve the hard-won draft schema of the unfortunate Missionary Commission.

3. THE SHORTER VERSION OF THE SCHEMA

On 23 April 1964, the Secretary General of the Council, Archbishop P. Felici, announced the decision of the Central Co-ordinating Commission that, in the interests of efficiency, all the schemata not yet discussed in the aula must be compressed into a few proposals and guiding principles. They would then be put to the Council's vote as *Schemata propositionum* without further discussion.

This presented the Missionary Commission with the almost contradictory task of reducing its schema to a few principles and at the same time incorporating in it the amendments suggested by Council fathers from all over the world. The commission was invited to Rome for 4 May and met from 8 to 13 May. At the same time each of the sub-commissions aided by *periti* worked on its own chapter of the draft schema. The material was condensed into a few essential propositions and the division into chapters omitted. After careful harmonization, the texts were submitted to the full commission for discussion. The final drafting was entrusted to Bishop Lokuang, one of the vice-presidents of the commission, assisted by the secretary and two experts. The full commission approved unanimously the draft of this truncated schema on 13 May 1964. The title *De Missionibus* was altered to *De activitate missionali,* because it seemed too pretentious for a few guiding principles, and also because some such change had already been requested by a number of fathers, on the grounds that the Council was speaking all along about the one single mission of the Church itself.

The document, amounting to six printed pages, contained a preface and thirteen missionary topics: 1. Necessitas missionis, 2. De evangelii praeconibus, 3. Labor missionalis, 4. Consilium centrale evangelizationis, 5. Debitum missionale episcoporum, 6. Debitum missionale sacerdotum, 7. Debitum missionale

Institutorum perfectionis, 8. Debitum missionale laicorum, 9. De oecumenismo et collaboratione cum non-christianis, 10. Formatio culturarum christianarum, 11. Formatio scientifica et technica, 12. Formatio catechistarum, 13. Instituta superiora.[21] The cardinal-president only took part in the first and last meetings of the commission, probably in order not to prejudice freedom of discussion. On 26 May, the schema was forwarded to Cardinal Cicognani; it was passed by the Co-ordinating Commission and distributed to the Council fathers dated 3 July.

When the third session began, the commission held three further meetings to examine the suggestions received in the meantime. The *propositiones* were extended from 13 to 14 (a section on the missions as a duty incumbent on the Church as a whole) and final preparations were made for the conciliar debate and vote.

On 5 November the Secretary General, P. Felici, surprised the Council with the news that on the following day the missionary schema would be presented for discussion at the 116th general congregation and that the Pope himself would be present at the opening of the debate.[22] Never before had the Pope, not even John XXIII, taken part in an actual working session. A great guessing-game set in about the significance of this extraordinary step. Pope Paul appeared, without ceremony, on foot, at the conciliar Mass, which was celebrated according to the Ethiopic rite with drums and clapping. After this he took his seat at the presidents' table[23] and gave a short opening address on the importance of the missionary schema. The salvation of the world, he said, depends on the fulfilment of the missionary command. New ways and means must be tried. He praised the shortened schema for its contents and composition, and recommended its acceptance. If necessary, it could, of course, be improved on. It would strengthen and renew zeal for extending God's kingdom, because it viewed the whole Church in a missionary light and summoned all the faithful to missionary activity. The Pope gave a special greeting to the missionary bishops and to all who devoted themselves to the missionary apostolate.[24]

---

[21] Conciliar printed matter: *Schema Propositionum de Activitate Missionali Ecclesiae (sub secreto)* (1964); detailed list of contents in *HK* 19 (1964–5), p. 233. As this schema was rejected by the fathers and a completely new document was presented by the commission during the final session, this reference may be sufficient.

[22] M. Lackmann, *Mit evangelischen Augen*, IV (1965), pp. 359 ff.; D. A. Seeber, *Das Zweite Vatikanum* (1966), pp. 210 ff.

[23] J. C. Hampe, *Die Autorität der Freiheit*, III (1967), p. 519: "This act was generally interpreted as an indication that he wished to act as head of the college of bishops, in accordance with the Council's Constitution on the Church, the final amendments to which were being voted on at that time."

[24] Pope Paul said, among other things: "Cum firmiter statuissemus saltem alicui uni ex generalibus vestris conventibus praesidere, hunc delegimus praesentiae nostrae diem quo in

Cardinal Agagianian thanked the Pope for having specially honoured by his presence the work of the messengers of faith and of the native clergy. The Pope had again shown his love for the missions by the recent canonization of the martyrs of Uganda, and by the announcement that he was to visit India. The Cardinal recalled the great progress made by the missions since Vatican I, Paul's journey to Africa as a cardinal, the development of papal missionary works, the efforts of the religious orders, and all the good works and self-sacrifice of priests and laity in the service of the missions. He greeted in particular the young Churches in the mission fields, and thanked all the Council fathers who in their deliberations had repeatedly emphasized the missionary character of the Church. The Pope exchanged a few words with the presidents and moderators of the Council, took his leave and left the aula. Then Bishop Lokuang read the Commission's report on the schema and the debate began. Cardinal Döpfner was moderator.

It was an open secret that the majority of the missionary bishops flatly rejected the schema if for no other reason than its meagre dimensions. This again stamped the missions as a marginal phenomenon. Better no text than a paltry one. In fact, however, the schema was better than its reputation. The theological foundation of the missions had found its appropriate place in the second chapter of the Constitution on the Church which deals with the missionary character of the Church as a whole. It had accordingly been dropped from the missionary schema. Nevertheless the schema stressed that all bishops are responsible for missionary work because of the collegiality of their office. It convincingly expressed the concern for adaptation to all civilizations and cultures, even if by the nature of the case it was impossible to go into details. Finally it had magnanimously found space for the establishment of an advisory council for the missions in the Curia. It would have been difficult to say more, or anything much better, in six pages. Even the final schema, five or six times as long, did not contrive to avoid all the faults found in this shortened text. Public opinion was firmly opposed to the truncated schema, however, and it had no prospect of acceptance by the Council.

At the 116th general congregation on 6 November, five fathers spoke, at the 117th on 7 November, seventeen, and at the 118th on 9 November there were six speeches. The debate had obviously been carefully prepared, the interventions carefully planned. A relatively large number of speakers represented entire continents, or at least very considerable groups.

Schemate Missionum disceptatio vestra versatur. Hoc quidem ut praeoptaremus, certe suasit Nobis singularis gravitas et magnitudo argumenti... Hoc schema ... cum perpendissemus, multum immo plurimum invenimus, sive materiae sive argumentorum pondus sive edisserendi ordo spectatur, quod dignum laude Nostra existimaremus. Qua propter opinionem profitemur facile fore ut, quamvis fortasse arbitremini hoc nonnullis in partibus perpoliendum et excolendum esse, idem adprobationem vestram consequatur."

On the first day the discussion was fairly calm. The draft was still regarded as perhaps acceptable but as seriously needing emendation.[25] The calm African Cardinal Rugambwa advocated its acceptance but considered a wider and deeper treatment of the question of adaptation to be indispensable. Cardinal Léger proposed that instead of forming a merely advisory body, the missionary council to be set up in Rome should be integrated into the Congregation of *Propaganda Fide*, with a full share in responsibility for decisions. Cardinal Tatsuo Doi wanted a clear definition of the term "missions" and its unambiguous restriction to the work of the Church in countries not yet Christianized. Cardinal Bea in a longer speech pointed out that the missions, today more than ever before, were suffering from a lack of vocations, and that even the urgent need for the missions was questioned; they therefore looked to the Council to provide new stimulus. The idea and theology of the missions must be thought out afresh and given a biblical basis. This could not be done by setting up new juridical forms. It is true that a native hierarchy had been established almost everywhere, but an influx of foreign missionary personnel continued to be indispensable, and the world episcopate had a common responsibility to provide for this. The first proclamation of the gospel to those who had never heard of Christ has always been most dear to the Church. To two thousand million human beings Christ had not yet come. According to Paul, the incorporation of all men in Christ is the goal of the mission, and this duty will last until the end of the world.

Despite wide-ranging criticism, these speakers did not reject the short schema as a whole, which, because of the brevity prescribed for it, could scarcely be expected to offer more than it did. The second day's debate, however, dealt it a mortal blow.[26] Despite the Pope's speech in its favour, a South Rhodesian missionary bishop (Lamont) described the text as dry bones, a skeleton which needed to be clothed with flesh and to have fresh life breathed into it. Many other missionary bishops expressed themselves to the same effect, if less vehemently. For them the schema was a great disappointment. Only one of the 17 speakers thought it good and sufficient.

With the great speech of Cardinal Frings who opened the second day's debate at the 117th general congregation on Saturday 7 November, all the

---

[25] The debate did not reach a very high level; there were many platitudinous commonplaces and repetitions. A survey may be had in M. Lackmann, *op. cit.*, pp. 361–70; 374–6. The best speeches, by Cardinal Bea, Bishop Zoa (Camerouns), Archbishop Gantin (Dahomey), Bishop Massa (expelled from China), Bishop Lokuang (Formosa), Cardinal Alfrink, Cardinal Frings, Bishop Moynagh (Nigeria) and Cardinal Suenens, were published in *ZMR* 50 (1966), pp. 11–25; and a few others in Hampe, *op. cit.*, pp. 522–31. Cf. also L. Dorn and J. Denzler, *Tagebuch des Konzils* (1965), pp. 303–25.

[26] Seeber, *op. cit.*, p. 211; Lackmann, *op. cit.*, pp. 366–70.

dykes burst and the waters swallowed up the helpless schema. "The problem of the missions is, in my view", Cardinal Frings began, "so essential for the Church, so important generally and especially in our time, that we cannot be satisfied with a few guiding principles. We must devote a special, complete schema to it, and discuss it in the fourth session. That is not only my personal opinion but the ardent desire of the superiors of religious orders and of many bishops from Africa and other missions. Consequently I humbly request that this wish be met." This broke the spell, and the floodgates opened.[27] Many of the subsequent speakers hammered away at the same point;[28] in other words a new, separate, complete missionary schema to be submitted during the fourth session.

Before the vote, six more fathers spoke at the 118th general congregation, all in favour of a new and improved schema.[29] By a masterpiece of skill and elegance, the president of the Missionary Commission, Cardinal Agagianian, contrived to extricate himself from the affair.[30] Directly before the vote at the close of the debate, the *relator,* Bishop Lokuang, declared that the com-

---

[27] He also expressed with great earnestness the Church's missionary duty and opposed the analogical use of the word "mission" for dechristianized countries instead of for the first evangelization of places where Christ has never been preached. He also gave his views on the establishment of a central advisory council in the Congregation of *Propaganda Fide* and proposed a yearly contribution from old Christian dioceses to the Church for missionary purposes. It was unworthy and unjust, he insisted, for missionary bishops to have to spend a lot of time and energy begging to meet their most essential financial needs.

[28] Special mention should be made of Bishop N. Geise of Bongor, who spoke for all the Indonesian bishops, Bishop Moors of Roermond, in the name of the Dutch Bishops' Conference, Bishop Riobé of Orleans, representing 70 bishops and heads of religious orders, Cardinal Suenens, in the name of all the African bishops, and Bishop Moynagh of Calabar (Nigeria), at the request of many African bishops.

[29] The wish for a theological basis for the missions to be included in the schema was repeatedly expressed. It was not sufficient to say that the Constitution on the Church answered this purpose, it was urged. Someone seeking guidance on the missions would not refer to the Constitution on the Church. The doctrine contained in the latter on the universality of the Church, the collegiality of the bishops and the catholicity of the local Churches ought to be made explicit in the missionary schema. It was a unique experience to hear the brilliant rhetoric and glowing enthusiasm of Bishop Fulton Sheen addressing the fathers: "Church and mission are one — what God has joined together let no man put asunder." As interventions had to be notified to the Secretary General five days before the beginning of the debate, the moderators were in a position to arrange the sequence of speeches not only hierarchically, but also for effect. Cardinal Frings's speech at all events could hardly have come at a better moment.

[30] "The ultimate reasons which prompted the Pope to be present at precisely this session and to recommend this particular schema have not been fully explained. It was obvious that the president of the Commission had marked interest in having the text accepted without much alteration" (Seeber, *op. cit.,* p. 212, note 56); see also Lackmann, *op. cit.,* pp. 361, 376.

mission was pleased and impressed that the Council fathers were so convinced of the importance of the work of the missions and consequently wished for a more extensive and weightier schema. In the name of the Cardinal-president he expressed willingness completely to redraft the schema, and asked for further suggestions for the improvement of the text. Thunderous applause. The routine question put to the vote was not whether the schema was approved or not, but "Do the fathers wish the schema on the Missionary Activity of the Church to be revised by the competent Commission?" Of the 1914 present, 1601 voted Yes, 311 No, 2 abstained. The way was thus open to what might prove eventual success.

4. THE FINAL FORM OF THE SCHEMA

Both the schemata produced by the Missionary Commission had thus been rejected, the first by the Central and Co-ordinating Commission, the short schema by the Council itself. A new starting-point had to be found and the work repeated. More than one member of the Missionary Commission was by no means displeased at this fatal development. But time was short, and new ways and means had to be found if a successful conclusion was to be reached.

At its full meeting on 16 November 1964, that is, during the third session of the Council, the commission decided to draw up a new schema taking particular account of the speeches or written interventions of the fathers,[31] as well as of the theological principles developed in the course of the Council. For this purpose a sub-commission, an editorial committee, was formed, consisting of Bishops Riobé of Orleans, Lokuang of Tainan (Formosa), Zoa of Jaunde (Cameroons), Lecuona of the Spanish National Seminary for Foreign Missions in Burgos, and the Superior General of the Society of the Divine Word (Steyl), J. Schütte. As *periti* they co-opted Y. Congar, X. Seumois, D. Grasso, J. Neuner and J. Ratzinger. Fr. Schütte presided. In the absence of Cardinal Agagianian, this working committee met without the *periti* for the first time on 20 November 1964 and agreed to take up the work "in seclusion" on 12 January 1965 in Nemi, in the college of the Steyl missionaries, the hospitality of whose house had been offered to the members and collaborators of the working committee by Fr. Schütte. Frs. Congar, X. Seumois, Grasso, Neuner and J. Glazik were called in as *periti*.

---

[31] Well over 1000 typed pages to clothe the "skeleton".

a) The first version [32]

In the rural tranquillity of Nemi, Cardinal Agagianian opened this cloistered session on Monday 12 January. All the members and *periti* had received methodically classified copies of the suggestions and amendments of the Council fathers.[33] All the members of the committee were present. Of the *periti*, Congar was not present; Ratzinger had expressed in writing his ideas on the theological basis of the missions. Mgr. Paventi and Fr. Peeters acted as secretaries. In whole day sessions from 12 to 26 January, a large programme of work was got through. The cardinal-president reappeared at the final session. In the next few days Fr. Peeters and his assistants put the texts into Latin. The draft was then sent for consideration to all members of the Missionary Commission and to a certain number of selected Council fathers whose interventions had particularly promoted the work. The plenary sessions of the Missionary Commission were then held in Nemi, from 29 March to 3 April.[34] The new text was approved unanimously, and Cardinal Agagianian named Fr. Schütte as the new and sole vice-president of the Missionary Commission.

Viewed superficially, this text, arrived at after much hard work, scarcely goes beyond the themes treated in the short schema. In fact, however, it is not a mere revision and emended version of the skeleton text, but represents a completely new, large schema. The 14 guiding principles loosely juxtaposed without intrinsic connection, have been systematically developed into a well-conceived composition and expanded fourfold. Whereas the truncated schema comprised 6 pages with 202 lines, the new text had 24 pages and 961 lines. There was also a quite marked improvement in quality. "Quantity and quality are of course interconnected. More can be learnt about the necessity of the missions from 239 lines than from 11; missionary work can be better described when 313 lines rather than 28 are available."[35] Above all, however, a serious attempt had clearly been made to meet the reasonable desires and concrete suggestions of the Council fathers.[36]

Great attention was devoted to the theological basis of the missions, and

---

[32] Conciliar printed matter under the title: *Schema Decreti de activitate missionali Ecclesiae (sub secreto)* (1965), containing: Text, pp. 5–28, Notes, pp. 29–32, *Relatio circa rationem qua schema elaboratum est*, pp. 32–38.

[33] *Steyler Missionschronik* 67, pp. 177 f.

[34] For details on their course from the technical and organizational point of view, see Paventi, *loc. cit.*, pp. 62–64; on the actual programme of work, A. P. Boland, *Église Vivante* 18 (1966), pp. 21–36, *Priester und Mission*, special number, July 1966, pp. 172–4.

[35] *Priester und Mission*, p. 175, note 6.

[36] Details in the conciliar printed matter: *Relatio super schema Decreti de activitate missionali Ecclesiae (sub secreto)* (1965), pp. 5–9; this is the first long Commission report given by Fr. Schütte when the first version was presented.

the collaboration of the Council theologians Congar and Ratzinger guaranteed its agreement with the Constitution on the Church. The idea of the mission was worked out more clearly, but no definition was given. The necessity of missionary activity was even more strongly emphasized and its motives better explained. The whole schema was consciously given a biblical, ecumenical and pastoral character; the hierarchical and institutional element was cut down, wherever possible, to the useful and essential. The local Churches are recognized as the basis of diversity in unity, and great possibilities are allowed for their development. Far-reaching plans are developed for the training of missionaries, for the running of the missions on the local level, but particularly on the highest level in the organization of the Congregation for the Propagation of the Faith *(Propaganda Fide)*.[37] The title *De activitate missionali Ecclesiae* was taken over from the short schema. As compared with those 14 propositions, the new draft contained 39 paragraphs composed as follows:

Prooemium
Caput   I: De principiis doctrinalibus
Caput II: De ipso opere missionali
            Art. 1: De praeambulis evangelizationis
            Art. 2: De praedicatione Evangelii et de congregando populo Dei
            Art. 3: De communitate christiana efformanda
            Art. 4: De ecclesiis particularibus
Caput III: De missionariis
Caput IV: De ordinatione activitatis missionalis
Caput V: De cooperatione

The schema received the unanimous approval of the Missionary Commission on 3 April; it was then forwarded to Cardinal Cicognani, was passed by the Co-ordinating Commission without objection, and by Pope Paul VI on 28 May, and was forwarded to all the Council fathers in the middle of June.

The response was small in extent and quality. The work of the secretariat of the Missionary Commission nevertheless continued practically without a pause.[38] It saw to the provision of copies of the few suggestions and comments sent in, and since time was short, it devised careful procedures for its further work. Cardinal Agagianian confirmed these on 9 September. The

---

[37] *Ibid.*, p. 8. The delicate question of the legal relations between the local ordinaries and missionary institutes was deliberately left open, because the situation had altered completely and circumstances varied from place to place. In the Commission's view a solution was to be found on the lines of agreements concluded between episcopal conferences and missionary institutes, with the approval of the Holy See.

[38] S. Paventi, *loc. cit.*, pp. 66 f.

Missionary Commission was to meet at the start of the fourth session; the five Nemi sub-committees were to handle proposed amendments; Fr. Schütte would be confirmed in his office as vice-president at full sittings of the Missionary Commission; the full commission would meet in the College of *Propaganda Fide,* the sub-commissions in the library of the Congregation; as regards the reorganization of that Congregation referred to in Chapter IV, Article 27, of the schema, a proposal would be put forward at the first full meeting of the commission; the *relatio* prepared by Fr. Schütte would be discussed.

The full commission met on 18 September in the Collegium Urbanianum under the presidency of Cardinal Agagianian. Fr. Schütte was confirmed in office as vice-president. No agreement could be reached on the modification of Chapter IV, Article 27; Fr. Schütte's proposal was not accepted. It was finally decided to entrust to Fr. Schütte the composition of the definitive text of this critical paragraph, taking account of the results of the discussion and the written suggestions received. The new text is printed as an appendix to the *relatio*[39] and contrasted with the formulation in the schema (p. 22, lines 17–22). This completed the preparations for the conciliar debate.

The debate began at the 144th general congregation (moderator: Cardinal Suenens) on 7 October about 11 o'clock, after the conclusion of the debate on the schema on the Church in the Modern World. Cardinal Agagianian introduced the missionary schema, Fr. Schütte read the long report of the Commission, and four speeches followed.[40] The debate was continued at the 145th general congregation (moderator: Cardinal Agagianian) on 8 October. More bishops spoke on Schema 13 in the name of at least 70 fathers, so that only 7 speakers could discuss the missionary schema. At the 146th general congregation on 11 October (moderator: Cardinal Agagianian), the third anniversary of the opening of the Council, 11 fathers spoke. The debate was officially ended at the 147th general congregation on 12 October (moderator: Cardinal Agagianian) to which 17 speakers contributed. The speeches were very uneven in quality and extremely mixed. Fatigue and even tedium spread in the assembly. When the president asked the fathers to show by rising from their seats their desire to end the discussion, a large majority did so. The Secretary General, P. Felici, put the following question to written vote: "Are the fathers ready to adopt the schema on the Missionary Activity of the Church as a basis for further revision in the light of their suggestions and comments?" Of the 2085 fathers present, 2070 voted Yes and 15 No. Thereupon further speeches were made in the name of more than 70 fathers.

---

[39] See p. 11, note 35.

[40] Lists of speakers and the main themes of their interventions are very accurately recorded in *HK* 19 (1964–65), pp. 674 f., 715–18.

In all, 49 fathers spoke on the schema, 39 of them from the missions. More than a hundred applications to speak had to be passed over. At the 148th general congregation on 13 October (moderator: Cardinal Lercaro), there were 10 more speeches. In conclusion, a regional secretary of the World Federation of Catholic Youth, E. Adjakpley from Togo, was allowed to speak as representative of the lay auditors. He spoke of the changed situation of the missions in the world of today, of the increased use of lay personnel from the old and young Churches, and on the special importance of ecumenism for the missions. [41]

A final summing up was given by Fr. Schütte in the name of the Missionary Commission. Although some points of the text still needed correction, he said, it had nevertheless been approved and accepted on principle by an overwhelming majority as the basis for a conciliar decree. The missionary character of the Church as a whole must be brought out more clearly, greater emphasis laid on the importance of the ecumenical movement in the missions, the laity must be employed very much more in the missionary apostolate, and dialogue with non-Christians must be substantially promoted. He gave an assurance that, in the revision of the text, all the amendments and comments put forward would be carefully examined, and that the proposals of the lay auditors and the suggestions of the observer-delegates would be taken into account.

b) The second version [42]

The Missionary Commission met again on 15 October to organize and co-ordinate the work of incorporating proposed amendments. [43] This delicate task of revision was entrusted to the committee which had drawn up the draft schema with such marked success. Its members, Bishops Lokuang, Zoa, Lecuona and Riobé, again worked under the chairmanship of Fr. Schütte. The periti co-opted were Congar, Ratzinger, X. Seumois, Neuner, Glazik, Moya, Buys, Greco, Grasso and Eldarov, two for each of the five sub-committees. The secretary was Fr. Peeters.

One hundred and ninety-three spoken and written interventions amounting to about 555 pages had to be classified and examined, incorporated in

---

[41] Text of the speech in Hampe, op. cit., pp. 529–31.

[42] Conciliar printed matter under the title: Schema Decreti de activitate missionali Ecclesiae: Textus emendatus et Relationes (1965). The text is given in two columns (pp. 5–58); the Textus prior is the first version, the Textus emendatus the second; the differences and improvement are clearly visible. The Commission's reports printed on pp. 59–87 refer to the Textus emendatus.

[43] Details on the meetings of the various commissions, sub-commissions and special commissions are given by Paventi, loc. cit., pp. 69–71. His account does not agree in all particulars with the brief indications of the official relatio, p. 65.

the revised text or rejected. All the petitions and proposals came before three tribunals: the committee, which once again was divided into five sub-committees, each responsible for a chapter of the schema; the five sub-commissions, and finally the full assembly of the Missionary Commission. The chief burden was once again borne by the committee, which made the most important alterations in the text at Nemi, from 19 to 22 October. From 22 to 26 October, the sub-commissions, meeting on the premises of *Propaganda Fide*, examined the results of this careful, conscientious work. Once again profound differences flared up over what was alleged to be the excessively narrow conception of the missions. In the interest of the bishops of Latin America, it was argued, this should be widened. The proposal was rejected. When the full commission met on 27 October in the Propaganda College, the revised text was unanimously approved in a secret vote taken on each of its chapters. On 3 November, the amended schema was submitted to the Co-ordinating Commission, and distributed to the Council fathers on 9 November. For purposes of comparison the new text and the first version were presented in parallel columns, each alteration clearly displayed by the print (pp. 5–58). Furthermore, all changes and emendations were explained and evaluated in detail in a general (pp. 59–64) and special (pp. 65–87) report of the commission.

It was immediately obvious that despite suggestions to the contrary, the title *De activitate missionali Ecclesiae* had been retained but the total length of the schema had grown from 39 to 42 paragraphs. The arrangement had undergone important modifications. Article 4 of the second chapter which deals with the local Churches, "De ecclesiis particularibus" (section 19), had been expanded (sections 19–22) into an independent main division (Chapter III), the subsequent chapters being numbered 4, 5 and 6. The title of Article 1 of Chapter II, "De praeambulis evangelizationis", had been replaced by "De testimonio christiano" in order to avoid the ambiguous term "praeambula". In addition the final section of the schema had been entirely rewritten.

This is not the place to list all the alterations and improvements, large and small, in the second version;[44] the more important ones will be discussed in the commentary. It is clear that the Missionary Commission had tried in a most praiseworthy way to satisfy the innumerable wishes and demands of the Council fathers as far as possible. The conciliar debate and the work of the commission had not been in vain. The basis of the missions was more clearly expressed (Article 7), greater stress was laid on the importance and urgency of the work of the missions, the theological connection with the Constitution on the Church (Article 7) and the Decree on Ecumenism (Articles 7, 15, 29, 36) was more clearly preserved, a more precise description

---

[44] Cf. *Relatio particularis seu de animadversionibus in Quarta Sessione factis*, pp. 68–87.

was given of the missionary mandate of the Pope and the universal episcopate in corporate responsibility, and of the missionary duty of the whole
People of God (Article 5).

The importance of the local Churches *(ecclesiae particulares)* at the present time and for the future is particularly well understood and clearly expressed (Article 6). A separate chapter is devoted to them (Chapter III,
Articles 19–23) in an expanded text (Articles 20 and 21). These local
Churches are not merely the object of missionary work, not merely recipients,
but are themselves agents of the proclamation of the gospel. The evangelized
must as soon as possible become evangelists. If this thought had been extended to the conception of the schema as a whole, it would have involved
numerous alterations in the various sections. The "Western outlook" deplored
by many fathers would have had to disappear completely. Where this was
obvious and could easily be remedied, alterations and improvements were
made; the rest remained. When "missionaries" were mentioned in the first
version, foreign priests were meant; the second version widened and clarified
this by adding: "whether they are natives or foreign, priests, religious or
laypeople". In the first version, dialogue with non-Christians is an obligation
incumbent on foreign missionaries; in the second, it is natives who, if not
exclusively, at least primarily, have to cultivate it. A similar remark may
be made about the missionary vocation of indigenous religious orders and
congregations and of the local diocesan clergy (Article 20). The importance
of the local laity for the proclamation and the planting of the Church is
placed in a correct light (Article 21).[45]

In purely juridical questions which would of course probably have ex-
ceeded the competence of the Missionary Commission, it exercised prudent
reserve, and only partly carried out or totally rejected the proposals of the
Council fathers,[46] e. g. that of extending the notion of missions on account
of the pastoral difficulties of South American prelates (cf., however, Article 6), or that of entrusting missionary territories to dioceses with a lot of
priests; this method had previously been employed in regard to the missionary institutes, but in the changed situation of the missions it was probably
out of date. In the reorganization of the Congregation for the Propaganda
of the Faith, the suggestion was not accepted that chosen representatives of
the various episcopal conferences should be included in the proposed secretariat of experts or to the central advisory council for evangelization "with",
"side by side with" or "under" *Propaganda Fide* (Article 29). This would
have made this supreme organization too big and cumbersome.[47] In the

---

[45] Cf. *Relatio generalis,* pp. 59–61.　[46] *Ibid.,* pp. 61–63.
[47] The Commission's report refers to the Decree *De pastorali Episcoporum munere in Ecclesia,* n. 5: "modis et rationibus a Romano Pontifice statuendis".

ticklish question of legal relations between local ordinary and missionary institutes, on the basis of the Decree on the Bishops' Pastoral Office (Article 35, section 5), the autonomous right of the bishops' conferences and of the missionary institutes independently to regulate their mutual relations by agreement without special approbation of the Holy See, was maintained (Article 32).

This revised version of the schema under the title *De activitate* missionali Ecclesiae was distributed to the Council fathers on 9 November, and the very next day put to the vote at the 157th general congregation (moderator: Cardinal Suenens).[48] A vote was taken on each section according to the double formula *(placet — non placet)*, and on the whole chapter according to the triple formula *(placet — non placet — placet juxta modum)*.

	Present	Yes	No	Invalid	Yes with reservations
1. Arts. 1–4 (Preface and theological basis)	2207	2183	21	3	
2. Arts. 5–6 (The missionary function of the Church)	2135	2012	117	6	
3. Art. 7 (Basis and necessity of the missions)	2114	2106	5	3	
4. Arts. 8–9 (History of the missions, eschatological aspect of missionary activity)	2128	2083	11	34	(27 of these voted Yes with reservations by mistake)
5. Preface and Chapter I (vote according to the triple formula)	2142	1858	7	5	272
6. Arts. 10–12 (Christian witness, presence, dialogue in the missions)	2161	2154	7		
7. Arts. 13–14 (Preaching of the gospel, gathering together the People of God)	2175	2138	37	1	
8. Arts. 15–18 (Formation of a Christian community in the missions)	2182	2165	9	7	
9. Chapter II as a whole	2116	1982	13	3	118
10. Arts. 19–20 (Growth of young Churches, missionary activity of local Churches)	2166	2160	4	2	

[48] Results of the votes in *HK* 20 (1966), pp. 30 f., and Paventi, *loc. cit.*, pp. 72–74; Paventi mistakenly speaks of 10 November and the 156th general congregation.

The General Secretary, P. Felici, drew the attention of the fathers who had voted "Yes with reservations" *(placet juxta modum)* to the fact that they could hand in the reasons for their reservations *(modi)* until the following day at latest. On 11 November, at the 158th general congregation (moderator: Cardinal Agagianian), the remaining 10 votes were taken:

11. Arts. 21–22 (Promotion of the lay apostolate in the missions, diversity in unity)	2209	2196	12	1	
12. On Chapter III as a whole	2209	2066	10	2	131
13. Arts. 23–26 (Missionaries, the missionary vocation, spirituality, theological and pastoral training)	2165	2138	18	9	
14. Art. 27 (Missionary institutes)	2151	2117	4	30	
15. On Chapter IV as a whole	2138	1816	11	2	309
16. Arts. 28–29 (Co-ordination of missionary activity, reorganization of the Congregation of *Propaganda Fide*)	2131	2064	53	14	
17. Arts. 30–31 (Local and regional co-ordination)	2125	2105	16	4	
18. Arts. 32–34 (The work of the missionary institutes, co-ordination between them, and between learned institutions)	2142	2101	37	4	
19. Chapter V as a whole	2153	1428	9	4	712
20. Chapter VI (on missionary collaboration) as a whole	2171	2006	6	1	158

The result of the vote was favourable.[49] All the chapters were accepted except Chapter V, where 712 votes were given with reservations and the necessary two-thirds majority was not obtained. In the votes as a whole on the six chapters, 1700 *modi* were handed in, many of them worthy of note, but most of them the result of canvassing. The schema returned once again to the Missionary Commission for the final examination and consideration of the reservations sent in.

[49] The results of votes 1–5 were announced at the 157th general congregation, of votes 6–10 at the 158th and of votes 15–20 at the 159th on 12 November.

5. THE PUBLISHED CONCILIAR DECREE

A great deal of work had to be done in a short time over the *expensio modorum,* the examination of the votes with reservations.[50] The rejected Chapter V had to be revised once again, but no substantial changes could be made in the chapters already approved. Directly after the votes on 10 and 11 November, the secretary of the Nemi committee, Fr. Peeters, started collecting and arranging the *modi.* Most of them had been handed in by the fathers at the same time as their voting cards in the aula. Pope Paul VI sent in an opinion on the schema. Where his wishes did not coincide with the *modi* of other Council fathers, his suggestions were classified under the heading "... from a single father". On 12 and 13 November the Nemi committee worked at a thorough consideration of the *modi.* At the plenary session of the Missionary Commission on 17 November, the emendations made were unanimously endorsed, and at a further meeting on 18 November the final report was approved.[51] The revised *modi* were printed with all speed, distributed to the Council fathers on 26 November for study, and put to the vote on 30 November at the 165th general congregation (moderator: Cardinal Agagianian) at the end of the ten-day break. Fr. Schütte read the commission's *relatio.*

A compact group of *modi* had concentrated on the rejected Chapter V dealing with the reorganization of *Propaganda Fide.* 461 fathers had requested that the missionary bishops sent as delegates to Propaganda should have a deliberative vote, that they should be nominated by the episcopal conferences, and that they should be nominated only for a limited term. In the view of these fathers, it was not sufficient to speak of "active and decisive participation"; there must be a clear and unambiguous grant of the right to a deliberative vote in the strictly juridical sense. After mature deliberation, the Missionary Commission decided for obvious reasons[52] on the formula: "They shall have an active share and a deliberative vote", when it is a question of decisions within the competence of Propaganda and of documents requiring the Pope's approval. The right of nomination by bishops' conferences was rejected because this would curtail the Pope's freedom considerably and would not encourage the dynamism necessary for large-scale

[50] Conciliar printed matter under the title: *Schema Decreti de activitate missionali Ecclesiae. Modi a Patribus conciliaribus propositi a Commissione de Missionibus examinati (sub secreto)* (1965), pp. 5–88: *Modi,* pp. 89–95: *Relatio generalis.*

[51] After this further *modi* were handed in by the Secretary General of the Council. These were examined with all speed by the Nemi committee summoned on 22 November, but could not be submitted to the plenary commission. A minute description of this last phase is given by Paventi, *loc. cit.,* pp. 74 f.

[52] Cf. *Schema Decreti* ... (see above, note 50), pp. 89 f.

planning. Nomination for a limited term was finally reserved to the post-conciliar regulations for implementing the Decree on the Missions.

Two hundred and sixty-five fathers wanted an explicit statement on close and uniform collaboration between *Propaganda Fide* and other Roman dicasteries, e.g. the Consistorial Congregation or the Secretariat of State, to which missionary territories in Asia, Africa and especially in some parts of Latin America are subject. The Commission, on the other hand, was of the opinion that since these were exceptional cases which might be suppressed by the Missionary Decree, a declaration to this effect had been introduced into the notes of the official conciliar text. In any case, such decisions were not a matter for the schema nor for the Missionary Commission but for the Holy See alone.[53]

In the section on the missionary duty of the bishops, 74 fathers did not want collegiality and the Synod of Bishops to be involved. This suggestion was rejected. The text would remain as it was. Missionary work would be an important responsibility of the Synod of Bishops, which would be a council of bishops for the whole Church. The authority of the Pope would not be limited in any way, as these fathers feared. The Pope would determine the matters to be discussed and the Synod would give advice in a worldwide perspective.[54]

As regards section 32 of Chapter V, which deals with the control of mis-sionary activity between local ordinaries and religious orders, many fathers had proposed that the agreements mentioned in the schema should be subject to the approval of the Holy See, since it was not right for every bishop and every religious order to settle these matters as they pleased (59 fathers). The reference to the Decree on the Bishops' Pastoral Office was not cogent, it was argued, for the missions are in an exceptional position (25 fathers). This proposal was justified in the interest of uniformity (6 fathers), and would be of particular advantage to institutes under papal jurisdiction and inter-national in character (16 fathers). The Commission expressed the view that the bishops should not have the burden imposed on them of having to refer to the Holy See and to seek the approval of *Propaganda Fide* for all these agreements. If any bishops wished, they would be free to do so. It was sufficient if the Holy See laid down general fundamental guidelines for such agreements.[55]

All the other amendments concerned the chapters already approved. These *modi* were mostly rejected or satisfied by insignificant modifications of the text, of a mostly formal kind. A relatively small number were incorporated, since they did not alter the substance of the schema. The result of the conciliar vote on the *expensio modorum* was as follows:[56]

[53] p. 91.   [54] p. 91.   [55] p. 92.   [56] *HK* 20 (1966), pp. 34 f.

	Present	Yes	No	Invalid
1. Art. 6 (Definition of the missions)	2229	2209	20	—
2. *Modi* on the other sections of Chapter I	2210	2189	18	3
3. *Modi* on Chapter II	2162	2133	26	3
4. *Modi* on Chapter III	2161	2142	16	3
5. *Modi* on Chapter IV	2169	2147	22	—
6. Art. 29 (Reorganization of *Propaganda Fide*)	2169	2112	54	3
7. Art. 32 (Regulation of relations with missionary institutes)	2168	2152	14	2
8. *Modi* on other sections of Chapter V	2195	2175	18	2
9. *Modi* on Chapter VI	2186	2159	24	3
10. On the revised schema as a whole	2182	2162	18	2

Thus the missionary schema had overcome all obstacles. The efforts made had been rewarded, the outcome surpassing the boldest hopes. The text was submitted to Pope Paul VI, finally voted by the Council fathers at the 9th general congregation of the fourth session and promulgated by the Pope "in common with the fathers"[57] under the title *Decretum de activitate missionali Ecclesiae*. 2394 fathers had voted Yes, 5 No. Thus it received the highest number of votes of all the decrees of Vatican II. A note appended to the document determined that the decree would not come into force *(vacatio legis)* until 29 June 1966.

The motu proprio *Finis Concilio* of 1 January 1966 established a post-conciliar Commission for the Missions,[58] which was to work out by that date the means for carrying out the decree. Surprisingly, the *vacatio legis* was extended indefinitely by the motu proprio *Munus Apostolicum* of 10 June 1966.[59] But as early as 6 August 1966 the motu proprio *Ecclesiae Sanctae* published the instructions for putting into effect the four decrees on the Bishops' Pastoral Office, and on the Ministry and Life of Priests (I), on the Appropriate Renewal of the Religious Life (II) and on the Church's Missionary Activity (III).[60] These norms came into effect on 11 October 1966, the fourth anniversary of the opening of the Council.[61]

[57] *AAS* 58 (1966), pp. 947–90.
[58] *Ibid.*, pp. 37–40.   [59] pp. 465 f.
[60] pp. 757–87.
[61] Cf. V. Dammertz, "Die Ausführungsbestimmungen zum Konzilsdekret über die Missionstätigkeit der Kirche", *AKK* 136 (1967), pp. 45–67.

111

Doctrinal Principles

Title. Both the Preparatory and the Conciliar Commission bore the title *De Missionibus,* and this was also used for the two first draft schemas (A and B). The short schema (C) was entitled "On the Missionary Activity of the Church" and this was retained even when the text was completely recast (D), and despite the protest of some fathers it was not changed in the final missionary decree itself. There were various reasons for the change of title in text C. The original title seemed too pretentious for the 14 meagre guiding principles of the truncated schema. Clearly the intention was to avoid the suspicion that the missions are a kind of religious colonialism. The theological reasons for the mission had been convincingly introduced and incorporated into the Constitution on the Church (Articles 16, 17) and this had clearly brought out the unity, the single and unique character of the Church's mission. Consequently the shortened schema was severely restricted to a few programmatic principles of missionary activity.[1] The title suited the contents of the document well enough. That was no longer quite true of text E, for here the speculative basis of the missions was not presented in the introduction. This text expounded theological doctrine in considerable detail in the first main section, which is also the most extensive chapter in the whole decree, but missionary activity in the proper sense is only dealt with in the following chapters. The Latinist will hardly find the style to his liking *(activitas?).* The excuse that by accepting text D the Council had also approved the title,[2] is not convincing. The more comprehensive term "missionary work" *(opus)* would have been more suitable than the vaguer expression "missionary activity".

[1] Inde Concilium, postquam de natura missionali Ecclesiae, de adaptatione missionali et de subiecto missionis in Schemata 'De Ecclesia' egerit, sequentia in mentem revocare vel decernere statuit *(Schema propositionum,* p. 7).
[2] *Schema Decreti ... Modi a patribus conciliaribus propositi a Commissione de Missionibus examinati* (1965), p. 5.

Article 1. The opening words "Ad gentes" and the description of the Church as "the universal sacrament of salvation" deliberately establish the intrinsic connection of the missionary decree with the Constitution on the Church, *Lumen Gentium.* The Church is sent by God to all men. As the quotation from St. Augustine recalls, the task of the apostles as Christ's disciples consisted in proclaiming the word of God and founding Churches. This states the two essential elements of missionary work, the proclamation of the word and the planting of Churches, and at the same time expresses the Christological and ecclesiological aspects of the mission. This task of proclaiming and establishing God's kingdom has passed to the successors of the apostles (an addition in text D 2) and has thus become a permanent obligation. Then the special urgency of the mission at the present moment in history is stressed. The point and purpose of the missionary decree is to lay down the principles of missionary activity and to arouse and mobilize all the energies of the People of God in accordance with the Church's renewed consciousness of its nature.

Chapter I is typically self-contained; it resembles a theological treatise in character and does not fit harmoniously into the missionary decree as a whole. It is not only the most extensive of the six chapters; it also contains the most footnotes, more than all the other chapters together. The patristic references are particularly numerous and excellently chosen, whereas the following chapters quote almost exclusively from conciliar texts and papal allocutions. Chapter I aims at giving in brief outline a theological theory of the missions. This had been urgently requested by a majority of the fathers; they thought that the pastoral statements of the Constitution on the Church were too general in character to do justice to the specifically missionary service.

The theological reasons which the decree presents as the basis of the mission have their ground in the mystery of the Trinity, in God's eternal saving plan. The Father's loving decree sends salvation to men in Jesus Christ and the Holy Spirit, through the instrumentality of the Church (Articles 2–4). The specifically missionary activity which transmits salvation is distinguished from the general mission of the Church; the concept, purpose and methods of the mission and its varying forms are described in detail and contrasted with the pastoral and ecumenical service of the Church (Articles 5 and 6). As motives of missionary endeavour it names the necessity of faith, baptism and the Church for salvation, love of God and glorification of God, and also the concrete fulfilment of human nature itself (Articles 7 and 8). Finally, the duration of missionary activity is given as the period between the Lord's first coming and his return, in which the Church works to gather together and convert the non-Christian nations (Article 9).

Article 2 lays down in the form of a thesis the lapidary principle which will be theologically developed in Articles 2 to 5:[3] "The pilgrim Church is missionary by its very nature", that is, its journey is that of an envoy. The inner Trinitarian processions in the primordial fountain of love, the *fontalis amor*, come forth *ad extra* in Christ's incarnation and in the mission of the Holy Spirit. It is from these divine missions *(missiones)* that the Church derives its missionary form according to the eternal saving design and decree of the Father.[4] It is rooted in God the Father as unoriginated origin and in the missions of the Son and the Holy Spirit. Through the incarnation and the Pentecostal event, the Father's saving will has become present and visible in the world. The Church has its ground in the life of the Trinity, and by its very nature is missionary.

This of course does not yet designate and exhibit the typically missionary function of the Church in the specific sense (unless all the Church's activity, its sacramental, pastoral, charitable and social works are to be called missionary, which would obscure and weaken the proper concept of the mission). The decree does stress, however, that God's redemptive plan does not simply call the individual human being to share in the divine life, but wills to gather men together out of their isolation into the People of God in the community of the Church.[5]

Article 3, pursuing the thought of Article 2, notes that even before the "missions" (of the divine persons) the Spirit of God could be at work by grace in men. Religious ideas and practices in the non-Christian world need, however, to be "enlightened and purified" even though in the providential plan they may serve to guide men towards the true God or as a "preparation for the gospel". It is striking how firmly and calmly the Council states and deals with the questions of missionary adaptation and the saving value of the non-Christian religions which had been regarded by missionary workers and specialists in missiology as the most important missionary problem of the present time.[6] The basis of this confidence can be found in a great theological tradition stretching from the speculation of the Greek Fathers of the Church[7] down to the doctrinal pronouncements of recent

[3] Detailed commentary by Y. Congar, who took part in the drafting of the text, in J. Schütte, ed., *Mission nach dem Konzil* (1967), pp. 134–72 ("Theologische Grundlegung").
[4] A. Rétif, "Trinité et Missions d'après Bérulle", *Neue Zeitschrift für Missionswissenschaft* 13 (1967), pp. 1–8; id. "Trinité et Missions", *Evangéliser* 6 (1954), pp. 179–89.
[5] Clement of Alexandria: "Just as the will of God is an act and is called world, so too his intention is the salvation of man and is called Church" *(Paedagogus,* I, 6, 27), quoted by Y. Congar, *loc. cit.,* p. 138.
[6] *Ad Gentes,* arts. 3, 8, 9, 14, 15, 17; *Gaudium et Spes,* arts. 22, 26, 38, 41, 57; *Lumen Gentium,* arts. 16, 17.
[7] A. Luneau, *L'Histoire du salut chez les Pères de l'Église* (1964), *passim;* W. Bierbaum, "Geschichte als Paidagogia Theou", *MTZ* 5 (1964), pp. 246–72.

Popes.[8] The mission, in fact, is not simply the proclamation of the word of God and the extension of Christ's dominion, but also the gathering, examination and purification of non-Christian preparations for and possible guides to the gospel. "What was not assumed by Christ was not healed."

All salvation has its ground in Christ's incarnation. He is the only mediator between God and man. In him God's saving action for men has become visible and effective. One of the additions to text D 2 laid particular stress on what was new and final in this visible revelation of God in Christ. The incarnation was a descent into the poverty and want, error and sin of mankind. And it involved not so much or merely a renunciation of the wise use and assistance of the good things of this life[9] as a true self-emptying (kenosis) in humility and mercy, the deliberate setting aside of any pretension to superiority, genuine regard for the conviction of others, the knowledge and recognition of the "true light which enlightens every man who comes into this world".

Only in this way can the work of Christ find lasting embodiment in the course of the ages until the end of the world. The incarnation is the origin and model of all missionary work, the sending of the Son by the Father into the world. This first mission remains the starting-point, the sole origin, the source of every other mission. In reality there is only one mission, that of the Son, and all others are only a participation in, and result of this. If we ascend to this source we find the origin of the whole missionary spirit.[10]

Article 4. No fully valid statements can be made about the person and work of Jesus Christ without mention of God the Father and the Holy Spirit. Because of numerous interventions, especially of Council fathers from the Eastern Church, draft D 2 improved the arrangement and substantially extended the text. The significance of the Holy Spirit as well as the collaboration of Mary in the economy of salvation was made clear, and the charismatic element in missionary work was emphasized. The Holy Spirit is the life-giving "soul" of the work of salvation, and impels the Church to expansion through missionary activity. Since Pentecost he has accompanied Christ's disciples and Church; Pentecost inaugurated the history of the apostles. Through the apostolic service the Church received a public character by the power of the Holy Spirit. Equipped with hierarchical and charismatic gifts, the saving work advances and the nations are led to the unity of faith in the community of the Church.[11]

[8] For example the encyclicals of Pius XII *Evangelii Praecones, AAS* 43 (1951), nn. 58, 62, and John XXIII, *Mater et Magistra: AAS* 53 (1961), p. 444.
[9] Cf. P. Gauthier, *Consolez mon peuple. Le Concile et l'Église des pauvres* (1965).
[10] See J. Daniélou, *Salvation of the Nations* (1962).
[11] Cf. A. Rétif, *Mission de l'Église et Mission de l'Esprit* (1958); N. Adler, *Das erste christliche Pfingstfest* (1938); P. Mondreganes, "Función misionera del Espíritu Santo", *Euntes*

The Council leaves no doubt and in fact expressly states, though without describing the mode of operation, that the Holy Spirit was at work for the salvation of the world even before Christ's return to the Father, and that he not merely accompanies but prepares the way for missionary activity.[12] Before the missionary begins his work by witness and preaching, the Holy Spirit, the giver of life, is already active. The missionary would do well to observe carefully what the Holy Spirit has already effected among his hearers, so as to link up with it and build on it. Generally, contact with other Christians or reading of the Bible will have preceded him. If the missionary is wise, he will take time to listen to these other human beings before he speaks. If he does so, he will probably find that in the life of his hearers there are experiences which, without any human planning, have smoothed the way and made it possible for them to accept the gospel. The moment will come when as Christians they will look back at these experiences and recognize them as the operation of the same Holy Spirit who spoke to them in the missionary's preaching and enabled them to perceive the word of God in his human words. The genuine evangelist knows that the faith of new Christians is not produced by his words. These merely serve as instruments of the action of the Holy Spirit which began before his arrival and will continue when he has gone, producing their faith as its fruit.[13]

Article 5 describes the Church's mission in general. A number of Council fathers complained of overemphasis on the hierarchical and institutional element, and wanted the basis to be the new awareness of the Church as the People of God. The text in fact can only be correctly understood if taken in conjunction with *Lumen Gentium*. It was not relevant here once more to define and expound the concept of the Church. The Constitution on the Church deals with the mystery of the Church, the missionary decree with the Church's mission.

The missionary mandate was first given to the apostles; the so-called "missionary command" (Mt 28:19 f.; Mk 16:15), a kerygma of the primitive Church, was therefore quoted verbatim (this was not yet included in text D 1). The apostles were the first representatives of the hierarchy and at the

Docete (Commentaria Urbana) 8 (1955), pp. 326–44; J. Capmany, "La communicación del Espíritu Santo a la Iglesia-Cuerpo místico como principio de su unidad", *Revista Española de teología* 17 (1957), pp. 173–204; Y. Congar, *Esquisses du Mystère de l'Église* (2nd ed., 1953), pp. 129–79, E. T.: *Mystery of the Church* (1960); id., *Les voies du Dieu Vivant* (1962), pp. 165–84; J. Daniélou, *op. cit.*, who observes that when we read the Acts of the Apostles, which might also be called the Gospel of the Holy Spirit, we see that every missionary work is attributed to the Holy Spirit acting through the apostles.

[12] Y. Congar, *Mystère du Temple* (2nd ed., 1964), pp. 310 f., E. T.: *Mystery of the Temple* (1962); G. Philips, *La grâce des justes de l'Ancien Testament* (1948).

[13] See L. Newbigin, *The Relevance of Trinitarian Doctrine for Today's Mission* (1963).

same time the first members of the Church. They and their successors, the college of bishops in union with the Pope, by Christ's will have the duty of spreading the faith. This task belongs to all the faithful as members of the Church; this is emphasized by the quotation from Ephesians 4:16.[14] The mission of the Church as the sacrament of salvation, in the obedience of faith to the Lord's command, must lead by witness and proclamation, sacramental action and missionary work, to "full participation in the mystery of Christ". Consequently Christ has given the Church by the power of the Holy Spirit the dynamic impulse to make present the sacrament of salvation in its full reality among all the nations.

The Church is therefore sent, has a mission; by its very nature it is missionary, i. e. journeying as an envoy (Article 2), on pilgrimage from the first coming of the Lord until his return. Since Christ continues his action in the Church, its mission must also bear the signs of Christ, poverty[15] and sacrifice, death and resurrection (cf. Article 3). No triumphant external successes are promised to this saving work of the Church, which has to live on the promise of its Lord, "I am with you always, to the close of the age" (Mt 28:20) and "the powers of death shall not prevail against it" (Mt 16:18).

Article 6 forms the transition to the specific theme of the missionary decree, passing from the Church's mission generally and its theological basis to the Church's missions, missionary activity in the special, technical sense. First a clear distinction is drawn between missionary activity and the various modes, levels and stages of the Church's mission. The latter is everywhere identically one and the same, a continuation of Christ's mission. "As the Father has sent me, even so I send you" (Jn 20:21). The conditions and circumstances under which the Church's work is done, however, are very varied, and change from nation to nation and age to age. The methods used and the kinds of activity employed must be modified and adapted to the particular situation in redemptive history.

The decree then gives the following definition of missionary activity in the narrower and special sense. "'Missions' is the term usually given to those particular undertakings by which the heralds of the gospel are sent out by the Church and go forth into the whole world to carry out the task of preaching the gospel and planting the Church among peoples or groups who do not yet believe in Christ. These undertakings are brought to completion by missionary activity and are commonly exercised in certain territories recognized by the Holy See."

[14] Y. Congar, *Lay People in the Church* (1964); D. Nothomb, "Qui portera l'Évangile aux païens?", *Spiritus* 18 (1964), pp. 3–17.
[15] J. Glazik, *Dekret über die Missionstätigkeit der Kirche* (1967), pp. 8 f.; P.-A. Liégé, "La pauvreté, compagne de la mission", in *Église et pauvreté*, Unam Sanctam 57 (1965), pp. 157–68.

Despite energetic endeavours and long controversies, Catholic missiology was long unable to agree on any generally recognized concept of the missions. This fact made collaboration difficult even in the Preparatory Commission, and continued to be a serious obstacle to the work of the Conciliar Commission for the Missions until the end. Two attitudes and views stood confronted, ultimately originating in two schools of missiological thought: 1) the concept of the missions held by the Münster school (J. Schmidlin) and 2) the curial-canonist concept (P. Charles, A. Seumois). These two fundamental and fundamentally different conceptions had been modified and further developed in the course of the years by a number of well-known missiologists, but no agreement had been reached.[16] This is not the place, nor is it our business, to adopt a position in regard to these theories; we are concerned to expound the definition set out in the missionary decree. Brevity is therefore essential. Putting the matter rather succinctly and without the necessary qualifications, we might say that the Schmidlin idea of the missions, strongly influenced by Protestant missiology (G. Warneck), chiefly emphasizes the proclamation of the gospel, the conversion of mankind, the salvation of the souls of non-Christians; it is Christocentric and personal in character. The canonist conception places the chief stress on the implantation of the Church, the establishment of the hierarchy, the foundation of particular native Churches, the winning over of non-Catholics; it is ecclesiocentric and territorial in character. Both conceptions view the Church chiefly as an institution, and the missionary as a foreigner who goes away to distant lands.

The Council refused on principle to contribute in any field to the triumph of particular theological theories or of freely disputed scholastic opinions. So it was here. The new definition in the missionary decree represents an expressive synthesis of the two above-mentioned tendencies and views, obtained by consistently applying the new understanding of the Church as the People of God. In fact each of those views of the missions, if affirmed exclusively, would be incomplete and in need of correction. The conciliar definition therefore represents a genuine advance and should bring the two positions closer together. In the Catholic view the proclamation of the gospel and the conversion of mankind necessarily lead to the administration of the

---

[16] Cf. J. Schmidlin, *Katholische Missionslehre im Grundriss* (1919); T. Ohm, *Machet zu Jüngern alle Völker* (1962); P. Charles, *Missiologie* (1939); T. Grentrup, *Ius missionarium* (1925); A. Perbal, *Premières leçons de théologie missionnaire* (1937); A. Seumois, *Vers une définition de l'activité missionnaire* (1948); id., *Introduction à la missiologie* (1952); id., "Le terme de Mission", *Scientia missionum Ancilla* (1953), pp. 54–65; E. Loffeld, *Le problème cardinal de la Missiologie et des Missions catholiques* (1956); J. Masson, *Fonction missionnaire, fonction de l'Église* (1959), a special reprint from *NRT* 80 (1958), pp. 1042–61, and 81 (1959), pp. 41–59. A detailed statement of the problems with abundant bibliography will be found in A. Freitag, *Mission und Missionswissenschaft* (1962), pp. 21–67.

sacraments and the formation of a Church. Conversely, it would be utopian to found a Church before the faith has been proclaimed and visible success has been had with conversions. The two views imply one another. The first is deeply rooted in the original Christian kerygma of the "missionary command", like most of the doctrinal statements of the great papal missionary encyclicals of modern times since Leo XIII.[17] The second view, on the other hand, is chiefly supported by numerous references from patristic writings, by the classical scholastic theologians (Aquinas, Albert the Great; also Bernard of Clairvaux and Francis Xavier), by innumerable curial documents of all dates and by impressive ecclesiological considerations.[18]

The definition contained in the conciliar decree attempts to be objective and balanced and so serve to link and correct the various views. The agents of missionary activity are the "heralds of the gospel sent out by the Church". Their field of activity is in principle the whole world, but in actual fact in their special sphere as missionaries they have to preach the gospel and plant the Church only among those "peoples or groups who do not yet belive in Christ". Consequently they are not sent to non-Catholic Christians (cf. *CIC*, can. 1350, § 2); ecumenical activity is dealt with later in the decree. They have to preach the gospel exclusively to non-Christians, that is, to people who do "not yet" believe in Christ. It is a mark of the missions that they are always the first proclamation of the gospel. The dechristianized countries and unbelieving masses of Europe and America create their own difficult problems for the apostolate but do not present a missionary situation. In those areas the Church is established as an institution and present through its hierarchy. Access to the Church is open to everyone. The relatively large number of priests, as compared with the missionary countries, ensures that the offer of salvation is publicly made. Missiologists as well as missionaries therefore decisively reject the use and transfer of the term "mission" to situations analogous to that of the missions,[19] e. g. expressions like "Germany a missionary country", or "French mission to the workers". Here the gospel was preached long ago; it is offered and accessible to men of goodwill. The decree emphasizes the "not yet" situation of the missions to which Cardinal

---

[17] Cf. K. Müller, "Praedicate Evangelium als Zentralidee der päpstlichen Missionsenzykliken", *ZMR* 44 (1960), pp. 161–74; "Innumerable references are made in the encyclicals to spreading the faith" (p. 173); the description of missionaries as *Evangelii praecones* "occurs at least 33 times in the six encyclicals" (p. 172). Strictly speaking, without straining the interpretation, only one passage in Benedict XV's encyclical *Maximum illud* supports the so-called implantation theory (*AAS* 18 [1926], p. 74).

[18] Cf. Y. Congar, "Theologische Grundlegung" in J. Schütte, *op. cit.*, pp. 153–56; A. Seumois, *Le Siège Apostolique et les Missions* (1959); A. Rétif, *Introduction à la doctrine pontificale des missions* (1953); E. Loffeld, *Le problème cardinal de la missiologie*, pp. 199–246; C. Journet, *L'Église du Verbe Incarné* (1942, 1951).

[19] J. A. Otto, "Missionsland?", *Die katholischen Missionen* 70 (1951), pp. 131–35.

Frings drew particular attention in his important intervention. "In the theology of the missions we should avoid all analogous use of the word 'mission' for territories which were formerly Christian but which are now dechristianized. The missionary idea must shine forth with its whole original clarity; it means the proclamation of our Lord Jesus Christ in places where this holy name has not yet been preached." [20] The recovery of dechristianized countries, of people who no longer *believe*, is a function of the Church's pastoral care. The conciliar missionary definition of "not yet" must, however, presumably be extended also to nations and groups where the gospel is no longer *preached*.

Finally the definition deliberately moves the centre of gravity of the prevailing concept of the missions from the geographical and territorial sphere to an almost exclusively human and sociological conception in harmony with the Council's ecclesiology. The mission is directed to human beings and peoples, not primarily to countries and territories. The Church is implanted in human beings; it is they who constitute the Church. The decree repeatedly designates as the object of the missions "peoples, groups or individuals", "groups and peoples", or "peoples or groups who do not yet believe in Christ", in whom the Church "has not yet taken root". When the Council says that the missions are "commonly exercised in certain territories recognized by the Holy See", this corresponds to the method of organization which has existed for the past three centuries and to the curial practice of the Congregation for the Propagation of the Faith.

The purpose of missionary activity by the evangelization of the nations is the implantation of the Church, i. e. of the vigorous, fully developed particular Church described in Chapters II and III of the decree. The most important direct means mentioned are the proclamation of the word of God and the administration of the sacraments (baptism, Eucharist). The choice of means and methods varies according to the stage and state of missionary work. The chief task is less that of establishing ecclesiastical institutions, organizations and hierarchical structures than of gathering together the People of God in active and living communities of faith.

The last part of the article distinguishes missionary activity from pastoral work and ecumenical endeavours. Rather disconnectedly (as is unfortunately quite often the case in the decree), missionary activity is again declared to be an essential and vital function of the Church, its intrinsic connection with the ecclesiology of the Constitution on the Church is emphasized and the mission is said to give expression to "the collegial awareness of the hierarchy", presumably in order to present the three fields of action mentioned as a duty incumbent on the universal episcopate.

[20] *ZMR* 50 (1966), p. 23.

In the view of the decree, missions, pastoral work and ecumenism are to be distinguished on principle, although in the concrete they are interconnected in a variety of ways. It is not said what constitutes their inner connection or what distinguishes them. Probably the intention was, at least in theory, to avert the danger that if missionary work were linked and confused with other domains of the Church's apostolate, a certain weakening of missionary enterprise might ensue. Except in the very earliest stages, mission and pastoral care are inseparable. The same man is often both missionary and pastor in the same place. In practice it is therefore often not possible to determine whether a situation is still a missionary one or whether regular pastoral conditions already prevail.

In this connection the Council took account of the views of a large and compact group of Latin American fathers who repeatedly and urgently asked for missionary status for their *praelaturae nullius* on the grounds of their special situation.[21] It is true that the missionary commission, out of regard for "genuine" missionaries and not least for reasons of principle, had refused any extension and consequent weakening of the missionary concept. Nevertheless in a note appended to the text of the decree, the special case and exceptional circumstances of these ecclesiastical territories were sympathetically recognized (note 17 to Latin text; note 21, p. 592 in Abbott).[22] They are in fact the only missions mentioned by name in the decree.

The concluding statement on ecumenical work in the missions inserted here in the definitive version (E) from section 8 of D 2, regrets the difficulties for missionary work which result from divisions in belief, and describes ecumenical efforts as indispensably needed in the interest of missionary credibility. It does not, however, outline any missionary programme, and simply refers to the guiding principles expressed in the Decree on Ecumenism.[23] The urgency of ecumenical efforts in the missions is also stressed in a different context in Articles 15, 16, 29 and 36.

Article 7 names as motives for the missions the necessity of faith, baptism and membership of the Church for salvation, love for Christ which extends to all men and seeks to incorporate them in his mystical body, and finally the glorification of God to which the whole of mankind is called and directed

---

[21] *Schema Decreti de Activitate missionali Ecclesiae: Textus emendatus et relationes* (1965), pp. 61 f., 71; *Modi a Patribus conciliaribus propositi, a Commissione de Missionibus examinati* (1965), pp. 18 f., 28.

[22] Cf. G. M. Grotti, "Die Missionen Lateinamerikas", in J. Schütte, *op. cit.*, pp. 82–93.

[23] *Parole et Mission* 28 (1965), pp. 3–98; M.-J. Le Gillou, *Mission et Unité* (1960); J. Glazik, "Die ökumenische Perspektive des Missionsdekrets", *Tatsachen und Fragen nach dem II. Vatikanischen Konzil. Ein Studienheft der Deutschen Missionshilfe* (1957), pp. 5–18; N. P. Moritzen, "Anzeichen von Änderungen im Verhältnis zwischen protestantischer und römisch-katholischer Missionsarbeit", *ibid.*, pp. 5 f.; E. Klappert, "Gedanken eines Missionars zur römisch-katholischen Mission", *ibid.*, pp. 98–104.

as God's People and family.[24] A large number of practising missionaries were disturbed about the all too favourable judgment on non-Christian religions and the possibility of salvation for non-Christians[25] which the Council seemed to them to have expressed in the Constitution on the Church (Article 16) and in the Declaration on the Relationship of the Church to Non-Christian Religions (Article 2). They asked for a clear statement on these problems and an official pronouncement on the necessity of the missions even after the Council, in order to have a solid theological basis for their laborious and responsible work. They were afraid that otherwise there would be a weakening of missionary spirit for lack of a firm standpoint. The Council gave no elucidation and certainly no decision on the value of the non-Christian religions for salvation.[26] It could not have done so. That difficult question is the subject of theological speculation and, to judge by what has been published, will not be settled for a long time.[27] At all events the traditional solution has not been utterly overthrown so far.

The necessity of the missions and the Church is directly and clearly founded on the unique and incomparable character of Jesus Christ. It is Christ's central function in the world and the cosmos which gives to Christianity among all religions its position and significance in the history of salvation. In this perspective, Christ and Christianity appear as "fulfilment, goal and accomplishment — as crisis and judgment" (H. Fries) of the non-Christian religions. Christianity is the universal and eschatological religion of mankind

[24] H. de Lubac, *Le fondement théologique des missions* (1964).

[25] K. Rahner, "Christianity and the Non-Christian Religions", *Theological Investigations*, V (1966), pp. 115–34; H. van Straelen, *Our Attitude towards Other Religions* (1965), pp. 81 to 109; L. Elders, "Die Taufe der Weltreligionen", *Theologie und Glaube* 55 (1965), pp. 124 to 131; H. Kruse, "Die 'Anonymen Christen' exegetisch gesehen", *MTZ* 18 (1967), pp. 2–29; F. Legrand, "Une conception moderne du salut des infidèles qui fait obstacle à l'élan apostolique d'après P. K. Rahner", *Le Christ au Monde* 8 (1963), pp. 457–65.

[26] The authentic teaching of the Church and the Council is presented by I. Auf der Maur, "Kirchliche Verlautbarungen über die nichtchristlichen Religionen", *Katholisches Missionsjahrbuch der Schweiz* (1966), pp. 31–43; A. Mulders, "Der missionarische Charakter der Kirche und die Sicht auf die nichtchristlichen Religionen", *Priester und Mission* (1967), pp. 257–71, in Dutch in: *Het Missiewerk* 46 (1967), pp. 1–20; H. Fries, "Das Christentum und die Religionen der Welt", in K. Forster, ed., *Das Christentum und die Weltreligionen* (1965), pp. 13–37.

[27] E. Cornélis, *Valeurs chrétiennes des religions non chrétiennes* (1965); I. Finsterhölzl, "Zur Theologie der Religionen", *Kairos* 7 (1965), pp. 308–18; J. Ratzinger, "Der christliche Glaube und die Weltreligionen", *Gott in Welt (Festschrift für K. Rahner)*, II (1964), pp. 287 to 305; H. R. Schlette, *Towards a Theology of Religions*, Quaestiones Disputatae 12 (1966) id., *Die Konfrontation mit den Religionen* (1964); id., *Colloquium salutis. Christen und Nichtchristen heute* (1965); H. Küng, *Christenheit als Minderheit* (1965); G. Thils, *Propos et problèmes de la théologie des religions non chrétiennes* (1966); J. Heislbetz, *Theologische Gründe der nichtchristlichen Religionen* (1967), with abundant bibliography; K. Müller, *Die Kirche und die nichtchristlichen Religionen* (1968).

because Christ is God's absolute and eschatological word to mankind. It is therefore impossible that the Christian religion should be essentially carried further or transcended within the religious development of mankind. We Christians, therefore, on principle can never accept that religions are merely relative, though we can certainly genuinely affirm that they can be inter-related. It is true that all religions can experience a certain enrichment and deepening through contact, dialogue and confrontation, but the old axiom *Extra Ecclesiam nulla salus,* though not very happily expressed, retains its validity even today, if correctly interpreted. It means that anyone who is saved finds salvation through Christ and the Church. Vatican II expressed this clearly and positively: "Ecclesia universale salutis sacramentum" (*Lumen Gentium,* Article 48). The old, frequently misunderstood and misapplied axiom must therefore be explained and modified: *Sine Ecclesia nulla salus,* or: *Extra Christum nulla salus.* This does not in any way state who, when and how many are saved, but how, in what way and by what means men attain salvation. Testimony to the complete universality of Christ and of Christianity is borne by St. Augustine in an astonishing passage of the *Retractationes:* "The reality itself which is now called the Christian religion, was also present among the ancients and was not lacking from the very beginning of the human race, until Christ appeared in the flesh. From then on, the true religion, which had always existed, began to be called the Christian religion" (*Retract.,* I, 12, 3: *Corpus Scriptorum Ecclesiasticorum Latinorum,* XXXVI, 58, 12–15).

Article 8 considers missionary activity in a general human light in the perspective of universal history. The mission, by its harmony with the realization of the plan of salvation and also that of creation, aims at leading men and mankind to its full development, unity and peace. It fulfils mankind's deepest expectations which can never be satisfied by men's own exertions in some kind of self-redemption. By its message of Christ, it tells men who they are and what their vocation is, and that of human society as a whole. The Church is essentially intended to be the Church of all mankind. By the proclamation of the reign of Christ, who in an Advent Antiphon (for 23 December) is praised as "the expectation of the nations, and their Saviour", the work of the missions is shown to be an epiphany of God. In this theological perspective and missionary dimension of earthly reality in time and space, world history and redemptive history converge.[28]

Article 9 names the period of missionary activity and indicates its eschato-

---

[28] Cf. C. Laufer, "Die Mission als geistiger Wiederaufbau der Menschheit", *ZMR* 34 (1950), p. 161; J. Daniélou, *The Lord of History;* H. U. von Balthasar, *Theology of History;* O. Köhler, "Missionsbefehl und Missionsgeschichte", *Gott in Welt,* II (1964), pp. 346–71; J. Feiner, "Kirche und Heilsgeschichte", *ibid.,* pp. 317–45.

logical character.[29] This period extends from the Lord's first coming until his return. In this age of the world between Easter and parousia, the sublime duty is entrusted to the Church of gathering together the People of God for Christ by missionary activity. Only then will Christ's return ensue (Mt 24:14; Mk 13:10). The mission is therefore a continuously eschatological process. In this interim period, men and nations are summoned by the message of Christ to make the decision to accept God's sovereignty, to unite under the one head, Christ, in accordance with God's saving plan, and to wait for his glory to be revealed. "Then comes the end, when he delivers the kingdom to God the Father after destroying every rule and every authority" (1 Cor 15:24). By missionary activity between the Ascension and the second coming, the accomplishment of salvation takes place in space and time as the "manifestation or epiphany and fulfilment of God's plan in the world and its history".

[29] L. Wiedenmann, *Mission und Eschatologie* (1965); J. Jeremias, *Jesu Verheissung für die Völker* (1956); D. Bosch, *Die Heidenmission in der Zukunftsschau Jesu* (1959); O. Cullmann, "Le caractère eschatologique du devoir missionnaire", *Revue d'histoire et de philosophie religieuses* 16 (1936), pp. 210–45.

CHAPTER II

Mission Work Itself

The theological foundations having been laid, Chapter II turns to the practical realization of the missionary duty, that is, missionary activity. This missionary work proper is described and presented in three main sections (the decree itself calls them "Articuli").

Section 1: Christian witness (Articles 11, 12)

Section 2: Preaching the Gospel and gathering God's People together (Articles 13, 14)

Section 3: Forming the Christian community (Articles 15–18).

The original title of the first section (in D 1) was: "The Preliminaries to Evangelization" ("De praeambulis evangelizationis"),[1] chosen on the analogy of the theological term of *praeambula fidei*. This title, however, was not to the liking of many fathers, especially missionaries, because to them the expression suggested merely a preparatory stage, an introduction to missionary activity, inserted prior to the actual proclamation of the gospel.[2] They claimed that it was not clearly stated that these preambles themselves have full missionary value and character and must accompany and support the entire work of spreading the faith at every stage and in every respect. The title was consequently altered (D 2 and E) to "Christian witness".

At first (D 1) this chapter had a fourth section ("De ecclesiis particularibus"). In D 2 this was removed from the text and expanded to become Chapter III, "Particular Churches".

---

[1] *Schema Decreti ... Textus emendatus et Relationes* (1965), pp. 19, 63, 73.

[2] Expressions such as pre-apologetics, pre-catechetics, pre-catechumenate, pre-evangelization have become fashionable; cf. H. Waldenfels, "Kritisches zu neuen missiologischen Begriffen", *ZMR* 52 (1968), pp. 97–103. Is it not questionable whether this does not make the problems more obscure rather than throw light on them, and postpone decisions and solutions rather than bring them nearer?

The aim of the decree here is simply to present the fundamental elements and constitutive features of missionary activity, not to provide the model of a new missionary technique. The method of preaching and spreading the faith varies very much from country to country and often changes very rapidly at the present time. If only for that reason a conciliar decree could not undertake to lay down a particular method but was concerned to establish guiding principles valid everywhere for the whole Church and applicable to the fundamental structures and main problems of all missionary work in all circumstances however varied.

Article 10 presents a brief preliminary balance-sheet of the gigantic missionary task. Two thousand million human beings do not yet know Christ. Sixty million non-Christians are added to their number each year. Despite great missionary efforts the percentage of Christians is decreasing. But the Council was not concerned with figures and statistics; it was thinking in sociological and cultural terms. When faith is offered, each individual is confronted with a free decision. This decision, however, is essentially co-determined by the forms of thought in which he has been educated, and by the social system in which he has grown up. The choices and decisions of men as historical beings are always grounded in and influenced by their environment, cultural categories and social conventions. Not merely in order to win the individual human being for Christ, but also and above all in order really to manifest the mystery of Christ by its very presence in a culturally non-Christian domain, the Church must allow itself to become part of "definite social and cultural conditions" and so continue, carry out and develop Christ's mission. Missionary activity is always an incarnational task (cf. Article 5).

Article 11 names as the fundamental form and starting-point of the mission, witness and dialogue, the influence of Christian life and the power of religious discussion.[3]

Christian witness is not to be regarded and judged merely as preparatory in character, for instance in places where the actual preaching of the gospel would be impossible or premature. The duty of bearing witness is incumbent on all who have been baptized and confirmed, "all believers in Christ wherever they live", even apart from any official missionary commission. More important than preaching is witness, without which the former would be unconvincing and ineffectual. Personal witness gives preaching a convincing justification. That does not prevent it serving as a necessary preparation and introduction in difficult circumstances when direct missionary work seems out of place. "Then missionaries can and must at least bear witness to Christ

---

[3] Cf. N. Neuner, "Mission, Dialog und Zeugnis", *Geist und Leben* 38 (1965), pp. 429–43; H. J. Türk, *Was sagt das Konzil über nichtchristliche Religionen, Mission, Toleranz?* (1967).

by charity and works of mercy with all patience, prudence and great con-fidence. Thus they will prepare the way for the Lord and make him present in esteem, respect and love with all men, whatever their race, language, cul-ceptible and recognizable in the atmosphere of Christian life; the true mean-ing of human existence and the all-inclusive bond of human fellowship must be perceptible to the non-Christian world around. Christianity has not simply to be taught, it has to be lived. Only then does it appear meaningful and convincing (cf. Mt 5:16). The existence of Christians in a nation, whether they are natives or foreigners, the presence of the Church through its mem-bers, must always have this character of witness. Present-day shifts in popu-lation, multiplication of cultural contacts and economic relations, present Christian witness with unimaginably numerous and favourable opportunities, whereas deliberate religious "propaganda" has no appeal but arouses inner resistance or even open hostility.

A fundamental condition for Christian witness to be effective is solidarity in some manner" (Article 6, cf. Article 12). The new man must become per-ture or religion. Christians as members of a Church community must not cut themselves off from their national community and lead an uprooted, in-sulated, separate existence in social isolation. This is a danger which partic-ularly threatens them if they form an extremely small minority; in such a case it is very hard and sometimes almost impossible to escape. They must not avoid contact and discussion with the traditions and religions of their non-Christian environment, either from imagined superiority or from an inferi-ority complex. In the spirit of the Council's Declaration on the Relationship of the Church to Non-Christian Religions (Article 2) they will now uncover the seeds of the word which lie hidden in those religions. But despite all their openness to the values and riches which "a bountiful God has distributed among the nations", all Christians must endeavour "to illumine these treas-ures with the light of the gospel, to set them free and to bring them under the dominion of God their Saviour" (cf. also Articles 3, 7, 9, 10, 11, 16, 18, 19, 20, 21, 22, 26, 40). Furthermore, in the present profound process of change which is shaking to their depths the ancient traditions of Africa and Asia and has affected them very much more than it has Christianity, faithful Christians can be a guide to their non-Christian fellow-citizens. By their firm-ness of religious outlook they can give an example of how to incorporate scien-tific knowledge and modern achievements meaningfully into contemporary life.

To the witness of life there must be added the witness of speech, religious discussion, dialogue.[4] The Christian who is confronted with another religion

---

[4] H. Pfeil, *Der Dialog der Kirche* (1966); S. Brechter, *De principiis fundamentalibus dialogi cum religionibus non christianis,* to appear shortly in the *Actus Congressus Internationalis de Theologia Concilii Vaticani II.*

may adopt three possible attitudes. He may criticize and attack it, he may shelter from it by avoiding any contact, cutting himself off and retreating to a ghetto, or he may enter into dialogue with it, seek contact, strive for collaboration and agreement. At Vatican II and since the Council, the Church has deliberately followed the last course. In former times the Church may indeed all too hastily perhaps have expressed condemnation of other doctrines and opinions, but today it is seeking dialogue with the world. In earlier days the Church may indeed have felt secure within the stronghold of its possession of the faith, but now it is venturing out into the open field of free discussion. Paul VI writes in his Encyclical *Ecclesiam Suam* (1964): "The Church must undertake a dialogue with the world in which it actually lives, the Church itself turns to speech, message, dialogue. This point of view is one of the most important in the present life of the Church; as is well-known, it is the subject of special and thorough study at the Ecumenical Council." [5]

Genuine dialogue is more than trivial conversation; it is an opportunity for bearing witness. According to Martin Buber, [6] genuine dialogue does not presuppose that the partners agree beforehand to treat their own convictions as relative, but that they accept one another as persons. It is not necessary for the two partners to be of the same opinion, or for them to be ready from the outset to arrive at a compromise whatever the circumstances. It is absolutely necessary, however, for each to meet his partner with great respect for his personality and convictions; without obtruding himself, each must place himself at the disposal of the other, be able to listen to him with a desire to learn from him. The closer each approaches and comprehends his partner, and the more honestly each presents himself as he really is, the richer and more fruitful the dialogue. On both sides dialogue involves bearing witness.

For the convinced Christian, dialogue is therefore possible with the convinced Buddhist or Moslem, and even with syncretists, without his having to abandon his fundamental conviction and dogmatic standpoint. Experience has shown that it is more rewarding to pursue discussions with people who hold firm religious convictions than with people whose views are vague and uncertain. For of course it is not the case that Christians, convinced though they are of being in full possession of the truth, have nothing to learn from people of other religious views. How often we Christians are put to shame by members of other faiths, by their self-sacrifice, fidelity and devotion to their ideals! Dialogue therefore permits both partners to bear witness. The Christian will speak about the Christian message and the Christ event; in fact he must speak of what he has experienced in Jesus Christ if he engages

[5] *AAS* 56 (1964), pp. 639 f.
[6] *Schriften über das dialogische Prinzip* (1954), p. 279.

128

as a Christian in religious discussion with a non-Christian. And from the start he must stress the grace-given character of belief in Christ; this excludes all arrogance but imposes the obligation on believers of speaking gratefully about Christ to all who are willing to listen. "Just as Christ himself searched the hearts of men and led them to divine light through truly human conversation, so also his disciples, profoundly penetrated by the Spirit of Christ, should know the people among whom they live, and should establish contact with them. Thus they themselves can learn what treasures a bountiful God has distributed among the nations of the earth."

Article 12 calls for no special explanation. It deals with the testimony of Christian love. This love is altruistic and does not discriminate; it is all-embracing and unselfish (first introduced in text D 2). In this love, Christ himself becomes present. He cared especially for the poor and oppressed, the afflicted and burdened. Christian love will therefore include all without distinction of age or sex, rank or race, religion or culture. It pursues no ulterior aims, is not a means to winning over and converting people; it is the spontaneous and unconditional expression, consequence and extension of Christ's love which comprises every human being wholly and entirely in every respect. Certainly this love primarily goes out to fellow-members of the Church, since membership of the Church involves special mutual rights and duties. But it would be incompatible with the universality of Christ's love if there were any intention of excluding and rejecting non-Christians on principle from works of charity solely because of their religious convictions. The numerous charitable institutions in the missions have not in themselves the task of attracting non-Christians into the Church and leading them to conversion. They are not directly missionary instruments; they are shining testimonies in a non-Christian country, to God's love, to redemption in Christ, to the new life of the redeemed.

The universality of love both demands and promotes Christians' social commitment and their collaboration with non-Christians in a common effort to master the great social and economic problems of the present day. This gigantic complex of problems is only briefly referred to in the decree, because the Council dealt with these matters in the Pastoral Constitution on the Church in the Modern World. If only to avoid waste of resources, the Church will not fail to collaborate widely with all constructive forces in the developing countries. The ethical attitude and religious conviction of intellectual workers will be even more important than material achievement and technical perfection. Special importance attaches to the educational field, to mission schools (not mentioned in text D 1). The text speaks of "different kinds of schools"; what are meant are all types from primary schools to universities, including all the intermediate kinds of specialized schools. They are not to be regarded simply as means of spreading the faith, as centres of catechetical instruction, as places of instruction for the next generation of Christians. Especially in the developing countries they should open their doors to all "as a service of supreme value to men". Christians are urged to collaborate in all organizations for development aid in the struggle against hunger, ignorance and disease, whether it is a question of private or public undertakings, national or international organizations, non-Catholic or non-Christian religious bodies. Here the Council throws wide open the door to collaboration with all men of goodwill. The new line will have to establish itself. There will be no lack of difficulties. Not without reason the decree warns that everything must be done prudently; however, the Church claims for itself no other right than that of ministering to men.

The influence and success of Christian witness are by the nature of the case difficult to assess, especially when that witness cannot directly serve missionary preaching. But it certainly has its own role and significance in the Church's mission. Authentic, clear witness is never in vain. It makes plain to everyone that Christianity is not a mere doctrine and law, but a new life, a transforming force and creative spirit. All Christians, even the missionary in an apparently hopeless situation (for none is really so) who has no possibility of proclaiming the faith, can and must take seriously Christ's command (Acts 1:8; Jn 15:27) to give testimony, to be his witnesses. Collaboration with all men in the most varied domains will not merely promote external progress, overcome material need and raise living standards. Above all, as a spiritual service to development, it will be concerned with man in his totality and will lead him to the ethical values of fraternal solidarity and mutual responsibility, until under the guidance of God's grace "the mystery of Christ himself begins to shine forth".

It is the special responsibility of the bishops, according to the Instructions for Implementing the Missionary Decree,[7] to impress on the minds of all Catholics their duty of bearing witness. "The decree of the Second Vatican Council *Ad gentes divinitus* (On the Church's Missionary Activity) applies to the whole Church. All are bound to observe it faithfully so that the whole Church may become truly missionary and the whole People of God conscious of its missionary duty. Consequently local ordinaries are to ensure that the decree is brought to the notice of all the faithful; by lectures for the clergy and sermons to the people a common consciousness of responsibility for missionary work should be explained and inculcated" (*Ecclesiae Sanctae,* III, Introduction).

[7] Motu proprio *Ecclesiae Sanctae* of 6 August 1966: *AAS* 58 (1956), pp. 757–87; the third part contains the instructions for implementing the missionary decree. The text is also contained in J. Glazik, *Dekret über die Missionstätigkeit der Kirche* (1967), pp. 126–41; commentary by V. Dammertz, "Die Ausführungsbestimmungen zum Konzilsdekret über die Missionstätigkeit der Kirche", *AKK* 136 (1967), pp. 47–67.

Article 13 introduces the actual essence and culmination of missionary activity, the preaching of the gospel and the gathering together of the People of God. At first sight it is surprising that only two articles (13, 14) are devoted to this. But the decree only deals with the most important problems of the missions, it does not attempt to teach new missionary methods. Problems are not the same everywhere and methods vary with place and time. The heart and centre of missionary activity is not witness, important as that is, but, in accordance with the Lord's plain command, proclamation. The Council gives no pedagogical instructions on the theological content and didactic form of missionary preaching.[8] It contents itself with noting that the gospel must be preached everywhere and to everyone with confidence and constancy, so that non-Christians may come to know the mystery of Christ as the fulfilment of their expectations and aspirations.

The purpose, goal and fruit of missionary preaching is conversion of heart, turning to God, devotion to Christ; it is the new man, conversion in the New Testament sense. Under the guidance of the Holy Spirit, this conversion usually takes place in stages. It is a spiritual course of religious development and growth, demanding sacrifices and bringing joys, leading from initial faith through aversion and conversion, to a new personal existence and life in Christ. The Church attributes the greatest importance to the non-Christian's taking this step with full freedom of mind, entirely without compulsion.

The Council plainly rejected the unfair principle that "error has no rights". Consequently the missionary will not only respect the religious convictions of non-Christians but will also recognize on principle that they too will wish to propagate their doctrines and views, that they too are engaged in a "mission". The right to missionary activity has a firm Christian basis in the doctrine of religious freedom. Anyone who claims this freedom for himself must also be ready to grant and allow it to the non-Christian. In the past and in practice it was unfortunately often the case that people claimed missionary activity for themselves but refused it to those of other faiths, or at least made it as difficult as possible by legal enactments and social pressure. Such an attitude is no longer possible today; the situation has

---

[8] T. Ohm, *Machet zu Jüngern alle Völker* (1962), pp. 552 ff. on the service of the word. The periodical *Parole et Mission* deals frequently with the problems of missionary preaching. J. Thauren, *Die religiöse Unterweisung in den Heidenländern* (1935); H. Kraemer, *The Communication of the Christian Faith* (1957); C. H. Dodd, *The Apostolic Preaching and its Developments* (2nd ed., 1956), on the New Testament model, terms missionary preaching for non-Christians "kerygma", sermons to the faithful "didache". D. Grasso, "Evangelizzazione, catechesi, omilia. Per una terminologia della predicazione", *Gregorianum* 42 (1961), pp. 242–67; id., "Il kerigma e la predicazione", *ibid.*, pp. 424–50; id., "Die missionarische Verkündigung" in J. Schütte, *op. cit.*, pp. 191–204.

fortunately altered. Faith can neither be forbidden nor compelled. The fundamental moral attitude of a person genuinely seeking truth is humility. Force and coercion are inappropriate and useless as means of finding truth. All triumphalism has to be renounced, as well as the temptation to snatch advantages and gain ground by dubious devices, allurements and over-clever methods after the fashion of the children of this world. The Christian Church is not the lord of the world and still less of its religions. The task it has received is not to conquer the world for Christ by every possible means, but to bear witness to Christ before men, to announce him, to declare and apply his message. It does this not by putting itself forward as knowing better about everything and as already in possession of everything, but by offering individuals, groups and peoples its saving and salutary services and doctrines while fully preserving personal freedom humbly and unselfishly.

Article 14 describes the catechumenate as the Church's missionary institution for gathering together the People of God. As well as examining the genuineness and purity of candidates' motives for conversion, it serves for instruction in Christian doctrine and for exercise in Christian life. The catechumenate as at present prescribed and usually followed lasts 1–4 years and on the whole has fulfilled these requirements quite well.[9] The Congregation of *Propaganda Fide* had not previously issued any universally binding regulations, and the Code of Canon Law merely prescribes that the adult candidate for baptism must be "sciens et volens probeque instructus" (can. 752). Everything depends on the mode of life and preparatory training of the candidates. Among primitive peoples the catechumenate will last longer than among those of higher civilization. At present, for example, the length of the catechumenate varies in exceptional cases from a few weeks to five years. "In practice two extremes are to be avoided, to admit to baptism after a hasty, insufficient conversion and preparation, which produces many baptized but few true Christians, or to baptize only after such a long, detailed and difficult conversion that this amounts to closing the door to most catechumens by discouraging them, and makes the mission a fruitless task."[10] The bow must not be bent too far. As regards the duration of the catechumenate, rules cannot be laid down to suit the whole world.

The missionary decree reorganizes the catechumenate and gives it even greater importance in harmony with the Council's teachings (Constitution on the Church, Articles 17, 14), liturgical principles (Constitution on the

---

[9] On the history and function of the catechumenate, cf. T. Ohm, *Das Katechumenat in den katholischen Missionen* (1959), with detailed bibliography; J. Hofinger, ed., *Katechetik heute. Referate und Ergebnisse der Internationalen Studienwoche über Mission und Katechese* (1961).

[10] A. Engel, *Die Missionsmethode der Missionare vom Heiligen Geist auf dem afrikanischen Festland* (1932), p. 62.

Sacred Liturgy, Articles 9, 64, 109, 66) and pastoral instructions (Decree on the Bishops' Pastoral Office, Article 14). In regard to non-Christians, the Church has the task of awakening faith by preaching the gospel and, in the catechumenate, of preparing adults to receive the sacraments of initiation. Reception into the catechumenate should take place by a solemn liturgical rite; the Congregation of Rites in 1962 had already divided the rites, ceremonies and exorcisms preceding adult baptism in a meaningful and appropriate way among the chronological and psychological stages of the catechumenate.[11] The catechumenate itself is entirely concerned with training and formation, habituation and exercise, development of faith and testing of morals, introduction to the liturgy of the Church and incorporation into the life of the Christian community. Special care is to be taken in teaching the saving effect of the sacraments. The Lenten and Easter seasons with the liturgical texts concerning the history of salvation, the traditional canonical examinations and mystagogic catechesis, should form its culmination and conclusion. The great sacraments of initiation, baptism and the Eucharist, perhaps confirmation also (cf. Constitution on the Sacred Liturgy, Article 71), should wherever possible be administered at the Easter Vigil in the presence of the whole community of the faithful, so that the neophyte may experience and learn the grace-giving reality of the paschal mystery of the commemoration of the death and resurrection of the Lord. Finally the decree requires the new order of Christian initiation to ensure a living and consciously responsible solidarity between the local community of the faithful, especially the sponsors, and the catechumens, and looks to the new Code of Canon Law to give a clear juridical definition of their membership of the Church.[12]

Article 15 leads to the third section of Chapter II which deals with the formation and building up of the Christian community, in four articles on the People of God (15), indigenous clergy (16), catechists (17) and religions (18). As the decree moves on, references to other conciliar texts become more frequent. The misfortune which dogged the composition of the missionary decree and delayed its promulgation until the final session at least had this great advantage.[13] On the other hand the reader is disagreeably jarred by the relatively frequent repetitions, overlapping and other unfortunate features. The various subcommissions obviously drew up the various chapters without close mutual contact, and the indispensable final revision of the text as a whole by the full commission could probably not be carried out with the

[11] *AAS* 54 (1962), pp. 310–38.
[12] According to the present Code of Canon Law, exorcisms may be pronounced over them (can. 1152), they can receive sacramentals (can. 1149) and ecclesiastical burial (can. 1239).
[13] J. Schelbert, "Das Missionsdekret des II. Vatikanums im Gesamtwerk des Konzils", *Neue Zeitschrift für Missionswissenschaft* 22 (1966), pp. 241–59; 23 (1967), pp. 18–26, 104–114, 194–205.

requisite care for lack of time (see above, "Origin and History of the Decree").

The Church is communion in Christ. The Holy Spirit is the inner principle of its life, and gathers together the People of God by awakening men to faith, and in holy baptism gathers the chosen race, the royal priesthood, into the Christian community. Consequently the Holy Spirit is already active even before the missionaries begin their work of witness and preaching. As God's co-workers and instruments of the Holy Spirit, they are entrusted with the formation and development of the local congregations. It is not sufficient to lead as many people as possible to faith by preaching and conversion, and simply to show them an individual way of salvation. Only as a Christian community is the Church implanted in a non-Christian land and becomes a sign of God's epiphany among men, united in brotherly love, filled with apostolic zeal and organized according to ministries and services. In developing these communities, farsighted planning must take into account from the start their future financial and intellectual self-preservation. Culturally they must be fully integrated into their nation, as was stressed earlier, and must make use of the riches of their own national culture. The danger of cultural uprootedness has to be faced and averted from the very start. Concrete instructions are not given. The importance of care for the family, maintenance of Christian schools and the work of associations for the lay apostolate is specially underlined and commended. Rather disconnectedly, the exhortation is inserted that charity should shine out between Catholics of different rites. This refers to the well-known difficulties of organization and coexistence among the Christian Churches of the Near East and of large parts of India.

Training in ecumenical spirit, the importance and urgency of which has already been mentioned in Article 6 (cf. also Articles 12, 29, 36), is now dealt with more expressly, on the basis of the norms of the Decree on Ecumenism. The framework laid down there is maintained, the limits set are adhered to, but the principles it establishes have to be transferred and adapted to the special conditions of the missions. The theological and religious reason for ecumenical work in the missions is not simply the increase in effectiveness which results from greater credibility; it is Christ the common Lord and baptism the common sacrament. This consciousness of a common faith must be strengthened in the young Churches, and also the awareness that we have other articles of faith in common with the separated brethren. By prayer together and joint Bible services a public profession of faith in Jesus Christ can be made "before the nations". Above all, co-operation in social and cultural enterprises (hospitals, schools) is possible; this should therefore be actively promoted. "Indifference and intermingling as well as unhealthy rivalry" are to be avoided. In the economic and technical sector, the problems and dangers are less than those raised by collaboration in the cultural and religious domains. It is therefore necessary carefully to cultivate the ecumenical spirit, to love the separated brethren as true disciples of Christ. The previously customary mode of thought and attitude will have to be profoundly modified and reformed to create in the young Churches the conditions for a common drive to spread the Christian message.[14] Texts D 2 and E also added that this ecumenical collaboration in the missions is not merely to be private in character but, subject to the judgment of the local bishop, is to be promoted among Churches and ecclesial Communities and their institutions (on ecumenism see also Articles 12, 16, 29, 36).

The whole Christian community in a non-Christian country must be actively missionary and develop a dynamic effectiveness. If only for that reason it must not withdraw into a ghetto existence, or cut itself off from its non-Christian neighbours in order to build up an exclusively Christian existence which has no further access to its socially and culturally heterogeneous environment. That danger was not always recognized and avoided in the past. The Christians of the young Churches must remain and increasingly develop as exemplary citizens of the States to which they belong, inspired with healthy patriotism, while employing all their strength for love of God and their nation to shape even earthly realities in a Christian way. This task especially belongs to Christian laymen, who in this context are not very felicitously described as "those who have been incorporated into Christ by baptism and live in the world" (the laity is also dealt with in Articles 11, 19, and especially 21, 29, 30).

The last paragraphs demand of the young Christian communities not only the silent apostolate of good example and witness but also explicit testimony to Christ by word and deed before their non-Christian fellow-citizens. And finally, from the People of God of the young Churches, when these are theologically and pastorally developed in the way the Constitution on the Church describes for the Church as a whole, the hierarchical and charismatic ministries will be raised up by divine vocation, as a necessary ecclesiological consequence, for these are indispensable to the indigenous development, consolidation and spread of the Christian community.

Article 16 is devoted to the training of a native clergy (education of priests and introduction of the diaconate). It is true that the missionary Church in every century has endeavoured to create an autochthonous clergy everywhere, though with varying interest and various degrees of success.[15] This pastoral

---

[14] M.-J. Le Guillou, *Mission et Unité* (1960); A. Gilles de Pélichy, "L'œcuménisme dans le décret sur l'activité missionnaire de l'Église", *Irénikon* 39 (1966), pp. 355–61.

[15] Cf. J. Beckmann, ed., *Der einheimische Klerus in Geschichte und Gegenwart (Festschrift für Laurenz Kilger)* (1950).

duty and central task of their ministry was, however, only imposed with increasing urgency on all missionary bishops by the encyclicals of Benedict XV, *Maximum illud* (1919), Pius XI, *Rerum Ecclesiae* (1926), Pius XII, *Evangelii praecones* (1951), and John XXIII, *Princeps pastorum* (1959).[16] At the present day in Africa a quarter of the priests are native to the country, in Asia already more than two-thirds; this is an astonishing success, the result of stubborn and self-sacrificing efforts. The decree notes with great pleasure the growth in the number of priests in the young Churches, for a numerous native clergy is essential if the Church is to strike deep roots in a country and attain the full development of its hierarchical structure. Text D 2 adds that the goal to be aimed at is the fully organized diocese with clergy native to it. The decree, however, lays chief stress on the careful, intelligent and appropriate education of this clergy, who are not simply to do auxiliary service, but already bear, or in the foreseeable future will bear, full responsibility for the spiritual life and independence of their Churches. Since the native clergy are completely equal in ecclesiastical function and pastoral responsibility with the clergy from the ancient Christian countries, they should receive the same thorough training, character formation and intellectual formation as the Council had just laid down in the Decrees on the Ministry and Life of Priests, on the Bishops' Pastoral Office (Articles 11, 22) and in the Constitutions on the Church (Article 28), on Divine Revelation (Articles 24, 25) and the Liturgy (Articles 16, 17, 18, 19).[17]

The missionary decree now makes supplementary provisions to ensure that the clergy of the young Churches are rooted in their national mentality and life. These aim at improving theological education and removing certain abuses which experience shows to have arisen in the course of time. Anyone acquainted with the missions as they really are, and who is able to read between the lines, will have no difficulty in recognizing here a criticism and reform of the existing state of affairs and of previous practice. By vocation and mission the priest is bound to dedicate himself entirely to the service of the Body of Christ and to the work of the gospel. He is not to be unduly concerned for personal or family advantage or place his ties with family and tribe, clan or caste higher than his duty of service to the family community of the faithful. He is ordained for the People of God and not for his ethnic group. Theology itself, which formerly was usually taught on the system and method of the West, must be based on the history of salvation and at the

---

[16] E. Marmy and I. Auf der Maur, *Gehet hin in alle Welt. Die Missionsenzykliken der Päpste Benedikt XV., Pius XI., Pius XII. und Johannes XXIII.* (1961); cf. in particular index under "Native clergy", pp. 169 f., on their formation, vocation, qualities, employment, necessity, influence, numbers, statistics, increase; J. Beckmann, *Der einheimische Klerus in den Missionsländern* (1943); J. Masson, *Vers une église indigène* (1944).

[17] See the commentaries in vols. I and II of the present series.

same time related to its milieu. The students should not become alienated from "the particular way of thinking and acting characteristic of their own people". On the contrary, their outlook must be opened and sharpened so that they may appreciate the cultural values of their nation, the possibilities of adaptation between the Christian religion and native traditions in religion and worship. Pastoral studies must be linked with local conditions, an ecumenical spirit deliberately fostered, and dialogue with non-Christians prepared for by appropriate training. Texts D 2 and E also recommend an indispensable instruction in administration and finance.

This is a formidable programme. It has long been recognized to be necessary, but has scarcely been seriously attempted. Detailed directions for putting it into effect are not given, it is true (cf. Articles 19, 20, 21, 23, 26), but at least a few indispensable conditions are created. In order to avoid cultural uprooting of the students, the basic theological formation should not be given in Rome, in fact it should not be given abroad at all; the experience of decades emphatically endorses this. Even spiritual direction and formation in a big international college with students of all kinds of countries and cultures presents a very difficult problem. The Council's emphatic call for a theology adapted to local conditions becomes a sheer impossibility abroad. Furthermore, long absence from home and the high standard of living in foreign countries beget habits and attitudes of mind which unfavourably affect the students' vocation and character and may be a serious and life-long handicap in their priestly service in poverty-stricken surroundings. Formerly, because of the lack of well-organized seminaries, the study of theology abroad was often unavoidable. The solution of the problem lies in the development of regional and central seminaries into fully-fledged theological institutions. The Church of the missions, however, today more than ever, needs specialists in the most varied branches of study. After they have done their theology in their own country and after a period of pastoral experience and testing, they should be trained at foreign universities and institutes[18] so that, as text D 2 added, they may be qualified to discharge more difficult duties in the Church of their own country.

The bishops generally and the missionary bishops in particular were divided at the Council, and still are divided, about the restoration of the diaconate as a permanent state of life. The indispensable services performed by the deacon, precisely in the missions, are succinctly described in the Constitution on the Church (Article 29): "For, strengthened by sacramental grace, in communion with the bishop and his group of priests, they serve the People

[18] A. Reuter, "Missionsklerus, Gedanken und Vorschläge", *ZMR* 49 (1965), pp. 120–26; id., "De Seminariis in Terris Missionum condendis et regendis", *Euntes Docete (Commentaria Urbana)* 18 (1965), pp. 161–74.

of God in the ministry of the liturgy, of the word, and of charity. It is the duty of the deacon, to the extent that he has been authorized by competent authority, to administer baptism solemnly, to be custodian and dispenser of the Eucharist, to assist at and bless marriages in the name of the Church, to bring Viaticum to the dying, to read the sacred Scriptures to the faithful, to instruct and exhort the people, to preside at the worship and prayer of the faithful, to administer sacramentals, and to officiate at funeral and burial services." The value of all this for the missions is evident. Deacons can hold services of the Word, where Communion is given, take charge of outposts in the absence of a priest, carry out the various stages of the catechumenate, assist the dying and bury the dead. Some of these tasks are performed by catechists. A deacon endowed with a sacramental grace of state would be an even more valuable help. The diaconate as a rank of the hierarchy can be restored at the discretion of a bishops' conference with the approval of the Pope. In general, deacons will be married men of mature age. There is no mention of the celibate deacon in the missionary decree (cf. Constitution on the Church, Article 29). The preparation and training of candidates would in some places present great but not insuperable difficulties. [19]

Article 17 deals with the missionary's indispensable assistants, the cate-chists. [20] The text speaks for itself. What would the missions of modern times have done without this army of tireless and self-sacrificing helpers? Their numbers rose from about 65,000 in 1925 to well over 100,000 today. The large-scale conversions in Africa would not have been possible without their work. Often the overworked missionary himself can only give the baptismal instruction. The whole catechetical preparation in the catechumenate is for the most part the responsibility of the catechists.

The Council gives high praise to this great host of faithful people for their "outstanding and absolutely necessary contribution to the spread of the faith", but at the same time it is aware that the present age with all its changes and advances demands a new type of catechist. Their level of education must be raised. Many catechists of the older generation are no longer capable of coping with the needs of the present day. Formerly their influence was chiefly a moral one, exerted on those around them by their exemplary lives, but today they have to satisfy certain intellectual requirements and cultural con-

---

[19] K. Rahner and H. Vorgrimler, eds., *Diaconia in Christo. Über die Erneuerung des Dia-konats* (1962); J. Hofinger, "Ist in der Mission ein eigener Stand der Diakone anzustreben?", *ZMR* 41 (1957), pp. 201–13; J. D. Reeper, "Restoration of the Diaconate", *African Eccle-siastical Review* 4 (1962), pp. 292–99; J. Hornef, "Die Erneuerung des Diakonats", *ZMR* 51 (1967), pp. 300–19 (with full bibliography).

[20] T. Ohm, *Das Katechumenat* (1959), pp. 31–39; St. Santandrea, "The Ideal Catechist", *World Mission* 14 (1963), pp. 64–74; R. Schoch, "Les Catéchistes", *Parole et Mission* 6 (1963), pp. 603–24; "Der Katechist nach dem Konzil", *ZMR* 52 (1968), pp. 63–69.

ditions. In seminaries for catechists on a diocesan or regional basis they must be familiarized with modern methods of religious instruction, receive a thorough grounding in holy Scripture and the nature and laws of the liturgy, and develop into exemplary personalities by constant practice and effort. Refresher and more advanced courses must be organized to deepen and develop their professional skills. This training is given in special catechists' schools, some of which accept only young candidates; many, however, are also designed for married catechists. The latter in particular have proved their worth and the future seems to belong to them.

Although the decree stresses the importance of catechists and their need for training, it is silent about the various uses that can be made of them and the range of their duties. Usually the catechists are the first to make contact with the missionary, and this is particularly important, especially for foreign priests. They live among the people, speak their language, know their manners and customs, share their troubles and sufferings, and consequently find it easier than priests to approach them. They are often better teachers, especially if they have suitable training, for they strike the right popular note and can draw apt illustrations from daily life. They gather people in Church for divine worship, admonish the lukewarm and indifferent, settle disputes, keep the missionary informed about important events and difficulties in the parish, work as itinerant preachers or take charge of outpost stations, hold services of the Word in the absence of the priest,[21] baptize in case of necessity, visit the sick, bury the dead and keep the parish registers. Catechists have become indispensable for missionary work, and it would be catastrophic to underestimate their importance. With the great shortage of missionary priests, only a relatively small circle of people could be reached if it were not for their constant collaboration.

The Council not only emphasizes the improvement of their training, but stresses that they should receive a just salary and social security. Previously most catechists worked for a pittance, because the necessary funds were simply not available. As few catechists as possible were employed and inevitably they were badly paid; native priests had to do without catechists altogether, usually for financial reasons. Missionary funds could not afford it and the young Christian communities were too poor or not yet accustomed to providing for the upkeep of their catechists.

The text refers to two kinds of catechists, full-time and part-time. The former must be provided with "a decent standard of living and social security

[21] J. Hofinger, "Der priesterlose Gemeindegottesdienst in der Mission", "*Neue Zeitschrift für Missionswissenschaft* 11 (1955), pp. 122–41; J. Kellner, "Priesterlose Gemeindefeier in den Missionen", *ibid.*, pp. 283–300; W. Promper, "Sind auf Missionsstationen, auf denen keine Sonntagsmesse gehalten werden kann, die Christen zur Teilnahme an anderen religiösen Übungen verpflichtet?", *ZMR* 41 (1957), p. 57.

through a just salary". With appropriate training and for regular work, on the very principles of social justice which they proclaim at the behest of the Church, they have a just claim to a salary which makes it possible for them to provide for a family and its education and training. Formerly a catechist's wage was only a fraction of that of a teacher; consequently it will have to be raised considerably. Simply to improve their position and standing, the aim should be, as circumstances and means permit, to make the index of teachers' salaries the basis for fixing those of catechists. Part-time catechists often perform their duties without pay or for only a small wage. In view of their large and growing numbers, the training, salaries and pensions of full-time catechists will require considerable funds, which poverty-stricken missionary bishops cannot possibly be expected to provide. Some Council fathers proposed the foundation of an *Opus Sancti Pauli* for catechists, parallel to the *Opus Sancti Petri* which exists for the native clergy. The decree expresses the Council's wish that the Congregation for the Propagation of the Faith should either provide special funds for the realization of this vitally necessary missionary programme or else arrange for the foundation of a special association on behalf of catechists.

Finally, the fully-trained catechists should receive their canonical mandate *(missio canonica)* by a solemn liturgical rite "so that they may enjoy greater authority in matters of faith in the eyes of the people". For the same reason several Council fathers wished catechists to receive minor orders. This is not a new idea. The question was raised as early as the *Monita ad Missionarios* (Rome, 1659: *De Catechistarum institutione eorumque ad ordines sacros promotione*). And even before the Council, theologians and practitioners had with good reason advocated a married diaconate.[22] The Council has opened the way to ordination as deacons on certain conditions to specially qualified catechists (Article 16) but has not conceded the conferring of all the minor orders or of one (perhaps that of lector). This decision is to be welcomed. As the law stands (*CIC,* can. 973, 976), tonsure and minor orders are preliminaries to the priesthood. The restoration of customs from the ancient Church is a doubtful proceeding.[23] And for various reasons any clericalization of catechists is to be opposed. These lay apostles represent a fortunate and necessary counterpart to the priest-missionary, and have quite specific possibilities of action. By the liturgical rite of induction into their office they receive, according to the theological view, a sacramental (analogous to minor orders, cf. Constitution on the Sacred Liturgy, Article 79), and consequently a grace of state and the supernatural helps necessary for the proper exercise of their office.

[22] Cf. J. Hornef, *Kommt der Diakon der frühen Kirche wieder?* (1959), pp. 166–83 (diaconate and the missions).
[23] B. Fischer, "Esquisse historique sur les Ordres mineurs", *Maison-Dieu* 61 (1960), pp. 58–69.

Article 18 completes the discussion of native clergy and catechists, by dealing with the position and importance of religious orders and congregations in the missionary development of Christian communities. In Chapter VI, on missionary co-operation, the decree gives the following summary: "Religious communities of the contemplative and of the active life have so far played, and still do play, a very great role in the evangelization of the world. This sacred Synod gladly acknowledges their merits and thanks God for all that they have done for the glory of God and the service of souls. It exhorts them to go on untiringly in the work which they have begun, since they know that the virtue of charity impels and obliges them to a spirit and an effort which is truly Catholic. By their vocation they are bound to practise this charity with a special degree of perfection" (Article 40; cf. Constitution on the Church, Article 44). In this article the term "religious" refers to priests, brothers and nuns, foreign but especially native members of religious orders and congregations — in all about 40,000 priests, 15,000 brothers and 80,000 nuns. The relevant provisions of the Constitution on the Church (Articles 43—47) and the Decree on the Appropriate Renewal of the Religious Life apply to all Christians following the evangelical counsels in the religious state. Here these provisions are expanded and applied to the special needs of the missions.

According to the Decree on the Religious Life, the *vita contemplativa* by its innermost nature is also essentially a *vita apostolica* (Article 1). The renewal of the life of religious orders must lead to an active participation in the life of the Church and its missionary function. Consequently all religious institutes must "promote among their members a suitable awareness of contemporary human conditions and of the needs of the Church. For if their members can combine the burning zeal of an apostle with wise judgments, made in the light of faith, concerning the circumstances of the modern world, they will be able to come to the aid of men more effectively" (*ibid.*, Article 2). "The manner of living, praying, and working should be suitably adapted to the physical and psychological conditions of today's religious and also, to the extent required by the nature of each community, to the needs of the apostolate, the requirements of a given culture, the social and economic circumstances anywhere, but especially in missionary territories" (*ibid.*, Article 3; cf. also Article 8). All religious must "combine contemplation with apostolic love ... by which they strive to associate themselves with the work of redemption and to spread the Kingdom of God" (*ibid.*, Article 5). Love of God and the following of Christ inspires and promotes "love of one's neighbour for the world's salvation and the building up of the Church. From this love the very practice of the evangelical counsels takes life and direction" and will prepare religious intellectually and at heart "to live and think with the Church to an ever-increasing degree and spend themselves completely on its mission" (*eiusque missioni totaliter se devoveant: ibid.*, Article 6). Even the strictly contemplative institutes, whose members live for God alone in solitude and silence, prayer and penance, "impart a hidden, apostolic fruitfulness", and contribute to the growth of the People of God. Chastity practised for the sake of the Kingdom of Heaven (*ibid.*, Article 12) brings liberty for apostolic action, and brotherly unity has an "apostolic influence" (*ibid.*, Article 15). All religious orders received from the Council the solemn charge: "The missionary spirit should be thoroughly maintained in religious communities, and, according to the character of each one, given a modern expression. In this way the preaching of the gospel among all peoples can be done more successfully" (*ibid.*, Article 20; cf. Article 25).

The missionary decree recommends special care in fostering the religious life even in the first stages when Christianity is being implanted in a non-Christian country. It does so not only because experience clearly shows that it "gives precious and absolutely necessary assistance to missionary activity", but above all because of its character as sign and its power as witness.[24] If the Catholic missions in the last hundred years have known greater development than ever before in history, and if all over the world young Churches have sprung up with a native clergy and hierarchy, this success is chiefly due to the tremendous expenditure of resources and personnel, the self-sacrificing efforts in every domain of pastoral work and education, by the missionary institutes.[25] Even more important because more direct and radical, is the missionary value of the religious life as sign, because "by a more inward consecration to God in the Church it luminously manifests and signifies the inner nature of the Christian calling". This witness points beyond man to a transcendent world and at the same time shines in a not yet Christian territory with the radiance of Christ's spirit.

The very controversial question whether native religious should be received into the foreign missionary institutes working in their country, or whether from the start plans should be made for the foundation of native religious institutes, is not dealt with; probably it was deliberately passed over. Instead, all the greater stress is laid on the need for adaptation; this is of the very greatest importance if the religious life is to take root and develop in a country with a non-Christian culture and social structure. The theological bases of the religious state are not affected; on the contrary, they should be

---

[24] J. Greco, "Les religieux et les missions", *Rythmes du Monde* 41 (1967), pp. 50–65; K. Siepen, ed., *Das Konzil und die Missionstätigkeit der Orden* (1966); P. Remy, "Valeurs missionnaires de la consécration religieuse", *Mission de l'Église* 42 (1967), pp. 16–22; M. Quéguiner, "Rénovation et adaptation des Instituts missionnaires", *Spiritus* 8 (1967), pp. 63–91.
[25] Statistical surveys, for example, in *LTK,* I, cols. 924 ff., VII, cols. 473 f.; J. Beckmann, "Roman Catholic Missions, 1965–66", *The International Review of Missions* 56 (1967), pp. 83–86; "Le Monde Missionnaire en 1966", *Église Vivante* 19 (1967), pp. 171–324.

reconsidered and deepened so that religious may be "enriched with the treas-ures of mysticism adorning the Church's tradition" (cf. Decree on the Appro-priate Renewal of the Religious Life, Articles 2, 6). Forms of life and exercises of piety conditioned by their age or social milieu must, however, be abandoned or adapted to the mentality and bent of each nation. The instructions for implementing the missionary decree (*Ecclesiae Sanctae*, III, 18) state: "In questions of the life of religious orders (n. 18) care should be taken not to pay more attention to outward forms (such as gestures, clothing, artistic styles) than to the particular religious character of the nations who are to be received or to the evangelical perfection which they wish to make their own." The seeds and traditions of the ascetical and contemplative life which exist in the higher civilizations are to be carefully examined and, where possible, incorporated into Christian conventual life. This difficult task is chiefly one for the study groups referred to in the Instructions for im-plementing the decree (*Ecclesiae Sanctae*, III, 18) "who are to inquire how the nations think about the cosmos, man and his relation to God; they must assimilate into theological reflection all that is good and true".

In accordance with these principles and maxims, a religious life is to be developed in the young Churches which will "display different aspects of Christ's mission and the Church's life". The decree therefore does not want uniformity and monotony in the religious orders in missionary countries, but a variety and colour similar to that of the orders and congregations which grew up in the course of history in ancient Christian lands, though of course without their historically conditioned features. They are not to limit them-selves to a single field of work but hold themselves open for various enter-prises in the service of the Church. This presupposes a careful all-round training of their members. The Council warns against dispersion of forces through the foundation of a number of congregations with the same apos-tolic aims (cf. also Decree on the Appropriate Renewal of the Religious Life, Articles 18, 19). Not every missionary territory should have its own congre-gations; supra-diocesan co-ordination will be undertaken by the bishops' conference.

In conclusion, the introduction and cultivation of the contemplative life is recommended, even in young Churches (cf. Article 40), precisely because this form of life "belongs to the fullness of the Church's presence". In its practical realization two tendencies have developed, both of which are approved and encouraged to further efforts: a return to the simple forms of ancient monasticism or the transplantation of Western monasticism with its rich traditions into new and quite different territories.[26] In both cases adap-

---

[26] J. de Menasce, "The Contemplative Life and the Missions", *International Review of Mis-sions* 56 (1967), pp. 330–37; G. Rathe, "Monks and Missions", *The Clergy Review* 52 (1967),

tation to local conditions and cultural traditions is obligatory and indispensable. The results achieved so far do not seem to promise much hope for the future. A series of such new foundations have had to be abandoned, others will not overcome the initial difficulties and will follow their example. Sometimes they set to work with too much romantic idealism and insufficient real practical experience. Nearly all these new foundations are still in an experimental stage. It may be noted that the missionary decree still equates contemplation and the monastic life. This terminology was abandoned in the final version of the Decree on the Appropriate Renewal of the Religious Life, thus recognizing apostolic work inside and outside the cloister as legitimate on certain conditions for monks.[27]

pp. 90–103; S. Frank, "Das beschauliche Kloster im Missionsland", *ZMR* 46 (1962), pp. 92 to 102; C. P. Tholans, "Monastische Missionsinitiative im Lichte des 2. Vatikanischen Konzils", *ZMR* 49 (1965), pp. 156–60; I. Auf der Maur, "Werden, Stand und Zukunft des afrikanischen Mönchtums", *NZM* 23 (1967), pp. 284–95, and 24 (1968), pp. 21–35; F. Mahieu, "Monasticism in India", *Clergy Monthly, Missionary Supplement* (1964), pp. 45–60; "Fondations bénédictines en pays de Mission", *Rythmes du Monde* 36 (1962), pp. 225–49.

[27] Cf. V. Dammertz, "Mönchtum und apostolischer Dienst in der neueren kirchlichen Gesetzgebung", which is to appear shortly in the *Mörsdorf-Festschrift;* S. Brechter, "Monastische Lebensform und moderner Missionsauftrag", to appear in *Liturgie und Mönchtum, Laacher Hefte.*

Particular Churches

Chapter III presents the particular Churches as the goal and outcome of specifically missionary activity. It sketches in four articles the growth and position of the young Churches in the universal Church (19), their share in missionary activity (20), the special mission of their laity (21) and their divinely-willed multiplicity within Catholic unity (22). This indicates the dimensions of evangelization, the stages on the road of all missionary work are marked out and measured. The task of the mission is not exhausted by individual conversions, even by mass baptisms; its goal is the creation of Christian communities, their rooted incorporation in non-Christian territories.

Text D 1 did not yet contain the whole of this chapter; only the chapters on the growth of the local Churches (Article 19, *De Ecclesiarum localium incremento*) and on their multiplicity in unity (Article 20, *De diversitate in unitate)* under the heading *De Ecclesiis particularibus* formed the concluding main section (entitled article) of the chapter. For Texts D 2 and E these two articles with insignificant alterations but numbered differently (Articles 19 and 22) were taken over, and two additional articles (21 and 22) were composed and combined under the title "Particular Churches" as Chapter III of the missionary decree. Was this rearrangement worth-while? The themes of Chapters II and III are not mutually exclusive. The article (21) on the role of the laity is hardly in its right place in the missionary decree as a whole. Only the intrinsic importance of the particular Churches as such is more clearly brought out, and this was the intention. The use of the plural, "Particular Churches", may seem rather unfamiliar at first to some Catholic tastes, for the traditional centralized concept viewed the Church not as pluralist but as monolithic. The plural is nevertheless perfectly legitimate especially since the Council, for the local missionary Church "mirrors the universal Church as perfectly as possible" (Article 20) in a way adapted to its environment. But the verbose and meaningless repetitions do not advance the thought; they are intrusive and irritating, and embarrassing in a conciliar document. Fewer words would have been more effective. As we have already noted, lack of time prevented adequate revision. The final draft lacked a co-ordinating hand and mind.

Article 19 deals with the growth of the particular Church and describes its position in the Church as a whole. At the fourth session many Council fathers wanted special emphasis laid on the particular Church with its specific functions. They urged that such a Church is no longer, as it used to be, merely the goal and object of evangelization but is already, and in the future will be even more, the subject and agent of missionary work. It does not stand on the periphery of the Church because it is served by foreign missionaries. In present conditions and in view of the missionary situation today it must develop a missionary dynamism of its own.[1] In contrast to the historically compromised concept of the established, national Church and in contradistinction to the local Church, the *ecclesia peculiaris* and *ecclesia localis* in the sense at present understood by canon law, the status of missionary particular Church exists[2] when a community of the faithful in a non-Christian society is provided with all that is "necessary if the People of God is to live and develop its life under the guidance of its own bishop". Nothing is said about the size of the community. It must not be supposed to be too small, since the particular Church represents a goal already reached (at least an important intermediate goal), "a certain end" *(certa meta)* in evangelization. It already possesses a sufficient degree of "stability and firmness", is to a certain extent socially rooted and adapted to the local culture (on acculturation and assimilation, cf. also Articles 8, 9, 15, 20, 22) and has already produced for itself a considerable, even if still insufficient, number of priests and religious. The conciliar renewal must also be carried out in the particular Churches, which will thus achieve increasing growth and maturity. The bishops of the particular Churches must regard themselves with their clergy and people as a member of the universal Church. "Let the young Churches preserve an intimate communion with the universal Church." Conversely, the universal Church will continue to give the particular Churches in the missions all necessary help, especially for the growth and maturation of Christian life, as long as this is urgently needed. It will also extend this help to particular Churches of long standing which are now in "a state of

---

[1] *Schema Decreti ... Textus emendatus et relationes* (1965), p. 78.

[2] J. Masson, *Decreto sull'attività della Chiesa* (1966), pp. 309–14; cf. E. Loffeld, *Le problème cardinal de la Missiologie*, pp. 78–196, on the local Church; J. Guerra, "Las iglesias locales como signo de la Iglesia Universal en su proyección misionera", *Misiones extranjeras* 14 (1967), pp. 181–94; A. Pirovano, "Le Chiese particolari secondo il decreto conciliare 'Ad Gentes'", *Le Missioni alla luce del Concilio. Atti della settimana di studi missionari Milano, 5–9 settembre 1966* (1967), pp. 68–78; R. Moya, "Giovani Chiese", *Euntes Docete (Commentaria Urbana* 19) (1966), pp. 186–208.

regression or weakness"; this refers once again (cf. Article 6, note 15) chiefly to the distress of the Latin American Churches. By a wide-ranging and well co-ordinated pastoral programme, which is not limited to trusting merely to the building of schools and seminaries for the recruitment, training and increase of native vocations to the priesthood and the religious life, the young particular Churches must be led to full independence.

Article 20 sees the equality and relative independence of the young particular Churches[3] confirmed and strengthened by their active participation in the mission to their fellow-citizens "who do not yet believe in Christ". Since they are a "faithful image of the universal Church", they also have the same missionary duty. As soon as the stages of planting and early growth are over, "the Church's missionary activity does not cease. Rather, there lies on the particular Churches already established, the duty of continuing this activity and of preaching the gospel to those still outside" (Article 6). This duty binds the whole People of God in the young Churches, bishops, priests and laity, but varies of course according to condition, office and vocation. Article 20 deals with the bishop and his priests, Article 21 with the laity. Here too we find ugly and unnecessary repetitions, platitudes and overlapping with Chapter IV on the vocation and training of missionaries and particularly with Chapter VI on missionary co-operation in the Church as a whole.

According to the Constitution on the Church (Article 25) to which reference is made in the text, "bishops are preachers of the faith who lead new disciples to Christ" (cf. also Decree on the Bishops' Pastoral Office, Article 12). The decree which emphasizes to satiety correct adaptation, appropriate catechetics, appropriate liturgy, appropriate theology, etc., as the chief earthly factors in all missionary success and obviously looks to these for the solution of the most difficult missionary problems, refers in this context, but only here, to a fact which deserves the greatest attention. Much more important than adaptation, though this latter must not be neglected in any way, are the changes which come about in pluralist industrial society as a result of urbanization, shifts of population, religious indifference, practical and militant atheism. The disintegration of traditional structures, the awakening of exaggerated national consciousness, the predominance of modern technological civilization create for missionary preaching a vis-à-vis which in fact no longer derives its vitality from the attitude of mind and forms of thought of the original indigenous cults and civilizations.

The native priests of the young particular Churches are ordained, like all priests, "to preach the gospel, and shepherd the faithful" (Constitution on

---

[3] G. Eldarov, "Dimensions communautaires de la responsabilité missionnaire dans l'Église", *Rythmes du Monde* 41 (1967), pp. 27 f.; X. Seumois, "Die Teilkirchen" in J. Schütte, *op. cit.*, pp. 255–8.

147

the Church, Article 28). Their "primary duty" as "co-workers with their bishops" is "the proclamation of the gospel of God" in fulfilment of "the Lord's command: 'Go into the whole world and preach the gospel to every creature' (Mk 16:15). Thus they establish and build up the People of God" (Decree on the Ministry and Life of Priests, Article 4). They are summoned to work together as a corporate body under the authority of the bishop. They are not to be satisfied merely to carry out their regular pastoral work, but also to be ready and willing for actual missionary enterprises. The native priest is therefore both pastor and missionary. In some places, contrary to expectations, the native clergy has developed little missionary initiative, claiming the normal pastoral work for itself and leaving the very much more burdensome pioneer missionary work to foreign priests. The Council opposes any such attitude. The native clergy should be generously ready for missionary work in districts of their own dioceses which have not yet been fully evangelized, or even for work in neighbouring dioceses outside their country which are short of priests or from which white missionaries have been driven, for example on racial or political grounds. If a specific vocation is necessary for the office of missionary (see Chapter III), complications could arise from such a requirement. The same readiness for actual missionary work should also be shown by native religious and laity. In view of the variety of changing circumstances, theological refresher courses are indispensable, and the bishops' conferences must organize these (cf. Decree on the Ministry and Life of Priests, Article 19).

For special tasks the particular Churches need special auxiliaries. Closely-linked, self-contained groups can be led to unity through dialogue, if necessary by means of the so-called personal prelatures. Bishops of the particular Churches should bear these possibilities in mind and not only not oppose such efforts but give them their full support.

These calls to missionary endeavour mainly refer to missions within a country, not abroad. In order to promote and strengthen solidarity and union with the universal Church, not only should the valuable traditional elements of the universal Church be harmoniously integrated into the legitimate individuality of the young Churches but the particular Churches themselves should as soon as possible be induced to share responsibility for the universal missionary work of the Church. Even grave shortage of clergy in their own country should not dissuade them from this. Active missionary enterprise always redounds to the good of the home Church, even of a young particular Church. Those who are concerned for all the Churches will grow in zeal for their own Church. By sharing in the universal missionary work, "communion with the universal Church reaches a certain measure of perfection".

Article 21 describes in generally clear and self-explanatory words the special advancement and role of the laity in the particular Churches (cf.

Articles 11, 15, 19). The laity everywhere have "the noble duty of working to extend the divine plan of salvation ever increasingly to all men of each epoch and in every land. Consequently let every opportunity be given them so that, according to their abilities and the needs of the times, they may zealously participate in the saving work of the Church" (Constitution on the Church, Article 33; cf. also in particular, Decree on the Apostolate of the Laity, Article 6). The extreme importance of an active laity for the mission needs no proof;[4] we need only recall what has already been said on Christian witness and religious dialogue (Article 11) and the work of catechists (Article 17).

The present article does not deal with foreign lay people who apply their knowledge and skill to the service of building up the young Churches, the so-called lay auxiliaries; they are dealt with in another context in Chapter VI (especially Article 41). The article is concerned with the laity as a constitutive and integral part of every particular Church with a vigorous life. Article 19 had in fact already spoken of the irreplaceable importance of the work of lay-people in the growth of the young Churches to maturity. "The congregations of the faithful must every day become increasingly aware and alive as communities of faith, liturgy, and love. The laity must strive by their civic and apostolic activity to set up a public order based on love and justice. The means of social communication must be used prudently and opportunely. By a truly Christian life, families must become nurseries of the lay apostolate and of vocations to the priesthood and the religious life." And in Article 20 where the witness of life and the proclamation of the Word is presented as the expression of the missionary vocation of the particular Church, it is specially noted that as well as the native clergy, "religious men and women and the laity too should burn with the same zeal towards their countrymen, especially the poor". And in all the statements of the missionary decree, in harmony with the new awareness of the missionary character of the Church and of the function of its members, the laity are also meant, or are even primarily addressed, especially when, as is the case from end to end of the decree, mention is made of the faithful, Christ's disciples, the members of the Church. Otherwise, the clergy or members of religious orders are explicitly addressed. Nevertheless many fathers wanted a summary statement which would clearly indicate the rank and role of the lay element in the young particular Churches. That was the origin in Texts D 2 and E of the present article which inevitably could hardly offer anything new.

The task of the mission consists in gathering together the People of God,

---

[4] *Fonction du laïc en milieu non chrétien. Rapports et Compte rendu de la XXXVIe semaine de Missiologie de Louvain* (1966); cf. A. Seumois, "Laïcat et Missions", *Rythmes du Monde* 41 (1967), pp. 66–75.

not in establishing a hierarchical clerical Church. Without an active laity there is no living Church with deep roots in the nation, no effective influence permeating the culture and society. Christian lay people belong to the nation in which they were born as well as to the Church in which they were reborn. As baptized and confirmed persons they have both the duty of bearing Christian witness in everyday life and of directly proclaiming the faith in their non-Christian surroundings. Here well-known things are said, and what has often been said is repeated. The Christian witness of the laity will manifest the newness of life, which, like a leaven and enriched with the values of their national culture, will gradually permeate and transform even non-Christian society according to the mind of Christ in fraternal love and universal unity. "They themselves must be acquainted with this culture. They must heal it and preserve it. They must develop it in accordance with modern conditions." The spreading of the faith must be undertaken in their immediate surroundings among relatives, acquaintances and colleagues, because most people, as experience shows, "can hear of the gospel and come to know Christ only by means of the laity who are their neighbours. Consequently professional missionaries and native priests will promote this ecclesiastical function of the laity and train them for such an important apostolate, so that by the common endeavours of pastors and laity the young particular Churches may become a shining beacon of salvation."

Article 22 concludes the chapter on the particular Churches with an ideal and grandiose vision of the future when the treasures of the nations in customs and tradition, wisdom and learning, arts and sciences, are brought into the young Churches for Christ and men's religious diversity is incorporated into the catholic unity of the universal Church.[5] A conciliar decree cannot give systematic and detailed instructions for such a vast process in the history of the human mind. Only a few guiding principles can be given but these can decisively influence in the long run the national position of a missionary Church and the Western structures of missionary organization. It is a depressing historical fact that, except in Western Europe and in the New World, the Church has not been able to incorporate and transform any alien culture. It has not become entirely native anywhere, but has everywhere remained Western.

Vatican II has recognized the legitimacy of pluralism in the Church and made adaptation a programme. "For all the faithful scattered throughout the world are in communion with each other in the Holy Spirit, so that

---

[5] X. Seumois, "Die Vielheit in der Einheit" in J. Schütte, op. cit., pp. 262–7; J. Neuner, "Arche der einen Welt. Die Verwurzelung der Kirche in den Kulturen und ihre Menschheitsaufgabe", Wort und Wahrheit 22 (1967), pp. 409–27; L. Luzbetak, The Church and Cultures. An Applied Anthropology for the Religious Worker (1963); T. Ohm, Machet zu Jüngern alle Völker (1962), pp. 691–709.

'he who occupies the See of Rome knows the people of India are his members'. Since the kingdom of Christ is not of this world (cf. Jn 18:36), the Church or People of God takes nothing away from the temporal welfare of any people by establishing that kingdom. Rather does she foster and take to herself, insofar as they are good, the ability, resources, and customs of each people. Taking them to herself she purifies, strengthens, and ennobles them. The Church in this is mindful that she must harvest with that King to whom the nations were given for an inheritance (cf. Ps 2:8) and into whose city they bring gifts and presents (cf. Ps 71 [72]:10; Is 60:4–7; Apoc 21:24). This characteristic of universality which adorns the People of God is a gift from the Lord himself" (Constitution on the Church, Article 13; cf. also Article 17).The particular Churches can "enjoy their own discipline, their own liturgical usage, and their own theological and spiritual heritage" (*ibid.*, Article 23). Adaptation is promised them in the manner of proclaiming the gospel, in the celebration of the liturgy and in the provisions of canon law. They are called upon to achieve this, so that in their own way they may "praise the glory of the Creator, glorify the grace of the Redeemer and shape their Christian life rightly" (cf. Constitution on the Liturgy, Articles 37, 39, 40; see also the Pastoral Constitution on the Church in the Modern World, Articles 44, 45, 58). For various reasons that need not be discussed here, this gigantic and exacting work will largely have to be done by the young Churches themselves. Previous isolated efforts were insufficient. The Council warns of two mortal dangers which must be consciously and clearly countered in this intellectual process, syncretism and particularism. The distant goals to be striven for by the efforts of the best minds are a theology drawing on the tradition of the universal Church and "using the philosophy and wisdom of the peoples", and Catholic unity with local and temporal diversity. Text D 2 introduced the important supplementary admonition that this high goal of adaptation can successfully be striven for only by the collegial collaboration of the bishops' conferences on a broad territorial and cultural basis (see also the instructions for implementing the decree, *Ecclesiae Sanctae*, III, 18).

Missionaries

After dealing with the theological basis of the missions (Chapter I) and the accomplishment of missionary activity (II & III), Chapter IV is entirely devoted to missionaries,[1] their vocation (Article 23), personality (Article 24), qualities (Article 25), training (Article 26) and organizations, the missionary institutes (Article 27). The text is based on the doctrines and instructions of the great missionary encyclicals of the last 50 years,[2] and is in line with the Constitution on the Church and the conciliar Decrees on Priestly Formation and on the Ministry and Life of Priests.

Article 23 states that to become a missionary a special vocation is needed, distinct from the universal missionary duty of Christ's disciples. (This was introduced in Texts D 2 and E). "And he went up into the hills and called to him those whom he desired; and they came to him. And he appointed twelve, to be with him and to be sent out..." (Mk 3:13 f.). The missionary vocation involves the following elements: God's gracious choice, candidate's human aptitude and inner inclination, missionary mandate from the Church. Personal willingness to undertake missionary work must therefore be combined with God's grace-given call and legitimate commission by the Church's authority.

Missionary work, as the proclamation of the gospel and the foundation of young Churches, is initiated and maintained by the universal Church,

---

[1] K. Müller, "Die Missionare" in J. Schütte, *op. cit.,* pp. 268–93; L. J. Lecuona, "La vocazione missionaria", *Euntes Docete (Commentaria Urbana)* 19 (1966), pp. 209–25; C. Papali, "Missionary Vocation", *Seminarium* 7 (1967), pp. 44–64; W. Burridge, "Post-Vatican Missionaries", *The Clergy Review* 52 (1967), pp. 868–76; B. Kelly, "The Missionary and His Formation. Reflections on Chapter IV of the Decree 'Ad Gentes'", *Ensign* (1967), pp. 13–20.

[2] E. Marmy and I. Auf der Maur, *Gehet hin in alle Welt. Die Missionsenzykliken der Päpste Benedikt XV., Pius XI., Pius XII. und Johannes XXIII.* (1961), with very good indices.

usually by Churches in ancient Christian countries. The missionaries are therefore sent from Christian lands to non-Christian peoples in foreign countries. The whole decree employs this traditional idea of the missionary. Only at this point, where a definition of the missionary is given, is the account framed more broadly, obviously in view of the statements about the native clergy in the young particular Churches. "For there are certain priests, religious, and laymen who are prepared to undertake mission work in their own countries or abroad, and who are endowed with the appropriate natural dispositions, character and talents. These souls are marked with a special vocation." Part of this was only added in Text D 2. The distinguishing mark of the missionary calling, therefore, is that a baptized and confirmed person with an express missionary commission from the Church, chooses the Lord's command to preach the gospel as his chief and in fact life-long task. He is a full-time missionary, not merely an auxiliary. All Christians are called to holiness, all have a missionary duty, because the Church is missionary. But the human being who responds to a special call from God becomes a member of a religious order by the acceptance of his profession on the part of the Church, and a missionary by receiving a definite mandate from the Church. The parish clergy have a pastoral function in the Church, they are not apostolic missionaries in the full sense of the word.

Since the missionary vocation is addressed to man by Christ in the Holy Spirit for the common good, the authentic missionary calling is in the theological sense a charism, which the Holy Spirit distributes to each in a special way as he wills (1 Cor 12: 11). By these gifts "he makes them fit and ready to undertake the various tasks or offices advantageous for the renewal and building up of the Church, according to the words of the apostle: 'The manifestation of the Spirit is given to everyone for profit'" (Constitution on the Church, Article 12). The missionary vocation is therefore a gift of the Holy Spirit for the benefit of the Church.

It is a special vocation, but this does not mean that it is rare, extraordinary and exceptional. Christ the Lord is *always* calling any he chooses from among the number of his disciples. No mystical illumination or perceptible inspiration is required for it. The seal and sign of vocation is present in anyone who, "endowed with natural dispositions and the requisite qualities and mental gifts, is prepared to undertake mission work". The final legitimation and authorization comes from the mandate given by the Church's hierarchy. "Sent by legitimate authority, they go out faithfully and obediently to those who are far from Christ. They are set apart for the work to which they have been called (cf. Acts 13:2) as ministers of the gospel."

Article 24 describes the missionary as a person of a particular kind and spirituality, as recipient and instrument of the missionary charism. When God calls, man must respond, like Paul, the highest model of all missionaries, who confesses, "But when he who had set me apart before I was born, and had called me through his grace, was pleased to reveal his Son to me, in order that I might preach him among the Gentiles, I did not confer with flesh and blood, nor did I go up to Jerusalem to those who were apostles before me, but I went away into Arabia; and again I returned to Damascus" (Gal 1:15 f.). The Spirit gave him insight and strength to respond. Similarly the chosen missionary expresses his readiness for radical imitation of Christ, even by total abnegation on the example of his master. This resolution is framed for a life-time (added in Texts D 2 and E: *ad vitam stare vocationi suae*), in order to be free from all earthly ties and human obligations so as to be "all things to all men" (1 Cor 9:22).

A good number of Council fathers wished to have *ad vitam* struck out and a milder expression (e. g. *generose*) substituted, presumably in order not to offend "temporary missionaries". (The latter are dealt with in Articles 26, 27, 38; from them, too, full resolve and total dedication are required.) The missionary commission rejected this suggestion on the ground that while the work of the temporary missionary is valuable and welcome, there is nevertheless an objective distinction between employment for a time and life-long consecration. And the dedication to mission service is all the more perfect, the firmer and more lasting the bonds prove to be (cf. Constitution on the Church, Article 44). Besides, the good of the Church requires life-long consecration (necessity of the mission, value of the missionaries' services). The full-time missionary needs an expensive training and lengthy adaptation. This mental potential must be employed in missionary work as long as its powers last. Part-time workers are dealt with in another passage; the real subject here is missionary spirituality.[3] At least the intention of devoting his whole life to the missions is, therefore, an essential feature of the full-time missionary. Those who do not fulfil this condition are auxiliaries, whether they are priests or laypeople.[4]

The decree demands of the missionary courage to preach the gospel and to bear witness by his example. This has already been dealt with in Articles 13 and 11. The genuine missionary will always have to be a man of action and energy, a man of prayer and brotherly love.[5] The sources of his strength lie in confident prayer and faithful obedience, "the hallmark of the servant

[3] *Schema Decreti ... Modi a Patribus conciliaribus propositi a Commissione de Missionibus examinati* (1965), pp. 65 f.
[4] Before the Council, lay brothers and nuns were regarded as missionary auxiliaries. The honorific title of missionary was reserved for priests. Cf. T. Ohm, *Machet zu Jüngern alle Völker* (1962), pp. 343–59 (choice and vocation of missionary agents), p. 359 (choice and vocation of missionary auxiliaries).
[5] O. Degrijse, "For a Spirituality of Apostolic Action. Some Fundamental Ideas", *Christ to the World* 10 (1965), pp. 425 ff.

of Christ". So that these well-springs of the spiritual life may not dry up, they must be constantly renewed by daily personal effort and by corporate days of recollection "if possible in houses specially established for the purpose" (an amendment introduced by Pope Paul VI himself).

Article 25 lists a formidable catalogue of virtues for the modern missionary in view of the difficulty of his task and the holiness of his mission. The most important qualities include both practical abilities and moral traits: initiative and enterprise, constancy and perseverance, patience and strength of purpose, openmindedness and knowledge of men, adaptability and objectivity, collaboration in team-work and sociability, by which "loneliness, fatigue and fruitless labour" are endured and mastered. These attitudes which the missionary needs, demand intensive mental and moral training and practical exercise in the long years of preparation. The real foundation, however, must be the missionary's religious attitude, which enables him to continue Christ's redemptive work in a spirit of faith and prayer, hope and discretion, love and sacrifice.

Article 26 determines the intellectual formation of the future missionary.[6] Several additions in Texts D 2 and E emphasized the pastoral orientation of the studies; too little attention had been paid to this in the earlier draft. The article distinguishes between basic training in the home country, practical training in the missionary country and specialist training for the mission. All the Popes of the present century have very markedly emphasized the intellectual equipment of the missionary, sometimes in the face of objections and resistance. Benedict XV wrote in his great missionary encyclical *Maximum illud* (1919): "Before the missionary can begin his apostolic work, he must thoroughly prepare himself, even though some people may declare that those who are going to announce Christ to quite uncivilized peoples do not need to be masters of many branches of learning ... Consequently even if the candidates whom the Lord calls to his holy service receive the standard training for apostolic work, they also absolutely need training in all the branches of religious and secular knowledge which may be of use to missionaries. We wish these provisions to be observed in the Urbanianum, the papal College of *Propaganda Fide*. We also order a chair of missiology to be established there."[7]

The fundamental training must be based on biblical theology and the history of redemption. The missionary, skilled in catechetics and experienced in teaching religion, has to announce the message of Christ, not to transmit

---

[6] J. Glazik, "Die Vorbereitung unserer Missionare für ihre Arbeit in der neuen Zeit", *Ordenskorrespondenz* 3 (1962), pp. 282–91; J. Schütte, "Die Vorbereitung der Missionare", *ibid.* 6 (1965), pp. 365–69.
[7] E. Marmy and I. Auf der Maur, *op. cit.,* pp. 17 f.; *AAS* 11 (1919), pp. 448 f.

a dogmatic system with all the refinements of logic. The missionaries' hand-book is holy Scripture, from which they must draw their preaching "as they study the mystery of Christ, whose heralds and witnesses they will be" (not yet in Text D 1). This corresponds to the Decree on Priestly Formation: "In the study of sacred Scripture, which ought to be the soul of all theology, students should be trained with special diligence" (Article 16).

All the branches of study are to be taught in the light of the universality of the Church and the diversity of the nations. Additional training in ethnology and the science of religions is recommended, for the missionary must know foreign peoples, their cultures and religions, their manners and customs, their past and present. Particular stress is laid on the study of mis-siology.[8] If it is to fulfil its important function, however, a certain rearrange-ment within the specialist branches of theological study will be necessary. The missionary must be thoroughly and comprehensively grounded in theo-logical principles, historical development and the contemporary situation, as well as in practicable and successful methods of missionary work.

Text D 2 added that pastoral instruction and especially apostolic training should combine lectures on theory with practical exercises. This directive is in full agreement with the intentions of the Decree on Priestly Formation: "Seminarians need to learn the art of exercising the apostolate not only in theory but also in practice. They have to be able to pursue their assignments both on their own initiative and in concert with others. Hence, even during their course of studies, and also during holidays, they should be introduced into pastoral practice by appropriate undertakings. Depending on the age of the seminarians and the local conditions, and given the prudent approval of their bishops, such programs should be pursued in a methodical way and under the guidance of men experienced in pastoral matters" (Article 21).

The decree also recommends in quite general terms, for as many religious brothers and nuns as possible, a thorough catechetical grounding and training for their even more effective employment in the missions. On occasion that may be true and appropriate even nowadays for foreign lay missionaries. In many places, however, it is certainly better to entrust this work to catechists or, where they exist, to native religious brothers and nuns. It ought to be taken for granted that temporary missionaries need appropriate specialist training (addition in Text D 2); no service is done to the missions by tourist missionaries.

Practical training can only be given in the missionary country itself. This

---

[8] Cf. T. Ohm, *op. cit.*, with abundant bibliography; A. Freitag, *Mission und Missionswissen-schaft* (1962); J. Glazik, "Missionswissenschaft" in E. Neuhäusler and E. Gössmann, eds., *Was ist Theologie?* (1966), pp. 369–84; H. Kösters, *Vom Wesen und Aufbau katholischer Theologie und Wissenschafts-theoretisches zur sogenannten Missionswissenschaft* (1954).

applies particularly to religious orders and congregations which work in several parts of the world or in areas of the same continent which differ greatly in society and culture. The training should consist of a concrete initiation into the history and customs, social structure and moral values of the territory where the work is actually to be done. Formerly it was usually given at home, or in some other territory. In the interest of a more thorough preparation and greater unity and system, more elaborate courses are desirable on the broader basis of a bishops' conference, if possible in collaboration with a pastoral institute. In some places experiments on these lines have proved successful.

The greatest importance attaches to learning the language thoroughly. A missionary who has not mastered the local language cannot develop his full potentiality, cannot make the necessary contact with people and remains a foreigner. Responsible superiors who deprive the new missionary of this practical training or curtail it severely for lack of man-power, do the missionary personnel and pastoral work a very poor service. Texts D 2 and E underlined the necessity of this instruction in "special pastoral requirements".

Specialist training of individual missionaries for special tasks is nowadays an indispensable condition of fruitful missionary work. Pius XII had already written in *Evangelii Praecones* (1951): "Furthermore even at home the candidates for this apostolate must not only be instructed and formed in all the virtues and branches of ecclesiastical study, but also acquire all the special sciences and knowledge which will eventually be of great use to them as messengers of the gospel among foreign nations. Consequently they must thoroughly master languages, particularly those they will specially need. They should also receive an adequate formation, both theoretical and practical, in medicine, agriculture, ethnology, history, geography and similar special sciences."[9] Versatility, but not at the expense of thoroughness, is now as always the aim of the missionary's training. In the future it is still they who will have to bear the chief weight of missionary work. At the present day, however, "so full of difficulties, but also of possibilities", specialists are indispensable. They advise their brethren in the solution of difficult missionary problems, and can also put their specialist knowledge at the disposition of regional bishops' conferences. According to the particular situation and stage in missionary development, specialists in different branches must be employed: missiologists, sociologists, linguists, ethnologists, etc. Technicians and publicists are expressly mentioned.

Article 27 recalls the valuable services of missionary institutes and emphasizes that they will continue to be indispensable in the future. Until now, members of religious orders have been the chief missionary agents. This is

---

[9] E. Marmy and I. Auf der Maur, *op. cit.*, p. 60; *AAS* 43 (1951), p. 507.

not surprising, for it corresponds essentially to their position and function in the Church. "Inasmuch as their self-dedication has been accepted by the Church, they should realize that they are committed to its service as well" (Decree on the Appropriate Renewal of the Religious Life, Article 5). To a large extent the history of the religious orders is the history of the missions, and vice versa. "The religious orders are as it were made for missionary activity, by their organization, unified direction, tradition, structure and experience... Furthermore, members of religious orders have to possess in a special degree the very qualities which are needed for missionary service: obedience, humility, spirit of sacrifice, love of the Cross, simplicity, poverty, purity and love of the neighbour. The spirit of the orders and congregations is a good basis for successful missionary work."[10] Even the necessary missionary training, to say nothing of missionary work, is beyond the powers of an isolated individual. Consequently Christians with definite missionary vocation in the Holy Spirit have founded missionary institutes or joined missionary orders and congregations[11] which, commissioned by the Church, have gathered together a new People of God all over the world and brought young particular Churches to a certain maturity and independence under a native hierarchy.

These missionary institutes, which "for centuries have borne the burden and heat of the day", stand at a turning-point which, it is true, is mainly juridical in nature but nevertheless has practical consequences. The so-called *Ius commissionis* by which missionary institutes were entrusted with ecclesiastical districts committed to them as their field of missionary work, is coming to an end. Of course the missionary institutes will continue to collaborate with the young particular Churches even though the legal situation has altered. According to opportunity and urgency, they will place personnel and resources at the disposition of the new dioceses, undertake special tasks, take charge of pastoral institutes, carry out special educational work or social programmes. In addition there will be no lack of regular pastoral work and strictly missionary tasks in regions or among groups "who perhaps for special reasons have not yet accepted the gospel message or who have thus far resisted it". Texts D 2 and E also added that the missionary institutes should make their experience available to temporary missionaries. The decree makes no statement about the employment of these missionary institutes in the future. It is content to say that "for these reasons, and since there are still many nations to be led to Christ, such communities remain especially necessary".

[10] T. Ohm, *op. cit.*, p. 802.
[11] On missionary institutes devoted exclusively or only partially to missionary work, see *LTK*, VIII, cols. 454 f.; 467—70; T. Ohm, *op. cit.*, pp. 803 ff.

CHAPTER V

Planning Missionary Activity

Chapter V presents the directing and organizing agents of missionary activity and describes their functions.[1] After a brief introduction (Article 28), it deals in detail with the central organization for the spread of the faith, the *Propaganda Fide* Congregation (Article 29), with the position and role of the bishop (Article 30) and the bishops' conferences (Article 31), in regard to the missions. Finally, the principles of co-ordination and co-operation between bishop and missionary institute (Article 32), missionary orders and congregations among themselves (Article 33) and centres of learning (Article 34) are determined.

Article 28 speaks of the manifold gifts of the Spirit varying according to profession and state of life, vocation and mission, which each believer must use in his own way to establish the reign of Christ and build up his Church. All these gifts of the People of God in their home countries and in the missions must be co-ordinated, so that the proclamation of the gospel may be carried out in an orderly, unified way.

Article 29 quotes the well-known saying of Benedict XV who called missionary activity "the supremely great and sacred task of the Church". This shows that it cannot be treated as peripheral, or as an obligation incumbent only on the missionary institutes. Responsibility for missionary work falls "primarily on the body of bishops". Certainly "as members of the body of bishops which succeeds the College of Apostles, all bishops are consecrated not just for some one diocese but for the salvation of the whole world" (Article 38) and "the task of proclaiming the gospel everywhere on earth devolves on the body of pastors" (Constitution on the Church, Article 23),

---

[1] J. Greco, "De ordinatione activitatis missionalis" *Periodica de re morali canonica, liturgica* 55 (1965), pp. 289–314; id. in J. Schütte, *op. cit.,* pp. 294–314; J. Masson, *Decreto sull'attività missionaria della Chiesa* (1966), pp. 375–411; S. Paventi and N. Kowalsky, "L'organizzazione missionaria", *Fede e Civiltà* 64 (1966), pp. 89–99; U. Poletti, "L'organizzazione missionaria della Chiesa", *Le Missioni alla luce del Concilio* (1967), pp. 165–77.

but "the individual bishops who are placed in charge of particular Churches, exercise their pastoral government over the portion of the People of God committed to their care, and not over other Churches nor over the universal Church. But each of them, as a member of the episcopal college and a legitimate successor of the apostles, is obliged by Christ's decree and command to be solicitous for the whole Church" *(ibid.).* In an intervention which testified to his ardent love of the missions, Cardinal Léger said, "We have now realized better than before that constant concern for the growth of the Church is not simply a supplementary obligation, but one which derives from our pastoral office itself. We are consecrated for a diocese and at the same time for the salvation of the world. For this doctrine to be effective, however, certain structures must first be created by which all we bishops, not merely each of us separately, can realize our corporate responsibility under the leadership of the Pope" (116th general congregation, 6 November 1964). Since the universal episcopate cannot for various reasons fulfil this duty to its full extent and with the necessary energy, it is entrusted in a special way to the Synod of Bishops, the "council of bishops concerned with the entire Church", which on behalf and in the name of the college of bishops and in conjunction with the pope "to whom the high office of spreading the Christian name is especially entrusted" *(ibid.)* will have to deliberate and devise solutions for the chief and great problems of evangelization.

Although many missionary bishops strongly criticized the juridical structure and methods of the Congregation for the Propagation of the Faith, the Council decreed that "for all missions and for the whole of missionary activity there should be only one competent Curial office, namely, that of the 'Propagation of the Faith'". But the demand was met for strong and active representation of the universal Church, especially of the missionary bishops, within the framework of the *Propaganda Fide* Congregation. On the whole, the highest missionary administration, the *Sacra Congregatio de Propaganda Fide,* actually emerged from this obstinate and emotionally charged struggle considerably increased in power. Its historical achievement was acknowledged and confirmed, and for the future it is to be renewed, better equipped and its powers are even to be increased and extended.

As before, this Congregation, under the authority of the Pope, who is to be effectively supported by the Synod of Bishops, holds in its hands supreme and undivided control of all missionary activity, both abroad in the missions and at home in work in aid of the missions. What the decree says about the functions of this Congregation constitutes both criticism and reform. Anyone who took part in the Council or is capable of reading between the lines, will have no difficulty in recognizing the urgent requests and insistent desires of the missionary bishops. From the remark, which for a conciliar document is a bold and even audacious one, that the Holy Spirit "often anticipates the action of those whose task it is to rule the life of the Church", we can conclude that the missions expect *Propaganda Fide* to display greater sensitivity to the changes of the age and more understanding of everyday needs. It must intensify the promotion of vocations, encourage prayer for the missions, modernize its out-of-date news service, increase the number of missionaries and employ them intelligently. The highest authority for the missions is expected to provide well-considered programmes of work and timely guidance, stimulating initiatives and active encouragement. And since the great papal missionary organizations, in particular the Association for the Propagation of the Faith, the St. Peter Association for Native Clergy, the Clergy Missionary Union and the Childrens' Missionary Association, are all under the Congregation for the Propagation of the Faith (cf. rules for implementing of the decree, *Ecclesiae Sanctae*, III, 13 § 2), its competence and responsibility also extend to collecting and augmenting the material means of existence of the missions. The basis of the distribution of missionary funds is to be re-examined, and account taken of the particular missionary situation in each territory. The *Propaganda Fide* Congregation thus controls the entire missionary activity of the Church throughout the world with one exception. The law of the Eastern Churches is to remain untouched. The authority of the latter in the Near East countries is accordingly recognized (cf. *CIC*, can. 257; *AAS* 30 [1938], pp. 154–9).

Until now, however, there have been some other ecclesiastical territories not under the jurisdiction of Propaganda. The dioceses of Angola and Mozambique and those of Goa, Macao, and Dili on Timor are subject to the Congregation for Extraordinary Affairs.[2] The Consistorial Congregation is responsible for numerous *Praelaturae Nullius* in Latin America.[3] These would prefer to work as missionary territories under the Propaganda Congregation like the existing apostolic vicariates and prefectures in South America[4] (cf. Article 6, note 21). All these exceptions are to be abolished and a unified arrangement aimed at. Since, however, justly-acquired and long-standing rights are involved, they cannot be abolished forthwith. The instructions for implementation (*Ecclesiae Sanctae*, III, 13, § 1) lay down as an interim solution and transitional measure, that in the said congregations special missionary sections are to be set up to work in close collaboration with Propa-

---

[2] On account of Portugal's right of patronage in its oversea provinces (colonies); Missionary agreement of the Holy See with Portugal: *AAS* 32 (1940), pp. 235–40, *LTK*, VIII, col. 634.

[3] The *Annuario Pontificio* (1966), pp. 712—32, lists 52 such *Praelaturae Nullius* for Latin America, 31 of them in Brazil.

[4] *Ibid.*, pp. 745–93; see *Atlas Missionum a Sacra Congregatione de Propaganda Fide dependentium* (1958), pp. 9 f., 11 f.; cf. L. Dorn and G. Denzler, *Tagebuch des Konzils. Die Arbeiten der dritten Session* (1965), p. 317.

ganda. The final aim is, however, to bring all missionary regions under the *Propaganda Fide* Congregation, in the interests of unified direction of missionary activity; the authority of the Congregation for the Eastern Church will, however, be unaffected.

Finally, the range of influence of Propaganda is extended even further by the obligation to collaborate with the ecumenical movement in the missions (introduced in Text D 2). What is widely recommended on the lower plane (Articles 6, 15, 16, 36) must also be practised and aimed at by the highest authority. For this reason it is laid down in *Ecclesiae Sanctae*, III, 14, that the cardinal in charge of the Secretariat for the Unity of Christians is *ex officio* a member of the Propaganda Congregation; that the secretary of the Secretariat for the Unity of Christians is to be a consultor of Propaganda and the secretary of Propaganda a consultor of the Secretariat for the Unity of Christians. Through this interlocking of personnel, fruitful collaboration of the two authorities is to be ensured.

The almost immeasurable abundance of tasks and the crushing magnitude of the problems, imperatively demands that the Congregation for the Propagation of the Faith should be "both an administrative instrument and an agency of dynamic direction", that it "should make use of scientific methods and of means suited to the conditions of modern times", profiting as widely as possible from the results of pastoral experience and scholarly research. Old lines must be abandoned in many domains, new ways and methods tried out and risks taken. To master this enormous task the Council has decreed that in the direction of Propaganda Congregation all who have the duty of co-operating in missionary work are to be represented and have a deliberative vote, i. e. the bishops of the whole world, superiors of missionary institutes and the heads of the papal missionary organizations (Texts D 2 and E; see above, in the "Origin and History of the Decree"). The decree gives no indications on the composition, legal status and mode of work of this body. It merely gives the ambiguous ruling that these representatives of missionary activity are to be called together at fixed intervals and "will exercise supreme control of all mission work, under the authority of the Supreme Pontiff". Viewed without prejudice, it might be thought that this body under the authority of the Pope represents the supreme direction of all missionary work. That, however, is impossible.

The instructions for implementing the missionary decree[5] (*Ecclesiae Sanctae*, III, 15) fixed the number of representatives in this body at 24. The missionary bishops with 12 members are most strongly represented, so that the

---

[5] Detailed commentary by V. Dammertz in *AKK* 136 (1967), pp. 45–67; J. Greco, "De momento missionali Litt. Motu proprio datarum 'Ecclesiae Sanctae' Pauli VI", *Periodica de re morali canonica, liturgica* 56 (1967), pp. 425–55.

various continents and territories each with their different missionary situation may have their turn and get a hearing. On the ground of corporate responsibility for the missions, the rest of the episcopate has four members, and the missionary institutes and the papal missionary organizations likewise have four members. These 24 members are to be nominated by the Pope at the suggestion of the bishops' conferences, missionary institutes and papal missionary organizations. Appointment is for five years, but an extension is possible. In order to maintain a certain continuity in this body and at the same time to avoid the danger of ossification, provision is made for change of members (about five each year). The body is to meet twice a year. No rules are laid down regarding the subject-matters to be discussed at these sessions, either in the missionary decree or in the instructions for its implementation. The members have a deliberative vote as a general rule, but in particular cases the Pope may simply request their advice.

The juridical status of this new body inside the Congregation for the Propagation of the Faith is not yet absolutely clear, especially its relationship to the full session of cardinals, for like the other congregations of cardinals (*CIC*, can. 246), *Propaganda Fide* consists of a determinate number of cardinals[6] with the Cardinal Prefect at their head. Usually once a month the full assembly of cardinals is convened[7] to deal with special matters such as the nomination of missionary bishops or the establishment and division of ecclesiastical dioceses, etc. It is true that among cardinals working for *Propaganda Fide* there are many from missionary territories as well as from ancient Christian countries.[8] Since, however, they can rarely take part in the regular full sessions, the decisions of the highest missionary administrative authority are largely in the hands of the relevant Curial cardinals.

The instructions for implementing the decree, it must be carefully noted, simply state colourlessly that the 24 members of the new body share in the direction of *Propaganda Fide:* "In moderatione Sacrae Congregationis de Propaganda Fide ... partem habent cum voto deliberativo"; similarly the missionary decree says: "In directione huius Dicasterii partem actuosam cum voto deliberativo habeant." They therefore have a role, and an active one, in the direction of Propaganda. But the missionary decree goes even further and confers on these 24 representatives supreme control of all missionary

---

[6] *LTK*, V, cols. 1344–9.

[7] The so-called congress usually meets weekly. It is composed of the Cardinal Prefect, the Secretary (usually of the rank of a titular archbishop), the Subsecretary and the "Adiutores a studiis"), who are appointed for particular missionary domains and questions and have to prepare in detail the problems awaiting decision. In addition in difficult cases, opinions (usually in writing) are collected from consultors nominated by the Pope.

[8] The present composition is given in the *Annuario Pontificio* (1967), p. 961 (16 Curial cardinals, 22 resident cardinal archbishops).

work: "Sub auctoritate Summi Pontificis supremam ordinationem totius operis missionalis exerceant." This would eliminate, from the supreme control of *Propaganda Fide*, the cardinals previously responsible. Here the Council obviously took a false step. The 24 representatives from all over the world are at no point termed members of *Propaganda Fide*, as for example in *Ecclesiae Sanctae*, III, 14, where the Prefect of the Secretariat for the Unity of Christians is listed as *ex officio* a member *(membrum)* of *Propaganda Fide*. The 24 representatives are not members of Propaganda but only of this new important body. As they are to meet only twice a year they could not possibly "exercise supreme control of all mission work". Such an interpretation would also contradict all the principles of the proposed reform of the Curia. The juridical position of the new body inside Propaganda Fide is not yet clearly determined. "The *S. C. Propaganda Fide* will therefore remain in the future a congregation of cardinals in which the cardinals have the decisive influence and it is probably more than chance that the ambiguous sentence is not repeated in the Instructions for implementing the Missionary Decree." [9]

In order to stimulate all missionary energies, the Council also decided on an expert advisory committee for *Propaganda Fide*. It was to be composed of men of great missionary experience with specialist qualifications, experts from various branches, endowed with the gift of discernment, able to analyse men and situations, deal critically with intellectual tendencies, provide fresh impulses and initiatives, and develop new methods of promoting missionary work. This important service of information and advice is also to call on the assistance of nuns, regional missionary bodies and lay organizations.

The instructions for implementing the decree provide more details on the establishment and function of this permanent staff of advisers. Bishops' conferences, heads of religious orders and the papal missionary organizations are instructed to propose suitable experts. Among them there should also be persons who live and work in the missions (*Ecclesiae Sanctae*, III, 15). Religious orders in the missions, regional organizations in support of the missions and lay organizations, especially international ones, can send representatives to take part and speak, but not vote, in the meetings of *Propaganda Fide* (III, 16).

In the missionary decree, only the representation of religious orders of women, "Instituta Religiosarum", was mentioned. The instructions for implementation speak of representatives "Institutorum Religiosorum in Missionibus". This is not intended to exclude the representation of nuns, the provision has simply been extended to include religious orders of men. It is true that the newly created committee includes four heads of religious orders

[9] V. Dammertz, *op. cit.*, p. 59.

with deliberative votes, but the advice of men religious with missionary experience can after all be very valuable. What is in question is the representation of members of religious orders in the missions, both missionary institutes and native communities.

According to the Council, supreme control of all missionary work lies with the Apostolic See (*CIC*, can. 1350, § 2) in conjunction with the Synod of Bishops. The exercise of this important task is entrusted to the Congregation for the Propagation of the Faith (can. 252) to which all missionary areas, i.e. all ecclesiastical territories where the regular hierarchy is not yet established, or where the particular Church has not yet attained full maturity and independence, are subject (or are to be subject) with the exception of those which fall within the jurisdiction of the Eastern Church (can. 257). *Propaganda Fide* is to be assisted in the discharge of its work by a newly created body with deliberative vote and by a permanent staff of expert advisers.

Article 30 sees in the missionary bishop the heart and strength, centre and driving force of the diocesan apostolate (cf. also Articles 19, 20). And whatever the personal dynamism necessary for the accomplishment of his task, he must also not fail to co-ordinate skilfully and support all available manpower. He must not discourage but promote personal initiative. In all apostolic work even "exempt religious" are subject to him (an addition made in Texts D 2 and E). A pastoral council consisting of clergy, religious and laity is to help him to co-ordinate the work and to deploy personnel to better advantage. He must constantly bear in mind that, as circumstances permit, personnel and funds are to be used above all for the evangelization of non-Christians. As well as placing on the missionary bishop the duty of establishing a pastoral council (*Ecclesiae Sanctae*, III, 20), the instructions for implementing the decree also make it his special duty to provide for the support of missionary personnel and care for lay auxiliaries (III, 24).

Article 31 emphasizes the importance of episcopal conferences (cf. Decree on the Bishops' Pastoral Office in the Church, Articles 36–38, Decree on Priestly Formation, Article 12, 22, Declaration on Christian Education, Articles 9–12) for the missions, where the difficulty of the work is visibly increasing and the problems are becoming more complicated. Individual dioceses very often have not the personnel or the funds to undertake larger projects. For particularly important questions, e.g. the problem of adaptation (Articles 10, 11), even the collaboration of neighbouring bishops' conferences may be necessary or advisable (cf. also Article 22). *Propaganda Fide* must encourage and in certain cases insist on collegiate collaboration of several episcopal conferences (*Ecclesiae Sanctae*, III, 18). Solutions must be sought and tried to enable Christianity to take proper root in a nation's culture and tradition (III, 18, § 1). Consequently study commissions are needed to undertake research in ethnology and comparative religion on the conceptions of the world, man and God held by the nations in question, and in this way to work out the theoretical presuppositions of an eventual solution to important problems of adaptation. A further commission should investigate questions of missionary catechetics. A third study group must examine the possibilities of liturgical adaptation and forms of life of native religious orders (III, 18, § 2). Seminary professors of the same socio-cultural region should meet regularly, exchange the findings of the study commissions and make use of them in their educational work (III, 18, § 3). In these circles too, it should be examined whether the missionary personnel, priests and catechists, are intelligently employed or might be more effectively distributed (III, 18, § 4).

Article 32 lays down guidelines for collaboration between bishop and missionary institute. From the juridical point of view, there are two very different positions in regard to the missions. A missionary territory may be entrusted to a missionary institute on the basis of what is called the *Ius commissionis,* or the young particular Church at a certain stage of growth and maturity may be already subject to a native local bishop (Article 27). When a territory was committed to a religious order, the missionary institute accepted the obligation of devoting itself with all its powers to the preaching of the faith, sending trained missionary personnel, sharing the financial burdens, obeying the responsible missionary authorities (apostolic vicar or prefect) and working deliberately at the development of the territory into an independent particular Church. On 8 December 1929, *Propaganda Fide* issued an instruction addressed to apostolic vicars and the superiors of missionary institutes, regulating the relations between those responsible for the missions and religious superiors. [10] The instructions given are no longer adequate in the present situation because the relationships between missionary bishop and religious superiors from the point of view of ecclesiastical law have undergone very marked changes. Since the end of World War II, the regular hierarchy has gradually been established in most missionary territories, many dioceses have been handed over to native residential bishops, and in some places the local clergy has shown a gratifyingly strong growth in numbers. The apostolic vicar was the representative of the Pope, an envoy of the Congregation for the Propagation of the Faith, delegate of a missionary institute; he possessed no direct powers, only a delegated authority. The diocesan bishop, on the other hand, is the regular holder of jurisdiction, with personal responsibility for the preaching of the gospel in his diocese in virtue of his consecration and appointment to the diocese. He is the head of a particular Church, which is in communion with the universal Church and the Bishop of Rome, and exercises his office in the name and on behalf of Christ. Consequently the responsibility and obligation of proclaiming the

[10] *AAS* 22 (1930), pp. 111–5.

gospel in a particular territory has passed from the missionary institute to the diocesan bishop. The bishop must now recruit his fellow-workers in the vineyard, and will ask the missionary institutes for their assistance as long as his own clergy is still numerically weak. In many places, the *Ius commissionis* has ceased to exist. The missionary institute has been relieved of its juridical obligation. New agreements and arrangements have to be made. The partners to them are no longer *Propaganda Fide* and the religious order, but the diocesan bishop and the missionary institute. The episcopal conferences must share in drawing up these agreements between local ordinaries and missionary institutes, and the Holy See may issue general norms and principles for their composition (cf. "Origin and History of the Decree"). These norms have not yet been issued, for mutual consultation between bishops' conferences and missionary orders will have to precede them in order to safeguard both the further fruitful development of missionary work and the just interests of the religious orders in the missions (*Ecclesiae Sanctae*, III, 17).

Article 33 wants to see co-ordination between the various missionary institutes and their close association with the episcopal conference. In the missions, as in other spheres, so many similar problems confront the religious orders that it is a need of the hour for them to meet for consultation and planning. The instructions for implementing the missionary decree accordingly lay down that in missionary territories and in ancient Christian countries, conferences of the heads of the religious orders and congregations of men and women should be formed as a working team including all the orders of men and women in the country or area (*Ecclesiae Sanctae*, III, 21). Seeing that in the missions even today the majority of priests belong to a religious order, experience shows that questions often arise which affect and concern both bishop and religious. The instructions for implementing the decree (*Ecclesiae Sanctae*, II, 43) therefore propose, on the basis of the Decree on the Bishops' Pastoral Office (Article 35) that such problems should be dealt with in mixed commissions. An institution of that kind should prove particularly useful and beneficial in the missions because of the mutual dependence there of bishops and religious superiors.

Article 34 acknowledges the importance of missiological institutes. They are indispensable for the education and training of missionaries, for missionary preaching, for dialogue with non-Christian religious, for contacts with foreign cultures. Fraternal and generous collaboration is recommended to these establishments, for example by study groups and refresher courses, exchange of publications and the results of research. General missionary training in the home country is, however, not sufficient; it necessarily has to be supplemented in the missionary country (Article 26). Even in the interest of missionary work itself on a broad territorial basis, specialized institutes for catechetics and pastoral work, sociology and ethnology, linguistics and the science of religions must be maintained. The instructions for implementing the missionary decree (cf. also Article 31) consequently lay down that "learned institutes should be established in the missions in greater numbers wherever possible and necessary. They should divide up and carry out the tasks of research and specialization on an agreed plan. The duplication of similar institutes in one area should, however, be avoided (no. 34)."

Missionary Co-operation

Chapter VI applies the theological principle that the whole Church is missionary, to the members and groups of the home Churches and deduces from it their responsibility and duty in regard to the missionary Church. Since evangelization is a basic duty of the Church, this consciousness of responsibility requires the employment for the preaching of the faith of all suitable personnel and available resources, by the whole People of God at home (Articles 35, 36), by Christian communities in diocese and parish (Article 37), by bishops and episcopal conferences (Article 38), by the pastoral clergy (Article 39), by the various religious orders and secular institutes (Article 40) and by apostolically-minded, active lay people (Article 41). The chapter and the decree conclude with a short word of greeting to missionaries.

Article 35 looks to the deep inner renewal of the Church to produce new stimulus and much-needed increase of aid to the missions from the Church as a whole.[1] This provides a correct and decisively important basis to start from. An intensification of missionary work will come less from a new theology of the salvation of the heathen and the salvific value of the non-Christian religions, or from the use of modern forms and methods of work and organization, than from the establishment of stronger faith and greater love in the whole People of God, the bishops, priests, religious and lay people, which is the aim of all the constitutions and decrees of the Council.

Article 36 gives the reasons which make missionary collaboration a duty

---

[1] D. Grasso, "Die missionarische Mitarbeit" in J. Schütte, *op. cit.*, p. 315–30; M. Quéguiner, "Théologie de la Coopération missionnaire", *A temps nouveau, mission nouvelle (le Congrès Miss. Intern. de Lyons)* (1962), pp. 97–121; J. Omaechevarria, "Responsabilidad de los membros del Cuerpo Místico en la salvación de todos los hombres", *Misiones Extranjeras* 9 (1962), pp. 56–68; J. Daniélou, "Nature missionnaire de l'Église", *Le Christ au Monde* 12 (1967), pp. 354–63.

for all Christians.[2] It is a basic duty and a central task which results from the Church's awareness that it has been sent to bring salvation to mankind. No member "of the living Christ" (Texts D 1, D 2, E: *membra Christi viventis;* an earlier draft read: *membra Christi viventia;* cf. Constitution on the Church, Article 33: *viva membra*) may evade this mission, whatever his position and function within the Church. Union with Christ through baptism, confirmation and Eucharist entails participation and collaboration in his mission to bring his mystical body to its full development. Baptism makes the Christian a member of the Church, confirmation empowers him to bear witness, the Eucharist calls him to proclaim Christ's death (cf. 1 Cor 11:26). He is essentially a member of the Church, only secondarily a member of a parish. It is a question, therefore, of showing a truly Catholic breadth of mind, of thinking in universal terms and of doing all in one's powers to spread the message of Christ. The first and most important missionary action is once again the witness of a Christian life (cf. Articles 11, 15, 21, 24, 41), displayed in zeal for the service of God and love of the neighbour.[3] This sign and witness will be more convincing and effective if given in unison with non-Catholic Christians[4] (addition made in Texts D 2 and E; see also Articles 6, 15, 16, 29). Through witness borne in common, Christianity becomes the "light of the world" and the "salt of the earth", and the Church the "sign lifted up among the nations". Christian life must therefore bear the convincing seal of truth. Those who have realized that the witness of "a profoundly Christian life" is the "first and most important duty in regard to the spread of the faith", will be ready to use all the means of aiding missionary work, natural and supernatural: prayer[5] and sacrifice for the missions and missionaries, encouragement of missionary vocations and the provision of financial resources.

In order to stimulate the missionary spirit as widely as possible, and to furnish information about the present state of affairs in the missions, their problems and difficulties, achievements and successes, a suitably designed

---

[2] G. Courtois, *La grande leçon de Vatican II: esprit chrétien, esprit missionnaire* (1967); A. Rétif, *Mission — heute noch?* (1968); K. Rahner, "Missionen dringlicher denn je!", *Die Katholischen Missionen* 86 (1967), pp. 3 f.; id., "Grundprinzipien zur heutigen Mission der Kirche", *Handbuch der Pastoraltheologie,* II/2 (1966), pp. 46–80; C. Papali, "Missionary Vocation", *Seminarium* 7 (1967), pp. 44–64.

[3] K. Rahner, "Über die Einheit von Nächstenliebe und Gottesliebe", *Schriften zur Theologie* VI, pp. 277–98.

[4] R. Lissy, "Mission im Zeitalter der Ökumenischen Bewegung", *Catholica* 9 (1967), pp. 19–26; "Catholiques et Protestants dans l'évangilisation", *Parole et Mission* 10 (1967), pp. 5–83; M. J. Le Guillou, "Missione in spirito d'ecumenismo", *Sacra Doctrina* 11 (1967), pp. 15–45; J. Glazik, "Die ökumenische Perspektive des Missionsdekrets des zweiten Vatikanischen Konzils", *Evangelische Missionszeitschrift* 24 (1967), pp. 19–30.

[5] T. Ohm, *op. cit.,* pp. 395 f.; J. Daniélou, "Vie d'oraison et présence au monde missionnaire", *Docum. UMC* 35 (1965), pp. 50–57.

campaign on behalf of the missions is indispensable, making use of the most modern mass-media, films and television.[6] The transmission of missionary news, which used mostly to be done by the various missionary territories or religious orders, must be reorganized, co-ordinated and internationalized through the episcopal conferences, apostolic delegations and the central authorities in Rome.

The instructions for implementing the decree stress the great importance of all the faithful hearing about the decree: "All are bound to observe it faithfully, so that the whole Church may become really missionary, with the whole People of God conscious of its missionary obligation. Local ordinaries must therefore ensure that the decree is brought to the knowledge of all the faithful" (*Ecclesiae Sanctae*, III, Introduction).

Article 37 extends this personal missionary duty of all Christians to the Christian communities in diocese and parish, which are dealt with in the two following articles, devoted to the bishops (Article 38) and to priests (Article 39). The Christian as Christian, as member of Christ's mystical body, always exists and lives in a community. The more vitally and inwardly he is linked with the People of God in the community of the Church, the more he is conscious of the missionary obligation which he has been given and of the love of Christ which impels him. It is no accident that most religious orders are very conscious of their duty in regard to the Church's missionary service (cf. Articles 18, 27, 32, 33, 40).

Diocese and parish are an image of the universal Church. Through them the Church becomes visibly present. Communal witness and missionary activity are necessary, not merely on practical grounds, because an isolated Christian cannot undertake and carry out the work of the mission, but for theological reasons. Missionary activity cannot be regarded as the hobby of a few, but must be shown to be a vital function of that Church which was described by the Council as "the universal sacrament of salvation" and as "missionary by its very nature", essentially an envoy. Christian love must be so universal in scope that it includes all, near or far. The renewal of the Church which the Council has called for and imposed as a duty will create not only stronger love for the missions but missionary activity itself, prayer, sacrifice and vocations. This will redound as a blessing on dioceses and parish, and in turn intensify and deepen the inner renewal.

The home Church is "active among the nations by those of its sons and daughters whom God has chosen for this sublime purpose". It regards these missionaries as its envoys and representatives who in its place have undertaken its responsibility in the outposts of the mission and are carrying out its missionary duty. Dioceses and parishes are therefore called upon to maintain

---

[6] J. A. Otto, "Zur Situation der Missionspresse in Deutschland", *ZMR* 52 (1968), pp. 15–27.

close contact with the missionaries, especially with those from their own ranks, or else to form a link with a parish or diocese in the missions. It is not said in what form these contacts should be established and maintained.

The draft schema of the Preparatory Commission for the Missions (fasc. 1, pp. 24–25) gave special recognition to the system of sponsorship which sprung up in the course of time between some home and missionary Churches. *Propaganda Fide* always regarded this practice with a certain amount of suspicion. This was due less to fear that, if numerous, these sponsorships might reduce the receipts of the papal missionary societies (practical experience has proved the contrary), than to anxiety lest they might bring inequality and rivalry into the missionary Church. It would be unacceptable for there to be poor and rich missionaries, needy and well-to-do missions, depending on whether one or even several sponsorships had been formed through personal contacts or special circumstances. The system of sponsorship is neither praised nor blamed, neither forbidden nor recommended in the decree, which does not in fact actually mention it. It is merely alluded to, though certainly tolerated "provided the universal scope of mission work is not thereby neglected", and all contacts and links "redound to mutual edification".

Article 38 recommends with particular urgency co-operation throughout the Church in aid of the missions.[7] Cardinal Bea said in his important speech on the missions during the third session that it is "our duty never to forget the fundamental truth expressed in the Constitution on the Church, namely, that all the members of the college of bishops, together and throughout the Church, have the task and grave duty of preaching the gospel to the whole of mankind".[8] The present article repeats and summarizes what the missionary decree has already largely declared regarding the missionary duty of the bishops (cf. Articles 5, 6, 19, 20, 29). They are "consecrated for the salvation of the entire world", the care of all the Churches is committed to them, "for the extension of the body of Christ is the duty of the whole College of Bishops". Article 29 had already emphasized that "the responsibility to proclaim the gospel throughout the world falls primarily on the body of bishops", and that consequently the Synod of Bishops "should give special consideration to missionary activity, as the supremely great and sacred task of the Church". Another expression of their corporate responsibility is the fact that in addition to 12 missionary bishops, 4 bishops as representatives of ancient Christian countries have been summoned to be members with deliberative vote of the newly created governing body of *Propaganda Fide*.

---

[7] A. Rétif, *Mission — heute noch?*, pp. 75–84 (on collegiality and the missions); G. Garonne, "Dioceses and Missions", *Washington Service* 18 (1967), pp. 18–21; "Les évêques dans une Église missionnaire", *Parole et Mission* 10 (1967), pp. 181–382.
[8] *ZMR* 50 (1960), pp. 13 f.

On the office and duty of bishops, the Council declared: "As lawful successors of the apostles and as members of the episcopal college, bishops should always realize that they are linked one to the other, and should show concern for all the Churches. For by divine institution and the requirement of their apostolic office, each one in concert with his fellow bishops is responsible for the Church. They should be especially concerned about those parts of the world where the Word of God has not yet been proclaimed or where, chiefly because of the small number of priests, the faithful are in danger of departing from the precepts of the Christian life, and even of losing the faith itself.

"Let bishops, therefore, make every effort to have the faithful actively support and promote works of evangelization and the apostolate. Let them strive, moreover, to see to it that suitable sacred ministers as well as assistants, both religous and lay, are prepared for the missions and other areas suffering from a lack of clergy. As far as possible, they should also arrange for some of their own priests to go to such missions or dioceses to exercise the sacred ministry permanently or at least for a set period of time.

"Moreover, in administering ecclesiastical assets, bishops should think not only of the needs of their own dioceses, but of other ones as well, for these too are part of the one Church of Christ. Finally, in proportion to their means, bishops should give attention to relieving the disasters which afflict other dioceses and regions" (Decree on the Bishops' Pastoral Office, Article 6; cf. also Articles 3, 5, 15; Constitution on the Church, Articles 23, 24, 27).

Article 38 of the missionary decree is practically a commentary on this part of the Decree on Bishops as applied to the missionary situation at the present day. The collegiate responsibility of the bishops for the Church in general and for the missionary apostolate in particular had already been taught by Benedict XV, Pius XI and especially by Pius XII;[9] the missionary decree merely draws the lines further and does not shrink from concrete demands. Since all bishops are responsible for the whole Church of God, the bishop has the duty of "stimulating, promoting and directing" work on behalf of the missions, and of imbuing the whole diocese with missionary zeal and spirit. He must call for prayers for the missions and encourage missionary vocations. He must not only provide priests for his own diocese but welcome vocations to the missionary institutes. Even when there is a grave shortage of priests, he is forbidden to hinder the development of a missionary vocation. He will call on the religious orders of men and women in his own diocese to pray for the missions and indeed to help with funds, and, if circumstances allow, to take part in missionary work. He must promote the

---

[9] E. Marmy and I. Auf der Maur, *Gehet hin in alle Welt*, pp. 166 f. (under the heading "Bischöfe").

missionary societies and charitable works of the missionary orders and congregations in his diocese, for the latter still bear the main burden of missionary work, in personnel and money. In particular he must support the papal missionary societies,[10] for they not only supply the necessary material resources but, what is equally important, imbue Catholics from childhood (Society of the Holy Childhood) with a worldwide missionary outlook (addition made in Texts D 2 and E). Finally, each bishop must be willing to allow some of his diocesan priests to go to work in the missions. In his encyclical *Fidei Donum*, 1957, Pius XII asked the bishops to release temporarily a certain number of diocesan priests to relieve the lack of priests in some areas in Africa. This initiative is now extended to the Church throughout the world, and appeal is made to the collegiate responsibility of the bishops. Such an exchange of priests would in general be on a temporary and voluntary basis. For missionary service they should, however, be "some of his best priests" and should not be set to work without appropriate preparation and training.

The decree does not raise the question of "missionary dioceses" which was discussed for a number of years.[11] Some dioceses with an intense missionary spirit have wanted, like the missionary institutes, to have an independent missionary area under their own control. *Propaganda Fide* was rightly opposed to such a scheme from the start. The future of the *Ius commissionis*, the entrusting and juridical concession of a missionary territory to a missionary institute, is now in doubt. There are missionary seminaries for secular priests in almost all countries. Since *Fidei Donum*, the employment of individual diocesan priests in the missions is possible and commended. The problem of missionary dioceses has therefore lost its topical significance.

In order to give greater emphasis to the missionary endeavours of the bishops and to preserve them from faulty planning and waste of effort, their financial assistance and provision of missionary personnel should be coordinated by the bishops' conferences, which are intended for dealing with supra-diocesan problems. At these conferences, all proposed and possible measures of assistance should be discussed: transfer of secular priests to the missions,[12] gift of a percentage of their own income to the missions,[13] excep-

---

[10] *LTK*, VII, cols. 481 f.; T. Ohm, *op. cit.*, pp. 823–31.

[11] S. Paventi, "L'azione missionaria delle diocesi", *Missionswissenschaftliche Studien (Festgabe Johannes Dindinger)* (1951), pp. 152–71; 164–71 *(Le diocesi missionarie)*.

[12] J. Bruls, "L'envoi en Mission du Clergé séculier", *Église vivante* 15 (1963), pp. 5–17; J. Masson, "Le départ aux Missions de prêtres diocésains", *Novella Ecclesiae Germina* (1963), pp. 110–18.

[13] "Every diocese must make an annual contribution for the missionary work of the Church. It is really unworthy and unjust that missionary bishops should have to spend months, or even half the year, begging to meet the needs of their dioceses. In our country, for example,

tional contributions for particularly important purposes, support of the missionary societies and of missionary seminaries for secular priests, new foundations if necessary, promotion of contacts between missionary institutes and the dioceses (addition in Texts D 2 and E). If these instructions are carried out as intended, the worst difficulties of the missionary bishops over personnel and finance would be removed overnight and the whole work of the missions would receive a powerful impetus. The bishops' conference is of course to determine the number of priests to be sent and the scale of financial aid. But since it is a matter of ideal recommendations, and the bishops' conferences are only to discuss these topics and cannot impose generally binding decisions, it will have to be seen what concrete effect results.

In conclusion, bishops' conferences are also charged with the care of foreign students and trainees.[14] Care for their human and pastoral welfare is not simple, but is of the greatest importance, since when they have finished their studies most of them will occupy key positions. Whatever the effort made and the willingness to serve them, it will not be easy to show them "the genuine face of Christ" (an idea expanded and given greater emphasis in Texts D 2 and E) in our industrial world and social system.

The instructions for implementing the missionary decree pick out those points which call for elucidation because of their immediate pastoral relevance. These chiefly concern Chapter V ("Planning Missionary Activity") and even more Chapter VI ("Missionary Co-operation"). It is characteristic that these instructions deal in reverse order, first with the responsibility of the whole Church (*Ecclesiae Sanctae*, III, 1–12) and only then with the planning and organization of missionary work (III, 13–24). In this way it emphasizes the importance of collaboration in the work of the missions as a fundamental duty of the People of God.

The attention of the bishops is drawn particularly plainly to this duty. They must tirelessly promote interest and zeal for the missions by making the missionary decree known throughout their diocese, by explaining the missionary task as a duty in conscience (III, Introduction) and by calling the faithful to prayer and sacrifice for the missions (III, 3). In every diocese a priest-member of the pastoral council must be appointed to take charge of the raising of funds for the missions. Every bishop (including those in missionary territories) must introduce and support the papal missionary societies

---

apart from the considerable voluntary contributions of the faithful and the dioceses, about DM 10 million from the Church tax could be raised for that purpose" (Cardinal J. Frings in the debate on the missions during the third session: *ZMR* 50 [1966], p. 23).

[14] G. Vilsmeier, "Missionsland Universität", *ZMR* 40 (1956), pp. 122—36; J. D. Merlo, "Les étudiants d'Afrique Noire en France et la religion catholique", *Parole et Mission* 6 (1963), pp. 127–38; H. Haas, "Foreign Students Abroad", *Clergy Monthly*, Miss. Suppl. (1960), pp. 304–9.

in his diocese, but without on that account restricting or eliminating the equally necessary societies and organizations which support the missionary orders and congregations. In this the prescriptions for the administration and forwarding of missionary funds must be observed (III, 7). The bishop is forbidden to distribute these funds on his own responsibility (*AAS* 21 [1929], p. 349). To arouse, promote and maintain zeal for the missions, he will have recourse to the missionary institutes (III, 11). In order to increase the efficiency of efforts on the diocesan level and to achieve the successful co-ordination of available resources, each bishops' conference must have a missionary section to collaborate with the missionary commissions of other bishops' conferences. The commission is to be particularly careful that missionary funds are fairly distributed (III, 9). Another particularly topical task is mentioned. For due pastoral care of people coming from the young Churches into the dioceses of Europe and America, collaboration with the missionary bishops is necessary (III, 23).

It is part of the official duty of the bishop to promote and foster missionary vocations. He must recruit and promote such vocations in his diocese (III, 11). He must not suppress them among his own clergy but, rather, generously encourage them (III, 6). The Decree on the Bishops' Pastoral Office (Article 6) and the Decree on the Ministry and Life of Priests (Article 10), as well as the instructions for implementing the missionary decrees (*Ecclesiae Sanctae*, I, 1–4), include new regulations for the incardination of priests (*CIC*, can. 111–17), and this may prove of great advantage to the missions.[15] The bishop must not refuse the application of a priest who wishes to help another diocese which is short of priests, provided the priest appears suited to the work and his own departure does not impose great hardship on his own diocese through lack of priests. An agreement must be arrived at concerning the rights and duties of such a priest (I, 3, § 2). The bishop can set a time limit (I, 3, § 4), but after five years' service as an auxiliary the priest can apply for legal incardination in the diocese where he works (I, 3, § 5). The establishment of personal prelatures (I, 4) might also have favourable results for the missions. "Above all the special vocation to life-long missionary service should be emphasized and explained by examples" (III, 6), for the missionary must "be ready to stand by his vocation for a lifetime and to renounce himself and all those whom he has thus far considered as his own, in order to become 'all things to all men'" (Article 24).

Finally, the bishops are in duty bound effectively to support the missions. Article 38, on the basis of the Decree on the Bishops' Pastoral Office, called upon dioceses to make regular annual contributions to the missions. *Ecclesiae Sanctae*, III, 8, specifies and extends this stipulation: "Since the voluntary

---

[15] V. Dammertz, *op. cit.*, p. 50.

contributions of the faithful are far from sufficient, it is recommended that as soon as possible a definite contribution should be fixed, to be made annually by the diocese itself, as well as from the parishes and other diocesan bodies in proportion to their own income; this will be distributed by the Holy See. The other alms of the faithful should not be affected by this." This demand for the contribution of financial aid by the dioceses was therefore extended to the parishes and other bodies in the diocese, e. g. Christian associations or religious orders and congregations which, in the words of the Decree on the Appropriate Renewal of the Religious Life (Article 13), are to bear "a kind of corporate witness to their own poverty" by almsgiving for the needs of the Church. Other missionary contributions of the faithful are not to be reduced by this, and all must recognize (111, 10) that the missionary institutes which "continue to be absolutely necessary", are not asking for money and resources for themselves but "have been entrusted by the Church's authority with the preaching of the gospel so that in this way the missionary duty of the whole People of God may be fulfilled". The bishops should therefore (III, 11) allow missionaries the opportunity of collecting alms for the missions in a suitable manner (AAS 44 [1952], pp. 549–51).[16]

Article 39 is an exhortation and urgent request to priests to join zealously in the work of the missions.[17] As "representatives of Christ and collaborators of the bishops" they have been "promoted by sacred ordination and by the mission they receive, to the service of Christ", in his threefold capacity, by which the Church is built up (Decree on the Ministry and Life of Priests, Article 1). "Since no one can be saved who has not first believed, priests, as co-workers with their bishops, have as their primary duty the proclamation of the gospel of God to all. In this way they fulfil the Lord's command: 'Go into the whole world and preach the gospel to every creature' (Mk 16:15). Thus they establish and build up the People of God" (*ibid.*, Article 4). There is therefore no exaggeration when the missionary decree declares that every priest's "life has been consecrated to the service of the missions". Priests must draw their missionary spirit and outlook from the Eucharist. From deep communion with Christ, the head of the mystical body, they will realize what is still wanting to its fullness and will feel impelled to undertake as their life's work the growth of the mystical body in extent and depth. Their pastoral activity and apostolic work will therefore have to be organized in such a way "that it will serve to spread the gospel among non-Christians."

Diocesan priests in their pastoral work will therefore strive to create

---

[16] J. Funk, *Einführung in das Missionsrecht* (1958), pp. 98–101; S. Paventi, *Breviarium iuris missionalis*, II (1960), pp. 241–52.

[17] J. Pohlschneider, "Priester und Mission", *Priester und Mission* (1963), pp. 55–70; A. Rétif, *Le prêtre et la mission* (1964); "Paroisse et Mission", *Parole et Mission* 6 (1963), pp. 23–112.

parishes which are missionary in outlook. They will instruct the faithful thoroughly about the importance of the evangelization of the world, encourage missionary vocations in families, promote the missionary spirit in schools and parish prayer for the missions, and collect alms for the missions, like beggars on behalf of Christ. A missionary parish will produce heralds of the gospel. Professors in seminaries and universities in their courses must convey a vivid and accurate picture of the religious situation in the world, and the whole of theology should be presented from missionary points of view and its missionary aspects emphasized.[18] Thus the future pastors will be able to form and develop a missionary outlook even during their studies (cf. Articles 26, 34), and come to realize that "every priestly ministry shares in the universality of the mission entrusted by Christ to his apostles" (Decree on the Ministry and Life of Priests, Article 10).

The instructions for implementing the missionary decree in their turn emphasize that the missionary character of the Church must become clear to the future priest during his training. In the new organization of studies, the theological foundations of the missionary decree (Chapter I) are to be taken into account, so that the proclamation of the gospel and evangelization will stand out as the essential activity which follows from the very nature of the Church. It is less a matter of lectures on missiology than of the close interweaving of fundamental ideas of the theology of the mission throughout all the various branches of theology. "Moreover the ways of the Lord in preparation for the gospel, and the possibility of salvation for those who have not yet heard it must be considered, as well as stress placed on the necessity of evangelization and incorporation into the Church" (III, 1). In addition to missiological study, personal contact with seminarists overseas is also recommended to seminarists at home (III, 5).

Article 40 repeats praise and gratitude for the religious institutes[19] and summons them to even greater efforts. Repetitions are frequent (cf. especially Article 18 with commentary) and even in ideas the decree is too markedly moving to its end.

In the missionary decree the term "instituta" is used collectively for all the orders, congregations, institutes and associations, as note 74 to Chapter IV expressly states. The distinction between the various forms which the religious life can assume is expounded in the Decree on the Appropriate

---

[18] T. Ohm, "Die Weltmission in den Lehrbüchern der Dogmatik", *ZMR* 38 (1954), pp. 80 f.
[19] J. Glazik, "Die missionarische Verantwortung der Gesamtkirche und die Ordensleute", in K. Siepen, ed., *Das Konzil und die Missionstätigkeit der Orden* (1966), pp. 61–66; A. Grillmeier, "Aus der Erneuerung des Ordenslebens im Dienste der Mission: Aus der Sicht eines Ordenstheologen", *ibid.*, pp. 67–68; "Aus der Sicht einer Ordensschwester", *ibid.*, pp. 79–86; M. Quéguiner, "Rénovation et adaptation des Instituts missionnaires", *Spiritus* 8 (1967), pp. 63–91.

Renewal of the Religious Life. After the directives for the "Instituta quae integra ad contemplationem ordinantur" (Article 7) and the "Instituta... variis apostolatus operibus dedita" (Article 8), there follows in that decree a separate article on the "venerabilis vitae monasticae institutum" (Article 9), guidelines for the "vita religiosa laicalis (Article 10) and for the "Instituta saecularia" (Article 11). It is noteworthy, and deliberate, that the monastic form of life is not discussed in direct connection with the contemplative institutes. But it is impossible here to go further into the history and interpretation of that text.[20]

The schema on the religious orders which was discussed by the Council in November 1964, the precursor of the final text, aroused the determined opposition of many fathers because of its rigid and unreal classification of the whole system of religious orders into active and contemplative institutes (there were 413 *modi!*). The decree as finally promulgated deliberately avoids dividing Christians who are following the evangelical counsels in the religious state into communities with contemplative, or active or mixed forms of life, and addresses all religious in virtue of their special vocation and consecration to God: "To this end, as they seek God before all things and only him, the members of each community should combine contemplation with apostolic love. By the former they adhere to God in mind and heart; by the latter they strive to associate themselves with the work of redemption and to spread the kingdom of God" (*ibid.*, Article 5).

All members of religious orders must therefore strive for a synthesis of apostolate and contemplation, though it will, of course, be different for each. Articles 7 and 8 of the Decree on the Appropriate Renewal of the Religious Life simply aim at characterizing the two chief types and basic models of the religious state. In actual life in the concrete, these are scarcely likely to be realized purely and completely, especially in institutional form. The various religious orders will therefore be organized more or less according to these two fundamental types and will strive to realize their particular ideals.

The present decree seems to recognize only two classes of orders and congregations, purely contemplative and exclusively active communities.[21] The contemplatives who live for God alone in prayer and penance, have indubitably great importance for the missions. Missionary work is always concerned with conversion, and every conversion is a work of grace. The prayer of contemplative monasteries and convents renders the work of the missionaries fruitful, awakens missionary vocations, opens the hearts of non-Christians to accept the gospel and promotes the growth of the missionary harvest.

---

[20] Cf. V. Dammertz, "Mönchtum und apostolischer Dienst in der neueren kirchlichen Gesetzgebung" (to appear shortly in the *Mörsdorf-Festschrift*).

[21] S. Brechter, "Monastische Lebensform und moderner Missionsauftrag", *Liturgie und Mönchtum (Laacher Hefte)*.

Consequently the communities which follow the contemplative life are asked to found houses in missionary countries, to adapt their form of life to the good traditions of the new environment and to manifest the Church as a community of the love of God and unity in Christ. "The contemplative life belongs to the fullness of the Church's presence" (Article 18).

All religious communities, whether they have worked in the missions before or not, are asked to examine conscientiously whether they could increase their missionary contribution or even introduce missionary work into their programme. Some tasks at home might be transferred to laymen in order to free their own members for the missions. For great orders and congregations to make relatively few of their members available for the missions, is an anomaly which ought to be investigated and remedied. All are appealed to, in line with the renewal of the Church and of the religious life, to adapt their constitutions to the changed conditions of the age as well as to the special character of the country and the work. The secular institutes too, which are specifically designed to deal with contemporary conditions, must make their contribution with the whole Church in support of the missions.

In the instructions for implementing the decree, the faithful are reminded that the missionary institutes are carrying out a mission and duty at the behest of the Church and are acting as representatives on behalf of the whole People of God (III, 10). The bishops are to introduce genuine missionary zeal into their dioceses by means of the missionary institutes, and give them the opportunity to seek vocations and collect funds. They must maintain contact with the missionary council of their country, to which the directors of the papal missionary societies and the superiors of the missionary institutes belong,[22] in order to organize the bishop's missionary aid systematically (III, 11). Finally each missionary institute "as soon as possible must set about its own opportune renewal with especial reference to its methods of preaching the gospel and initiating into the Christian life, as well as in regard to the actual mode of life of its communities" (III, 12).

Article 41 summarizes the importance of the laity's support for the work of the missions throughout the Church (cf. Articles 11, 15, 19, 21, 29).[23] It

---

[22] K. Siepen, "Die Vereinigung Deutscher Ordensobern nach Akten und Berichten des Generalsekretariats", *Ordenskorrespondenz* 5 (1964), pp. 104–25.

[23] E. Marmy and I. Auf der Maur, *Gehet hin in alle Welt*, p. 181 (under the heading "Laien"); T. Ohm, *op. cit.*, pp. 813–18, 840–50; J. A. Otto, "Die gottverfügte Stunde, Überlegungen zu einer brennenden Frage", *Die Katholischen Missionen* 86 (1967), pp. 75–82; K. Siepen, ed., *Das Konzil und die Missionstätigkeit der Orden:* M. Oberhoffer, "Aus der Sicht einer Missionsärztin", pp. 87–99; J. Schmauch, "Mission und Entwicklungshilfe", pp. 100–7; J. Chiflet, *Les Laïcs en coopération internationale* (1964); J. Daniélou, *Les laïcs et la mission de l'Église* (1962); G. Koenen, *Laïc et Missionnaire* (1961); J. Chiflet and V. Barbieri, *Il laico a servizio delle missioni* (1962); Y. Congar, "Laie" in H. Fries, ed., *Handbuch theologischer Grundbegriffe*, II (1963), pp. 7–25.

repeats in part what Article 36 had said about the missionary responsibility and task of the People of God, and the theological basis for the work of the laity in the Church and missions (see also the Constitution on the Church, Articles 33, 35). Their missionary commitment assumes particular religious depth "if, called by God, they are used for this work by the bishops" (addition in Texts D 2 and E.). If some undertake the work for life, they can be termed lay missionaries, if temporarily, missionary auxiliaries. "Now, the laity are called in a special way to make the Church present and operative in those places and circumstances where only through them can she become the salt of the earth. Thus every layman, by virtue of the very gifts bestowed upon him, is at the same time a witness and a living instrument of the mission of the Church herself, 'according to the measure of Christ's bestowal' (Eph 4:7)" (Constitution on the Church, Article 33). Their tasks in the service of the mission are of many kinds.

In gratitude for the gift of faith, they keep alive the idea of the missions at home, stimulate and encourage vocations, collect funds for the extension of God's reign. In the missions the tasks of lay people, both native and foreign, are becoming more numerous and extensive. They teach, administer and organize secular affairs and attend to temporal needs, take an active part in the various branches and organizations of the apostolate, and do all they can to make the young Churches independent and self-sufficient. Special mention and approval is given to economic and social assistance in developing countries. The laity have two tasks in particular to fulfil in this respect: to build up fundamental social structures and to train an élite. This would not merely meet momentary needs but give real help with long-term development. The solution of these difficult problems demands collaboration with all men of goodwill, Catholics, other Christians, non-Christians and not least the great international organizations. An indispensable condition for fruitful and successful work by the laity in the missions is solid technical and religious training as well as a special intellectual and spiritual formation and preparation. Experience shows that this must not be neglected and is best given in special courses.

Since all possible resources have to be assembled and mobilized to intensify the work of the missions, praise and recognition is given to the learned researches of laymen in the service of evangelization. They support the work of the missionaries and facilitate dialogue with non-Christians.

Article 42 concludes with a greeting (reformulated in Texts D 2 and E) to missionaries throughout the world and with sentiments of confidence and hope for the fulfilment of Christ's rule through the intercession of the Queen of the Apostles.

Decree on the Ministry and Life of Priests*

History of the Decree

by
Joseph Lécuyer

The history of the decree *Presbyterorum Ordinis* concerning the ministry and life of priests can be traced back to the questionnaire sent all over the world by John XXIII immediately after he had announced the decision to convoke a Council on 25 January 1959.

The replies to this questionnaire, collected and classified in fifteen large volumes, contain many requests touching the life of the clergy. A supplement to the second volume, entitled *Disciplina cleri* provided a general survey.[1] Chapter One, entitled *De clericis in genere* in fact summed up the most important points subsequently taken up in the preparation of this decree. Generally speaking we might say that the perspective at this stage was essentially different from that reached at the later stages of the Council. It manifested a juridical rather than a pastoral tone, thus making it clear that many of the bishops were preoccupied mainly with the duties of the clergy, their discipline, their obligatory pious exercises, the associations designed to advance their spirituality, and so on. All of this revealed a common concern among the bishops for the spiritual life of the clergy and for the increasingly fruitful fulfilment of their office.

1. The Preparatory Commission

Meanwhile on 5 June 1960 the Pope had appointed the Preparatory Commission by his decree Superno Dei nutu. The third Commission was given the title *Commissio de Disciplina Cleri et Populi Christiani*,[2] its chairman

---

* *Translated by Ronald Walls*

[1] *Acta et Documenta Oecumenico Vaticano II apparando*, Series I (Ante praeparatoria), Appendix volumnis II, Pars I (Typis Polyglottis Vaticanis, 1961), especially pp. 255–335.

[2] Cf. *Pontificie Commissioni Preparatorie del Concilio Ecumenico Vaticano II* (Tipografia Poliglotta Vaticana, 7 December 1960), pp. 10 and 53–62.

was Cardinal P. Ciriaci, Prefect of the Congregation of the Council, and its secretary was P. C. Berutti, O.P. The Commission numbered thirty-two members, of whom ten were archbishops or bishops, twenty priests of the Western rite, and thirteen ordained religious. As well as the members thirty-four consultants were named, of whom twelve were archbishops or bishops.

The Commission met for the first time on 16 November 1960. In all there were nine general sessions, the last of which ended on 7 April 1962. This corresponded to fifty-one plenary sessions of the Commission running to a total of 170 hours. The work of the general sessions was prepared by twenty sub-commissions composed of regular members and consultants, each of whom had to examine a special problem. This preparatory work came to light in a number of schemata, several of which were to serve as starting points for the preparation of the decree on priests. Special mention must be made of three schemata: a) *De clericorum vitae sanctitate;* b) *De distributione cleri;* c) *De officiis et beneficiis clericorum.*

The Council began its first series of sessions on 11 October 1962 before the findings of the Preparatory Commission had been printed and circulated to the fathers. The whole work was taken up afresh by the Conciliar Commission.

2. The Conciliar Commission up to the second series of sessions of the Council

By 16 October the Council had appointed sixteen members to the Commission *De Disciplina Cleri et Populi Christiani,* and their names were published on 20 October. Nine more were appointed by the Pope, and the names of these were published on 29 October.[3] The chairman was still Cardinal Ciriaci, but a new secretary, the Rev. Alvaro del Portillo of Opus Dei, was appointed, and remained in office until the end of the Council. The Commission was composed of two cardinals, nine archbishops and fourteen bishops. Only two of the members were religious. During the first period of the Council the new Commission had no real work to do. Not until shortly before the end of the first series of sessions were the texts formulated by the Preparatory Commission distributed to the fathers in the fourth volume of schemata. The Commission met for the first time on 3 December 1962. First of all they compiled an agenda of work that had to be done and determined general rules for revising the schemata produced by the Preparatory Commission. Three of these prepared schemata were to be conflated in one entitled *De clericis.* The schemata in question were 1) *De clericorum vitae*

---

[3] Cf. *Commissioni Conciliari, a cura della Segretaria Generale del Concilio* (Tipografia Poliglotta Vaticana, Ia ed., 30 November 1962), pp. 29–32.

sanctitatae; 2) *De officiis et beneficiis clericorum;* 3) *De distributione cleri.* It was agreed that all the members of the Commission would keep strictly to the directives issued by Pope John XXIII on 5 December[4] and send in their written comments on the proposed schemata by 8 February 1963. These *animadversiones* were to be collected to provide the starting point of a fresh redaction.

The fathers did indeed send in numerous comments: 129 on *De clericorum vitae sanctitate;* 64 on *De officiis et beneficiis clericorum;* and 102 on *De distributione cleri.*

Meanwhile, however, a new circumstance had emerged, which affected future work in a somewhat new way. On 17 December 1962 John XXIII had formed a new Commission of Cardinals for Co-ordination, headed by the new Secretary of State, Cardinal A. G. Cicognani. In a letter dated 6 January the Pope announced this to the bishops and explained the competence of this new Commission,[5] which met between 21 and 29 January 1963. On 30 January they announced that no more than seventeen schemata were to be presented to the Council. Further, they ordered the Commission *De Disciplina Cleri et Populi Christiani* to produce a decree entitled *De Clericis,* consisting of three chapters: 1) "De vitae sacerdotalis perfectione"; 2) "De studio et scientia pastorali"; 3) "De recto usu bonorum ecclesiasticorum". The original pre-conciliar schema was to be revised and become an admonition in an appendix to the decree *De Clericis.*

The Commission set to work on these foundations. From 12 to 23 February the four Commissions met, composed as follows:

1. Sub-commission entrusted with chapter I ("De vitae sacerdotalis perfectione"); *relator:* Mgr. F. Marty, Archbishop of Reims; secretary: J. Lécuyer, C.S.SP.

2. Sub-commission entrusted with chapter II ("De studio et scientia pastorali"); *relator:* Mgr. H. Janssen, Bishop of Hildesheim; secretary: S. Sigmond, O.P.

3. Sub-commission entrusted with chapter III ("De recto usu bonorum ecclesiasticorum"); *relator:* Mgr. H. Mazerat, Bishop of Anger; secretary: Mgr. G. Onclin.

4. Sub-commission entrusted with the exhortation to be contained in the appendix ("De distributione cleri"); *relator:* Mgr. V. Enrique y Taracón, Bishop of Solsona; secretary: Mgr. G. Violardo.

The four sub-commissions worked from 12 to 23 February 1963, having in all twenty-six sessions lasting altogether ninety-two hours. The fruit of

---

[4] *Ordo Agendorum tempore quod inter conclusionem primae periodi Concilii Oecumenici et initium secundae intercedit* (Tipografia Poliglotta Vaticana 1962), no. 1, 2 and 3.
[5] Cf. *AAS* 55 (1963), p. 152.

this work was the first draft of a schema for the decree *De Clericis*. This schema was presented to the General Secretariat of the Council on 9 March, which passed it on to the Commission *De Concilii laboribus coordinandis*, which in turn approved the schema *De Clericis* at its session on 25 March, at the same time suggesting some very minor emendations. A special commission was appointed to examine these suggestions. This commission prepared the final text which was handed to the Secretariat of the Council on 18 April. On 22 April 1963 at an audience given to the Secretary of State, the Pope decided to have the document printed and circulated to the fathers. This was done during May 1963.[6]

The publication appeared in the form of a brochure of 28 pages bearing the following title: *Schemata Constitutionum et Decretorum de quibus disceptabitur in Concilii Sessionibus. Schema Decreti de Clericis*. (Typis polyglottis Vaticanis, 1963). The contents were as follows:

Caput I: "De vitae sacerdotalis perfectione" (nn. 1–14), pp. 5–11.

Caput II: "De studio et scientia pastorali" (nn. 15–26), pp. 12–17.

Caput III: "De recto usu bonorum" (nn. 27–39), pp. 18–23. "Exhortatio de distributione cleri" (nn. 40–43), pp. 24–26.

The text was presented to the Council fathers along with a request that they send in their comments to the General Secretariat. By 1 October 237 fathers had sent in a total of 464 comments. These were printed in a single volume which was circulated and used as the basis for revision.

3. Emendation of the schema *De Clericis* and the production of the schema *De Sacerdotibus*
(27 November 1963)

The compilation of the *animadversiones* ran to 99 pages and was sent to the consultants at the beginning of the plenary sessions which took place on 7 and 8 October 1963. On both of these days it was decided to leave the examination of the fathers' comments and suggestions to the four sub-commissions, so that those which seemed to merit substantial adaptation might be presented to the Commission. And so every comment was examined and answered either by rejection or by being proposed for acceptance. The Commission examined the work of the sub-commissions in the plenary sessions of 18, 25, 26 and 27 November 1963. As a result a new text of the schema was produced bearing the title *De Sacerdotibus*.[7] On the model of the

[6] For a complete history of this period we refer to the report of the secretary of the commission in the brochure: *Schema Propositionum de Sacerdotibus* (Typis Polyglottis Vaticanis, 1964), pp. 15 f. We shall refer again to this brochure in another place.

[7] This text, along with a review of the *animadversiones*, was published in pp. 17–46 of the above-mentioned brochure.

previous schema *De Clericis,* the chief alterations touched the following points.

At the request of fifteen East African bishops the title was changed. They pointed out also that the schema spoke only of priests. Likewise the title of the first chapter was changed to "De vita spirituali sacerdotum". The question at issue was not perfection in respect of the life of the clergy alone, as the original title might have implied, but rather of the special obligation of the priest to strive for that perfection which is the goal of every Christian.

Many bishops would have liked to see a theological dissertation on the nature of the priesthood and of the priestly office in the first chapter or even in an introduction. The Commission unanimously rejected this proposal, for their interest centred in discipline (cf. *Commissio de Disciplina Cleri et Populi Christiani*), and they felt that it was impossible for them to meddle in the sphere of the Commission on Doctrine which simultaneously was at work on the schema *De Ecclesia,* which was to include a special chapter devoted to the hierarchy. At the same time a fairly large number of changes were proposed in order to make the text appear less juridical and more theological and pastoral. A number of bishops had expressed the opinion that the priesthood is in itself very much a state of perfection already; but there was divergence of opinion on this point and the Commission felt that it could not commit itself in this controversy, which had for so long exercised theologians, unless some solution were found acceptable to all. Instead, it formulated this fundamental idea: the priestly office, performed under the beneficent direction of the bishops, is a true exercise of the love of God and of one's neighbour, and this is a sure method of striving for perfection.

At the request of several fathers the threefold office of Christ as teacher, priest and pastor was discussed right at the beginning of the prologue (n. 1). This drew a distinction that had already been accepted in describing the hierarchical functions in the Constitution on the Church. First to be named among the functions of the priest was preaching the word of God. N. 2 ("Fundamentum exigentiae sanctitatis sacerdotalis") was scarcely altered. N. 3 ("Ipsum ministerium postulat sanctitatem in sacerdote") was fairly radically altered, the priestly office being there described in terms of the threefold function of teaching, worship and pastoral direction. Further, mention is made of the role of love in this office, for love is the source of all perfection. N. 4 ("Sacerdotis sanctitas proprii muneris adimpletione alitur atque augetur") was the target for 52 *animadversiones.* According to the order mentioned in the previous section everything ought — it was said — to be re-arranged; moreover, what had been the subject of n. 5 ("Sacerdos fratribus servire satagat, quo melius eos Christo adducat") and also n. 9 ("Instanter orandum et adlaboreandum pro vocationibus") were interpolated at this place. Finally, one paragraph dealing with the attitude to be adopted to those who had been unfaithful to their vocation was deleted. The new n. 5 comprised the parts omitted from n. 4 and the substance of the old n. 7. It dealt with unity and the sense of community under the new title: "Sanctibus in unitate Ecclesiae vivenda". N. 6 ("Subsidia ad sanctificationem adhibenda") had provoked numerous comments; almost every bishop wanted to mention some pious practice particularly dear to his own heart; others wanted deletions. In the end the following principle was observed: only the really important obligations, common to the clergy of the whole world, East and West, were to be mentioned. This was to become n. 7, following the new n. 6 containing the substance of the old n. 8 ("Consilia evangelica sectanda"), now altered and expanded so as not to be confined merely to the evangelical counsels appropriate to the religious life. The new title of the new n. 6 was "Vita secundum evangelium componenda". The old n. 10, scarcely altered, became n. 8: "Crux in apostolatu cum gaudio amplectanda". N. 11 of the first schema became n. 9 ("Semper se paratum praebeat ad perfungendum quolibet munere a superiore commissio"). N. 12 was removed and the substance of n. 13 taken over into chapter III. Thus the final section of chapter I was now n. 10 ("Mors in spe et tranquillo animo recipienda"), corresponding to the original n. 14.

Chapter II ("De studio et scientia pastorali") embraced nn. 11–22 of the schema, and it remained very largely unchanged, having elicited fewer comments.

Chapter III ("De recto usu bonorum") was the target for 95 *animadversiones*. A number of the fathers wanted more precise rules governing the execution of the following general principles of the schema: an end to the classification of religious ceremonies, simplification of vestments of bishops and prelates, suppression of honorific titles, etc. The Commission decided that it was not for the Council to go into such practical details which were predominantly the concern of the Commission for the Reform of Canon Law, or of the episcopal conferences. It was, moreover, a task to be undertaken with knowledge of the conditions prevailing in different countries. N. 28 of the original text became n. 24 and was substantially expanded: it dealt not only with emoluments received in the performance of a sacred office, but with the manner in which clergy ought to use their personal property. The precepts, once contained in chapter I (n. 13), concerning the obligation to make a will in good time, were now included in this text. N. 29 of *De Clericis* pointed out that the system of benefices is now obsolete. The new n. 25 took account rather of the diversity of situations and did not repeat the above affirmation. However, it retained all that was said about the necessity of giving pride of place to fulfilling ecclesiastical duties.

The exhortation on the distribution of clergy was revised from the stylistic angle. In the process it took on a more pastoral character. Certain rules, formerly contained in footnote 8, were now included near the end of the text. These concerned the formation of national and international seminaries designed to allow the easier distribution and specialization of the clergy.

4. The reduction of the schema *De Sacerdotibus* to ten guiding principles

The schema *De Sacerdotibus* had scarcely been drawn up when the Central Co-ordinating Commission made an important decision. At the two sessions which took place on 28 December 1963 and on 15 January 1964 it was decided that the decree *De Sacerdotibus* was to be reduced to its essential content and given the form of a few guiding principles which alone would be put to the vote in the Council. This decision was announced on 23 January 1964 and the Commission had forthwith to begin work all over again.

Immediately a special sub-commission was appointed including in particular the secretaries of the previous four sub-commissions. This sub-commission met on 28, 29 and 30 January 1964 in Rome. A text containing ten guiding principles was produced and circulated to all members of the Commission and consultants on 1 February 1964. Thus they had time to study the proposals before the plenary session scheduled for March. This session lasted from 3 to 5 March — thirteen hours in all. The Commission approved the final text with ten guiding principles which attempted to sum up the essential doctrine contained in the schema *De Sacerdotibus*. We shall mention briefly the title and headings of the ten guiding principles.

1. "Exigentia sanctitatis sacerdotalis eiusque fundamentum". This first proposition corresponded to nn. 1 and 2 of the schema. The priest is exhorted to sanctify himself not merely because of the general call to sanctity addressed to all Christians, but because of his special share in the priestly office which demands of him a total self-oblation for the good of the whole body, as Christ had done.

2. "Sacerdotis sanctitatis proprii muneris adimpletione alitur atque augetur". This proposition summed up nn. 3, 4 and 7 of the previous schema. The priestly office, if performed with generosity, is a perfect exercise of love for God and one's neighbour, and thus a specially effective means of attaining perfection. Nonetheless, priests, while avoiding all exaggeration, ought not to neglect the traditional instruments of the spiritual life such as mental prayer, for these instruments are necessary for the effectiveness of the priestly office.

3. "Vita sacerdotalis ad evangelii normas componenda". The priest's life must be modelled on the gospel: self-abnegation; total surrender to the kingdom of God; fraternal unity with other priests; genuine poverty which renounces all gratification of vanity (in dress, titles, honours, etc.) and which

189

aids him in putting himself at the disposal of the poorest; chastity and obedience. This proposition summed up nn. 5, 6 and 9 of the previous schema.

4. "Studium ad essentialia officia status sacerdotalis pertinet". This insisted on the necessity of study as an essential and life-long duty of the priestly state. The theological sciences are what it has principally in mind, but secular studies are included especially in so far as they are related to the priestly office. Cf. nn. 11–16 of the schema.

5. "Scientia pastoralis pro locorum adiunctis acquirenda". Priests must be equipped with the necessary means of fulfilling their obligation to study. Some of these means are specified. This was a summary of nn. 17–21 of the schema *De Sacerdotibus*.

6. "Cleri distributio apte fovenda". This contained a summary of the exhortation that had been appended to the schema; a revision of the rules governing incardination and excardination; the better distribution of the clergy; possible specialization for specific forms of apostolate; international seminaries, personal dioceses or prelacies, etc.

7. "Fines ad quos bona in Ecclesia destinatur". This is a summary of nn. 23 and 24 of the schema *De Sacerdotibus*.

8. "Officiis ecclesiasticis princeps locus in iure tribuatur". This alluded to the laws governing benefices. First place must be given to the ecclesiastical office or ministry, which is defined thus: any function which must be performed permanently in respect of a spiritual end. This statement corresponded to n. 25 of the schema.

9. "Aequa remuneratio clericis providenda". The duty of the bishop to provide adequate sustentation for his priests or to lay down regulations to achieve this. Greater equality in the treatment of all points: cf. nn. 26 and 35 of the schema of *De Sacerdotibus*.

10. "Massa communis bonorum in singulis diocesibus constituenda". This contained a summary of nn. 27–32 of the schema.

These ten guiding principles were placed before the Co-ordinating Commission on 16 March 1964. They were approved by the Commission and also by Pope Paul VI on 17 April. The new project was sent out to the Council fathers during April. In addition to the ten guiding principles (pp. 5–8) the publication[8] contained also the *relatio* of Mgr. Marty concerning the preparatory work (pp. 11–14), an account of the evolution of the schema *De Clericis* (pp. 15–16) and the complete text of the schema *De Sacerdotibus* (pp. 17–46).

---

[8] The brochure mentioned in footnote 6.

5. The twelve propositions: *De vita et ministerio sacerdotali*
(2 October 1964)

Before the third series of sessions began on 14 September 1964 the fathers had sent in a list of written comments. There were fifty-three requests for alterations, including some of the greatest importance. In particular the German-speaking and Scandinavian bishops, who had met in Innsbruck, sent in a notable report, which exerted a decisive influence on the direction of subsequent work. On 14 September these *animadversiones*, contained in a sixteen-page pamphlet, were passed on to a special sub-commission, which prepared the work of the full Commission, which met on 29 September 1964 to examine and discuss the new text produced by the sub-commission. Thus a total of twelve propositions were approved by the Commission on one day. The new production contained a considerable number of very important alterations.

Most important of all, the title had been changed at the request of three French bishops. The original title, *De Sacerdotibus*, had seemed too general and too pretentious in relation to the few problems dealt with in the schema. On the other hand there were other texts at that time being studied by the Council — *De Ecclesia*, for example — which contained important material on the subject of the priesthood. The introduction explicitly mentioned this text which the Council had already studied.

The first proposition ("Sacerdotum cum laicis conversatio") was completely new and in substance corresponded to the text suggested by the German-speaking and Scandinavian bishops. According to this the priest is primarily a member of the Christian community and must behave like a brother among brethren, for he is above all an example of those human qualities that are so important in all human relationships. The second proposition corresponded to the original n. 3. At the request of several fathers there was included an important addition on the meaning of clerical celibacy. Cardinal Lercaro, who was one of those who made this request, also asked that the special obedience which a priest owes to his bishop should be shown to derive from his share in the same priesthood and mission as his bishop. In content n. 3 corresponded to the original nn. 1 and 2 and was entitled: "Quae in ministerio sacerdotali eluere debent". This avoided enumerating things already discussed in the Constitution on the Church. A fairly long addition, proposed in part — as we have said — by the German and Scandinavian bishops, strongly underlined the mystical value of the priestly, apostolic life. Several fathers had gone further and requested that the rosary or a daily visit to the Blessed Sacrament or daily examination of conscience be specially mentioned among the duties of the priest. In order to avoid endless discussion the Commission decided to mention only mental prayer, which had clearly emerged in the enumeration of specific devotional practices. A feeling for the liturgy and, in a general way, veneration of the Eucharist and of the Mother of God were briefly mentioned also. Finally, it was said that the life of the priest must itself be a witness to the faith. N. 4 developed a few propositions contained in the original n. 3 under the title: "Sacerdotum inter se confraternitas". These dealt with the fraternal spirit among the clergy, the bishops' care of their clergy, commendation of community life. N. 5 took up the material of the original n. 4 and dealt with the obligation to study. The text described this as essential to the office of the priest, although the title had not previously expressed the thought. The proposed n. 6 (formerly n. 5) once more took up the theme of pastoral science and its acquisition. At this point a new seventh proposition was introduced under the title: "Sacerdotum sollicitudo omnium ecclesiarum". At the request of three fathers the text was taken up again from n. 37 of De Sacerdotibus. N. 8 repeated the original n. 6 almost without change. N. 9 was the former n. 7 with an excerpt from De Sacerdotibus (n. 24) added. The concluding guiding principles remained almost unaltered.

This text together with the original was printed in a brochure of 24 pages entitled: "Relatio super schema emendatum propositionum De Sacerdotibus quod nunc inscribitur De Vita et Ministerio Sacerdotali". It included the report of Mgr. Marty, the two texts in parallel — textus prior and textus emendatus, and the report of the Commission concerning the alterations. The text was dated 2 October 1964 when it was circulated to the Council fathers.

6. Plan for a message to priests (29 September 1964)

The reduction of the schema De Sacerdotibus to but a few guiding principles caused pain among many bishops. They got the impression that priests might feel neglected by the Council, especially as so much attention had been paid to the bishops and the laity. This uneasiness found an echo in the Commission De Disciplina Cleri et Populi Christiani. On 29 September the members of the Commission unanimously agreed to intervene with the moderators of the Council and request that the idea of a message from the fathers of the Council to all the priests of the world — debated the previous year — be taken up again.

This request was accepted. On 8 October the Commission De Disciplina Cleri et Populi Christiani was officially entrusted with the composition of such a message. During the second Council period a draft had already been produced, but this was found to be inadequate. And so they set about composing a fresh text. As it turned out, however, the course of events made this projected message unnecessary.

7. The first discussion in the Council hall
(13–15 October 1964)

Discussions on the twelve guiding principles *De Vita et Ministerio Sacerdotali* began in the Council hall on 13 October 1964. Between that date and 15 November forty-one fathers spoke.

On 13 November, after Mgr. Marty had read the report in the name of the Commission, Cardinal Meyer from Chicago was the first to speak. He complained of the inadequacy of the text, thus reduced to a few guiding principles, and he demanded the production of a truly comprehensive schema comparable with that on the bishops or the laity. The rest of that day's interventions recognized the value of the text before them, it is true, but all expressed the same concern: the text must be given a richer content if it were to satisfy the expectations of the priests of the whole world.

Next day this dissatisfaction became still clearer. Like Cardinal Meyer, Cardinal de Barros Camara too demanded a comprehensive and detailed schema on priests. Speaking in the name of 112 bishops of Brazil and other countries, Mgr. F. Gomes (Goa) went so far as to say that the text was a great disillusionment for, and injustice to, priests. If the Council was able — he continued — to say such beautiful and even noble things about bishops and laity, how could it be content with such pitiful and incomplete affirmations about priests? He did not call in question the good intentions of those who had produced the text, but he did complain about the result of their labours. The tone of the schema was paternalistic and it shirked the serious problems of the poverty of the clergy, of community life, of clerical dress and of vanity within the Church. He concluded with an appeal not to come to a hasty decision that would be injurious to their work, and moved the postponement of voting, scheduled for the following day. The text should be returned to the Commission for expansion and revision. The latter proposal was accepted by the moderators on 14 October.

Those who had intended to speak on the schema, however, continued to do so in the course of the following morning. Cardinal Alfrink of Utrecht complained of the absence in the text of any missionary spirit and of the awareness of real world problems. He proposed the erection in every diocese of a pastoral council composed of priests and laymen. Mgr. Köstner (Gurk) underlined afresh the disparity between this much abbreviated schema and that on the laity. Mgr. Jenny, Bishop of Cambray, reminded the Council of the mystery of the priesthood and of its mediatorial function, and asked that the schema be not set aside, but returned to the Commission for thorough revision, so that a more positive and optimistic text might be provided. In the same vein, Mgr. V. Sartre, titular Bishop of Beroe, demanded a thorough reconstruction of the schema, for which he suggested the main outlines, laying special stress upon the missionary character of the priesthood. Last to speak was Cardinal Lefèbre of Bourges. He spoke in the name of seventy bishops and his special objection to the text was that it did not bring out clearly enough the tremendous greatness and efficacy of the priesthood which had been designed for the sanctification of mankind. Finally, Mgr. Marty, the official *relator* of the Commission, summed up the result of the debate, pointing out that the schema could not take account of the wishes of everyone if it was to remain contained within the framework of a few guiding principles. He added that the Commission would be able to prepare a fuller and richer text if asked to do so. He invited the fathers to send in written observations and suggestions both for the schema and for a message to priests.[9]

In the course of discussion at the Council the fathers had publicly expressed their comments, and now they sent in a whole list of written observations. All of this was collated at the secretariat for the Commission and printed in two volumes of 156 and 94 pages respectively. Volume I was ready by 26 October, volume II on 15 December 1964.[10]

The wishes expressed by the fathers in the course of the discussion were used by Mgr. Marty, *relator* of the Commission, as the starting point of a letter in the name of all members of the Commission to the moderators of the Council. He requested that the schema on priests be presented to the fathers of the Council in the full length that had been desired and that the compulsory twelve guiding principles be abandoned. A reply to this intervention came on 12 October: the basis for a complete re-casting of the schema was accepted.

8. The decree *De Ministerio et Vita Presbytorum* (first schema, 12 November 1964)

Time was short, for the third phase of the Council was nearly over, and the Commission wanted to put a new draft before the fathers before they departed, if that were at all possible. Already the sub-commissions had been at work and on 29 October, at a plenary session, the Commission approved the draft of the new schema. The working out of separate sections was handed over to special sub-commissions which then sent on their results to

[9] Cf. G. Zizola, "Uno Schema da rifare" (ed. by R. La Valle) in *Fedelta del Concilio* (2nd ed., 1965), pp. 279 ff.

[10] Sacrosanctum Oecumenicum Concil. Vatic. secundum, Commissio de Disciplina Cleri et Populi Christiani, *Animadversiones in Schema Propositionum "De Vita et Ministerio Sacerdotali" a Patribus Conciliaribus factae* (duplicated paper) (26 October 1964); Pars altera (15 December 1964).

a central sub-commission which blended everything into a unity before presenting the text to the plenary Commission. This met on 5, 9 and 11 November 1964; the new text was examined and then ratified at the final session; the new draft was thus produced in fourteen days, thanks to the enormous effort of the experts and of the secretariat of the Commission. The text was sent immediately to the secretariat of the Council, but the fathers did not receive copies until 20 November, one day before the end of the third phase of the Council.[11] Mgr. Felici, general secretary of the Council, announced the distribution, at the same time asking the fathers to send in written comments by the end of January 1965.

The new schema was presented in a 44-page brochure. The contents were: 1) the general report by Mgr. Marty; 2) the totally revised schema set parallel wherever necessary to the original text of propositions; 3) the report of the secretariat of the Commission on individual sections of the schema. The schema was constructed as follows: Introduction; Part I: "De presbyterorum ministerio" (nn. 1–11); Part II: "De presbyterorum vita" (nn. 12–19); Summary in the form of a short exhortation to priests (n. 20). This was an almost completely fresh text, in terms not only of content, but of tone and style. A brief analysis proves this beyond doubt.

The title is different: the subject indicated is no longer the priesthood (including the bishops) in itself, but the second order of priests, the presbyterate. First place is given not to their life but to their ministry, thus hinting that the priest's life must be determined by the requirements of his ministry and not vice versa.

The Introduction takes up the theme of the exalted *ordo* of the presbyterate, of its participation in the office of Christ as teacher, priest and king, for the good of the Church. This whole Introduction is new, but has similarities with n. 1 ("De natura presbyteratus"). At the request of 124 fathers the nature of the presbyterate is expounded within the framework of the universal mission of the Church. The nature of the official priesthood is explained in distinction to the general priesthood of all the faithful on the one hand and to the episcopate on the other. Following the plea of 116 fathers, n. 2 ("Presbyteri, verbi Dei ministri") starts off with an exposition of the three great functions of the priest: the priest is a co-worker with the episcopate in their task of preaching the word of God not only to the faithful, but to the whole world. There is also a brief explanation of the link between this function and the ministry of the sacraments, especially the Eucharist. This number is completely new. N. 3 ("Scientia presbyterorum sacra") takes up and expands the idea contained in the original guiding principle n. 5.

[11] *Schema Decreti De Ministerio et Vita Presbyterorum, Textus emendatus et Relationes* (Typis Polyglottis Vaticanis, 1964).

According to n. 2 this exposition on the obligation to study was introduced on account of the connection between the duty to teach and the duty to learn. This arrangement, however, interrupts the exposition of the priestly functions, and was in the end rejected. N. 4 ("Presbyteri, sacramentorum et eucharistiae ministri") likewise is completely new, its most important topic being a fairly long exposition of the Eucharist. N. 5 ("Presbyteri, populi Dei rectores") is completely new and expounds the twofold aspect of the priest's role in the education of the individual Christian and of the congregation as a whole. At the request of many fathers the formation of a Catholic and missionary spirit is also mentioned. A few sentences allude to the spirit of dialogue which ought to prevail between the priest and his people. Above all this section points out the importance of the celebration of the Eucharist in the formation of true Christian community. N. 6 ("Scientia et ars pastoralis pro diversis adiunctis") reproduces the essence of principle n. 6, but some things are focussed up more sharply. In relation to the whole schema the position of this section may seem odd. N. 7 ("De habitudine inter episcopos et presbyterium") is almost completely new. Only a few lines remain of the original guiding principle n. 2. Account is taken in this section of the desire of numerous fathers who wanted a fairly thorough exposition of the relation between priest and bishop. The required unity is founded in the grace of the sacrament itself. Bishops must see their priests as true assistants and advisers, as friends bound to them by a multiple bond of functions which both have to fulfil. Priests, for their part, must recognize that the fullness of the priesthood resides in the bishops. They must exhibit an attitude of honest co-operation and obedience, first towards their bishops, and then towards the entire episcopate in whose universal task they all share. At the request of several fathers the setting up of a council of priests in every diocese was prescribed. N. 8 ("Confraternitas et co-operatio inter presbyteros") is almost wholly new with the exception of a few sentences from the old n. 4. Fraternal charity among priests, already expressed in the liturgical ceremonies, is required for the sake of the example this gives to the faithful, and because of the unity of the priestly commission which, despite diversity of function, is always the same commission.

Life in community is recommended, as circumstances allow, and so are associations for priests. N. 9 ("Presbyterorum cum laicis conversatio") follows the main outlines of the original n. 1, and then goes on to speak of the special function of the laity, which must be recognized and respected, of the need to listen to what the laity have to say, and of the priest's duty to provide a centre of unity and love for the laity. N. 10 ("Apta presbyterorum distributio") reproduces the original propositions nn. 7 and 8. A few pastoral recommendations are added concerning priests sent to unfamiliar regions. N. 11 ("De vocationibus sacerdotalibus") is quite new and was introduced on the plea of seven fathers. It reminds us of the duty of all of the faithful to foster priestly vocations; and priests, too, are admonished to remind the faithful of this duty. A few remarks are included on how to recognize the signs of a true vocation, and on co-operation between dioceses and even between episcopal conferences to ensure the recruitment and education of the clergy. This brings us to the end of Part I of the schema.

Part II (" De presbyterorum vita") begins with a description of the foundation of the doctrine on the spirituality of the priesthood. N. 12 ("Peculiaris exigentia sanctitatis in vita sacerdotali") is thus completely new. N. 13 ("Triplicis muneris sacerdotalis exercitium sanctitatem requirit simul ac fovet") contains the ideas embodied in the original proposition n. 3, expanded here and there. At the request of 115 fathers mention was made of the significance of the priestly ministry as itself an obligation to, and source of, sanctification. Taking up a request of 114 fathers n. 14 ("De unitate et harmonia vitae presbyterorum") considers the serious problem of the integrity of the priest's life, which is so often damaged by the conflict between the duties of his office and the needs of his own interior balance. This integration must be sought in an ever growing assent to the will of God, through union with Christ, who fulfilled the Father's will on earth. This, too, makes clear the central significance of the Eucharist in the life of the priest. This number is completely new. N. 15 ("De castitate perfecta ceterisque consiliis evangelicis") picks up certain elements out of proposition 2 of the guiding principles, but the text has been reconstructed and substantially augmented. There had been long discussion in the Commission on this section, especially on priestly celibacy. On the one hand 121 fathers had asked for an exposition of the foundations of the Church's doctrine and of the appropriateness of priestly celibacy; on the other hand 118 fathers wanted a clear statement that there was no fundamental incompatibility between the priesthood and matrimony. On the latter point the text mentions specially validly married priests who can obviously be exemplary priests ("optime meriti"), and adverts also to the first apostles who were not all unmarried. Both of the arguments for celibacy are based first upon the counsel which Christ and St. Paul gave and second upon the direct connection between the priestly function and the eschatological reign of God when there will be no longer any marriage. Current law concerning celibacy is then mentioned and ratified by the Council. There follow a few sentences on poverty and obedience among priests. N. 16 ("Media ad vitam interiorem fovendam") reproduces the old guiding principle 3 in a fresh form. N. 17 ("Aequa remuneratio presbyteris providenda") resumes the old nn. 10 and 11. N. 18 ("De recto usu bonorum") represents the old n. 9 in an improved style. On the plea of two fathers this speaks only of ecclesiastical property or of those goods which priests receive in return for the exercise of an official ecclesiastical activity, and not of any personal property they may happen to possess. N. 19 ("Praevidentia socialis in favorem presbyterorum") again speaks of common possession, which was provided for but not made obligatory in guiding principle 12.

9. The schema of the Decree on the Ministry and Life of Priests — second version (1 April 1965)

By the end of January 1965, 157 Council fathers had sent in their written comments on the text which they had received just before the third phase of the Council ended. These comments were collected and arranged in the form of 466 supplementary proposals contained in a 165-page booklet. This was ready on 26 February 1965,[12] and sent to all members and experts of the Commission on 28 February. The Commission was called to meet on 29 March. A sub-commission of experts was to meet on 22 March and prepare the work of the Commission. During the preparatory sessions this small group of experts examined the proposed alterations and prepared a draft answer to each comment. In addition they edited a draft text which already incorporated all of the supplementary material which the sub-commission had approved.

When, on 29 March, the Commission met, it found its work already fairly well advanced. The *relator* of the sub-commission placed a summary of the requested additions along with the findings of the sub-commission before the fathers. And so they were able to ratify a new text on 1 April. Most of the comments had to do with the external form of the text: length, pointless repetition, quotations that were not always pertinent. Such faults could be explained by the haste with which the first draft had been prepared, and they were relatively easily put right.

The new text is slightly shorter, as can easily be seen from the parallel sections of text provided in the edition of 25 May 1965.[13] This was accomplished through the avoidance of double mentions and the use of a more succinct and powerful style. Another important change that is immediately obvious concerns the arrangement of sections, especially in Part I. The following analysis makes this quite clear:

Part I: n. 1 (= 1), 2 (= 2), 3 (= 4), 4 (= 5), 5 (= 3 + 6), 6 (part of 7), 7 (= 8), 8 (=9), 9 (=part of 7 + 10), 10 (= 11); Part II: the arrangement remained the same, but the numbering was displaced by one: nn. 11–19

---

[12] *Animadversiones in Schema Decreti "De Ministerio et Vita Presbyterorum" a Patribus Conciliaribus factae* (26 February 1965) (duplicated).
[13] *Schema Decreti de Ministerio et Vita Presbyterorum, Textus recognitus et Relationes* (Typis Polyglottis Vaticanis, 1965).

(= 12–20). Whereas Part II retained the same order as before, Part I was completely re-cast in many places. The main alterations in the text must be briefly mentioned, leaving out those which do not affect doctrine. We must also point out that with this version the opening words now become: "Presbyteratus ordinis".

One important change affects n. 1, which is a definition or description of the presbyterate. Forty-eight fathers, including the bishops of Indonesia, fourteen bishops from West Africa and Mgr. Garrone, had requested that this statement stick more explicitly to the doctrine of the constitution *De Ecclesia* on the presbyterate, which takes as the starting point the task handed on to the bishops, and in which the priests co-operate. The first section was altered along these lines. The second section takes up the residue of the old text in summarized form, the comment having been made that this was too one-sidedly orientated towards the liturgical ministry. At the request of numerous fathers a third section is interpolated on the dialectical situation of the priest who is in this world but not of it, is not separated from men, and yet stands somewhat apart.

Following the request of Mgr. Gufflet (Limoges) explicit reference is made to the sacrament of penance in the service of the priest; and, in response to fourteen bishops from western France, the priest's use of liturgical prayer is also mentioned. In response to the plea of a few of the fathers, n. 6 expresses the view that priests are co-operators with the *ordo* of bishops and not merely with their own bishops. The first lines of n. 7 have been altered in accordance with the wishes of several fathers, and from now on a distinction is to be made between the ordo of the *presbyterium* to which all priests belong and to which entry comes through ordination, and that *presbyterium* shared in by all priests who have dedicated themselves to serve a particular diocese under the authority of its bishop. N. 12 contains two important additions. On the one hand, in accordance with the desire of fourteen French bishops, the daily celebration of Mass is recommended, even if none of the faithful can assist; while on the other hand, in accordance with the request of Mgr. Rusch (Innsbruck), a few lines are added on pastoral asceticism which with unremitting confidence strives towards fresh advances and new undertakings. N. 13 has been substantially shortened.

On the question of priestly celibacy (n. 14), the comments by the fathers had been more numerous than on any other question. These comments by no means followed one pattern; often they expressed diametrically opposed views. The Commission had tried to find a formula that would satisfy the majority, and so, in accordance with the wish of several fathers, the married apostles were not mentioned, for, in leaving all to follow Christ these men had most probably left their wives also. This, at all events, was the opinion of several fathers. There was another group who did not want to mention the married priests of the Eastern Church either; but the Commission would not allow this deletion because it might have been interpreted as a slur upon the Eastern Church. At the request of Mgr. Renard (Versailles) a few lines were added on voluntary celibacy as a sign of the total self-oblation of the priest in the service of Christ. Observations on the eschatological meaning of this voluntary celibacy were abbreviated and re-phrased in order to avoid any hint of Manichaeism or of disparagement of sex. The same section discusses poverty as a means to greater apostolic freedom.

In addition to the aids to the spiritual life of the priest already mentioned n. 15 adds first the reading of holy Scripture, then devotion to the Eucharist — which had accidentally been omitted in the earlier draft. In an important expansion we are reminded of the freedom there must be to choose, under the inspiration of the Holy Spirit, from all the other pious practices which are available to the Christian; but first place must always be given to the public worship of the Church.

10. Discussion in the Council during October 1965

The new text, the report of Mgr. Marty and the report of the secretariat of the Commission on the supplementations were ready at the end of May 1965 and sent to the Council fathers. The fourth phase of the Council began on 14 September of the same year, but the schema, "The Ministry and Life of Priests", was not debated until 14 October. Meanwhile something special had happened at the session on 11 October. About midday Cardinal Tisserant, chairman of the presidential council, had had a letter read out by the general secretary, which he had just received from the Pope. Paul VI had learned that some of the fathers intended to initiate discussion at one of the sessions on the law governing celibacy in the Latin Church. The Pope publicly declared his opinion: "It is not opportune to discuss this topic in public because it requires great prudence and is of great importance." The Pope asked those fathers who felt it to be their duty, to express their views in writing to the presidential council, who in turn would pass them on to the Pope. On the following day, 12 October, the Paris newspaper *Le Monde* published the substance of the intervention which Mgr. Koop (Lins, Brazil) had prepared on this topic. In view of the shortage of priests and of the needs of the constantly increasing population, this bishop advocated that episcopal conferences be authorized to admit men of mature age, who had been married for not less than five years, to the priesthood. Even in Rome rumours were going around. This novelty, for example, it was said, was so widely accepted that the bishops of Latin America no longer shared the conservative view of the canonical regulation concerning celibacy. In order to silence these rumours the president of the Latin American episcopal council, Mgr. Larraín, sent a telegram to the Pope on 13 October, in which he declared the complete agreement of his council with the desire which the Pope had expressed in his letter to the Dean of the College of Cardinals on 11 October.

On the same day, 13 October, towards the close of the general congregation, Mgr. Marty read out his report on the new schema that had been placed before the fathers. Discussion began on the following day. Cardinals Mèouchi, Ruffini, De Arriba y Castro, Colombo, Quiroga, Léger and Richaud and several bishops spoke. Many interventions supported the schema — with occasional requests for improvements in detail. Cardinal Léger complained that there was no exposition of a specifically priestly spirituality, the point of departure seeming to be the spirituality of the religious orders, especially in respect of the evangelical counsels. Next day the discussion continued. Cardinal Döpfner spoke for the German bishops. He pointed out the necessity of seeing the problem of priests in the actual context of the difficulties of the modern world. Like Cardinal Léger, he would like Part II to be more clearly thought out with regard to the special situation of priests. Instead of speaking of the evangelical counsels the following points might be considered instead: 1) the spirit of humility and obedience; 2) poverty and the proper use of this world's goods; 3) celibacy. Other speakers on this day were Cardinals Doi, Alfrink, Laudazuri, Suenens, Jaeger and Herrera, and ten bishops. On 16 October the speakers were Cardinals Lefèbvre, Rugambwa, Roy, Florit, Bea, Shehan and Rossi, and several bishops.

About midday on 16 October the moderators asked the fathers to decide whether they considered that discussion had been carried on long enough and could now be closed. The fathers agreed that it could be closed. Thereupon the following question was put to them: "Do the fathers agree to make the schema, which has been discussed during the past days, the basis of a final revision, to be undertaken in the light of the verbal and written comments made?" The result of the voting was: present 1521; yes 1507; no 12; invalid 2. Mgr. Marty thanked the fathers in the name of the Commission and promised that their comments would be carefully considered.

There were, however, still to be public interventions concerning this decree during the three general congregations on 25 to 27 October. A number of bishops spoke in the name of over seventy fathers and were granted the right of intervention. The last bishop to intervene was Mgr. Pellegrino, Archbishop of Turin, who gave an excellent account on priests and the theological sciences. On 27 October the last voice of all was heard, that of the auditor Mgr. Thomas Falls, parish priest of the Sacred Heart in Philadelphia. Other parish priests had sent in written comments.[14]

---

[14] A great number of the contributions to the discussion in the Council were published. See, for example, DC 62 (1965), pp. 2183–2202; 63 (1966), pp. 329–348 (all in French).

11. The revision of the schema (17 and 29 October 1965)

After the voting had taken place on 16 October the Commission set to work again. The comments sent in by the fathers were examined and the schema amended correspondingly. Six sub-commissions deleted proposed additions from the text and returned their results to the central sub-commission, whose task was to co-ordinate the revision and reduce it to a common denominator. In this way they prepared things for a plenary session of the Commission.

The Commission met on 27 October and sat also on the two following days. Each member had a copy of the 43-page booklet in which the secretariat of the Commission had collected all of the suggestions sent in by the fathers before 19 October.[15] The interventions made after this date were disposed of as soon as possible, but were kept in mind during the work of revision. To begin with it was decided to divide the schema into three chapters, chapter II and chapter III each falling naturally into three sections. The general structure, suggested by Cardinal Suenens, looked like this:

Prooemium (n. 1)
Caput   I: *Presbyteratus in missione ecclesiae*
Caput II: *Presbyterorum ministerium*
    1. *Presbyterorum munerum* (nn. 4–6)
    2. *Presbyterorum habitudo ad alios* (nn. 7–9)
    3. *Presbyterorum distributio et vocationes sacerdotales* (nn. 10–11)
Caput III: *Presbyterorum vita*
    1. *Presbyterorum ad perfectionem vocatio* (nn. 12–14)
    2. *Peculiares exigentiae spirituales in vita presbyterorum* (nn. 15–17)
    3. *Subsidia pro presbyterorum vita* (nn. 18–21)
Conclusio et exhortatio.

Besides the slight change of the first word from "Presbyteratus" to "Presbyterorum", the Introduction has undergone significant expansion. It is explained that the decree is addressed specially to diocesan priests, but that, with appropriate adaptation, it could be applied to the regular clergy who are engaged in pastoral work. The text which follows speaks of the presbyterate. At the request of numerous fathers it is divided into two parts: the first deals with the presbyterate itself, the second of its situation in the world. Two viewpoints had become evident among the Council fathers du-

[15] *Animadversiones in Schema Decreti "De Ministerio et Vita Presbyterorum" oretenus vel in scriptis factae* (19 October 1965) (duplicated).

ring the definition of the presbyterate. A large number wanted to proceed simply from the idea of *co-operators with the bishops* to the threefold levels of teaching, of worship and of pastoral ministry, corresponding to the lines laid down in *De Ecclesia*. This broad outline had been followed in the previous version. Others complained that the relationship to the Eucharist was not being given pride of place, and wanted the sacerdotal character of the presbyter to be more strongly underlined. These two conceptions were not diametrically opposed and so the Commission sought a compromise. Part of the text of November 1964, which put the liturgical aspect in first place, was used again. In the following section which speaks of the situation of the priest in the modern world, the chief deletion is the statement about the priest's function in respect of all mankind, including non-Christians. In describing the functions of presbyters (nn. 4–6) their share in the mission of the bishops is the thing mainly stressed, as in a general way is the universal and missionary character of the priestly ministry.

The text which suffered most alteration was n. 12 dealing with the priest's vocation to holiness. The new text makes a closer connection between the spiritual life of the priest, his mission and his functions. To achieve this end part of the text of November 1964 was resumed at the request of numerous fathers.

The next section contains a clearer expression of the fundamental idea: the very exercise of his ministry is a means of sanctification for the priest himself. The section which deals with the unity in the life of the priest is clearer and better arranged. In it a few lines are added on the objective norm of loyalty to the will of God, which is loyalty to the Church.

The most significant changes are those affecting the old n. 14 which deals with the evangelical counsels in the life of the priest. A large number of fathers had asked for a thorough re-casting of this part. Above all they wanted to avoid any transference to the spirituality of the priesthood of elements that were normative purely of the religious life. It would be better to speak of evangelical virtues than of evangelical counsels. These virtues must, moreover, be seen in close connection with the duties of the priestly ministry and not primarily as means towards personal perfection. Thus spoke Cardinals Léger, Döpfner (in the name of 65 fathers), Suenens and Roy, as well as 35 Italian bishops. Others wanted a greater stress to be laid upon the spirit of poverty: Cardinal Rossi and 43 Brazilian bishops, Cardinal Florit and others. Yet another group wanted to see the virtue of obedience linked with that of humility. In view of so many requests the Commission thought it proper to distribute the material among three sections. In the new draft n. 15 deals with humility and obedience, which are indispensable to a pastoral ministry that is filled with love. The text has been completely re-cast. N. 17 speaks of the use of this world's goods and of voluntary poverty, which is a means of achieving greater freedom of dedication to the work of the priestly commission. This section covers the old n. 17 and part of n. 14.

Section 16 presents the problem of celibacy. Until the very end it had been treated with great caution, not for internal reasons only, but out of regard for the common practice in the Eastern Church.

The Commission agreed upon the following structure: 1) celibacy is a gift of God that is not demanded of the priesthood, but which is specially appropriate to his state; 2) this appropriateness possesses, first, a theological character: celibacy expresses the essence of the priestly mission in a very special way; 3) the appropriateness has also a pastoral character: celibacy brings greater freedom for complete devotion to a ministry for the kingdom of God; 4) the current legal prescriptions of the Western Church are ratified; 5) all priests are enjoined to prize celibacy very highly; 6) all the faithful are invited to pray that this gift shall be poured out upon the Church in rich measure.

Several details became the subject of long discussions. Proof of the fact that celibacy is not an essential mark of the priesthood was seen both in the tradition of the Eastern Church and in the practice of the ancient Church. At the last moment Cardinal Bea, president of the Secretariat for Christian Unity, had sent a written petition through the Secretary of State to the Eastern Church asking them to make some positive statement on married priests, on the special style of their vocation, on the example they give to all Christians of marriage and family life. On 16 October Cardinal Bea had already made an intervention in the Council when he said: "It seems to me that this Ecumenical Council ought to treat both priestly states in the same way: the state of complete continence in celibacy and the state of full (if not exactly ideal) marriage in the married clergy. It ought to be shown how both types, each according to its state, are to be carefully chosen, educated and formed..." [16] There had been a very long discussion on this topic in the Commission. On the one hand it seemed to be impossible to deal with the celibate and the married state in the one document, as though the Church had never shown any preference for one rather than the other; on the other hand they dared not give the impression that the priesthood of the married man was less a priesthood than that of the voluntary celibate. In the end it was decided to add a few lines in which married clergy were encouraged "to give an example of love, faithfulness and conjugal chastity, as also of the Christian up-bringing of children" and to devote themselves fully to the flock entrusted to them.

N. 18 speaks of the aids to the spiritual life of the priest. Some difficulties arose over this article. Cardinals Spellman, Ruffini and Florit, Bishop Sán-

[16] Text in DC 63 (1966), pp. 333 f.

chez Moreno and Bishop Tomé had asked that frequent reception of the sacrament of penance be specially mentioned. It was most important that none of the aids mentioned appear to be imposed externally, but that their interior relationship to the priestly ministry be demonstrated. Other bishops (Mgrs. Charue, de Provenchères, Shehan) wanted to see greater emphasis placed upon mental prayer and adoration in the life of the priest. The earlier text was almost totally altered to allow these observations to be incorporated.

The two sections dealing with the material circumstances of the priest (nn. 20 and 21) were changed very little. Five bishops (Mgr. Nabaa and four French bishops), however, asked for the addition of a few lines on the duty of the faithful to supply the material needs of the clergy, if other provision has not been made. Forty-four Council fathers from Brazil had wanted the word "stabiliter" deleted from the definition of the "Officium ecclesiasticum" because of the difficulty of defining this stability, but the Commission decided to retain the word, which already occurs in can. 145, para. 1, and has not given rise to difficulties. The concluding exhortation was expanded. The reproach had been levelled against the schema that it was inopportune and seemed to be ignorant of the real problems facing the priestly ministry (Cardinals Mèouchi, Rugambwa, Suenens, Alfrink, Döpfner and others). In his intervention in the Council Cardinal Florit had already answered this difficulty in principle, saying that the problems facing priests today can be solved basically only through faith and a life lived by an ever deepening faith. And so, he added, the schema must provide above all the theological principles which are for ever valid for the life of the priest; and this had been sufficiently accomplished. There was nothing to stop the Council from prescribing practical guide-lines which could be evaluated in terms of given circumstances and adapted as required. The Commission, however, thought it proper to lay more stress upon the difficulties facing the priestly ministry today; and so two sections were interpolated at the beginning of the concluding exhortation.

The text, thus prepared, was printed in a 72-page brochure.[17] This contained the report of Mgr. Marty (pp. 5–7), the previous text *(textus prior)* and the improved text *(textus emendatus)* set in parallel columns (pp. 9–51), the report of the Commission on the improvements (pp. 53–67) and, finally, the summary according to which the fathers would be asked to vote (p. 69). This brochure was sent out to the fathers on 9 November 1965.

[17] *Schema Decreti de Ministerio et Vita Presbyterorum, Textus emendatus et Relationes* (Typis Polyglottis Vaticanis, 1965).

12. The voting on 12 and 13 November 1965 and the *modi*

The schema was presented to the Council for voting on 12 and 13 November 1965, without further discussion. In all there were fifteen votes: one on Chapter I; seven on Chapter II; seven on Chapter III. At the end of each chapter or section there was a general vote with *placet, non placet, placet juxta modum*. The result was as follows:

	Present	Yes	No	Yes with reservations	Invalid
Intro. & Ch. I	2154	1772	16	361	5
Ch. II	2129	1548	9	568	4
Ch. III, n. 1	2134	2037	2	95	0
n. 2	2076	1434	11	630	1
N. 3 & Concl.	2058	1510	4	544	0

187 of the *modi* affected the title and 43 the general structure of the decree. The rest were distributed as follows:

Number and content	*Number of modi*
1. Introduction	376
2. Nature of priesthood	383
3. Situation of priests in the world	61
4. Ministry of the word of God	115
5. Worship and sacraments	256
6. Leaders and pastors	146
7. Relationships with bishops	280
8. Relationships with each other	762
9. Relationships with laity	15
10. Distribution of priests	101
11. Vocations to priesthood	104
12. Call to holiness	78
13. Sanctification and ministry	142
14. Integrity of priest's life	27
15. Humility and obedience	89
16. Celibacy	1331
17. Use of possessions and poverty	56
18. Aids to spiritual life	972
19. Study and pastoral science	68
20. Just remuneration of priests	19
21. Common property and social security	6
22. Conclusion	54
	5441

Adding to this the 187 *modi* to the title and the 43 to the general structure we arrive at the grand total of 5671.

The Council was to come to an end on 8 December, and so the Commission had little time left to examine all of these comments by the fathers and arrive at an answer which would satisfy them all. For this reason the work during this period was particularly intensive. The secretariat of the Commission (Alvaro del Portillo assisted by Giuliano Herranz) presented a lucid arrangement of the *modi,* and their indefatigable industry led to a satisfactory result. By this arrangement the *modi* were entrusted to a special sub-commission which, in addition to its president, Mgr. Marty, included the following members: Y. Congar, O.P., Mgr. G. Onclin, A. del Portillo, G. Herranz and J. Lécuyer, C.S.Sp. All of the *modi* were examined and all received a reply. The *modi* were then either accepted or rejected, the last word being reserved, naturally, to the plenary Commission. A precise reason was sought for every acceptance or rejection. In this way the reflections and intentions of the Commission were made clear for any future interpretation of the text, and the fathers were given the opportunity to vote with full knowledge of all the issues.

The plenary Commission met first on 19 November and then on 22 November. The fathers studied the work of the sub-commission and discussed the proposals which were then accepted, altered or rejected.

There were many suggestions concerning the title: "Constitutio" instead of "Decretum"; "De Ministerio et Vita Presbyterorum speciatim diocesanorum"; "De Presbyterorum Ministerio et Vita" (accepted because couched in better Latin than "De Ministerio et Vita Presbyterorum"). A few words were altered in n. 1 (Introduction) so as to make clear that this decree concerned all priests, especially those engaged in pastoral work. The few alterations accepted in nn. 2 and 3 did not affect the general sense of the text. In n. 5 the various sacraments administered by the priest were briefly mentioned. There was a short addition to n. 6 dealing with the pastoral responsibility of priests for members of religious orders. One sentence in n. 7 stresses the responsibility of the bishop for the spiritual education of his priests. In n. 9 the obligation of recognizing the charisms of the laity was more clearly stated, and a few lines were added about the duties of the faithful towards their priests.

Once again the most difficult problem was the celibacy of the clergy. The first addition reminds us that voluntary celibacy for the sake of the kingdom of God is no monopoly of priests and members of religious orders. At the request of 110 fathers the passages from the Pastoral Letters which mention married bishops were cited (1 Tim 3:2–5; Tit 1:6). The few words about the married priests of the Eastern Church had elicited a flood of reactions. 71 of the fathers would have preferred to see no mention at all of this variation in law from fear that the brightness of celibacy might be dimmed. 68 rejected any positive address to married priests, thinking, perhaps, that their duties as husbands and fathers were the same as those of other married men, or, perhaps, that any such exhortation might be taken to imply that they had to be reminded of their duties. In contrast to this there were two fathers who wanted a special treatment of the question of married and unmarried clergy. These fathers emphasized that the two categories contained complementary aspects of the priesthood, the first representing the matrimonial aspect of the Church, the second the virginal. Finally, there were 5 fathers who wanted the Council to recognize the law current in the East as fully as it recognized the law current in the Latin Church. The suggestion was adopted and the exhortation to married priests to be good fathers and husbands was deleted. A certain number of *modi* which aimed at affirming the superiority of the celibate over the married priesthood on the level of the priesthood itself had to be turned down. Obviously such a discrimination could not be tolerated for the sacrament is indivisible and consecration to voluntary celibacy is not on the same level as the sacrament of holy orders in itself.

It was in respect of these reasons favouring celibacy that opposition became liveliest. 289 fathers rejected the distinction made in the text between theological and pastoral motives. The basic motive for celibacy, they said, is the special consecration to Christ which it embodies, and by which a man is liberated to place himhelf wholly at the service of the kingdom of God. The text was altered, therefore, along these lines. A small change, advocated by 35 fathers, was also accepted, in order to harmonize with a decision the Council had made concerning married deacons in the Latin Church. 123 fathers had wanted the Council to be content merely to mention the current canon law without explicitly assenting to it. The Commission was unable to accept this change for it affected a text approved by a considerable majority. One father proposed that the Council declare that the law of the Latin Church requiring celibacy contained an implicit vow of complete and permanent chastity. On this topic the Commission had before them an even more far-reaching proposal from the Secretary of State: the candidate for the priesthood should be asked to take an explicit and public vow, provisionally on receiving the subdiaconate and permanently on receiving the diaconate or priesthood, and this vow ought be renewed on Maundy Thursday each year. The Commission was unable to accept this proposal because it would have represented a substantial addition to a text already approved by the Council. More than 400 fathers had wanted to see a few more lines on devotion to the Mother of God, and so an addition along these lines was made to n. 18. Two suggestions were taken up affecting the next section. The first recommended study and knowledge of the documents produced by the magisterium, of the Councils especially; the second laid upon the bishops the obligation to foster more intensive theological study among some priests.

13. The voting on 2 December 1965 and final approbation
on 7 December 1965

The improved text was printed in a 136 page volume.[18] In it were the general report by Mgr. Marty (pp. 5–7), the improved text itself, with emendations in italics (pp. 9–13, 28–40, 79–92), and the detailed report on the *modi*, provided with the reasons for acceptance or rejection by the Commission (pp. 14–27, 41–78, 93–135). The Council fathers were invited to make known their opinions on the alteration made by the Commission on the basis of their examination of the *modi*. The results of the voting on 2 December 1965 were as follows:

	Present	Yes	No	Invalid
Intro. and Ch. I	2298	2291	5	2
Ch. II	2301	2262	38	1
Ch. III, n. 1	2278	2261	15	2
n. 2	2271	2243	27	1
n. 3 and Concl.	2268	2254	11	3
On the whole schema	2257	2243	11	3

And so the decree was now ready for approbation and promulgation. In its final form, but without sectional titles and without the report appended, it was printed in a boaklet of 38 pages.[19] At their public session on 7 December the assembly was invited to give its final assent. The result of this was:

Present	Yes	No
2394	2390	4

Pope Paul VI thereupon promulgated the decree according to the ritual formula.

---

[18] *Schema Decreti de Presbyterorum Ministerio et Vita, Textus recognitus et Modi a Patribus Conciliaribus propositi a Commissione de Disciplina Cleri et Populi Christiani examinati* (Typis Polyglottis Vaticanis, 1965).

[19] *Decretum de Presbyterorum Ministerio et Vita de quo agetur in Sessione publica diei 7 decembris 1965* (Typis Polyglottis Vaticanis, 1965).

Commentary on the Decree

Articles 1—6 by Friedrich Wulf
Articles 7—11 by Paul-J. Cordes
Articles 12—16 by Friedrich Wulf
Articles 17—22 by Michael Schmaus

Title. The fact that the title had to be changed so often — *De Clericis, De Sacerdotibus, De Vita et Ministerio sacerdotali, De Presbyterorum Ministerio et Vita* — throws an initial light upon the evolution of the decree. To begin with the subject under discussion was the clergy in the most general sense. In reality, however, even the first draft was concerned specially with clergy who had the care of souls. And so henceforth the decree spoke of "priests", "sacerdotes", and finally — because attention was turned to priests of "the second rank" — of "presbyters", corresponding to the traditional hierarchical ladder of bishops, presbyters and deacons, that appeared early in the Church — hinted at in the Pastoral Letters, fully developed in the letters of Ignatius. Thus the very title of the decree presents a linguistic and also a material problem of decisive importance for our understanding of the ministry in the Church.

The word "presbyter" comes to us from the vocabulary of the primitive Church. Taken over from Hellenistic Judaism where, following ancient Jewish tradition, it was used to describe the elders of the community, we find it used in the New Testament, along with the name of the bishop, to describe the office of leader.[1] As is well known to describe this office and any ministry in the Church, the word ἱερεύς *(sacerdos)* was avoided. One spoke of "teachers", "evangelists", "shepherds", "deacons" or simply of those "who labour" or are "over you" (1 Thess 5:12), and of "leaders" (Lk 22:26; Acts 15:22), but never of ἱερεῖς *(sacerdotes)*. Not until the end of the century, in a letter of Pope Clement to the Church at Corinth (*c.* 93 to 97), is the word ἱερεύς used to describe the leaders and ministers at Christian, eucharistic worship. By analogy with Old Testament priestly hierarchy,

---

[1] G. Bornkamm in *TWNT*, VI, pp. 662 ff.; W. Michaelis, *Das Ältestenamt in der christlichen Gemeinde im Lichte der Heiligen Schrift* (1954); M. Guerra y Gómez, *Episkopos y Presbyteros* (1962).

the high-priest (ἀρχιερεύς: bishop), the priests (ἱερεῖς) and the levites (λευῖται) are differentiated from the laity (ὁ λαικὸς ἄνθρωπος).[2] The use of the Latin word "sacerdos" to describe bishop and presbyter cannot be proved before the end of the 2nd century with Tertullian.

What is the explanation of this hesitancy, in spite of the fact that the leaders of the early Christian communities probably very soon assumed the presidency of liturgical assemblies, especially that of the Lord's Supper?[3] First we must note that the Christians of the earliest Churches did not feel that they were adherents of a *new* religion, or that in their assemblies they were performing actions that could be compared either with the activities of the heathen cults around them or with the Jewish temple cult. They had no temple of their own,[4] no special rites and ceremonies, no sacrifice; their leaders wore no special vestments or insignia and were not regarded as specially consecrated and hence holy persons, who alone were permitted to approach the sphere of the holy and the divine — to enter the Holy of Holies. Even at the Lord's Supper there was an atmosphere of complete normality. Quite simply: there was no place to attach the idea that one had to have, in the community of faith, priests in the cultic sense — ἱερεῖς: *sacerdotes* — as in Judaism or in the other religions.

In the primitive tradition Christ himself was not ἱερεύς. He made no claim to be a priest, and the witnesses of his life remembered him not as "priest", but as "prophet" (Mt 13:57; 21:11; Lk 1:76; 7:16; Jn 4:19; 6:14; 9:17; Acts 2:30); for there was no apparent similarity between what he had done and what the priests of the Old Testament did. After the Resurrection they called him *Kyrios*, Lord, expressing belief in his exaltation. It was only later that they became aware of the full breadth and depth of his mission. Not only had he preached the message of salvation as a prophet sent by God, but had fulfilled the promise of salvation by "giving himself up for us, a fragrant offering and sacrifice to God" (Eph 5:2, 25; Gal 2:20), becoming a "sin-offering" for us so that we might be reconciled to God (Rom 3:25; 5:18f.; 1 Jn 2:2; 4:10). This was priestly activity in a pre-eminent sense; it outstripped all that men knew of priesthood in the history of religion and of salvation. It was quite natural, therefore, that Christ should eventually become described explicitly as "priest". This was done by the author of the

---

[2] 1 Clem 40:5. This does not mean, however, that here the New Testament ministry was seen simply as following the lines of the Old Testament priesthood. The analogy merely consists in the fact that in both cases there was a true ministry of sacrifice (cf. 1 Clem 40:2 ff.), performed by those men whom God himself appointed.

[3] Not strictly demonstrable from the New Testament, but implied by later practice (*Did.* 15:1; 1 Clem 44:4).

[4] At first the Jewish Christian congregation at Jerusalem took part in the Jewish temple worship (cf. Lk 24:53; Acts 2:46; 5:42).

Letter to the Hebrews probably about A.D. 80–90 — that is, fairly late. But this author states that Christ's priesthood is unique, far superior to even the Old Testament priesthood, as reality is superior to shadows (Heb 8:5; 10:1), fulfilment and consummation to promise (Heb 9:15). Since his redemptive death on the cross Christ is the one true priest, high-priest, the priest par excellence, mediator of the new and eternal covenant (Heb 8:6; 9:15; 12:24). By a single sacrifice (Heb 9:26, 27, 28) he has reconciled men with God (Heb 7:27; 10:10) "once for all" (ἐφάπαξ). In virtue of this sacrifice he has "once for all" entered into the Holy of Holies where God alone has the right to dwell, so that those also who believe in and follow him will for ever enjoy direct access to the Father. Christ and his redemptive act have thus put an end to all previous, provisional priesthood. If there is still a priesthood in the Church it will have to be essentially distinguished from all priesthood before and apart from Christ. We must still bear in mind that of all the titles of honour given to Christ in the New Testament that of priest remains the exception: it is found only in Hebrews.

In the Lord's Supper of the early Churches the historical event of Christ's sacrificial death was commemorated and repeatedly made present and, in virtue of the Lord's own ordinance, made effectively present. Thus it came about that people saw the eucharistic action also as a cultic sacrificial act and regarded the memorial meal as a sacrificial meal. That this had already begun in the New Testament is implied by the related liturgically stylized accounts of the institution which, in the Mark-Matthew version, recall the covenant at Sinai which was sealed with sacrifice, and which, both in Mark-Matthew and in Luke-Paul, recall the atoning suffering of the Servant of God of Isaiah 53, who offered himself in place "of many".[5] It was but one short step further from this understanding of the Eucharist to calling the presidents at the Lord's Supper ἱερεῖς: sacerdotes. There was good reason for this, for these had been authorized to act by Christ himself; they acted on his commission and in his name, in his very person; but there was also great danger of misunderstanding, for they could so easily fall back into line with the traditional Old Testament priesthood, thus exposing the unique character of the New Testament priesthood to the risk of being disguised.[6] History shows that the Church failed to overcome this danger. First of all we see how the sacerdotal element in the episcopal and presbyterial offices —

[5] Cf. J. Schmid, *Das Evangelium nach Markus* (3rd ed., 1954), pp. 262–5; H. Schürmann, *Der Abendmahlsbericht Lukas 22:7–38* (1963), pp. 34–35; J. Ratzinger, "Is the Eucharist a Sacrifice?", *Concilium* 3 (1967).

[6] The problem lies here: the office of president at eucharistic worship neither follows the line of the Levitic priesthood nor can it be understood apart from some reference to it. On the question of the uniqueness of the New Testament priesthood cf. J. Colson, *Ministre de Jésus-Christ ou le sacerdoce de l'évangile* (1966).

their cultic function — quickly became the essential and definitive element in these offices, and the other elements, especially that of the commission to preach, fell disproportionately into the background.[7] In addition the exaggeration of the sacral character of sacramental ordination resulted in the subjects of the spiritual office being regarded as specially holy persons,[8] who had to keep their distance from all profane (i. e. unholy) things[9] and who were given in return a unique, almost exclusive status in the Church. The Council tried to correct this line of development by refraining, even in the title, from speaking of clerics or of *sacerdotes*, and returning to the New Testament word "presbyter", which commended itself among other things by its collegial and fraternal associations, expressed in the concept of the presbytery. This commentary will show whether or not this correction went far enough. This intrinsically laudable attempt suffers, however, from the circumstance that the translation of the Latin "presbyter" into modern European languages does not at all express what is wanted, because the corresponding loan-words while deriving from "presbyter" *(priest, prêtre, priester, presbitero)* are in fact all imbued with the notion of a cultic priesthood.[10] A change in the connotation of the word according to the mind of

---

[7] It is significant that at an early date Chrysostom entitled his tractate on the clerical state simply: περὶ ἱερωσύνης, *De sacerdotio (PG, XLVIII, 624 ff.)*. At the height of the scholastic period the three major orders were differentiated by their different closeness to the altar — to the consecrated species (Thomas Aquinas, *Summa Theologica*, Suppl., q. 37, a. 3 R). The priesthood was defined by the *potestas in corpus eucharisticum*, but the episcopal office possessed in addition the *potestas in corpus Christi mysticum (ibid.,* II–II, q. 184, a. 6 ad 1; III, q. 67 a. 2 ad 2; q. 82, a. 1 ad 4). Trent began its exposition on the sacrament of orders with these words: "Sacrifice and priesthood are, by divine ordinance, so closely linked, that both are to be found in every ordinance of salvation" *(D 1764)*.

[8] Anyone who commits a sin against them, therefore, commits a sacrilege *(CIC,* can. 119). In respect of the objective holiness of the priest the fact is significant that on the question of the effect of the sacrament of orders the first things to be mentioned are the increase of sanctifying grace and the character of orders; only then are spiritual powers mentioned. The latter find their ontological foundation in the sacramental character (thus Thomas Aquinas, *op. cit.,* Suppl., q. 35, a. 1 and 2). In the measure in which the ontological aspect was not interpreted personally, but was materialized, a "metaphysical clericalism" emerged (thus P. Fransen in H. Fries, ed., *Handbuch theologischer Grundbegriffe,* II, p. 348). Conversely, from the greatness of the spiritual powers the eminence of the objective sanctity of the ordained was deduced. Well-known in this respect is the saying of John Chrysostom: "As though already translated to heaven, as though they had already put off human nature, as though free from our human passions — so high, to such a dignity have they been raised" *(De sacerdotio,* III, 5: *PG,* XLVIII, 643).

[9] The objective, cultic sanctity of the priest is the chief basis for celibacy of the clergy. Cf. L. Hödl, "Die Lex Continentiae", *ZKT* 83 (1961), pp. 333 and 339; E. Schillebeeckx, *Der Amtszölibat* (1967), pp. 43 ff.

[10] The clearest expression of this is to be found in the term *presbyterium,* no longer understood as the college of presbyters but as the area around the altar. Only in Italian is the

213

the Council will have to be brought about through people living out in future a fresh concept of the spiritual office and its status.

With each change in title there resulted a concomitant change in the content of the decree. Originally it dealt mainly with the spiritual life, with the priest's striving to attain sanctity — as did the corresponding schema prepared at Vatican I[11] — thus resembling the various exhortations and encyclicals addressed to priests by recent Popes. Without any connection, two extra chapters were added: "On the Distribution of Priests" (Article 10 in the present decree) and "On Offices and Benefices" (now Articles 20 and 21). As early as the first session of the Co-ordinating Commission, established towards the end of the first period of the Council in January 1963, Cardinal Urbani demanded that a chapter entitled: "On Studies and Pastoral Science" (now Article 19) be added to the decree. The expansion of the title into its present form only occurred after the abridged schema had been rejected by the Council fathers (October 1964) and a more comprehensive decree had been requested. The first draft of the title spoke, however, first of the *life* and then of the *ministry* of the priest. The transposition is significant and reveals the very conscious intention of the authors: the office of the priest is to be viewed first and foremost in terms of its function and not of its status. It has a dynamic not a static nature.

PREFACE

Article 1. In this very first article, which serves as a kind of introduction, the basic outline of the image of the priest as sketched in the decree is visible. It confirms the tendency apparent in the title itself: not the consecration and sanctity of the priest, but his ministry and function within the Church are the things which stand in the foreground of study. We detect, however, as in Article 28 of the Constitution on the Church, a certain uncertainty and vagueness in terminology, which leads us to conclude that the theological concept of the priesthood presented by the decree is not quite homogeneous.

The concept of *ordo*[12] in the introductory words of the article comes from Roman official terminology and originally signified a position of leadership over against the people. It was adopted into ecclesiastical usage by Tertullian. From the 4th century onwards it was also used in the sense of grades of rank and of consecration within the Church's official hierarchy. An earlier draft

word "presbyter" in the title of the decree not translated by the corresponding modern loan-word. The title of the decree is translated *Ministerio e Vita dei sacerdoti*.

[11] "De vita et Honestate Clericorum", *Collectio Lacensis: Acta et Decreta Sacrorum Conciliorum Recentiorum*, VII, pp. 649 ff.

[12] Cf. P. Fransen, "Ordo", *LTK*, VII, cols. 1212–20.

had spoken of the "priceless" *(inaestimabilis)* dignity of the priestly state. This epithet, like many others of the same species, was deleted in order to destroy the false nimbus with which in the past Catholics have tended to invest the priesthood. As the post-conciliar years have seen this destruction reach the proportions of a radical crisis of order, such an epithet would by now have appeared quite anachronistic.

In the second half of the article a first attempt is made to describe the essence of the priest's office: this is conferred through ordination and the mission received from the bishop; it consists in the service of Christ the teacher, priest and king; it is a participation in his ministry and thus includes the competence upon earth to build up the Church throughout the ages to become the People of God, the body of Christ and the temple of the Holy Spirit. One or two questions must be asked at this point. What is the relationship between ordination and mission?[13] Is mission canonical mission *(missio canonica)*, which is an act of the power of jurisdiction, or is it something more fundamental as in the office of bishop — mission being understood as belonging along with ordination to the constitutive element of the office (independently of its concrete exercise), as a direct participation in the mission of Christ, so that it is already given with the sacramental conferring of the office?[14] The text in itself allows of both interpretations. Comparing this text with other conciliar texts, however, it appears that, from the theological point of view, there is no essential distinction between the office of bishop and that of presbyter. It is said of presbyters as of bishops that they are "consecrated by the anointing of the Holy Spirit and sent by Christ."[15] It is explicitly emphasized, moreover, that "all priests,

[13] In this context *ordinatio* and *consecratio* are interchangeable, as the ordination rite in the Roman *Pontificale* shows. This passage of the conciliar text makes it even clearer by adding the phrase "sacra ordinatio".

[14] Quite simply, the content of the episcopal office is said to be participation in the mission of Christ (Constitution on the Church, art. 21), and an explicit distinction is made between this fundamental, sacramentally conferred mission and canonical mission *(ibid.,* art. 24). On the question of how in this case the sacramentally conferred mission, embracing all three offices of Christ including the pastoral office, is related to canonical mission, and what the precise content of the latter is, or, in other words, on the question of whether the classical distinction between *potestas ordinis* and *potestas iurisdictionis* does not require re-thinking, cf. K. Rahner in his commentary on the Dogmatic Constitution of the Church in vol. I of this series. In view of what has been argued here can one still say, following *CIC,* can. 109, without qualification: "The power of order is conferred through ordination and in consequence of the indelible character is irremovable. Pastoral power, however, is conferred by canonical mission and is removable" (K. Mörsdorf, "Grundfragen der Reform des kanonischen Rechtes" in *Münchener Theologische Zeitschrift* 15 (1964), p. 8; *ibid.,* in *LTK,* VI, cols. 218 ff.)? This may be doubted because the power of order — as participation in the indivisible mission of Christ which includes his pastoral office — and the pastoral power cannot be adequately distinguished from one another.

[15] *Presbyterorum ordinis,* art. 12, sec. 2.

together with bishops, so share in one and the same priesthood and ministry of Christ that the very unity of their consecration and mission requires their hierarchical communion with the order of bishops". [16] If, therefore, this passage lays special emphasis on mission by the bishop, this need not necessarily refer to the *missio canonica* (although comparison with Article 17, which shows that the priest shares in the bishop's office through ordination and canonical mission, implies that it does). It might equally intend to stress that the sacramentally conferred mission of the office of presbyter is always and only a participation in the mission of the bishop (who as successor of the apostles [17] alone possesses the authority of Christ [18]), and can be theologically understood only in that sense. In what follows we shall frequently and in more detail refer to this union between the order of presbyter and the order of bishop (Articles 2 and 5 and especially 7). Participation in the *mission* of Christ is the same thing as participation in his *ministry (ministerium)*. This ministry, according to the conciliar text, embraces the three well-known offices: the teaching office (prophetic office), the priestly office (office of sanctification) and the royal office (pastoral office). [19] These attempt to represent the redemptive work of Christ in terms of its three main functions. This is evidenced in Scripture, [20] has been familiar to the Catholic tradition since the time of the Fathers, but was first systematized by Calvin. Through the mediation of Lutheran theology it was taken into Catholic theology in this fixed form towards the end of the 18the century, and has gradually, found its way into papal doctrinal statements. [21] Throughout all of its documents Vatican II built the doctrine of the priesthood upon this concept, [22] in order to retrieve this from its centuries-old restriction to the realm of cult. Praiseworthy as this is, there is no clear reference anywhere to the fact that the so-called three offices can be distinguished only partially, and are by no means meant to be exhaustive (Scripture and tradition fly to a multitude of titles in order to grasp and express the richness of the mission and commis-

---

[16] *Ibid.*, art. 7, sec. 1.

[17] Dogmatic Constitution on the Church, arts. 20 and 28; *Presbyterorum ordinis*, art. 2, sec. 2.

[18] Article 21 of the Dogmatic Constitution on the Church speaks of the "fullness of the sacrament of orders" and of "the high priesthood" and of "the apex of the sacred ministry".

[19] Cf. M. Schmaus, "Ämter Christi", *LTK*, I, cols. 457 ff.

[20] A favourite text in reference to the conferring of the three offices of Christ upon the apostles is Mt 28:19 f.

[21] Cf. J. Fuchs, *Magisterium, Ministerium, Regimen. Vom Ursprung einer ekklesiologischen Trilogie* (1941). On the application of this trio in papal documents, see principally *Mystici Corporis; AAS* 35 (1943), p. 209; cf. also addresses of Pope Pius XII on the threefold office: *AAS* 46 (1954), pp. 303 ff.; pp. 666 ff.

[22] Dogmatic Constitution on the Church, arts. 25–28; 34 ff. (for the laity); *Presbyterorum ordinis*, arts. 1, 4–6, 7.

sion of Christ). The boundaries between the titles are fluid; in many ways they overlap. For example, one might hand over the teaching office to the pastoral office; likewise there is a reciprocity between the teaching and the priestly office: the word of preaching has a sacramental character and the sacramental action becomes efficacious only in and through the word. Probably it is precisely at this point in the co-ordination of word and sacrament that we see the characteristic theological basic structure of the redemptive activity of Christ in the Church. A final word is said in this introductory article on the theology of the New Testament priesthood: participation in the mission and ministry of Christ is so deep and so real that by his action the priest, as servant of the Redeemer, the Teacher, the Priest and the King, contributes to the building up of the Church on earth into the people of God, the body of Christ, the temple of the Holy Spirit.[23] The "with Christ" (σὺν χριστῷ), which in the New Testament denotes community of life and destiny with the crucified, risen and glorified Lord,[24] the unity between him and his many brethren in the fellowship of one body, the Church, assumes sacramental visibility and palpability in the ministry instituted by Christ himself. Finally, it is always Christ himself who effects redemption in and through his ministers, but he does this truly through them, so that their ministry and operation within the Church is indispensable. In the concluding sentence at least a hint is given about the increased difficulties of the pastor in the turmoil of the times we live in. If one reflects on the crisis which has fallen upon the priesthood so soon after the Council (for theological, anthropological, sociological and pastoral reasons), then it would seem that one or two more energetic interventions would not have been out of place, in order to draw attention — as is done chiefly in Article 22 — to the crisis that was already simmering at that time. The original tone of the decree was chiefly designed to remind the priest of his duty to lead a model life.[25]

---

[23] This idea is frequently expressed, with reference perhaps to 2 Cor 10:8; 13:10. It is essential to the Catholic understanding of the sacramental ministry.

[24] Cf. W. Grundmann, "σὺν χριστῷ", *TWNT*, VII, pp. 780 ff.

[25] Cardinal Alfrink in his intervention of 15 October 1964 and Cardinal Döpfner in his of 15 October 1965. The latter devoted a whole section to this topic.

The Priesthood in the Mission of the Church

Article 2. The first chapter of the decree (Articles 2 and 3) can be traced to the frequently expressed request that the separate statements on the ministry and work of presbyters be prefaced by a concise theology of the priesthood — although such a theology had already been provided in Chapter 3 of the Constitution on the Church, particularly in Article 28. This preface was to expound the nature and the necessity of the official sacramental priesthood in the Church in contrast to the general priesthood of all the faithful, and describe the relationship of the priest to the laity and his position in the world.

The title itself is significant, for it links the priesthood with mission, that is, with the missionary task of the Church. This immediately indicates that the priesthood in the Church too is primarily missionary in character.

Article 2 begins with a statement about the one and unique priesthood of Christ. This too is defined in the language of St. John's Gospel in terms of the two factors: consecration and mission.[26] It is here that the consecration and mission of the priesthood in the Church find their origin and their model. What is the substance of these two factors and how are they related to each other? The basic concept is undoubtedly that of mission; but mission must not be conceived in a purely external sense, as a positivistic jurisdictional act that does not affect the person. It is a personal happening which creates a spiritual relationship between the one sent and the one to whom he is sent, and confers the status of a representative with corresponding authority. If even human commissioning posits varying degrees of existential-ontological reality, how much more does commissioning by God! He who is

---

[26] According to our decree, art. 12, sec. 2, "sanctification" in Jn 10:36 means the same as "consecration". The same passage had already been cited in the Dogmatic Constitution on the Church, art. 28.

sent by God acts with the authority and power of God. God's call gives what it commands, and so the one sent is, *ipso facto,* empowered and equipped to perform that which he is commissioned to do. This applies pre-eminently to Christ, the eschatological messenger and ambassador, *the* one sent by God, who stands in closest fellowship of life with the Father. Thus John the Evangelist, with the help of the category of *mission,* is able to expound and illumine the whole (priestly) redemptive activity of Jesus.[27] What then does consecration signify in addition to all this? According to Jn 10:36, "sanctification" (= "consecration") denotes nothing other than the election and setting apart of Jesus by God, to fulfil his mandate and mission. (In practice it is co-extensive with mission.) We can, however, consider the special fitting out, and filling with grace, which was granted to Jesus to enable him to fulfil his Messianic task. (Even this is not to be separated from mission.) This is probably what the decree has chiefly in mind when, in note 1 to the first sentence, it cites Mt 3:16; Lk 4:18; Acts 4:27; 10:38. According to these passages, "sanctification" or "consecration" denotes that anointing with the Spirit, by which the man Jesus was endowed with the Spirit of God and with special gifts of the Spirit appropriate to his mission. This anointing with the Spirit took place — really and symbolically — at his baptism. This explains its more exact meaning also.[28] Jesus' baptism came at the beginning of his public activity. The anointing with the Spirit which he received on that occasion is thus linked with his prophetic mission, the preaching of the eschatological message and the announcement of its fulfilment. Thus did Jesus interpret himself when he read from the book of Isaiah (61:1 f.; 58:6) in the synagogue at Nazareth, and applied to himself what Isaiah said about the mission of the prophet (Lk 4:18 f.). And this was how the early Church, too, understood things, as Peter's sermon outside the house of the centurion Cornelius proves (Acts 10:37 f.). Jesus, the one who is sent, is primarily the revealer and preacher, the "great prophet" (Lk 7:16). To this mission corresponds first the bearing witness to, the manifesting of, the love of the Father.[29] But as his word was essentially a deed-word (he himself was God's final, irrevocable deed-word to man and the only valid reply of man to God) and his witness the witness of life, therefore the sacrifice of his life was all part and parcel of his mission: it sealed the word of the Father and the response of man in blood — the perfect *martyria.* Correctly, therefore, the

---

[27] For him Christ is the "one sent" par excellence, through whom man, living in this world's darkness, receives the light — i. e. faith (cf. Jn 1:4–9). In the synoptic gospels the concept of the mission of Christ in the sense of his messianic function is found less frequently (cf. Mt 15:24; Mk 9:36; and the parables like Mk 12:1 ff.).
[28] Cf. I. de la Potterie, "L'onction du Christ", *NRT* 80 (1958), pp. 225 ff.; summarized in *Vocabulaire de Théologie Biblique* (1962), p. 720.
[29] In St. John's Gospel the concepts *mission* and *witness* are correlative.

primitive Christian kerygma, recalling certain words of our Lord (Mk 10:38; Lk 12:50), connected the anointing with the Spirit, manifested in the baptism, with his death on the cross (Acts 4:27; Rom 6:6 ff.). What happened on the cross was the sacrifice of life in the Spirit and the acceptance of this sacrifice by the Father in the Spirit. And so priestly action in the sense of sacrifice and cult is also part of Jesus' mission. Hence the Letter to the Hebrews (3:1) admonishes Christians to look to "Jesus, the apostle and high priest of our confession" — referring no doubt to the solemn confession of Jesus by the congregation at the Eucharist.

The text of the decree then goes on to say that the Lord Jesus "has made his whole Mystical Body share in the anointing by the Spirit with which he himself has been anointed". This happened par excellence in the event of Pentecost, described in Acts 1:5, 8, as the baptism of the assembled faithful with the Holy Spirit (reception into the baptism of Christ is death in the sense of Rom 6:3–6) and as the descent of the Holy Spirit in order to impart his power for the sake of the witness all are called upon to give (analogous to the anointing of Jesus "with the Holy Spirit and with power", Acts 10:38). For this reason the whole body of Christ, the Church, as the place of the sacramental redemptive presence and activity, is a "spiritual house" (temple), and all the faithful, united in one fellowship with Christ, are a "holy, royal priesthood", equipped and called to "offer spiritual sacrifices (i. e. in the Spirit) acceptable to God through Christ" and to "declare the wonderful deeds of him who called you . . ." (1 Pet 2:5, 9). All of the redeemed are empowered "to enter the sanctuary by the blood of Jesus"[30] who is our "great priest over the house of God" (Heb 10:19, 21), to speak freely with our Father and to offer themselves and their lives to him in sacrifice. Here again, in the last section of the article, the decree lays the stress upon the mission of the Church, upon its prophetic mission, the basis of which is the confession of Jesus (1 Pet 3:15) and the testimony of Jesus (Rev 19:10). The priesthood of the Church must possess, first and foremost, a prophetic character: its basic commission and fundamental authorization is to preach, in the power of the Spirit, the one and ultimately valid redemptive act of Christ, which was performed vicariously for the whole world. This preaching, because authoritative, is sacramentally efficacious.

This allows the decree to move on to statements about the special, official priesthood. Unfortunately the spiritual, theological unity between the official priesthood and the priesthood of the Church is not made sufficiently clear. It is not stated that the fundamental priesthood in the Church is that of the Church, the whole People of God, and that hence the official priesthood, in spite of its institution by Christ — not by the Church —, finds its immediate

---

[30] Reference to the Eucharist.

theological setting within the priesthood of the Church. It represents the priesthood of the Church and makes this palpable in the sacramental and social reality of the Church. The special powers given by Christ to the priest in the sacrament of holy orders, and not possessed by every member, are primarily powers of the Church. They are given to him, not as an individual official, but as representative of the Church, and hence only through the mediation of the Church. (The ordaining bishop, as successor of the apostles and member of the college of bishops, acts not only in the name and person of Christ, but in the name of the Church and as its representative.) Through him the Church fulfils her essential nature, her priestly mission, as through a sacramental instrument.[31] St. Augustine beautifully expresses the power to remit sins in the name of Christ in these words: "So does the Church act in blessed hope through this troublous life; and this Church, symbolized in its generality *(figurata generalitate)*, was personified in the Apostle Peter *(ecclesiae personam gerebat)*, on account of the primacy of his apostleship. For, as regards his personality, he was by nature one man, by grace one Christian, by still more abounding grace one, and yet also, the first apostle; but when it was said to him, 'I will give unto thee the keys of the kingdom of heaven . . .' (Mt 16:19), he represented *(significabat)* the universal Church . . . The Church, therefore, which is founded in Christ received from him the keys of the kingdom of heaven in the person of Peter, that is to say, the power of binding and loosing sins. For what the Church is essentially *(per proprietatem)* in Christ, such representatively *(per significationem)* is Peter in the rock *(petra)*; and in this representation Christ is to be understood as the Rock, Peter as the Church."[32] The collegial nature of the priestly office likewise is to be seen in terms of its ecclesiological character.[33] The college of bishops under its head, the Pope, as successor of the apostolic college under Peter, is a sign of the unity of the Church and of the foundation of its unity in Christ. Insofar as the presbyter is incorporated and remains in this college — in virtue of the unity and link between the episcopal and the presbyterial offices —, he too represents the Church, the people of God, as well as Christ the one Lord of the Church.

The idea that the special priesthood sacramentally and socially embodies and represents the priestly Church, becoming its organ of fulfilment, is scarcely expressed in this article — as we have already remarked. The office is first viewed in itself, in terms of its own peculiar authority and dignity, for the sake of the Church and her members, it is true ("in order to join them

---

[31] Cf. K. Rahner, "The Various Sacraments as Acts in which the Church's Nature is Fulfilled", *The Church and the Sacraments*, Quaestiones Disputatae 9 (1963), Part II: pp. 76 ff.

[32] *On St. John*, 124, 5 (PL, XXXV, 1973 f.; CC, XXXVI, pp. 684 f.).

[33] Cf. Dogmatic Constitution on the Church, art. 22.

together in one body"; "they would perform their priestly office publicly for men in the name of Christ"), but without any explicit reference to the mystery of the priestly Church. Its relational, executive, and representational character is restricted to its reference to Christ ("qui sacerdotale officio in nomine Christi fungerentur"; "the priestly office shares in the authority by which Christ himself builds up, sanctifies, and rules his Body"; the peculiar stamp of their office makes them "so configured to Christ the Priest that they can act in the person of Christ the Head"). Thus the priest is distinguished from all of the rest of the faithful; he is a member of the hierarchical Church — sharing in the consecration and mission of the bishop, although always subordinate to him and dependent upon him in the exercise of his ministry[34] —, and as such stands on the side of Christ the Head, facing the Church of the faithful. However true this may be,[35] it is nonetheless one-sided: it isolates the priest, as history has shown. This, too, is no doubt the reason why in this article (sections 2 and 3) the traditional, rather static image of the priest, determined by the sacerdotal-cultic idea and the concept of the power of order and of absolution, predominates: "These ministers in the society of the faithful would be able by the sacred power of their order to offer sacrifice and remit sins", says the text, following Trent. The essence of the sacramental priesthood is seen not in the missionary mandate to preach and sanctify, but in ordination and the character conferred by order, the ontic preconditions of spiritual power.[36]

This view, however, is significantly supplemented in the fourth section of this article, which brings into the foreground the missionary aspect, the commission to preach and to sanctify addressed to the New Testament ministry. Here, too, the general priesthood of all the faithful and the special priesthood of the sacramental order are traced back to their ultimate unity in a universal view. For the first time we see how radically the priesthood of the New Testament is distinguished from all other non-Christian priesthoods, even that of the Old Covenant, and how much it has been turned into a spiritual-personal thing, an offering of the heart and of the person's whole existence — adumbrated by the prophets of the Old Testament —, and how much all priesthood has lost its autonomy as a result of the one and only priesthood of Christ. The New Testament ministry derives essentially from the office of the apostles.[37] According to St. Paul, who is quoted at this point

---

[34] *Ibid.*, art. 28, sec. 1.

[35] Cf. O. Semmelroth, "Das priesterliche Gottesvolk und seine amtlichen Führer", *Concilium* 4 (1968); id., *Das geistliche Amt* (1965).

[36] The character of order can also be understood functionally as an irrevocable setting apart and authorization for Christ's mission.

[37] Hence it is not accidentally that Peter (1 Pet 5:1) compares his apostolic ministry to that of the presbyters of the congregation, in that he calls himself their co-presbyter.

(Rom 15:16), the apostolic ministry in its entire scope is a holy priestly ministry (his words are deliberately taken from the cultic sphere and can be understood only so in the context: λειτουργὸς Χριστοῦ; ἱερουργεῖν τὸ εὐαγγέλιον; προσφορὰ εὐπρόσδεκτος), a ministry of the gospel, of the word, of the message of God which has been declared to men in Jesus Christ[38]. Fundamentally it is a ministry (λειτουργία) of *the* minister, Christ himself (Heb 8:2, 6), whom Paul, called by God to do so, represents. The object of this message is to lead the heathen (ἔθνη), the nations — specially entrusted to Paul — to faith so that they may become a sacrifice sanctified in the Holy Spirit, well-pleasing to God. This terminology of sacrifice is justified; for in the obedience of faith a man denies himself, renounces sin, selfishness, concupiscence, inordinate trust in his own strength, and yields himself to the merciful and loving God, confident in his forgiveness. Or, again in St. Paul's language, he presents his whole existence "as a living sacrifice, holy and acceptable to God" (Rom 12:1).[39] He is able to do this only because Christ the sole mediator has reconciled him to God by the sacrifice of his life upon the cross. The sacrifice of Christ on the cross is the basis of his trust and his hope. Now, when the priest, the apostle and minister of Jesus Christ, to whom "the sacred task of the gospel" has been entrusted, solemnly proclaims the Lord's death in the Eucharist (1 Cor 11:26) and presents it before God in the name of the Church, then not only his own offering, but that of the faithful is united — through his ministry which is exercised as representative of all the people — with the one sacrifice of Christ, and the Church presents herself, in and with her immolated Head, to the Father.[40] In virtue of the sacrifice of her Lord on the cross she has become his body, participating in all that he is and does. Thus the Eucharist only makes plain, in symbolic and sacramental efficacy, the goal towards which the whole apostolic ministry of the priest is directed: preaching the faith and pastoral care as well as administration of the sacraments. It makes it plain that "the whole society of the redeemed, the assembly and fellowship of the saints are offered as an all-embracing sacrifice to God through Christ the high-priest" (Augustine). This demonstrates the height of priestly action: by his ministry the priest contributes to the handing over the kingdom, the sovereignty and all things, by the Son to the Father, at the end of history (1 Cor 15:24), so that "God may be all in all" (*ibid.*, 15:28). The priest's ministry has two foci: the pasch

[38] Similarly Phil 2:17: "Even if I am to be poured as a libation upon the sacrificial offering of your faith".

[39] Cf. P. Seidensticker, *Lebendiges Opfer (Rom 12:1). Ein Beitrag zur Theologie des heiligen Paulus* (1954).

[40] Cf. H. U. v. Balthasar, "Die Messe als Opfer der Kirche?", *Spiritus Creator. Skizzen zur Theologie,* III (1967), pp. 166–217; T. Schneider, "Das Opfer der Messe als Selbsthingabe Christi und der Kirche", *GL* 41 (1968), pp. 90–106.

223

of Christ, from which all that he can effect as a priest flows, and the glory of the eschatological kingdom, which proclaims the glory of God. His life moves between these two things.

What are the chief marks of the theological image of the priest as sketched by Article 2 of the decree, and how does this image differ from that of Catholic tradition — at least of the Middle Ages? The following are probably the decisive points, although they may not always be worked out with complete clarity and logic. [41]

1. Once again the uniqueness of Christ's redemptive mediation — in the sense of Hebrews — is taken really seriously. Christ alone is the priest, and his priesthood is an eschatological priesthood. He is a priest because he was raised up on the cross and passed through death to heaven where he approaches the Father for us (Heb 9:12, 24 f.). The primary purpose of the priesthood in the Church must therefore be to preach the salvation accomplished once for all by Christ (so that "men knowingly, freely, and gratefully accept what God has achieved perfectly through Christ, and manifest it in their whole lives" — Article 2, last paragraph). But because this preaching is given authoritatively in the name and in the person of Christ, it signifies also a being "with Christ", in Christ it becomes redemptively efficacious; and because Christ's word was always a response of obedience to his Father's commission (most explicit in the *martyria* on the cross), therefore the making present of the Lord's death, proclaimed in the Eucharist (1 Cor 11:26) includes also the co-sacrifice of the Church, the body of the Lord, wherein the priest acts as the Church's representative (a fact that has at times become lost sight of in our present-day emphasis on the sole mediatorship of Christ).

2. Whereas from the Middle Ages until Vatican II the presbyterate was seen as the fundamental priestly order, to which something extra was added by jurisdiction in order to produce the episcopate, now it is the episcopate that is seen as basic, the presbyterate being a participation in the episcopate as the plenitude of the official ministry.

3. The one-sided cultic character of the Catholic priesthood has been absorbed into the wider apostolic ministry, which has found expression above all in the doctrine of the three offices of Christ. In the process the linking of word and sacrament has pointed to a deeper theological structure of priestly operation. As a result, too, the missionary character of the New

---

[41] Cf. on what has been said here, the following works which take up and develop the statements of Vatican II (or have anticipated them): K. Rahner, "Priesterliche Existenz", *GL* 17 (1942), pp. 155–71; *ibid., Theologische Überlegungen zum Priesterbild von heute und morgen* (1968); *Das moderne Priesterbild. Dogmatische Grundlagen des priesterlichen Selbstverständnisses* (1958); J. Ratzinger, "Zur Frage nach dem Sinn des priesterlichen Dienstes", *GL* 41 (1968), book 5.

Testament ministry, which is traced back to its origin in the mission of the apostles, has once again become more strongly stressed. This corrects the one-sided concept of holy orders as a static, personal prerogative of the priest.

4. The tracing back of the general and the special priesthood to their deeper theological basis of unity has not been entirely successful. It is true that the general priesthood of all the baptized has become clearer than in any earlier theological literature. It is presented as a genuine, effective participation in the priesthood of Christ, although obviously the mode of this participation is qualitatively differentiated from the participation appropriate to the special priesthood;[42] and it is also explained how the priestly operation both of the official ministry and of the laity are brought into a unity or made to complement one another in the celebration of the eucharist or in the field of the apostolate;[43] but it is never made sufficiently clear that the fundamental priesthood is that of the Church, the community of those who believe in Christ, and hence that the special priesthood essentially grows out of the mystery of the priestly Church, without simply being under the control of the Church.

Article 3. This article makes plain that the new image of the priest favoured by the Council and sketched above, was not always consistently maintained. The traditional theology of the priesthood was never quite authentically integrated into the new view of the Council.

This article deals with the correct relationship of the priest to the world and to men, as this arises on the one hand out of his hieratic office and on the other from his apostolic commission. As a result of an exaggerated concept of the dignity of the priest (the consecrated man of God), in the past the priest was often far too much isolated from the people. As mediator of redemption and forgiver of sins he stood above the people; and he was to be a model for men in all things. In contrast now the necessity of greater closeness between the pastor and the faithful is stressed — and for theological reasons. Like Christ he has been sent from the Father to men and is man's appointed representative in the presence of God. For this reason, as St. Paul said of himself, he must be "all things to all men, in order that all might be saved". Nonetheless his position in the world remains ambivalent. "By their vocation and ordination, priests of the New Testament are indeed set apart in a certain sense within the midst of God's people" (for that reason he must become even less conformed to the world than other Christians), but

---

[42] Dogmatic Constitution on the Church, art. 10; *Presbyterorum Ordinis,* art. 2, sec. 1.
[43] The Eucharist: *Presbyterorum ordinis,* art. 2, sec. 4; the apostolate: Dogmatic Constitution on the Church, art. 34; Decree on Laity, art. 3.

at the same time he must live among men, meet them as his brothers, and share in their lot.

The article expresses this rather pompously and piously, using arguments that are not free from a paternalism that has theological and religious roots. Even the introduction uses an argument that is theologically suspect: Hebrew 5:1 is quoted *verbatim*, and although this verse occurs over and over again in traditional theology of the priesthood, it is surprising to find it cited by the Council in this context. Hebrews 5:1 is speaking unambiguously about the Aaronic priesthood which came to an end with Christ. The New Testament priesthood is orientated solely upon Christ, whose priesthood is no earthly, temporal priesthood, but a heavenly, eschatological, eternal priesthood ("Now if he were on earth, he would not be a priest at all" Heb 8:4).[44] The definitive thing, therefore, about the priest of Christ is not that he has been "taken from among men" (this would make his priesthood merely from below, from men); the precondition of his priesthood is, rather, that he has become a new man through baptism. For Aaron, genealogy was indispensable, for the priest of Christ, the indispensable thing is descent by grace (mission) from Christ who "has become a priest, not according to a legal requirement concerning bodily descent but by the power of an indestructible life" (Heb 7:16). Because Christ alone "is able for all time to save those who draw near to God" (Heb 7:25), the role of the priest in the Church can only be that of a minister of the one priest who is Christ, and the priest's function to stand ready to fulfil Christ's priestly mission of redemption. His priesthood possesses no kind of autonomy. The following sentences of the article, which remind us that Christ is the model to be copied by his apostles, were also theologically erroneous in their original draft. They showed how the author of the text took as his starting point too exalted a notion of the dignity of the priesthood. The too direct parallel that was drawn here between the priest and Christ, who was sent by the Father from the heights of divine majesty into the world of men, suggested the notion that the priest has to climb down from the heights of his consecrated status to meet the men who are entrusted to his care.[45] The present text does not indeed allow of this interpretation, but the image of the Good Shepherd is not sufficient by itself to portray the relationship between priest and faithful. From the theological point of view it would have been more fitting to recall at this point the general priesthood of all believers, the priesthood of the Church, through which both priests and laity are entrusted with the same mission, and which

---

[44] The chief thing to be expounded is the intention of the Letter to the Hebrews, as has been shown by F. J. Schierse in *Verheissung und Heilsvollendung. Zur theologischen Grundfrage des Hebräerbriefes* (1955).

[45] Thus Cardinal J. Döpfner in his intervention of 15 October 1965.

unites both as brothers in a common effort. Such a conception is in harmony with a Church of the faithful, a community Church, to which we are drawing closer and closer at the present moment; but the article still proceeds one-sidedly from the traditional folk-Church, a Church of leaders and those who are led. Other conciliar statements — even in this same decree — go much further in correcting this inadequate concept.[46]

[46] Cf. Dogmatic Constitution on the Church, chap. IV, art. 32, esp. sections 3 and 4; *Presbyterorum ordinis*, art. 9, esp. section 1.

The Ministry of Priests

I. PRIESTLY FUNCTIONS

Article 4. Chapter II of this decree begins by naming the three offices. As we have said (Article 1), this does not intend to provide an exhaustive statement on the priestly ministry or its theological structure. The Council wanted, rather, in this way to depict merely the whole wide scope of the priestly commission. The order in which the offices are listed, however, is not without significance. The commission to preach comes first. The Dogmatic Constitution on the Church (and independently the Decree on the Bishops' Pastoral Office in the Church) gives only the very general reason that the preaching of the gospel is "among the principal duties of bishops";[47] but this decree probes deeper. It tries at least to make a start with a concise but meaty theology of the word, of preaching. Preaching — faith — the Church (community of the faithful) are seen in their close connection. The kerygma of the priest, whose office can be described as a "ministry of the gospel" (cf. Rom 15:16), is the kerygma of the Church. It emerges out of the faith of the Church and her tradition; it puts this faith into words and is addressed first of all to the Church herself, to the community of the faithful, in order to strengthen the bond of faith as the bond of her unity. In those places, too, where it is a missionary word, addressed to the "nations" or the "heathen", those who do not believe, it is not only borne by the Church, but has for its aim the awakening of faith and the creation of communities of believers, the increase of the people of God, the building up of the Church as the body of Christ. Thus in actuality preaching is the start of all priestly activity as it is its centre also; for in the kerygma of the Church as the society of believers the Lord himself, crucified, and risen, the one who unites all in faith and creates unity, is effectively present.

On those terms the priest must be aware of himself not only as the servant

---

[47] Dogmatic Constitution on the Church, art. 35; Decree on the Bishops' Pastoral Office, art. 12.

of Christ, who commissioned him, but also and precisely as commissioner and representative of the Church, whose faith he has to preach. This ecclesial aspect of the priestly ministry is inadequately expressed at this point — as throughout the decree. It is true that there are several references to the priest's duty to preach, but the source of this duty, according to what the decree says, is solely the commission of the Lord (Mk 16:15) to the individual officials, who stand over against the laity of the Church and to whom they give a share in "the gospel truth in which they themselves rejoice in the Lord", as though they possessed the truth and had control of it. [48] Such a notion forces us to suspect that the authors of this article thought of preaching primarily as imparting knowledge, handing on dogmatic statements, as concerned with the correctness of the faith. But the tenor of the decree as a whole tends, rather, to stress the existential faith of the priest, for his word ought indeed to arouse and nourish faith in the hearts of men. "The task of priests is not to teach their own wisdom but God's Word, and to summon all men urgently to conversion and to holiness." The priest properly fulfils his task of preaching only if he himself is imbued with faith and speaks out of his experience of faith. He should be more of a mystic than a teacher if he would utter "the Word of the living God" in the Church and let its sacramental effect be known.

This applies above all to preaching within the liturgy, especially at the celebration of the Eucharist. This would have been the place to speak of the interrelation of word and sacrament and demonstrate their deep unity. [49] Only a hint of this is given. However, the last sentence of the article reads: "In this celebration (the Mass), the proclamation of the death and resurrection of the Lord is inseparably joined to the response of the people who hear, and to the very offering whereby Christ ratified the New Testament in his blood." This could be developed into a theology of the double polarity of the unity of word and sacrament, and might have been made the centre of gravity of the article.

Mention is made of the various modes and occasions of preaching the faith and special mention is made of the difficulty of preaching today. What is said goes no further than the remark that "such preaching must not present God's Word in a general and abstract fashion only, but it must apply the

---

[48] That our interpretation has not gone off the rails is shown by the original draft of this passage: "The presbyters are obliged to share out with all whatever they have of faith and of grace, and all the fullness they possess in the Lord."

[49] On the sense in which preaching, understood in terms of redemptive theology, can be made the fundamental concept of the priestly ministry, under which even the cult, the sacrifice of the Mass and the administration of the sacrament, would be subsumed, cf. K. Rahner, "Priesterliche Existenz", loc. cit.; id., Theologische Überlegungen zum Priesterbild heute und morgen (1968).

perennial truth of the gospel to the concrete circumstances of life". The whole burden of the problem as it has emerged since the Council is never disclosed. The Council could not yet see that we are no longer concerned with this or that detail in the fabric of the faith, nor yet with finding a modern language adapted to the conceptual and experiential world of modern man, but with the foundations of faith — of faith in God itself. At all events this was not seen. The hermeneutic question both in respect of the discovery of biblical and historical-dogmatic truth and in respect of linguistic articulation of transcendent (divine) truths in general scarcely appeared as a subject of debate; but here lies the crux of the problem for the preacher of today.

Article 5. According to the decree and to every related statement of the Council, the substance of the priestly office in the narrower cultic sense is the work of sanctification. The priest is a minister of the work of sanctification, founded by God in Christ and continuing through all ages. He himself, therefore, must be *consecrated* and *sanctified* in order to be able to act as minister and instrument of the holy and sanctifying God. According to this article, his ministry through the sacraments must be conceived along the same lines.

True as this view is — and it is the view of tradition —, it leaves a few questions open and requires a little supplementation. Is the work of sanctification a matter only for the *priestly* office and not also for the *preaching* office, if preaching is to be more than just handing on objective truth? That which the sacraments signify and symbolically contain — the *res sacramenti* — can be obtained even apart from the sacraments: in every act of faith, hope and love. It is precisely to this that preaching ought to lead us. Not less than a sacrament, it is an offer of grace; for this, too, is not grace itself, but merely its offer, requiring free acceptance by a recipient, in faith, hope and love. From the first section of this article one could all too easily form the impression that man's sanctification is too exclusively bound up with the reception of the sacraments. It is not made sufficiently clear, that the sacraments are but the socially palpable form, instituted or inaugurated by Christ (through his institution of the Church), the visibility of the mediation of redemption as rooted in the sacramental character of the Church, which remains fundamentally and essentially tied to faith. What is missing from this article is a clear, if short, exposition of the relationship between faith and the sacraments.[50] In its final version it could mislead non-theologians into conceiving the sacraments in too materialistic a way, especially as the text stresses only the ordination of the priest as a precondition

---

[50] Cf. K. Rahner, "Personal and Sacramental Piety", *Theological Investigations*, II, pp. 109–133.

of the administration of the sacraments (is mission required only for preaching?), as though a "holy" person were required in order to hand on the grace of Christ. Of course none of this is directly stated. We merely draw attention to the danger of a false interpretation of the text — and practice proves how necessary such a warning is. There can be no doubt, however, that the decisively important personal aspect of the process of sanctification receives very short shrift in this article. We might mention also, that the work of the priest as a liturgical minister, as leader of the congregation at prayer (adoration, praise, thanksgiving and supplication) and sacrifice (Eucharist) is insufficiently expounded (Article 2, sec. 4 and 5, did, however, discuss this in respect of sacrifice). This might also be the reason why here, too, as in what precedes, nothing is said about the sacraments as self-realizations of the Church, as redemptive events in which not only the administrator and recipient as individuals, but the Church as such, essentially participates. It is precisely in the ecclesiological interpretation of the sacramental action that contemporary theology has made a decisive step forward.[51] The concluding sentence about the special bond between presbyter and bishop in celebrating and administering the sacraments once again draws attention to the unity of the official ministry, in which the unity of the Church herself is reflected. This unity must show itself to exist pre-eminently in the manifest realization of the deepest mystery of the Church, which is "a kind of sacrament or sign of intimate union with God, and of the unity of all mankind".[52] On the other hand, at this very point the sentence seems to lay too one-sided a stress on the role of the hierarchy in the sacramental life of the Church.

The second section of the article, following the teaching of St. Thomas on the Eucharist as centre and goal of all the sacraments, and as the climax of the priestly life, describes the eucharist as "the source and the apex of the whole work of preaching the gospel". This recalls Article 10 of the Constitution on the Liturgy, which says that "the liturgy is the summit towards which the activity of the Church is directed; at the same time it is the fountain from which all her power flows". At this point, too, the context makes plain, that it is the eucharist above all that is meant — otherwise the statement would be open to misunderstanding.[53] This is a profound statement; but it has to be interpreted aright and one may not apply it literally to a celebration of the Eucharist regarded in isolation. One must look for the *res sacramenti,* for "Christ himself, our Passover and living bread. Through his very flesh (i. e. through the most intimate communion with his whole life) . . .

---

[51] K. Rahner, *The Church and the Sacraments* (1963), esp. pp. 21 ff. and 76 ff.
[52] Dogmatic Constitution on the Church, art. 1.
[53] Cf. J. A. Jungmann's commentary on the Constitution on the Sacred Liturgy in vol. I of this series, pp. 15 f.

He offers life to men. They are thereby invited and led to offer themselves, their labours, and all created things together with him." When it says that "the most blessed eucharist contains the Church's entire spiritual wealth", this does not mean that this wealth is to be found only in the sacrament as though in a single vessel from which alone men can draw this wealth. It is merely the most concentrated form, instituted by Christ himself, in which the mystery of the Church becomes visible and present and is communicated to us. According to the decree the whole "work of preaching the gospel" must, therefore, be orientated towards this spiritual wealth which is Christ, and from that wealth it must draw its strength. (The phrase "preaching the gospel" or "evangelization" is borrowed from modern French pastoral theology. It denotes the whole scope of missionary pastoral care, the confrontation of man with the gospel in life, word and deed and is not restricted to preaching.)[54] Unfortunately the decree (in the concluding sentence of the second part of this article) restricts this preaching the gospel to the preparation of catechumens for Communion and to the reception of Communion by the faithful, and so the whole breadth and dynamism of the idea just enunciated is destroyed.

The third section picks up the central importance of the Eucharist for the life of the Church and draws the logical conclusion (est ergo ...) that the corporate celebration of the Eucharist is "the very heartbeat of the congregation of the faithful". This thought — so important for pastoral practice — is not developed until Article 6, section 5. This ist symptomatic of the theoretical and actual inseparability of the three offices: fundamentally these simply unfold the one, single office of Christ. At this point we find an allusion to the indispensable effort of the priest to encourage the faithful to participate fervently in the sacrifice of the Mass and to receive the sacraments with deep interior devotion, so as to exclude every sort of magical abuse. The very proper admonition to celebrate the liturgy in such a form as to lead the faithful into genuine prayer, provides the occasion for speaking about education in prayer in general. What is said belongs to the sphere of spiritual direction, a task that is often neglected in the bustle of modern pastoral work. A special chapter could be written on "the appropriate exercise of the evangelical counsels". What is really meant by the "evangelical counsels" is not something extraordinary and additional, going beyond the requirements of the commandments, but simply the serious realization of the Christian faith itself.[55] This concept, however, has become lost to the average

---

[54] This is done by J. Ratzinger in his essay on the question of the meaning of the priestly ministry, loc. cit.

[55] Cf. commentary on the Decree on Religious in vol. II of the present series, pp. 309–14 and commentary on the Constitution on the Church in vol. I, pp. 273–9.

Christian mind, not least as a result of the customary portrayal of the counsels by traditional spiritual writers. The accent of the concluding sentence falls upon the "hymns and spiritual songs" which the faithful sing "in their hearts". The Christian's whole life ought to be a hymn of praise and thanksgiving.

The last two sections of this article deal for the most part with the personal duties of the priest in respect of his pastoral commission: the Divine Office, care for the dignity of the house of God and familiarity with the theory and practice of the liturgy. While in prosperous countries too much care has at times been expended upon the building and furnishing of churches, the Divine Office, despite the high compliments paid it in the Constitution on the Liturgy,[56] and despite promised reforms of the Breviary, has become a serious problem. The question is this: how can we provide a uniform official, common prayer suitable both in content and form for our modern pastors? The proper celebration of the liturgy, too, very largely depends upon the measure in which the liturgy (still not completely reformed) is in harmony with the sentiment and cultural expressions of the man of today, thus endowing it with spontaneity. In an aside, which alludes in the footnote to the encyclical *Mysterium Fidei* of Pope Paul VI, there is a theologically well expressed reminder of the profound significance of visiting the Blessed Sacrament, a practice that is no longer valued, and certainly no longer performed, as it used to be.

Article 6. Of all three offices, that of the pastor, the guide, is least distinctly differentiable from the other two.[57] This article demonstrates this fact. What it says applies more or less to the whole scope of a priest's activity, with special reference to the office of leader, first in respect of the care of individuals and then in respect of the building up and the life of the congregation.

The fundamental question — already briefly described above, Article 1, note 14 — that arises here is this: does the pastoral office included within the power of orders contain a special power *(potestas)* or is this power only conferred through a special juridical act, through canonical mission *(missio canonica* — jurisdiction)? If the former is the case, what is the relationship of the sacramentally conferred pastoral power to that (autonomous) pastoral power which the priest may exercise only in virtue of canonical mission, of the jurisdiction imparted to him? Although — as we can understand — the article makes no direct statements on this topic, and has no intention of

---

[56] Chap. IV, arts. 83–101.

[57] This lies in the nature of the office. According to J. Ratzinger (on the question of the priestly ministry, *loc. cit.*) the pastoral office is the all-embracing and fundamental office, from which the other two (the ministry of the word and the priestly ministry) emerge as two modes of the articulation of its execution; and these two are always contained within the pastoral office.

doing so, and although it quietly presupposes what has been said on the subject in other conciliar documents, notable in the Constitution on the Church,[58] some inferences can be drawn from the text. In general it states first of all that the priest represents Christ as head and shepherd, to the congregation. The word "shepherd", following Jesus' statement about himself in John 10, chiefly signifies the manner in which authority ought to be exercised within the Church. At all events the office of presbyter contains genuine if subordinate authority in the Church *(pro sua parte auctoritatis)*, which may not be called in question by the legitimate, timely demand of the laity for collegial collaboration and fraternal dialogue. It is a question, however, of a special type of authority, of spiritual authority, which requires and includes the function of ruling, necessary in every human society, but is not that in essence. It has its roots in something deeper — in the sense of being an instrument, a minister, of him who alone is head and shepherd of the congregation. This is underlined once again by the statement that "For the exercise of this ministry, as for other priestly duties, spiritual power is conferred upon them for the upbuilding of the Church". The very text itself leaves open the question whether this power, which is obviously the authority to lead and direct, is already contained in the power of holy orders, is conferred sacramentally, that is, or is only conferred through a special juridical act. We might at first infer the latter, because in the celebrated *Prefatory Note* to Article 22 (last sentence of section 2) of the Constitution on the Church an explicit distinction is drawn between function *(munus)* and power *(potestas)*, in order to obviate the misunderstanding that the functions conferred through ordination are "ready to go into action" *(potestas ad actum expeditae)*. This is not to deny but to affirm, that the power of order — and that includes the pastoral authority to rule — is a real power. Moreover, the text of this article confirms that this applies not only to episcopal consecration, but to the ordination of the presbyter, for it draws a parallel between the pastoral authority conferred upon the presbyter and the powers of the other two offices, and traces this power back to its origin in Christ, quoting 2 Cor 10:8 and 13:10 (cf. note 21). This sort of (sacramentally) conferred pastoral power denotes nothing less than an existential-ontological sharing in the mission of Christ, a sharing that essentially and irrevocably determines the person of the ordained priest. On account of the social and hierarchical structure of the Church, for its actual, legally valid exercise it requires specific regulative presuppositions, that is special commissioning by those authorized to give it *(missio canonica)*, the forms of

---

[58] Constitution on the Church, arts. 21, 22, 24, 28 and the Prefatory Note 2 on art. 22, par. I (cf. commentaries in vol. I of this series by K. Rahner, A. Grillmeier and J. Ratzinger; also the Decree on the Bishops' Pastoral Office, arts. 2 and 3).

which are different for the office of presbyter and that of bishop. Whereas the bishop, insofar as he stands in "hierarchical communion with the head and members of the body",[59] is a successor of the apostles *sui iuris,* acting, therefore, neither as the Pope's representative nor in his name, but in his own authority, conferred upon him directly by Christ,[60] the presbyter shares directly only in the mission and authority of the bishop's office and acts, therefore, only in the name of the bishop, whom he represents by special functions in the local congregation. The essence of his office is defined in a phrase from the preface of the ordination mass: he is the "worthy fellow-worker" of the bishop. The sacramental handing on of pastoral power in the hierarchically structured Church thus, of its nature, requires more precise legal regulation, but this regulation does not add something to the power as such, but releases it according to specific norms so that all may be done decently and in order (1 Cor 14:40).[61] Basically it is one and the same mission to the pastoral ministry, the conferring of which, by reason of the order that is necessary within a graduated society of divine right, results from various acts. These acts must be seen, however, in their essential unity and must never be torn asunder.[62]

Throughout the detailed exposition of how the priest ought to exercise his proper authority, his power of ruling, the model of the Good Shepherd is constantly kept in mind. The priests' authority is a spiritual authority, "conferred upon them for the upbuilding of the Church". The priest ought, therefore, to "treat all with outstanding humanity, in imitation of the Lord", and regard all who are entrusted to his care as "God's family" and "as a brotherhood of living unity". Priests must never "put themselves at the service of any ideology or human faction. Rather, as heralds of the gospel and shepherds of the Church, they must devote themselves to the spiritual growth of the Body of Christ." One could say that his authority is all the greater the more he becomes the servant of all. This does not prevent him from admonishing and commanding in the name of Christ and of the gospel. He must never

---

[59] Constitution on the Church, art. 22, section 1; also the Prefatory Note.

[60] *Ibid.,* art. 27: "Bishops govern the particular Churches entrusted to them as the vicars and ambassadors of Christ ... This power, which they personally exercise in Christ's name, is proper, ordinary, and immediate, although its exercise is ultimately regulated by the supreme authority of the Church, and can be circumscribed by certain limits..."

[61] For this reason we consider that M. Schmaus's solution is not a particularly happy one. He says that in the power of orders "a certain basic element of pastoral authority is conferred", but that "the fullness of pastoral authority" is conferred through *missio* (cf. "Hirtengewalt", *LTK,* V, col. 387.

[62] J. Ratzinger is right when he says: "Insofar as the idea of law is isolated from or associated with the sacramental idea, law in the Church will be a thoroughly centralized affair or an intrinsically collegiate one." (See vol. I of this series, p. 301.) This has consequences also for the relation between bishop and priests.

desire "to win favor". As herald of the gospel he has a special obligation to
the poor and the lowly and to all who require his help in a special way. He
must have some knowledge of spiritual direction so that he can help men to
recognize the concrete will of God. He must be able to discern spirits, a
function exercised not least in his pastoral care of religious, both men and
women. Two things are stressed in respect of the leadership of the congregation. 1. The building up of the congregation proceeds from the altar. Thus
the foundation and centre of the congregation must be the celebration of
the Eucharist. This requires more than "ceremonies however beautiful". The
genuineness and life of pastoral care that centres on the altar is proved by
its leading men to "the attainment of Christian maturity", and bringing alive
a sense of community among the faithful. 2. Wherever such community of
faith in the one Lord grows and rallies round the Lord, the corporately celebrated eucharist urges on not only to manifold ministries of love within the
community itself, but to missionary activity beyond the bounds of that community; for the congregation knows that it is responsible for the whole
Church, for the whole of mankind. Both of these things presuppose a congregation of genuine believers, a congregation that will remain small — the
"little flock". At this point a fresh question emerges: in future will pastoral
care be so exclusively parochial as it has been in the past? Will the many
voluntarily constituted societies within the Church not become increasingly
important, without necessarily calling the validity of the parochial congregation in question?

The problem of the concrete form of the exercise of authority in the
Church, of the concrete form of leadership, is of critical importance for the
future social status of the priest. Does not the decree still see this in too
paternalistic a light (even under the image of the Good Shepherd)? And what
will happen if in the days to come more lay people are drawn into functions
of leadership?

II. PRIESTS AS RELATED TO OTHERS

In structure and content the exposition of this section can be traced back to
a stimulating and theologically productive critique of the draft of this decree
dated 2 October 1964, by Mgr. Pironio of La Plata, Argentine, in the name
of eight members of the Council.[1] Under this title we might expect to find
certain regulations of conduct arising out of the priest's concrete sphere of
action. Then we would expect to find in the text of the decree an indication

---

[1] *Animadversiones in Schema Propositionum De Vita et Ministerio sacerdotali* (26 October
1964), pp. 33–36.

of the relation of the priest to his congregation and to all whom he would like to embrace within this congregation. We would look for a second section dealing with the relationship of priests to each other, and finally an exposition of the relations between priests and their bishop.

Regard for the evolution of the decree would likewise seem to lead to the above sequence of ideas, and away from the sequence in the text before us. The central idea of Article 7 emerged as an attempt was made to adapt the propositions contained in the *De Sacerdotibus* of 27 April 1964 to the theological scheme of the Constitution on the Church. In its second chapter, however, *Lumen Gentium* demonstrates that the basic sacramental *datum* even of the official priesthood is their membership of the people of God. And so an exposition of the relationships affecting the official priesthood would do better to start with the relationship of the official priesthood to the baptized, as the draft decree of 2 October 1964 already proposed. In this way the image of priestly activity presented by the decree would have given a clear reflection of the characteristic insight of Vatican II: more important than all differentiations is the fact that first and foremost the Church is the community of all the faithful.

It is correct, therefore, to attribute significance to the present arrangement of the text of this section and to infer from it that the subject is not simply the conduct or spiritual requirements of the clergy. Something else is being described here. By an exposition of the relationships affecting priests the text illumines the new sphere of life and activity into which the ordained man enters. This sphere emerges out of a threefold relation: the priest knows himself to be a man orientated towards the bishops, towards his fellow presbyters and towards all served by his ministry. His relation to the bishop ranks first because the bishop is the real representative within the diocese of the priesthood of Christ and all official priestly activity is always generically and actually (Articles 2 and 5) related to him. The relation to the presbytery provides the framework of official activity *(cooperatio)* and both relationships are directed towards the ministry which leads men to live the gospel to the glory of God.

We may conclude, therefore: the sacramental definition of the official priest, given in Article 2, receives important supplementation in Articles 7–9. To begin with the delineation of the ordained is expressed in ontological categories; now it appears in existential abstraction. To begin with the ontological foundation of the priestly ministry is analyzed; now its tangible actualization is described. The text describes this as relation to others *(habitudo)*. Both perspectives mutually determine one another so that the full form of holy orders is neither truncated in actuality nor prejudiced on the ontological level. The existential statement includes the ontological and vice versa. The two dovetail into one another. The ontic stamp of the official priest is concretized in his spiritual self-fulfilment in which he finds himself thrown upon others. Consecration and function are two aspects of the one reality that constitutes holy orders, and they belong together.

Article 7 explains that through consecration and mission those who belong to the priestly grades of holy orders are responsible for a ministry to the people of God and so are mutually dependent. This sacramentally based community and common commission demand — especially today — that bishops and priests feel their reciprocal obligation.

When the Commission entrusted with producing the text of this decree began its work on the first attempt, *De Clericis* of 22 April 1963, the theological judgment of *Lumen Gentium* (Article 21) that "by episcopal consecration is conferred the fullness of the sacrament of orders" had not yet been formulated. For this reason the first draft of the decree sought in vain for a distinguishing and theologically fruitful statement about the relationship of priest to bishop, founded upon ordination. In the first draft the bishop was mentioned only with reference to obedience on the part of the priest. Thus the dependence of priest upon bishop followed the model of the relation of the religious to his superior.

The draft of 22 April 1964 abandoned this notion — at least in the section now before us: "quae sacerdotalis oboedientia natura sua differt ab illa quae religiosis ... convenit" (Article 2). The relation of priest to bishop and of bishop to priest is determined by the fact that the priesthood subsisting in the bishop and in the priest is the one priesthood of Christ: "unitas consecrationis missionisque". But there is a distinction between *consecratio* and *missio:* "real participation in the episcopal ministry is conferred upon presbyters through the sacrament; the exercise of the ministry, however, comes through canonical mission."[2]

Thus the necessity of the unity between bishop and priest is derived "not solely from the bishop's power of jurisdiction" (Cardinal Lercaro of Bologna). This thought permeated the ideas before us so that they are less juridically phrased than the corresponding statements in the Constitution on the Church (Article 28).

From this unity with the bishop arises the invitation to the presbyter to enjoy "communio filialis" with his own particular bishop. Later, when the text was applied to the episcopate as a whole, the phrase was altered to "communio hierarchica" with the episcopal state.[3] The changed numbering

---

[2] Reply of the Commission to a *modus.* Cf., with reference to the discussion of the juxtaposition of *potestas ordinis* and *potestas jurisdictionis*, K. Rahner in vol. I of the present commentary series, pp. 192–5; J. Ratzinger, *ibid.*, pp. 300 ff.; K. Mörsdorf in vol. II of the present commentary series, pp. 206 f.

[3] Here it is the *Ordo Episcoporum* that is under discussion and the statements made about the bishop have mostly the plural form. The reason for this is as follows: whereas in early

of the text necessitated a more positive form of expression. Behind "hier-archica", however, used here to explain the meaning of "dependence" (Mgr. Ancel of Lyon), we must see the word "filialis". As in *Lumen Gentium* (Article 22) "communio" characterizes "the sense of a permanent bond".[4]

A striking expression of this "communio cum Ordine Episcoporum" is seen in *concelebration*.[5] The mention, too, of the name of the Bishop of Rome and of the local bishop in the Canon of the Mass is also interpreted as a public profession of union with the episcopal order.[6] Our text points, then, to two elements which articulate a central aspect of the Eucharist: the idea of unity. In a special way this aspect of the Eucharist lays an obligation on both grades of the official priesthood. "In ancient times men were vividly aware of the community associations of the Eucharist. In particular, the Eucharist for long played a large part in community relationships in the spatial sense. The community, which the Catholic Church in its spatial extension over the world had to embrace, was assured if the pastors of the separate congregations remained united with their superiors, the bishops, and if these remained united among each other."[7]

Participation in the priesthood of Christ is declared neither by a posi-tivistic definition nor by a juridical act. It consists rather in a gift of the Spirit (Article 2: "unctio Spiritus Sancti"; Article 7:" donum Spiritus Sancti"; Article 10: "donum spirituale"). In orders this is conferred, along with its permanent character, upon the presbyter by the bishop.[8] Through this per-

---

Christian times ordination was always associated with consecration to serve in a particular Church — consecration apart from induction being rejected (Council of Chalcedon, can. 6) — later the translation of priests from the Church of their ordination became quite usual. Hence the priest was no longer regarded as an assistant of one particular bishop seen in isolation from the rest of the bishops. While a priest is consecrated to serve with a partic-ular bishop in a particular Church, he is the assistant of the whole college of bishops within the whole Church *(cooperator ordinis nostrae)*. Cf. J. Colson, "Fondement d'une spiritualité pour le prêtre de 'second rang'", *NRT* 73 (1951); S. Ryan, "Episcopal Conse-cration", *Irish Theological Quarterly* 33 (1966).

[4] K. Rahner in vol. I of this series, pp. 196 f.; likewise J. Ratzinger, *ibid.*, pp. 301 ff.; also G. d'Ercole's article on research concerning the collegiality of bishops in *Concilium* 4 (1968).

[5] Cf. with reference to the historical development of concelebration: J. A. Jungmann in vol. I of the present commentary series, pp. 42 f., esp. footnote 23; see also K. Rahner and A. Häussling, *The Celebration of the Eucharist* (1965), pp. 106 ff.

[6] Cf. J. A. Jungmann, *The Mass of the Roman Rite* (1959).

[7] id., "Fermentum", *Pastoral Liturgy* (1962), pp. 287 ff.

[8] On the biblical and dogmatic basis cf. H. Schürmann, *Die geistlichen Gnadengaben in den paulinischen Gemeinden* (1965), pp. 33–40: "...Paul was obliged to recognize other per-manent ministerial functions besides his own, as manifestations of the operation of the Spirit. This explains why Paul understood the two types of phenomenon — the *official* and the *free* — as interrelated things requiring uniform classification and incorporation in

manent spiritual endowment the presbyters become genuine, serious, necessary partners of the bishops in the task of leading the people of God. The use of the indicative ("habent") indicates that we are dealing with a theological proposition and not with a wish that the Council is addressing to the bishops.

In support of this statement the decree argues neither biblically nor systematically, but accepts as basic that the *lex orandi* corresponds to the *lex credendi*.[9] In the *Traditio apostolica* attributed to Hippolytus of Rome (d. 235), we have our oldest extant rite of consecration. In this formulary the bishop prays at the ordination of presbyters for the Spirit of grace and of counsel to come down upon the candidates, enabling them to share in the leadership of the Church.[10]

The interrogation in the prayers of ordination then leads to a comparison of the bishop and his priests with Moses and the seventy wise men. Numerous objections by the Council members focussed attention on the problems arising from this Old Testament image and called for the rejection of the text. Even at the second last draft 22 Council fathers wanted to delete the passage because the parallel left unclear whether it was a human spirit (of Moses or of the bishop) or the Spirit of God that was being conferred. Others maintained that, in contrast to the formulation of the decree, the Book of Numbers and the *Pontificale Romanum* make it quite clear that God is the active subject. God himself sends his Spirit.

The Commission wanted to retain the analogy and, without completely committing itself, appealed to the *Pontificale Romanum* and to traditional texts quoted in footnote 37. This exposition of the Old Testament and the allusion to Moses as type was meant to express that it is the same Spirit that animates the presbyters and that within this group of leaders the bishop holds responsibility for leadership and is mediator of the competence to lead.[11]

The spiritual bond of *communio* binding these two grades of orders together is then expressed in the customary terms. In spite of an allusion to the Constitution on the Church this text does not contain the formulation used in that document to describe the closeness between bishop and priests. In addition to the concept *amici*, which appears in both decrees, in the Constitution on the Church and in the decree *Christus Dominus* (Article 16) we find the concept *filii*, while in the Decree on Priests we find that of *fratres*.

---

a common catalogue" (p. 40). See also K. Rahner, *The Church and the Sacraments*, Quaestiones Disputatae 9 (1963).

[9] Cf. C. Vagaggini, *Il senso dommatico della liturgia*, and also J. Lécuyer's contribution in Y. Congar and A. D. Dupuy, eds., *L'Épiscopat et l'Église universelle* (1962).

[10] Cf. B. Botte, *L'ordre d'après les prières d'Ordination;* L. Guyot, *Études sur le sacrement de l'ordre* (1957), pp. 13–35.

[11] L. Guyot, *op. cit.*, pp. 38–44.

In October 1964 Mgr. Sartre of Madagascar had pointed out that "not even the idea had been expressed that the presbyterate (in the draft) is the form of brotherhood between priests and between priests and the bishop". The term "fratres" was first adopted in the draft of 30 November 1965. The Commission accepted the *modus*, subscribed by 27 fathers, arguing that: "the community in the priesthood of Christ, for bishops and for priests, must find expression as the foundation of Christian brotherhood. It is necessary for the schema to advert to this brotherhood at least in one place."

The practical consequences of the *communio* affect bishops and priests. The bishops must accept responsibility for the material and spiritual well-being of the members of the presbyterate. The text refers to detailed definitions of this function by recent Popes and in the schema on the pastoral function of the bishops. The decree we are studying now takes up this topic in Articles 19–21, and the motu proprio *Ecclesiae Sanctae* sketches the first lines of its concretization.[12]

The thought expressed here derives from a petition presented by the German-speaking and Scandinavian bishops. In remarking on material well-being they certainly were not thinking primarily of their own obligation or of priests in our own regions. Allusion to the *bonum spirituale*, however, leaves us with the problem of how our bishops propose to fulfil their own obligations and erect solid institutions to deal with the *grave onus sanctitudinis* through pastoral care of the pastors. It is not enough simply to make a few arrangements in respect of young priests or to show genuine solicitude in isolated cases.

The admonition to bishops to co-operate with their priests arises from some spirited opinions provoked by the draft of 2 October 1964. Mgr. Théas of Lourdes said: "It is obvious to us that we cannot at all fulfil our mission as teachers and pastors and the work of sanctification without the co-operation of our priests. If we have eyes to see our own limitations we know that we can do nothing without our priests." Mgr. Garaygordobil of Ecuador said: "Priests must be real co-workers with the bishops and not just executors . . . On important issues the bishop ought to be obliged to consult his presbytery and come to a decision either after this consultation or after voting."

It says much for the realism of the fathers that they demanded the erection of a solid diocesan institution for the carrying out of these suggestions. The Commission maintained their proposals in face of objections which expressed a fear of democratizing tendencies. Some bishops rejected the phrase "presbyterium repraesentantium" and objected to the idea of a *senatus*, for such formulations would imply the notion of a parliamentary government of the Church. But the Commission added a cautious statement on the form of this

[12] Cf. K. Mörsdorf in vol. II of the present commentary series, pp. 232 ff.

consultation. The sentence ran: "... a group or council ... which is able effectively to support the bishop." The addition said: "... *suis consiliis* — in making his decisions".

The name *(consilium presbyterale)* and the structure of this new council of priests were given in the motu proprio *Ecclesiae Sanctae* — On the Norms of Execution of Some Decrees of the Second Vatican Council, dated 6 August 1966. The structure is described in I, n. 15, paras. 1–4.[13] Footnote 41 of the decree shows that this group is not subject to the cathedral chapter or the council of diocesan consultants. Rather, these two ought to be "overhauled in such a way that they come more into line with modern conditions and needs". The newly erected colleges ought indeed to become equal in standing to these.[14] Because a pastoral council including lay members is to be instituted also,[15] the question arises of the mutual interrelation of all these episcopal consultative committees.

Mgr. Höffner of Münster tried to clarify this problem.[16] According to him the pastoral council took precedence over the council of priests because it gave a voice to the whole People of God. This argument would be convincing only if both councils were meant to represent the interests of different groups to the bishop. Their function is, however, to advise the bishop on the way to lead his diocese. Similar considerations are pertinent in respect of the assertion of F. Klostermann that the pastoral council is "the true study, planning, co-ordinating, and advisory organ of the bishop in all problems of the diocese and its direction.[17]

Such a view is not in harmony with the motu proprio.[18] It overlooks the dogmatic and historical significance of the presbyterate.

1. The council of priests is a prescribed institution (I, n. 15, para. 1) to which the bishop must listen in certain cases (I, n. 22, paras. 2–3); the pastoral council is "strongly recommended" (I, n. 16) and is consulted by the bishop when such consultation seems appropriate (I, n. 16, para. 2).

2. The council of priests is concerned with the presbytery, reduced on grounds of functional efficiency *(presbyterium repraesentatum)*. It is precisely to the presbytery that the function belongs of supporting the bishop in leading his diocese. For the ministry of leadership the bishop is sacramentally empowered by orders *(Lumen Gentium,* Article 21). Priests of the second rank receive a similarly orientated gift of the Spirit in order to build up the People of God

---

[13] Cf. *ibid.,* pp. 252 ff., esp. footnote 45.

[14] Cf. *ibid.,* p. 252.

[15] *Christus Dominus,* art. 27.

[16] Cf. with reference to the theology of the pastoral and priests' council the supplement to the official journal of the diocese of Münster: *Unsere Seelsorge* 17, no. 6 (1967), pp. 1–4.

[17] On new diocesan structures see F. Klostermann in *Diakonia* 2 (1967), pp. 257–70, 267.

[18] Cf. K. Mörsdorf, *op. cit.,* pp. 253–5.

by their ministry (*ibid.*, Article 28). By this charism conferred through the sacrament they are distinguished "in essence and not only in degree" from those who share in the general priesthood, and thus become pre-eminently qualified to be co-operators with the bishop.[19] This notion finds support in the tradition of the Fathers who laid much stress upon the part played by the presbytery in the direction of the diocese.[20] Such historical and sacramental foundations stand irrespective of whether or not the auxiliary function of the presbytery in government is approved and defined juridically.[21]

The idea of a council of priests and the regulations for its institution — in contrast to the pastoral council — point to the need for a comprehensive and continuous source of information at the disposal of the bishop concerning the life of his diocese and concerning sensitive points within the local Church. This supplements the present locally sited consultative organs which, because indirect and patchy, are bound to give a one-sided picture. To arouse a spirit of co-operation with the plans and decisions of the bishop and his collaborators and to encourage the will to brotherly co-operation among priests cannot, therefore, be the sole purpose of the council of priests,[22] even although care of the presbytery may well be of prime importance to this council.

In its first draft the decree deliberately relied, in its attempt to describe the ideal of perfection in the secular priest, upon the evangelical counsels. "Because ultimately the evangelical counsels were proposed to all as the most efficacious means of perfection, priests were exhorted to follow them to the best of their abilities."[23] And so in formulating the text the dependence of the priest upon his bishop was neither based upon his common orders nor limited to the bishop. Article 3 of the *Propositiones* dated 27 April 1964 requires that the priest shall "obey in a childlike and magnanimous spirit not only the commands but the requests of his superiors." The expression "superior" gives the impression that the terminology and spirituality of religious orders is being discussed.

In our text, which is further concretized in Article 15 of the final redac-

---

[19] Cf. H. Denis, "Approches théologiques du sacerdoce ministériel", *Lumière et Vie* 76—77 (1966), pp. 145–74. "It is true that the whole community of Christians together display the visible sign of the Church; but it is the ministerial office alone that has the power and authority to be a guarantor, in the name of Christ himself; and it has this through vocation and consecration" (p. 155). Cf. also O. Semmelroth's contribution on the priestly people of God and its leaders in *Concilium*, no. 4 (1968).

[20] Cf. *Presbyterorum ordinis*, commentary on art. 8; also K. Rahner, "The Presbyterium and the Individual Priest", *Theology of Pastoral Action*, Studies in Pastoral Theology 1 (1968): "We can say, therefore, that history proves that a bishop must always by divine right be surrounded by a presbyterium" (p. 96).

[21] F. Klostermann, *op. cit.*, p. 267.

[22] Cf. K. Mörsdorf, *op. cit.*, p. 253.

[23] *Relatio* on article 3 of the *Propositiones* of 27 April 1964.

tion of *Presbyterorum ordinis,* obedience is no longer regarded as an ascetic instrument. "Oboedientia cooperationis spiritu perfusa" gives the text a pastoral slant. The official ministry of the Church demands the co-ordinated action of all those taking part in it. Organic work is possible, however, only if all submit to the direction of those having ultimate responsibility. [24]

A new concept of obedience and a pastoral perspective by no means necessitate a structureless Church. There is a graduated sharing of bishops and priests in the priesthood of Christ. This is a sacramental fact, quite undisturbed by the democratic tendencies of our times. Priests are official ministers of the second rank, bishops on the other hand have received "the fullness of the sacrament of orders". Indeed, "in the bishops, therefore, our Lord Jesus Christ, the supreme High Priest, is present in the midst of those who be-

---

[24] Cf. K. Rahner, *Servants of the Lord* (1968), pp. 130 f.: "Of themselves authority and obedience to authority have a 'functional' role in society ... Obedience does not really subject the person who obeys to the person who commands, but rather orientates the 'subject' to the goal and good of the society concerned... This is no less true of authority and obedience in the Church... Therefore men can command and obey only within the sphere of the authority concerned, which is delimited by the goal and business of the society. Now that goal and business require that the ruler be obeyed so long as he commands within the sphere which they delimit, even though the subject himself may think the command ill-suited to further the good of the society. On the other hand if a command clearly and positively conflicts with the goal and business of the society it is immoral and may never be obeyed."

In view of the complex problems arising from the topic of obedience one is amazed at the simple attitude of a Dutch Catholic sociologist: "First, then, we must affirm that the Catholic Church in principle approves disobedience, has indeed canonized disobedience." Such simplification leads to crass errors.

We lack the preconditions for testing the logic of sociological proofs. For example, when Francis of Assisi is cited as a proof of canonized disobedience one asks if the concept of disobedience is not equivocal in this case, being used in the sense of "nonconformist behaviour" or "critical initiative". It is true that the latter must never break loose from a controlling authority — as the example of St Francis of Assisi makes clear. And so in this case we must request the use of more appropriate forms of expression in order to avoid confusion.

Even if sociologists had established the fact that the constant reform of social systems is only guaranteed by the disregard of authority, this fact could not be reduced to the simple formula that "disobedience is a virtue". Such global and unqualified transposition blurs the distinction between empirical sociology and theology. The renewal of the system comes about — in New Testament terminology — not by disobedience but by "opposing to his face" (Gal 2:11), not defying authority but arguing with it. The believer knows that salvation is to be found not in disobedience but in obedience (Rom 5:19; Phil 2:18). His whole life of faith is moulded by this truth. "And so, faith is essentially obedience, as disbelief is essentially disobedience" (O. Kuss, *Der Römerbrief* pp. 138–9). "Every act of obedience within the Church is a sign of obedience towards Christ. 'Encounter with Christ' is thus the deepest mystery within the command-obedience relationship within the Church" (A. Müller, "Authority and Obedience in the Church", *Concilium,* 5, no. 2 [1966]).

lieve." [25] For priests, too, Christ is present and at work in the bishops as his servants. It is through the ministry of the bishops especially that Christ's action becomes sacramentally and historically palpable. [26]

This representation of Christ is not operative everywhere and in every action, but manifests itself as fundamentally a ministry and therefore relative. And so the authority of the bishop, which the presbyters must acknowledge with faith and reverence, in limiting cases is linked with service to the Church, so that there is always the possibility of too strictly binding directives being given.

Not only in its understanding of authority, but in the exposition of the qualities characterizing the relation of priest to bishop, our text is far from giving an absolutist picture of the bishop. A mechanical and apodeictic demand for obedience is incompatible with "sincere charity". Obedience can be animated by this "caritas sincera" only when there is the sense of being esteemed and an awareness of mutual goodwill, which makes merely outward submission quite unthinkable.

There is an abrupt transition from this concept of obedience to that of unity. To demonstrate this unity the decree follows a pastoral and pragmatic argument. It dispenses with supernatural motivation and is at once obvious. It is true that one must begin from the fact that not all necessary, certainly not all possible, co-ordination of apostolic functions at the supra-parochial and supra-diocesan level has yet been accomplished; but the indirect encouragement of such co-ordination is so general in tone that it must remain ineffective unless supported by practical directives. [27] The ideas appeal to the conditions of our times and thus raise the question as to the extent to which the sciences, which analyze our society and age, can be fruitfully used in the apostolate.

Article 8 develops the relationship of priests to one another. First of all several possible embodiments of the priesthood are described. The text then touches on the problem of disparity in age, the social side of this unity founded upon orders, and the mutual responsibility priests have towards each other.

The sacrament of holy orders is the clamp which binds all priests together in a single community, in spite of all their individuality and their variety of functions. At the level of the diocese this sacrament creates a specially close-knit group around the bishop. This is his *presbyterium*. [28]

---

[25] *Lumen Gentium*, art. 21.

[26] K. Rahner in vol. I of the present commentary series, pp. 192 ff.; cf. also G. Baraúna, ed., *De Ecclesia*, II (1966), pp. 24–43.

[27] Cf. K. Mörsdorf in vol. I of this series, pp. 259 f.

[28] K. Mörsdorf points out that the *LTK* under the title "Presbyterium" merely mentions the so-called dwelling place: *loc. cit.*, p. 256. By its frequent use of this word Vatican II

In the New Testament the word πρεσβυτήριον denotes a college of elders in Hellenistic-Jewish society (Lk 22:66; Acts 22:5) or in Christian society (1 Tim 4:14).[29]

The distinction between *episkopos* and *presbyteros* may not always be very clearly drawn in the Acts of the Apostles,[30] but it is true that in the Pastoral Letters *episkopos* appears in the singular whereas the presbyters form a college.[31] To this official committee fell the task of leading the community.[32] At Timothy's installation they joined in by laying on their hands (1 Tim 4:14). These could not have been the natural representatives of the congregation because the presbyters were appointed by the apostles (Acts 14:23) or their successors (Tit 1:5).[33]

This biblical germ of the presbytery grew in the time of the Apostolic Fathers. In the First Letter of Clement of Rome (d. 101) to the Corinthians (44:1–6) and especially in the letters of the martyr, Ignatius (d. 107), this process of evolution finds an echo.[34] Thirteen references to the presbytery give us a very clear idea of how the Bishop of Antioch regarded their function. This group was composed of men who, under the bishop and set above the deacons, engaged in the ministry of official instruction, of public worship and in leading the local Christian congregations. There are many examples of lists of the three ministries in which the committee of presbyters appears between the bishop — always in the singular — and the deacons (Ign., *Magn* 13:1; Ign., *Trall* 7:2; Ign., *Phld* 4; 7:1; Ign., *Sm* 8:1; 12:2). Often they are mentioned simply with the bishop (Ign., *Eph* 2:2; 4:1; 20:2; Ign., *Magn* 2; Ign., *Trall* 2:2; 13:2). It is quite beyond doubt that the bishop was always president of this group. "It is unseemly, however, to take advantage of a bishop's youth. In deference to the power of God one ought, rather, to show him all reverence" (Ign., *Magn* 3:1). In another passage Ignatius says: "Whoever undertakes anything apart from the bishop, serves the devil" (*Sm* 9:1). The presbytery, however, share in the leadership of the Church and all of

---

turns our attention to the social connotation behind the local one (*Sacrosanctum Concilium*, art. 41; *Lumen Gentium*, art. 28; *Christus Dominus*, arts. 11, 15, 28; *Presbyterorum ordinis*, arts. 7, 8; *Ad Gentes*, art. 19). In what follows this will be discussed at least in outline.

[29] Cf. G. Bornkamm, "πρέσβυς", *TWNT*, VI, pp. 654–83; On the early apostolic period see H. Schürmann, "Das Testament des Paulus für die Kirche, Acts 20:18–35", *Unio Christianorum* (1962), pp. 108–44; G. d'Ercole, "The College of Priests in the Early Church", *Concilium* 2 (1966).

[30] D'Ercole, *op. cit.*

[31] Bornkamm, *op. cit.*, p. 667; Schürmann, *op. cit.*, pp. 139 f.

[32] Bornkamm, *op. cit.*, p. 666; Schürmann, *op. cit.*, pp. 137 ff.

[33] Bornkamm, *op. cit.*, p. 668; Schürmann, *op. cit.*, p. 133.

[34] Cf. the article by J. Lécuyer entitled "Le Presbyterium" which appeared in the collection *Les Prêtres, Commentaire des Décrets Presbyteriorum ordinis et Optatem totius*, Unam Sanctam 68 (1968).

the faithful including the deacons must obey them (Ign., *Magn* 2:1). Ignatius compares the presbytery to a senate and to the college of the apostles (*Trall* 3:1). Ignatius knew that harmony would prevail only where bishop and presbytery exercised their authority in fundamental unity. The unity of the servants of the hierarchy was for him the source of unity in the congregation and between the congregation and God: "There is but one flesh of our Lord Jesus Christ and one cup which unites us with his blood; there is but one altar, just as there is a single bishop with the presbytery and the deacons" (*Phld* 4).

The *Traditio apostolica* of Hippolytus of Rome (d. 235)[35] throws light on the liturgical function of the presbytery. The presbytery is specially mentioned along with the congregation in connection with the election of the bishop.[36] They do not take part in the consecration of the new bishop, but after his consecration along with him they extend their hands over the gifts, thus exercising their priestly ministry. The bishop alone recites the offertory prayer.[37] At the ordination of a new priest they lay their hands upon him after the bishop has done so,[38] "because of the same common Spirit of the clergy".[39] "They are not solitary individuals each with his own special mission to fulfil; they are a college which shares in the function of the bishop."[40]

Finally, we may deduce from the letters of Pope Cornelius (d. 253) and of Bishop Cyprian of Carthage (d. 258) that the presbytery took part in leading the Church. Cyprian emphasizes that from the start of his episcopate he had made it a rule to undertake nothing solely on his own personal initiative without the advice of his presbyters and the agreement of his people (*Ep* 14:4). In Rome Cornelius assembled the presbytery in order to decide about the adherents of Novatian and heal the schism (Cyprian, *Ep.* 49:2).

The close bond holding the presbytery together loosened as time went by. During the Decian persecution Cyprian permitted the members of the presbytery to celebrate the Eucharist by turns along with a deacon (*Ep* 5:2). The Synod of Sardica (343) forbade the erection of episcopal sees in places where a single presbyter sufficed (can. 6). About the end of the 4th century a move began to try to restrict the direction of presbyters by the bishop. Thus the bond of the presbytery became weaker and the bishop was regarded as *primus inter pares*.[41] The writings of Jerome strengthened this tendency and

---

[35] Cf. B. Botte, "Caractère Collégial du Presbytériat et de l'Épiscopat", *Études*, pp. 97–124.
[36] B. Kleinheyer, *Die Priesterweihe im römischen Ritus* (1962), p. 15, n. 10.
[37] Botte, *op. cit.*, p. 99.
[38] Kleinheyer, *op. cit.*, p. 15.
[39] *Ibid.*, p. 17.
[40] Botte, *op. cit.*, p. 100.
[41] *Ibid.*, pp. 105 f.

through Rabanus Maurus and Amalar influenced the medieval view of the ordained priest. The priesthood was no longer centred around the bishop, but around the presbytery. The link with the bishop became looser and looser and the concept of the presbytery faded.

In contrast Vatican II can rely upon a sound biblical and patristic foundation when it once again attributes some importance to the presbytery.[42] By this term it denotes neither an ecclesiastical building nor the totality of priests in the whole world. It denotes, rather, the group of priests in a particular diocese who, under the authority of their bishop, serve the Church in this locality. In the course of the Council the view had at first been expressed that "a person becomes a member of the presbytery in virtue of ordination and hierarchical communion with the head and members of the presbytery" (Mgr. Pourchet, St.-Flour, France); later it became clear that incorporation in the presbytery is *iuris ecclesiastici,* whereas one is bound to describe the community which orders create between priests and bishop as *iuris divini.*[43] Thus the act of consecration creates a sacramental link between bishop and priest, but does not create membership of the presbytery. It is only canonical mission by which the bishop grants the faculty to exercise a ministry that incorporates a priest into the community of the presbytery (Cardinal Döpfner, Munich), for "the welding of priests into a community is required by the unity of the ministry itself" (Patriarch Mèouchi of Antioch).

The presbytery finds, therefore, the basis of its existence in the commission of priests to serve. Within the community which thus arises the bishop must be seen as "tamquam ratio unitatis Presbyterii in unaquaque diocesi".[44]

This concept of presbytery implies that even those secular priests and religious who are not incardinated but work in the diocese are drawn within the community of the presbytery, finding within it their "spiritual home".[45] All stand ready to fulfil the same task; all become participants — "cooperatores veritatis".[46] The motu proprio *Ecclesiae Sanctae* (I, n. 15, paras. 1–2) numbers the priests commissioned for service by the bishop among the presbytery. In the case of non-incardinated priests, however, there are difficulties. The bishop has not full control of them, for they have ties beyond his particular presbytery; and priests in religious orders may suffer because of a conflict of types of spirituality. It is always desirable, therefore, that priests

[42] J. Lécuyer, *op. cit.*
[43] Reply of the Commission to a proposed alteration.
[44] Reply of the Commission to a *modus.*
[45] Cf. K. Mörsdorf in vol. II of the present series, pp. 255 f.
[46] The citation of 3 John is inapplicable on exegetical grounds. According to Schnackenburg, *Die Johannisbriefe* (1953) this letter was addressed to the layman Gaius (p. 284), who gave hospitality to itinerant preachers (p. 288). In virtue of this contribution to the mission the presbyter describes him as a fellow labourer in the truth (p. 290).

engaged in pastoral work be incardinated into the diocese in which they are working.

By stressing the presbytery as the responsible community within the diocese, the Council did not mean to suggest that there should be uniformity or a stereotyped way in which priests must live and perform their ministry. They were underlining, rather, that the mastery of the one task demands differentiation of function. It is true that the text does not contain concrete suggestions as to how this desired plurality is to be realized, but a stimulus to reflection on the differentiation in priestly function and behaviour is given. Cardinal Roy of Quebec, said: "The more modern starting-points and the diverse forms of pastoral work — as, for example, associations for the apostolate — which extend beyond parochial boundaries are not sufficiently in evidence." This gave rise to the suggestion in our text that today "multiplicia officia necnon novae accommodationes" are necessary.

This is all the more heartening, because "... the demand for uniformity, for sheer identity in behaviour imposed an unnecessary psychological burden upon the priest, who felt acutely the inadequacy of a formalized approach in so many pastoral situations."[47] It is heartening also because it opens up the possibility of escape from the "professional underdevelopment of the priestly vocation."[48] Admittedly in this context we must not accept unqualified the sociological affirmation of the professional underdevelopment of the clerical vocation. Sociological laws can do justice to the total reality of the Church and the priesthood, as understood by faith, only when applied with caution. The absolutizing of sociology would reduce the priest to a functionary. G. Hansemann has drawn a picture of the priest from his own experience: "The priest makes quite a good job of his profession: his heart is in it. But a profession is not a thing which takes possession of the innermost soul. We can see all too well how the whole problem of the priestly personality is determined by this question: is priesthood a personal relation to Christ or not?" ("Wandel im Verständnis der Seelsorge", *Der Seelsorger* 37 [1967], p. 236). The priest who today thinks of himself as no more than a functionary of the social group known as the Church, contradicts the spirit of the decree, which demands the right to control the testing of faith and the relativization of all analyses and reform proposals provided by empirical science (1 Jn 4:1). Specialization and the authority of the expert might increase the joy and self-confidence of many priests and demonstrably make more attractive the vocation of the secular priest.

As well as diocesan specialists such as are required for educational estab-

---

[47] G. Siefer, "Zur Soziologie des Priesterbildes", *Diakonia* 2 (1967), p. 131.
[48] O. Schreuder, *Gestaltwandel der Kirche* (1967), p. 83; see also the same author's, "Der professionelle Charakter des geistlichen Amtes", *Der Seelsorger* 36 (1966), pp. 320–35.

lishments, business and factories, for pastoral care of priests, sailors, police and the army, one can think of division of labour and specialized tasks at the deanery level: family care, adult education (theological and biblical, seminars on marriage and society), charitable organizations and social service, work in unions and for ecumenical solidarity, catechesis and youth-work, publicity and expert knowledge in social legislation. In these and other fields priests — and often laymen too — might specialize. For all of these specialities training courses would have to be provided.[49] The dean would be responsible for the co-ordination of all this pastoral work, as indicated in the motu proprio *Ecclesiae Sanctae:* "Equipped by the bishop with the necessary authority, the deans should be in a position to encourage and direct appropriate co-operation in pastoral work within their areas" (I, n. 19, para. 1).[50] The priests involved would have to be relieved of their parochial duties, especially as the priest is directly "first a member of the presbytery of a diocese, and his primary office is to accept responsibility for the Church at large rather than to exercise a mission in this parish or to that group of people or even in some supra-parochial ministry. The 'functional principle' of his participation in the function of the bishop takes precedence over the 'territorial principle' or the 'personal principle' in the exercise of his office."[51] Progress has already been made along these lines at the city level in, for example, Verviers in Belgium and in Eindhoven in Holland. In these days local mobility is so great in country districts, too, that supra-parochial work is scarcely hindered at all by distance.

One concrete reference in our text to special forms of the apostolate concerns priests as manual workers. This reference was made at the Council by a group of vicars apostolic from Oceania (Juillard, Martin, Darmancier, etc.) and by the then Galilean Melchite Archbishop, now Patriarch, George Hakim. Such a suggestion would have been inconceivable, however, apart from the experiment of the worker-priests in France.[52] This will always be associated with Cardinal Suhard of Paris, J. Loew, O. P., and the C. A. J. chaplains, H. Godin and Y. Daniel, who sparked off the movement by their analyses of the situation published in 1943: *La France, pays de Mission?*

The story of the gradual suppression of this movement is well-known:[53] first the recommendation by the Congregation for Religious to withdraw the worker-priests (29 August 1953), then the order of the Nuncio Marell to 26 bishops and religious superiors to suspend the experiment (23 September

---

[49] *Optatam totius,* art. 18.
[50] Cf. K. Mörsdorf, *op. cit.,* p. 261.
[51] H. Schuster in *Diakonia* 1 (1966), p. 357.
[52] Mgr. Hakim's theological adviser was at one time a professor at Dijon — Paul Gauthier.
[53] Cf. the detailed sociological dissertation by G. Siefer, *Die Mission der Arbeiterpriester* (1960).

1953), then renewed approval under special conditions (5 November 1953), and finally the prohibition of factory work in a letter by Cardinal Pizzardos on 15 September 1959, published through an indiscretion.

The vicars apostolic and Mgr. Hakim saw in manual work a means whereby priests could earn a living — following St. Paul's example (1 Cor 9:15–18). The motive the decree has in mind is that the priest might share in the life of the workmen ("operariorum ... sortem participantes") and it takes up Cardinal Suhard's reasons: "His work ... is an act of becoming at home among people to whom hitherto he had been a stranger. In suffering and with a sacrificial spirit he shares in human existence."[54]

In this way Cardinal Suhard and the Council contradict the alarming arguments which Cardinal Pizzardo had used in his letter: "It is indeed fitting that the priest should be as the apostle was ... He bears witness above all by his word and not through manual labour among factory workers as though he were one of them."[55]

An intelligent application of our text in terms of Cardinal Suhard's motivation is bound to turn our attention to men and groups to whom the priest is a stranger and with whom he must become at home, taking part in their life through suffering and in a sacrificial spirit.

Until the last minute the inclusion of reference to worker-priests in the text of the decree was disputed. Traces of this dispute remain. In opposition to the context which clearly emphasizes the competence of the bishop over his presbytery it is asserted here that the permissibility and manner of this type of apostolate is to be decided by an "auctoritas competens". The text does not make clear who is meant by this authority. The phrase is the expression of a compromise. 72 Council members proposed an emendation saying that permission for priests to undertake manual work should be granted "iussu et iudicio Episcopi" and not "probante competenti Auctoritate"; for it is the bishop who has the right to determine whether this or that work is consonant with the authentic and necessary mission that priests have undertaken. Another divergent proposal was that the passage about worker-priests be deleted. 368 bishops signed this petition which was sent in on 11 and 12 November 1965, just before the Council ended.

The reply to these two *modi* plays these two proposals off against each other. The "iussu et iudicio Episcopi" was rejected because bishops could not be left to decide to send on such a difficult mission priests who might not be disposed to undertake the work. The bishops, indeed, had no intention of doing any such thing. Those who wanted to insist that the Council was not in a position to legislate on such untested matters where disaster

[54] Cardinal Suhard, *Le Prêtre dans la Cité* (1949), p. 49.
[55] *HK* 14 (1959), p. 77.

could so easily befall, would have to keep an open mind: "Auctoritas, cum probat, dat normas ut pericula vitentur". Hence the formulation of the text lacks conviction in this place; but its substance shows that the bishops are aware of their responsibility towards all mankind, and are prepared to revise past errors of judgment.

The remaining sentences of the first section are imbued with the thought of the unity of priests with each other. As with the relation between priest and bishop, first mentioned is the experience in the liturgy and then some forms of priestly intercourse, because both can deepen the living experience of unity. Finally the decree speaks of the foundation of unity. A central theme from the High Priestly Prayer gives the mandate and provides the pastoral reasons: in order that they can bear witness to the Son. This thought from St. John's Gospel affects all of the faithful but it can very properly be applied to priests. Unity is at times of more importance than the attempt to find new forms of pastoral care, for schism cripples the power of witness.[56]

The problem of disparity in age among priests can provide a real threat to unity. Even within a presbytery the natural difference in outlook and judgment between men of different ages can cause estrangement. The Council sought to obviate this danger by a few rules of conduct addressed to all priests. In so doing they granted to each age its own privileges: the young are encouraged to try experiments (incepta), which the older are to test (experientia) and encourage (benevolentia).

Unfortunately this section contains no suggestions for reducing the tensions between old and young priests by means of a new and favourable pastoral structure. A prime requirement here is that only specially fitted parish priests should be chosen to initiate young priests in pastoral work. Not every parish priest is a good mentor. This curate relationship should be dissolved only for weighty reasons, and the duration of such a curacy should be limited to what is necessary. A man past forty with no genuine responsibility is bound to become discontented. This certainly means that far more posts must become available where younger priests can have relative independence. The specialization already mentioned might be a way of achieving this end at the supra-parochial level and the primary ordering of priests around the deans.[57] If the dean is elected by vote[58] he might well bring the required sympathy

---

[56] At this point we should note the wealth of references and formulations concerning the relation of the priest to others, which attach to the concept of unity: unus, unire, unio, unitas, communis, communio.

[57] Cf. the Church Anzeiger of the diocese of Aachen 37 (1957), p. 167: "In future we should see the appointment of a priest to a parish thus: he is appointed to take up residence and fulfil his primary ministry in this parish church, under the direction of the dean of the district, and also to fulfil extra parochial duties."

[58] "Deans are to be appointed for a specific period, according to particular law."

and mental flexibility to his office which could maintain harmony between young and old priests. In this way the dialogue we are striving to conduct with the world would not break down within the ranks of the presbytery itself.

The text of the decree does not forget the consequences this unity has at the human level. It seems out of place to cite the New Testament in order to provide such natural things with a religious motive (Cardinal Döpfner). The text simply calls to mind those features which make up the image of real brotherly love: kindness, especially towards the underprivileged; unselfish companionship and all the forms of community life that circumstances allow. [59]

The ideas about the *vita communis* and *associationes* received their present expression only after much alteration and refinement of the text. In the first draft they were there but with the primary intention of warding off the moral dangers a secular priest faces through loneliness. Even the final formulation still gives this negative reason for associations, but it is not now the chief motive. It is striking, nonetheless, to find in the forefront here — in contrast to the customary tone of Council utterances — not the pastoral task of the priest *(ministerium)* but spiritual aids *(vita)*. No reason is given why, when mentioning such associations, the improvement of pastoral opportunities was not more clearly indicated (team work, *pastorale d'ensemble*). Suggestions along these lines, made by a few of the fathers (Cardinal Alfrink in the name of the Dutch bishops, Mgr. Pironio of La Plate in Argentine, Degrijse, Superior General of the C. I. C. M., etc.), were reproduced in a very abstract form *(cooperatio)*.

On the question of the intensity with which community life should be recommended the fathers of the Council were divided. On the one hand it was emphasized that in community life serious difficulties could arise for priests if love and tolerance were lacking (49 Argentinian bishops), and so the recommendation of this form of life "quam maxime fieri possit" was rejected (Mgr. Hengsbach, Essen). On the other hand Cardinal Lercaro of Bologna observed that the formulation of the decree need not simply reiterate the ideas contained in *CIC* (can. 134). He wanted a stronger stress upon community life, "even if it is not yet possible to prescribe a *vita communis* for the clergy". Another, very correctly, spoke of the danger of celibate priests becoming practically and psychologically out of touch with human society and thus losing the power of communication with the people to whom they

---

[59] On *Vita communis* (including permanent form) cf. M. Arneth, *Bartholomäus Holzhauser und sein Weltpriesterinstitut* (1959); also J.-F. Six, *Un Prêtre. Antoine Chevrier* (1965), the biography of the too little known founder of the priestly community at Prado, esp. pp. 269 to 278.

must preach the good news.[60] "For this reason the lack of community life is immeasurably regrettable" (Mgr. Gufflet, Limoges; likewise Zaffonato, Udine; Elchinger, Strasbourg; Schmitt, Metz, etc.). Mgr. Baudox of Saint Boniface, Canada went furthest of all by proposing the *vita communis* not only for religious, but for clerics, "as a special sign of the mystery of the Church".[61] This people of God are characterized no less by the sign of the love of all the members for one another (Acts 2:44–47) than by the sign of eschatological exile given by celibacy.

The legal status of associations[62] became a topic of fairly long discussion by the Council. Many bishops supported the view that such associations should be subject to episcopal jurisdiction. They had in mind primarily their independence of pastoral responsibility within their dioceses. For other reasons some objected to priestly associations arising in a diocese without episcopal approbation. One member pointed out that in many countries associations were being formed with the intention of separating priests from their bishops: "The more or less avowed intent is to form a so-called national Church separated from the Holy See."

In countering this, the Commission pointed to the juridical and practical reasons against the institution of priestly associations by episcopal legislation. For one thing, in such a case the *forum internum* and the *forum externum* would not remain separate. Moreover, many priests would feel morally bound to join an association directed by the bishop so as to show their loyalty to their own bishop. The danger would arise also of a split developing in a diocese between those who were members of the association and those who were not.

The Commission refused to concede to the rejection of these reasons by 30 bishops and to the renewed demand for associations established by diocesan law. They opposed the desire of 124 members of the Council to make such associations subject to episcopal conferences, on the grounds that it was inter-diocesan and international associations that were under discussion. In the end it was decided that associations should be recognized by the *auctoritas ecclesiastica*.

The conclusion of Article 8 is at once surprising and realistic. It mentions all the priests whose ministry is endangered by difficult circumstances, or who have failed in some way. In most modern ecclesiastical documents not a word is said about such priests — apart from the comprehensive penal regulations contained in the *CIC*. Exhortations to give fraternal assistance

[60] Cf. Mgr. J. Stangl, *Priester und Gemeinschaft: Priesterlicher Lebensstil in der Gegenwart* (1962), pp. 213–40.

[61] Cf. art. 6: "instrumentum efficax quo nondum credentibus vita ad Christam eiusque Ecclesiam indicatur."

[62] Cf. N. Greinacher, *Priestergemeinschaften* (1960).

referred to cases of material hardship, illness and age.[63] The fact that the obligation to celibacy gives rise to difficulties is evident if at all in the negative background to the picture of the greatness of the priesthood[64] or in the directions for those responsible for the education of priests.[65] And so most Catholics have tended to despise priests who fail publicly.

During the Council a few bishops (Spülbeck of Meissen and Gottardi of Trent) turned their attention to these priests. They demanded that these men should not "be treated as men for whom it were better had they never been born, whose only course is despair" (Gomes Dos Santos of Goians, Brazil), and that ways be discovered to enable them "to share again in the life of the sacraments" (Angelelli of Córdoba in the Argentine). These wishes, which meanwhile have been very largely acted upon, for the most part are concerned with the practice of canon law, but they do contain an element affecting the presbytery. It is there in a critical situation that brotherly love must be maintained and provide genuine assistance, tactful admonition and prayer so that none be allowed to fall.

It is not true of Germany to say that "in recent years the number of priests giving up their office has greatly increased",[66] but even if smaller numbers default the basic attitude of other priests and of the faithful towards them is bound to change. Those who were behind this text of the decree would seem to have had some such intention. Mgr. Bluyssen expressed this when appealing to his priests: "1) to employ every means of destroying in the faithful the attitude of unthinking misunderstanding and suspicion; 2) to seek as far as possible to give positive assistance, with full recognition of the special agencies through which a defaulting priest seeks employment."[67]

Article 9 discusses the relation of the priest to all whom he serves. The text starts from the fact that those enjoying the general priesthood and those bearing the official priesthood are equal in the sight of God. Hence the laity possess a genuine dignity and can claim areas of special competence and responsibility within the Church. Among them the priest preserves the bond of unity, and with them he keeps open for others a way into the community.[68]

Anti-Lutheran polemics in the end led to the stifling of the biblical truth that all the baptized are priests. Before the Council a reaction to this polemic had set in (Y. Congar) and the Council carried the process further, adverting

[63] Pius XII, "Menti nostrae", AAS 42 (1950), p. 698.
[64] Pius XI, "Ad Catholici Sacerdotii", AAS 28 (1936), p. 19.
[65] For example, Pius XII, op. cit., pp. 690 f.
[66] J. Bluyssen, Analecta des Bistums Den Bosch 5 (1967), pp. 250–2.
[67] Ibid., p. 251.
[68] Cf. the decree Apostolicam actuositatem, esp. arts. 6, 10, 25; constitution Gaudium et spes, art. 43.

255

repeatedly to the fact that the whole People of God are called to a real ministry of the gospel. The evolution of this decree shows that this truth was very slow to spread, for something intellectually deduced takes a long time to find its echo in all affected areas of life.[69]

The schema *De Clericis* of 22 April 1963 confined lay priestly activity in the service of the apostolate to prayer, financial support and to regions where there was a scarcity of priests (Article 42). An important stimulus towards changing this conception came from the conference of German-speaking and Scandinavian bishops in Innsbruck, 19–22 May 1964. Inspired by what happened there, Article 1 of the draft of 2 October 1964 states that the priests along with all who believe in Christ are "disciples of the Lord"; the priest is a "brother among brethren and with them a member of the body of Christ, the building up of which is the task of all who have been reborn in the bath of baptism and signed with holy chrism, of each according to the measure of the grace and endowments bestowed upon him".

This strong emphasis upon the equal claim laid upon all of the baptized and, at the same time, the absence of an illumination of the special commission and life of the priest provoked many objections to the draft. Some reflection upon the ministry and functions of the priest was demanded (Cardinal Alfrink, Utrecht) because "some priests are seriously asking themselves if they would not have been better to remain as laymen in order to fulfil their vocation of serving and preaching the gospel to men" (Mgr. Hakim, Damascus).[70] The true evaluation of the function of the laity, it was said, had sparked off a chain reaction: a confused idea of vocation, depreciation of the special priesthood, lack of interest in the case of young men called to the priesthood (Mgr. Lefèbvre of Bourges in the name of 80 French bishops).

And so it turned out that the content of Article 1 was pushed into Article 9. At the beginning of the decree it was indeed assumed that the common priesthood of all the baptized provides the basis for any theology of the official priesthood (Article 2).

Criticism of later drafts, too, again revealed the opposing attitude to the problem of how to define the relationship between priest and laity. Cardinals Suenens, Heenan, Cardijn and other bishops wanted a stronger stress laid upon the spiritual fatherhood of the priest and his function as a leader. Cardinal Döpfner warned against clericalism and quoted Mt 23:10 in order to emphasize the special responsibility of the laity in the apostolate. Thus the final redaction contains statements about the role of the ordained ministers

[69] Cf. also F. Wulf, "Stellung und Aufgabe des Priesters nach dem Zweiten Vatikanischen Konzil" in *GL 39* (1966), pp. 45–61.

[70] Cf. A. Brunot, *Prêtres pourquoi?* (1964), esp. pp. 23–37.

as leaders alongside unrelated statements about the equal dignity of all members of the People of God.[71]

J. Ratzinger has a report[72] on how the official minister has to be understood within the body of the baptized. He takes a saying of St. Augustine as his starting-point: "Pro nobis episcopus sum, cum nobis christianus." Augustine is not indulging in meaningless rhetoric about humility, but means to elucidate the true nature of his office. He draws upon an illustration from the theology of the Trinity. This states, it is true, that in God each of the three Persons "subsists only in turning from himself to the others, so that Person and relation are identical ... If I look upon him I see simply God; Father, Son or Holy Spirit, is there only in relation." Augustine applies this notion to the doctrine of spiritual office: "Official minister is a relational concept. Seen in itself and for itself alone each man is simply a Christian and cannot hold a higher status ... 'Pro vobis', i.e. in relation to others, he is an official minister, although this ministry is indeed irrevocable and affects his whole being. Official ministry and relationship are thus identical. Office and relation coincide. Office is the relation of *being for*. Thus we say how the strict identity of the Christian, which we call his general priesthood, exists simultaneously with the strict reality of the official ministry, and how this irresolvable paradox, around which Catholic-Protestant controversy keeps on revolving, becomes entangled in itself, becomes welded together and remains real, analogous to the paradox of the Threeness and Oneness of God."[73]

On account of the "strict identity of being a Christian" the Council chose the word "brother" to describe the priest. At the same time it describes the "relation of *being for*" by the word "father". Is it correct to use such a formula in violation of our Lord's explicit prohibition (Mt 23:9)?

The decree does not say unequivocally that the priest is a father. The brotherhood of the priest is affirmed unequivocally, but his fatherhood applies only to his official capacity *(munus patris)*. This mode of statement sets the statements about the fatherhood of the priest in parallel with the text about his *repraesentatio Christi*. The affirmation that the priest acts like a father is true in the same sense as the affirmation that in his official activity he acts "in the person of Christ the Head" (Article 2). Moreover, the writings of St. Paul prove that the apostle claimed to stand in the relation of father to the Church (1 Cor 4:15; Gal 4:19; Phm 10), thus expressing the "fact that he transmitted life".[74]

---

[71] Cf. F. Wulf, *op. cit.*, pp. 46–48.

[72] "Das Konzilsdekret über den priesterlichen Dienst" — delivered at the annual diet of the principals and directors of the German-speaking seminaries for priests and theologians in Brixen, 2–4 August 1967. Text in the minutes of the diet, edited by J. Mayr, Brixen.

[73] J. Ratzinger, *op. cit.*, pp. 44 ff.

[74] Schrenk, "πατήρ", *TWNT*, V, pp. 1006 f.

In this interpretation of the fatherhood of the priest it seems that our Lord's saying is not being disregarded. The question remains, however, whether the title "father" ought to be the everyday form of address for a priest. Certainly we cannot find the answer to that question in St. Paul.[75]

Any concretization of that which is meant by fatherhood or ministerial authority remains tied to the fact that the priest is an envoy. In this capacity he is thrown back upon the form in which Christ lived out his mission.[76] This implies that for the priest, "being for others is constitutive" and, moreover, is a being that depends upon others and is orientated towards others. The origin and the goal of being sent imply the double burden of withdrawing oneself. It means to make the one who sends present in word, deed and will *(non quae sua sunt quaerentes),* to be a prophetic signpost that does not come between the seeker and the sought. It means also that one thinks only about those to whom one is sent. The I of the ambassador loses all importance in comparison to them, it is a mere pawn, there only to serve *(non venit ministrari, sed ministrare).* If the concept of the ambassador becomes filled with the image of Christ, it signifies "the colossal, almost explosive opening up of one's own existence on two sides".

The concept of *being for* or of envoy more or less rules out the possibility of drawing a line between laity and priests. A verbal announcement by Cardinal Darmajuwana of Central Java brings us to the root of the problem. Of a later revised version of this article he remarked, "the text distinguishes almost fussily between the official priesthood of the presbyter and the general priesthood of all believers; this fuss seems to arise from fear — quite without foundation in the Church of today — that the laity want to take over the prerogatives of the priests. Such fear and suspicion, which disfigure the Church of Christ and give rise to anti-clericalism, are bad counsellors."

The pastoral design of the Council likewise influenced the formulation of its decrees. Thus we always see most plainly in them the tendency to give all groups within the Church a positive indication of their function, and of necessity there is a lack of clear delineation. Many would rather have been given a specific definition of their function within the apostolate as a whole. For this, too, is a presupposition of clarification in self-understanding and of the place of the clergy in the Church.

Our text makes a start at discussing the definition of spheres of competence within the Church. This is necessary if there is to be "serious co-operation of the laity with the presbyters in the common apostolate" (Cardinal Döpfner, Munich). In connection with the Constitution on the Church (especially

---

[75] *Ibid.*
[76] On what follows cf. Ratzinger, *op. cit.,* pp. 21–23.

Article 37) it roughly stakes out the area into which the priest ought not to trespass: "dignitas, propria pars in missione Ecclesiae, libertas, experientia et competentia in diversis campis humanae actionis."

In this context, however, the function of the layman is given a very vague profile, and the statements remain ineffective.[77] Change of mentality requires stronger stimuli than are given here. Without such strong stimulus the traditional outlook on the relationship of priests to laity, conditioned as it is by the image of a clerical Church, will not change. A new mentality which looks upon the Church as one's own concern gains ground very slowly. That the clergy themselves are not least to blame can be seen from the reply to the question in preparation for the Third World Congress of the Lay Apostolate.[78]

In spite of the autonomous involvement of the laity, which consists "not simply in the administration of temporal goods or in consultation, but in initiative, in a share in the Church's mission" (Patriarch Mèouchi of Antioch), the ordained priests carry the principal responsibility within the people of God. The endowment of the Spirit which they possess enables them to articulate the demands of God. The text adverts to the double way in which men today are able to perceive God's dealing with men. The suggestion that God can be experienced in the outward (signa temporum) or interior life (spiritus) of man is worth examining. In our times it is in the end this experience alone which is able to support faith[79] and give theological systems their credibility.[80] A central task of the priest is, therefore, to interpret the signs of the times (Lk 12:54 ff.). "It may be, indeed it is certain, that it is only possible to read the message of Jesus Christ with any clarity and fullness in the book of the world if it has first been read in the book of the Scriptures. But after that it can and should be read in the book of the world and of man's life as well ... It would be a good thing if direction in the spiritual life given to lay people were to take more explicit account of this possibility, which is obvious enough in itself."[81] In France Action catholique with its révision de vie has tried to develop a method that might help us on this point.[82]

The text tells us something, too, about the second way in which we expe-

---

[77] Cf. F. Wulf, op. cit., p. 57.

[78] Cf. the congress report: "Das Volk Gottes auf den Wegen der Menschheit" (1968), p. 27.

[79] Cf. Apostolicam actuositatem, art. 24; also K. Rahner, "Frömmigkeit heute und morgen", GL 39 (1966), pp. 326–42.

[80] Cf. K. Rahner's contribution on the trinitarian God as transcendental primal cause of the history of salvation in Mysterium Salutis, II.

[81] K. Rahner, Mission and Grace, I, p. 109.

[82] Cf. J. Loew, Tagebuch einer Arbeitermission (1960), pp. 349–52; also F. Hillig, Die 'Révision de vie' — eine neue Übung aus neuem Geist", GL 37 (1964), pp. 376–83.

rience God: by the impulse of the Spirit of God given to the individual or the congregation, an impulse which strengthens faith. This awareness of God does not come about automatically or mechanically: only an emphatic decision for him in face of the burdens of everyday life can disclose a glimpse of his presence to us.[83]

The priest must be on the alert not only for occasional impulses of grace, but for every manifestation of special endowment (*charismata, attrahentes altiorem vitam spiritualem*). It is his function "to test the spirits, not to manage or rule them" (Mgr. Gufflet, Limoges). Nor must he lack courage and patience to delegate to laymen tasks in the service of the Church, so that they can act upon their own responsibility. The Latin text uses the word "officia" to denote these functions, thus making clear that it is not an externally imposed obligation which leads to action (*munus*), but voluntary service or practical necessity.

The priest finds his place at the centre of the circle of the life of the laity (*in medio laicorum*). Thus all the distinctions in form of life that formerly derived from the opposition between sacred and secular become invalid.[84] At this point the mutual interrelation of priests and laity is again taken up (cf. Article 6, para. 6), so that the unity between them can be stressed afresh. Not only the presbytery (Article 8), but the People of God in their totality are obliged to maintain this unity,[85] for the mystery of the Church[86] can be manifested[87] in the unity of priests with their people even more than in the community of life among priests. Priests must be solicitous for the common good, never allowing true doctrine to be distorted out of opportunism.

The local congregation is the Church in microcosm, but it must never lead a narcissist life of self-satisfaction. Its members cannot be content to maintain the static continuance of those who practise. They must go out to those who have fallen from the Church and bring them back to faith and life within the congregation; they must be ready to converse with brethren in other confessions; and they must have a missionary spirit towards all who do not recognize Christ as their Redeemer.

---

[83] Cf. K. Rahner, "Reflections on the Experience of Grace", *Theological Investigations*, III (1967), pp. 47–57; id., "The Logic of the Knowledge of Religiously Important Concrete Particulars in Ignatius", *The Dynamic Element in the Church*, Quaestiones Disputatae 12 (1964), pp. 115–70.

[84] Cf. A. Liégé, "Baptême et Sacerdoce", *Prêtres Diocésains* (Feb.–March 1962), pp. 7–64. The desire of one bishop to include a prescription concerning clerical dress in the text of the decree was denied with a reference to *CIC* and to the particular laws of several regions.

[85] Cf. *Apostolicam actuositatem*, art. 10.

[86] Cf. Constitution on the Liturgy, art. 42.

[87] For the reason stated some reflection on the structure and size of the parish would certainly be appropriate. Cf. K. Rahner, "The Parish", *Theology of Pastoral Action*, pp. 100 to 105.

The text which follows is close to that of *Lumen Gentium* and was accepted only in the final draft. It can be traced to the motion of one bishop and is designed to prevent the rest of the text of this article from appearing "too hard, because it describes only the obligations of the presbyter and does not assure him of any legitimate response".

III. THE DISTRIBUTION OF PRIESTS AND PRIESTLY VOCATIONS

Article 10 bases the responsibility of priests for the whole Church upon the commission given to the apostles. It urges projects and initiatives designed to relieve the lack of priests and the hardship of priests through the proper distribution of ordained priests and seminarians. Some practical hints are then given to those sent as pastors into strange lands.

The beginning of this article provides a striking contrast to Article 2. In Article 2 it is stated that every member of the body shares in its mission. In this passage the mission seems to apply only to priests. If the comprehensive command to go "to the ends of the earth" had been addressed exclusively to priests, the laity might indeed be apostolically active, but only "permanens in suo loco" (Patriarch Mèouchi, Antioch). But this is contradicted by *Lumen Gentium* (Article 33) and by the practice of the Church (catechists, pastorally employed nuns, etc.). It may be that the text is redolent of the inappropriate notion that the anointing as a member of the body of Christ becomes intensified through orders. Or it may be that the terms "mission" and "ends of the earth" have associations solely with priest-missionaries.

Three bishops proposed changes in the text at this point, designed to express the fact that orders do not prepare *(praeparat)* for mission but confer it. The Commission rejected this proposal on the grounds that the text was clear enough. In this passage it might have been explained that the word "mission" or "sending" is used in various senses in the decree. The text speaks of the mission of Jesus by the Father and of the apostles by Jesus (Article 2: "missis Apostolicis sicut ipse missus erat a Patre"). Clearly it is the biblical concept of mission that we have here: ἀποστέλλειν, πέμπειν.[88] It means "to send out with authority (derived from God) to serve the kingdom of God".[89] Such mission surpasses any authority which orders can confer, and includes it. The Council also used the expression to describe the apostolic function of the Church, in which every member shares (Article 2). That this sharing does not

---

[88] St. John uses the two concepts interchangeably: cf. K. H. Rengstorf, "ἀποστέλλειν", *TWNT*, I, pp. 403 f.; also J. Giblet, "Der Priester 'zweiten Grades'", in Baraúna, ed., *De Ecclesia*, II (1966), pp. 195–7.
[89] Cf. K. H. Rengstorf, *op. cit.*, p. 405.

include all of the authority of the official ministry is forbidden by the customary and theological interpretation of the official ministry.[90] Finally the term means legitimate commissioning *(missio canonica)* by the bishop to execute the authority conferred in orders (Article 1: "missio quam ab Episcopis recipiunt"). Because today this is the sense in which the Church understands "missio", the Council fathers formulated the text before us, which says that the gifts of the Spirit given in orders merely "equip for mission".

When in this passage the relationship of the ordained to the priesthood of Christ was being textually fixed, again it became apparent (cf. Article 9) that there was confusion as to how the essence of the priesthood was to be defined. The formula "priests have acquired a share in the fullness of the priesthood of Christ" was meant to mark off the distinction from the general priesthood. Sixty bishops, however, pointed out that the fullness of priesthood can be attributed to Christ alone. One of them remarked also that the fullness of orders as a sacrament is imparted to the bishops. And so emerged the text we now have, wherein the little word "vere" has to express the distinction between official and general priesthood, thus casting a shadow upon the latter.

The text takes the figure of Melchisedech as a prefiguring of the universality of the priestly mission, alluding to Heb 7:3 which speaks of the King of Salem who was "without father or mother or genealogy, and has neither beginning of days nor end of life". The author of Hebrews reaches this description of Melchisedech by applying a principle of rabbinical exegesis to the data of the Old Testament (Gen 22:16; Ps 110:4): if the scriptures are silent there is nothing there *(quod non in thora, non in mundo)*.[91] As a result, Melchisedech's priesthood is taken to be not of human origin. It cannot be explained, in terms of membership of a priestly line, but is derived directly from God.[92]

It is true that this verse holds no key position within the context of the Letter to the Hebrews, but the Fathers and also heretics of later days paid great attention to it. For them it had this significance: Jesus did not belong to the clan of Levi, but to that of Melchisedech, i.e. he was begotten by God. The "order of Melchisedech" does not state, therefore, that "the priesthood of Christ is not restricted by race, nation, or in time" but that, as an eternal priesthood, it could not have originated in time.[93]

The type of the King of Salem seems to have been misunderstood in the

---

[90] Cf. H. Zeller, "Amt", *LTK*, I, col. 451; also K. Rahner, "Priester IV", *ibid.*, VIII, col. 745: "Over against the individual Christian as such, the ministry — as that of the whole Church — is thus something higher (D [32nd ed.] 3850), because the Church as a whole possesses powers (even if invested in persons) which the individual as individual does not."
[91] Cf. O. Kuss, *Der Brief an die Hebräer* (1953), p. 55; also H. Rusche, "Die Gestalt des Melchisedek", *MTZ* 6 (1955), pp. 230–252.
[92] Cf. H. Rusche, *op. cit.*, p. 236.   [93] *Ibid.*, p. 237.

present context. Cardinal Döpfner wanted the allusion to the *vexata figura Melchisedech* deleted, but unfortunately his wish was not granted.

In the first draft dated 22 April 1963 in its exhortation entitled "De Distributione Cleri", the decree had set itself against all group egoism in the work of salvation, and against all unwillingness to offer services to bishops in need. This missionary initiative *(sollicitudinem omnium ecclesiarum cordi esse debere)* became more and more specific as the composition of the decree progressed. The final text presents quite a wealth of detail, unusual in this decree, for the Commission frequently rejected expansions on the grounds that such refinements ought to be left to the revised *CIC*. The detailed treatment, therefore, accentuates the importance of the theme. This must be said all the more clearly as there has been no response to these suggestions — apart from material assistance — from the German-speaking area, to which the suggestions were no doubt addressed. The quotation from St. Paul at the end is worth noting. This enjoins human closeness between the missionary and those to whom he is sent. Separation dulls the missionary's sensitivity and obstructs his preaching — as Article 9 has already pointed out with reference to the priest's relation to the laity. There were a few verbal interventions which did not affect the final text but are important as an indication of the viewpoints of those who made them. Eleven bishops from Central Africa emphasized that only mature, prudent and steady men should be sent to do pastoral work in foreign lands, and not men motivated by the desire for excitement or by over-activism. Cardinal Darmajuwana of Central Java proposed that secular priests who move to another diocese might remain joined to their own diocese and return there after five or ten years. In addition he warned against the multiplication of international seminaries, for then a rootless clergy might emerge, and this would precipitate serious dangers.

The Council turned the eyes of priests and seminarians towards their responsibilities for the Church as a whole (the decree *Christus Dominus* [Article 6] did the same for bishops), but no reproach of laziness was thereby implied against any diocese. "It does not seem right, however, to support dioceses that show no signs of trying to support themselves" (Cardinal De Barros Camara, Rio de Janeiro). Moreover, the so-called "Catholic" mentality demands that we shun all particularism. There would still seem to be Churches in which the jurisdiction of the priest runs only as far as the boundaries of the diocese and does not cover the whole country or language-area (Mgr. Peireira, Coimbra, Portugal).

The distribution of recruits to the priesthood was again tackled in the motu proprio *Ecclesiae Sanctae* (I, nn. 1–5) where it was given canonical form.[94]

---

[94] Cf. K. Mörsdorf in vol. II of this series, p. 204.

Article 11 declares that priests, who will always be there in the midst of the People of God, themselves bear the responsibility of ensuring an adequate supply of young men to fill up their ranks. Priests, however, can fulfil this obligation only if they receive widespread support from their congregations.

In the Catholic view the priestly office in the Church is *iuris divini*.[95] Without going into systematic arguments, the text before us accepts this view, choosing for its formulation one or two biblical concepts, so that the official minister appears under the image of the shepherd. In all this it remains clear that the true eschatological shepherd is Christ himself *(Pastor et episcopus animarum nostrarum)*. Mt 9:36, which sets the shepherd and the labourer in the vineyard in parallel, supplies the basis for applying the shepherd image analogously to the priest.[96] The Latin word for priest in this context is *sacerdos,* a word which the decree uses to embrace bishop and presbyter.[97]

The need of official ministers in the order of salvation, met for the faithful by our Lord's institution of the priestly ministry, finds empirical corroboration from sociologists[98] who say that a large-scale community could never realize its intrinsic potential without the formative example of a senior, centralized leadership,[99] capable of co-ordinating the efforts of the members. In this context sociology does not speak of an isolated individual but of a group. For the functioning of a larger community such a group seems to be indispensable, especially when it is a case of models according to which each rising generation must conform, or of problems of a way of life in the broadest sense.

The quotation from the Second Letter to Timothy concerns the safeguarding of tradition. "That which is attributed automatically (in Col 1:28; 3:16) to all Christians can now be attributed (in the Pastoral Letters) only to specially suitable Christians, chiefly to the leaders of the congregation."[100] The Catholic doctrine of tradition sees in this the foundation of the system whereby through a "public, solemn act of the Church" a commission is given to hand on to other suitable men the "capacity to teach and the traditional doctrine". "According to the commission the apostolic office is to be continued

---

[95] Cf. *D* 966; also H. Zeller, "Amt", *LTK,* I, col. 454.

[96] Cf. Acts 20:28 ff.; Eph 4:11, etc., and also J. Jeremias, "ποιμήν", *TWNT,* VI, p. 497, who emphasizes that in the early Churches people "were constantly aware of the image of the leaders of the Church as 'shepherds'".

[97] Cf. Relatio de singulis Propositionibus, *De Prooemio,* of 2 October 1964.

[98] Cf. P. R. Hofstätter, "Eliten und Minoritäten", *Kölner Zeitung für Soziologie und Sozialpsychologie* 14 (1962), pp. 62 ff.

[99] In sociology the concept of the elite has a neutral connotation. The leader is he who best fulfils the group norms and contributes most to the accomplishment of the group aims.

[100] K. H. Rengstorf, "διδάσκειν", *TWNT,* II, p. 150.

in the Church."[101] The text of the decree does not trace this commission back to an explicit command of our Lord, but to the will of Jesus as interpreted by the Holy Spirit *(suggerente Spiritu Sancto ... duxerunt).* The commission is given to all officials including the presbyters.

The emphasis upon the responsibility of the official Church, which comes to the fore in this place undoubtedly because the text is addressing itself precisely to these officials, finds its needed supplement in an image from the *Pontificale Romanum.*[102] A concern to provide priests for the future is laid upon all. The text referred to in *Optatam Totius*[103] then appeals separately to families, parishes, teachers, priests and bishops, to make their contribution to furthering vocations, without imputing superior responsibility to any one group. In regard to priests, our context makes it abundantly obvious that a priest's labours are fruitless if "the special witness of his life" does not make his "ministry of the word" credible.[104]

Various bishops presented *modi* asking that the subject of vocation be treated. The Commission declined to do so and referred to the treatment of clerical vocation in general in *Lumen Gentium* and *Perfectae Caritatis* and to the treatment of priestly vocation in the papal encyclicals *Ad Catholici Sacerdotii* and *Menti Nostrae.* Our text is not supposed to deal with the *natura vocationis* but with the signs of it that might be useful for priests, parents and teachers.

Among such signs — according to Cardinal Darmajuwana of Central Java — are unconditionally included personal inclination for, and delight in, spiritual activity. In addition, "generose Domino vocanti respondere" must certainly be mentioned. J. Ratzinger[105] at all events sees in this generosity the chief point of contact in all efforts to point young men the road to the priesthood. "And I believe that this would be important also for that which we call recruitment to the priesthood. Such recruitment must appeal to generosity and not to love of ease, otherwise it brings the wrong results.[106]

After commending diocesan and national projects to gain vocations to the priesthood and after the appeal to spread the idea of the necessity and value of the priestly ministry through homilies, catechesis and publicity channels, the article ends with a thought from the writings of the Fathers. Two texts

---

[101] O. Karrer, "Tradition", *HTG,* II (1963), p. 695.
[102] This is the image with which the bishop begins his address to the faithful when he wishes to evoke their assent to the approaching ordinations. Cf. B. Kleinheyer, *op. cit.,* pp. 95 f. and 192–4.
[103] Cf. also J. Neuner's commentary on the Decree on Priestly Formation in vol. II of this series, pp. 380–2.
[104] Cf. art. 8, footnote 21.
[105] The conciliar decree: cf. art. 9, footnote 5.
[106] *Ibid.,* 46.

interpreting Jn 21:16 f. are cited and directly applied to the priestly ministry. [107]

With the support of these passages the text arrives at the formulation: "maximum testimonium amoris" — to be understood in the light of the patristic texts not as superlative but at most as elative.

---

[107] John Chrysostom: "The question arose in order to show us how much he had the guidance of these flocks at heart. If this, then, is now obvious, it must be equally obvious that a greater, an unspeakable, reward is prepared for him who labours for that which is so dear to Christ ... For he was not at pains on that occasion to show how much Peter loved him ... but intended to demonstrate to Peter and to all of us how fervently he loves his Church, in order that we too will throw ourselves into her service with all fervour." Gregory the Great: "If, then, pastoral care is a witness of love *(dilectionis est testimonium cura pastionis)*, anyone who is equipped with the power but declines to nourish the flock of God demonstrates that he has no love for the supreme Shepherd."

The Life of Priests

Article 12. In discussing the title of the decree it has already been stressed that in forming a notion of the office of the priest it is important first to think of his ministry and only then of his life. It was affirmed that the office of the priesthood would be viewed primarily in terms of its function and not of its status. A consequence of this is that the priest's whole life — his spiritual life, his spirituality, his relationship to the world, to things and to men — must be decisively defined and stamped by his ministry, his function, his mandate and mission. The purpose and content of chapter 3 of the decree is to demonstrate precisely these things. First of all the priest's spiritual life in general is discussed (12–14), then some of the particular human and religious demands that the office brings with it (15–17), and finally the helps and means that are available or are required for his spiritual life, for his continuing formation and for his material sustenance (18–21).

Article 12 is built up as follows. By way of introduction, the special obligation of the priest to strive for perfection is explained; then comes the first definition of the peculiarity of his road to sanctification and of the specific nature of his spirituality. The central idea of this article is the special union that must exist between the presbyter and Christ the High Priest, and hence between the presbyter and Christ's mission, destiny and redemptive work extending through time. For the non-theologian, the statement: "By the sacrament of orders priests are configured to Christ the Priest", requires further explication. The configuration here mentioned is ascribed by theological tradition, especially since St. Thomas, to the *character* of orders, understood as a supernatural quality physically inhering in the soul — more exactly, as a spiritual potency to undertake the performance of divine worship. Quite apart from the implied restriction of the priestly ministry to the liturgy, the man of today finds it hard to use concepts taken from the material order to describe processes and conditions in a personal spirit. It is time, therefore, for us to translate the undoubtedly profound speculation of

267

high scholasticism into personal categories, as has been successfully attempted some time ago with the tractate on grace. If this is not done, what is really meant will no longer be understood and will be rejected as nonsensical. The further statement, that "priests are bound by a special claim, since they have been consecrated to God in a new way by the reception of orders. They have become living instruments of Christ the eternal priest, so that through the ages they can accomplish his wonderful work", likewise requires more precise explication; for the priest's state of consecration has very commonly been misunderstood in the past, and for many the priest is, purely and simply, the consecrated man. What, by contrast, is the true meaning of the statement? As the citation of Jn 10:36 in the following section implies, "being consecrated" means first of all "being set apart" for the special priestly ministry.[1] By irrevocably calling a man to such a ministry, God sets him apart, lays his hand upon him, claims him for himself and for his work, so that the one who is called and commissioned has to put himself, as an instrument, at God's (Christ's) disposal. In this sense he is consecrated to God. At the same time, this being consecrated means that God grants the one called and set apart his authority and grace to perform the ministry laid upon him. He inclines in love towards him, gives him his Spirit. This is precisely what is meant in biblical-patristic tradition when it speaks of the anointing of the priest with the messianic-prophetic Spirit, or when the more sober language of theology speaks of the grace of the sacrament, which confers upon the priest the power to place his whole life in the service of Christ and enables him to perform "the priestly service of the gospel of God" (Rom 15:16). But the call and the consecration of the priest are rooted in the fundamental call of the Christian to faith and in the consecration of baptism, which are unsurpassable and than which, in the objective order, there is no higher gradation — a fact which in no way denies the special dignity of the sacramental priesthood, and even less calls in question the increase in justifying grace. All special calls and consecrations are already embraced within this fundamental call, and represent merely the articulation and unfolding of this fundamental vocation and fundamental consecration for the one service of Jesus Christ in the various dimensions of ecclesio-charismatic life. The decree draws attention to the connection between the consecration of baptism and that of the priest, although unfortunately it adverts one-sidedly to the *perfection* contained in the two vocations and not to the call to *ministry* (as would have been in harmony with the tenor of the decree). This emphasis could mislead us into separating perfection from ministry. The concluding sentence of the first section does, however, obviate this misunderstanding by

---

[1] On the concepts of *consecration* and *mission* in conciliar statements and on their mutual relationship cf. A. Grillmeier's commentary on the Constitution on the Church, art. 28, in vol. I of this series, p. 220, and also my exposition of art. 2 of this decree.

saying that it is precisely the *ministry* taken up by the priest as commissioner and representative of Christ, which gives him the opportunity to imitate Christ better. It is unfair to the psychological make-up of the priest of today to stress so strongly (as this article does) that the priest is under obligation to strive for the perfection of Christ in a special way ("To the acquisition of this perfection priests are bound by a special claim, since they have been consecrated to God in a new way by the reception of orders"), for today the priest feels the burden of his own imperfection far more acutely than did the priest of former days.[2]

The second section explains more precisely wherein the perfection, that is determined by this ministry of representing Christ, consists. It consists in nothing other than the dedication of the priest's whole life to the service of mankind, in the style of Christ who gave himself for us. In order to express adequately the "Passion" that is necessarily attached to such a dedication, that is, to define the characteristic quality of the priest's *mortificatio*, as a striving and suffering with Christ the High Priest, the text makes the general statement: "Priests mortify in themselves the deeds of the flesh." Such asceticism, however, is not specifically that of the priesthood. It would have been more appropriate, therefore, to have said something like this. "For the sake of total dedication to the service of men, they mortify all private desires and plans for their own lives." The allusion to Eph 4:13 in the last sentence of this section is hardly apposite, for in all probability this passage is not saying "that *we*, the members of the body of Christ become the 'perfect man' (ἄνδρα τέλειον, *virum perfectum*, Vg), but that we, through the movement towards unity in faith and knowledge, arrive at Christ the Head".[3] Nonetheless, this passage, like other passages in this article, correctly emphasizes that the sanctity of the priest — like that of every Christian — is primarily a gift of grace, a fruit of the holiness of Christ, whose Spirit "vivifies and leads them". The first precondition of his sanctity is, therefore, that he keep his eyes fixed on Christ, that he remain in union with him, being "docile to the impulse and guidance of the Holy Spirit". As the third section in particular argues, where this happens there is an interaction between "the ministry of the Spirit and of justice" (cf. 2 Cor 3:8 f.) and sanctity. (The allusion is

---

[2] The original formulation of the idea presented an even greater danger of placing too high an ascetical demand upon the priest — as do many phrases in the papal encyclicals and exhortations to priests from Pius X to Pius XII. It runs: "Because every priest, according to the saying, 'as the Father has sent me so I send you', represents Christ in person, he must try to achieve the perfection of him whose ministry he represents, and must — having become a 'man of God' (Tim 6:11) in a special way — appear among men as though bearing the radiance of him who lived among us 'holy, sinless, without blemish, separated from sinners and exalted high above the heavens'."

[3] H. Schlier, *The Epistle to the Ephesians* (1957), pp. 200 f., who is followed in this view by M. Dibelius, *To the Ephesians*, Handbook to the N. T. 12 (1953), pp. 82 f.

to the priest of the new covenant as a servant of the Spirit and of the righteousness of grace, in contrast to the mechanical ministry of the Old Testament.) This is what makes apostolic work fruitful, while the priestly ministry
in its entire scope is "directed towards perfection of life".

The concluding paragraph once again emphasizes the critical importance
of holy priests for the spiritual renewal of the Church, aimed at by the
Council. This is undoubtedly justified in essence, but, in the weariness and
crisis of faith which not a few priests are experiencing during the post-conciliar development of the Church, the constant admonition to strive for "that
greater sanctity" does not always exert a beneficial psychological effect.

Article 13. The idea, already expressed in general terms in Article 12, that
the way of sanctification peculiar to the priest lies in the perfect fulfilment
of his priestly ministry, is now thematically developed in terms of the three
offices.

In respect of the teaching or preaching office, the first section is dictated
by the re-discovery of holy Scripture and the present high esteem accorded
to the word of God. The opening words of this section echo the opening
words of the Dogmatic Constitution on Revelation, but they make use of
the term "ministers of God's Word" — popularly used by Protestants to
describe their clergy, and hitherto suspect in Catholic circles.[4] Holy Scripture alone is explicitly named as the source of preaching. This does not, it is
true, exclude the theological and spiritual tradition of the Church, but allows
it to recede into the background. In this way the decree becomes clearly
distinguished from all that has been officially published to the pastoral clergy
in the recent past on the subject of preaching. In this the article merely draws
the conclusions implicit in the statement of the Decree on Priestly Formation,
that holy Scripture "ought to be the soul of all theology".[5] Two requirements
are now put forward in respect of the sanctification of the priest through
study and preaching of the word of God. 1. The priest must prayerfully
make the word of God in holy Scripture his own. 2. His preaching must not
be mere instruction, but must be a spiritual word. The first requirement asks
for the re-discovery of the "prayerful theology" so often inculcated in recent
years. For this, daily Scripture reading and constant recourse to fresh scripture study are indispensable. At the same time we must consider how the
word of Scripture is to be translated into the concepts and mentality of the
man of today, with his experience of the modern world, his difficulties and
doubts in matters of faith. In carrying out this translation we must take
care — as the decree points out — not to push into the forefront our own

---

[4] The Council of Trent correctly rejected the view that the priesthood was "only the office
and mere ministry of preaching the gospel" (*DS* 1771).
[5] Decree on Priestly Formation, art. 16.

wisdom, the all too human reflections of the preacher, in an effort to get close to our times, but to sound out the pure and undistorted word of God. This only happens if — as the decree says — the priest remembers "that it is the Lord who opens hearts and that sublime utterance comes not from themselves but from God's power". This already hints at the second requirement: preaching must be confused neither with a religious lecture nor a one-sided moral sermon. It is never a word that comes, as it were, "down from above". At all times the preacher must be conscious that he is a disciple of the Lord, so that his word is addressed to his co-disciples, to his brethren. On the other hand he has to offer real help to his brethren; he must be their spiritual guide into the depths of the gospel, of the mystery of Christ, that has been hidden from all eternity; he must lead them into the mystery of the unfathomable love of God. He has to be a mystagogue who initiates them in the ways of spiritual accomplishment. Whenever he succeeds, his preaching will most certainly contribute to his own spiritual progress: it becomes a road to sanctification. Much as we applaud the return of the central mystery of the Christian revelation, of the gospel, to the heart of preaching, a warning has to be uttered against biblicism. It is true that theological tradition must be thought out afresh, but today's sermon cannot dispense with theological penetration. To the first main section of this article we might add, therefore, that the theological effort involved in a study of tradition contributes no less to the sanctification of the preacher, provided it is inspired by the Spirit of Christ.

The second main section on the ministry of sanctification or the priestly ministry describes the offering of the eucharistic sacrifice as the priest's "chief duty" *(munus praecipuum)*, whereas the Council says of bishops that preaching "occupies an eminent place" *(eminet)*[6] among their chief duties *(inter praecipua munera)*. The discrepancy here is only apparent, for this article is discussing explicitly only the *sacerdotal* functions of the presbyter: "Priests fulfil their chief duty in the mystery of the eucharistic sacrifice." The avoidance of the word "presbyter" is deliberate. In the Dogmatic Constitution on the Church it is affirmed even more plainly of priests that "they exercise this sacred function *(munus sacrum)* of Christ most of all *(maxime)* in the eucharistic liturgy or synaxis".[7] It seems illuminating and in need of no further proof, that ministering in the "sacred realities" the priest contributes more directly and powerfully than in any other of his functions towards his own sanctification. (For this reason many exhortations to priests used to quote the sentence from the bishop's address at the ordination of priests: "Imitate what you handle; and as you celebrate the mysteries of the Lord's

---

[6] Constitution on the Church, art. 25; Decree on the Bishops' Pastoral Office, art. 12.
[7] Constitution on the Church, art. 28.

death, be earnest in ridding your members by mortification of all vices and lusts." The present article repeats this exhortation.) And yet, one may doubt that this is so. The priest's most powerful engagement seems to be guaranteed in pastoral work, and preaching likewise automatically demands the priest's personal participation, whereas — as experience proves — the sacramental actions, holy Mass most of all, are exposed to the danger of impersonalism through habitual use. This may be the very reason why personal engagement is urged so vehemently at this point. "As ministers of sacred realities, especially in the sacrifice of the Mass, priests represent the person of Christ in a special way." "In it the work of our redemption continues to be carried out." "While being nourished by the body of Christ, their hearts are sharing in the love of him who gives himself as food for his faithful ones." Ever and again the admonition is given to have one's heart in the sacred act: priests must "unite themselves with the act of Christ the Priest", must "offer their whole selves every day to God", and "they are joined with the intention and love of Christ when they administer the sacraments". All of these indicatives have an admonitory character. Very properly, the priest's constant readiness to hear confession is stressed above all else. This is indeed the mark of the "intention and love of Christ" especially for the busy priest of our own day. Even the "private" daily celebration of Mass — taken for granted by the older generation of priests, and theologically fully justified, as the Council emphasizes — is of high spiritual value; but one cannot disguise the fact, that with the reform of the liturgy, especially with the use of the vernacular, this has become psychologically more difficult for many. As has been stressed already in Article 5, the spiritual fruitfulness of the Breviary depends very largely upon its timely revision.

Pastoral care in the narrower sense contributes to the priest's own sanctification (third main section) whenever the priest succeeds in maintaining an attitude of selfless integrity over against those — especially the individual — entrusted to his care, and refrains from seeking his own fulfilment. This is where he can put to the test the measure of his genuine desire to live for others, to be used by them, and to allow his own wishes and plans to fall away into insignificance. Thus the pattern of priestly perfection popular in former days — the priest as model of all the virtues — is no longer so highly esteemed, for we are all too well aware of our own and each other's weaknesses. The only decisive thing is that the priest throw his whole being into the service of men. Wherever there is any distress he must be at hand to give effective help — that costs him something. The pastoral love, so much extolled in this article, takes on a different shape today from the shape it used to have. It has to be companionable and brotherly, free from all semblance of paternalism. In our days, therefore, when men have become more down to earth, more secular, more disillusioned and sceptical, it is more difficult to utter a spiritual word that fits man's psychological situation. And when ultimate things are at stake, where his pastoral work compels the priest to accept oppression and suffering, even to risk his life, there undoubtedly the pastoral *manner* has no longer any part to play; all that counts is genuine witness, the action that flows from faith and love. For this reason, in spite of all the hardships, it is much easier for priests in countries where the Church is persecuted, to become more selfless and closer to Christ in a simple pastoral ministry — the spiritual help that one human being gives another. In these places weariness of faith, discouragement and despondency are recognized as temptations, whereas elsewhere these things often creep up unobserved and overcome the priest. The seeming futility of his activity can gradually destroy him; in such circumstances he must protect his pastoral love. Unrest in the world and in the Church today constitutes a threat to the pastor, as it is also a stimulus to a life of faith. This article is only partially successful in realizing what pastoral love means in the present day.

Article 14. The problem that now emerges is this: if the priest's road to sanctification is as profoundly determined by his office, his ministry, his pastoral work as the previous article explains, does he not run into the danger — if he acts upon this principle — of becoming so absorbed in his work that he has no energy left for prayer, recollection and an interior life, which are prerequisites of the true inspiration of his pastoral activity, and thus also of the fruitfulness of his pastoral ministry in respect of his own striving for perfection? Is this danger not all the greater the more hectic life, with its increasing and varied demands, becomes — even for the priest? Are not more and more pastors complaining that the sheer volume of their duties is preventing them from facing up to themselves, from taking themselves in hand, is threatening the centre of their own personal lives? The first section of this article puts this question by asking how the priest of today can once again bring his exterior activity into harmony with his interior life. The terminology in evidence here itself hints at some of the underlying causes of the present crisis in traditional priestly spirituality — although this was not the intention of the authors. The concept of *interior life* in the specific sense it has in modern spirituality, emerged only in the seventeenth century. It ousted the much broader concept of the spiritual life that embraced the whole of human life, and restricted the spiritual more or less to recollection and prayer.[8] Human activity thus became regarded as purely outward or even external. At all events it had nothing directly to do with spiritual life. Even the predominance of the interior life among religious had led to that externalistic piety against which the first section of the article declaims: "No merely external arrangement of the works of the ministry, *no mere practice*

---

[8] Cf. H. Sanson, *Spiritualité de la vie active*.

of religious exercises can bring about this unity of life, . . ." The premises may be false, but the polemic is justified. There has to be a more organic unity of action and contemplation, and the concept of interior life does not promote this, because it encourages a misunderstanding.

The so-called "practice of religious exercises" arose in the monasteries. In harmony with the contemplative ideal, which still remains normative for modern active religious orders, spiritual exercises dictated the daily rhythm, and the religious life was very largely practised in the form of practices and devotions. This style of piety was held up before secular priests and the laity as the model of a more intense Christian life. The spiritual regulation of the seminary was regarded, more or less, as the pattern of the later life of the priest.[9] In a more tranquil age, when things and events were still manageable, this may have been helpful. Today that is no longer the case — not even for the religious orders. On the contrary, the fixed spiritual exercises that used to be taken for granted as part of the priest's life, that were at least never seriously disputed although perhaps not always carried out — daily meditation, examination of conscience, visiting the Blessed Sacrament, the recitation of the rosary, regular retreats (*CIC,* can. 125, 2; 126) — have long since ceased to be cherished and even less to be practised. Not even the Breviary retains its immovable place in the daily routine of the priest of today. By many it is regarded as a burden, as a stint that must be got through, as something for which one has no time or energy left over. In their traditional forms these spiritual exercises, for their part, seem to provide too small a stimulus for the true *pensum* that is required of the modern pastoral priest, for the simple reason that all relaxation and recollection has gone from them. Undoubtedly there is today an undisguised suspicion of a piety based upon spiritual exercises. Life itself, it is said, everyday life with its contingencies and obligations must determine the stuff, the form and the rhythm of the

[9] In the first draft of the Preparatory Commission in 1961: "On the holiness of the life of the clergy" the following aids to the priest's spiritual life were listed: 1. Continuous reading of and meditation on holy Scripture, study of the Fathers and of theology. 2. Attentive and devout participation in liturgical life, principally the offering of mass and the saying of the Breviary, as well as fervent love of Christ especially in the Eucharist. 3. Docility to the inspirations of the Holy Spirit. 4. Love for the mother of God. 5. Daily meditation. 6. Retreats — annual in the early years, then every second year. 7. Monthly day of recollection, daily examination of conscience, spiritual reading, frequent confession, spiritual direction . . . In the draft of 1963 the following list occurs: 1. A set time each day for mental prayer over and above vocal prayer. 2. Spiritual reading from holy Scripture, the Fathers, the lives of the saints. 3. Veneration of the Mother of God by daily meditation of the rosary and other prayers. 4. Daily examination of conscience. 5. Monthly day of recollection, frequent confession, spiritual direction . . . 6. Annual retreat. The decree in its present form deals with these aids in Article 18, although in a much abridged fashion. Once again freedom of choice of the most suitable method of prayer for the individual is specially mentioned.

spiritual life. Otherwise one runs the risk of fleeing into a world of religious illusion and letting the real world pass by. And equally, it is life itself that provides the decisive opportunities for sacrifice and self-denial. Self-chosen sacrifices always run the risk of avoiding the demands of everyday life and neglecting the commandment that the hour brings with it. In other words: pious practices are too easily indulged in for their own sake and tend to erect a religious world alongside the secular world. Basic rethinking is required on this point. In fact it is absolutely necessary that the pastoral priest of today adapt his prayer-life, in respect of time, place and form, to his priestly work, for this must take priority. That is not to say that he can do without spiritual exercises, without practice in spiritual activity.[10] This is as necessary for him as it has been in all ages. Without it his spiritual life would all ebb away; he would no longer succeed in making of his priestly activity itself a spiritual act — a loving sacrifice to God and his neighbour, as Article 13 described it.

This article does not, however, follow up the idea of a practice of spirituality appropriate to the situation of the pastor of today. It turns, rather, directly to the topic of pastoral activity itself, and mentions a basic idea taken from the sphere of priestly spirituality, which might mould the imagination and motives of the priest, and provide his life, in spite of its variety and distractions, with a unifying line. This is the idea of fulfilling the will of God by following and imitating Christ. The notion of mission is always there in the background. The article never loses sight of a missionary image of the priest. The priest, in all he does or in all that he encounters, keeps his eyes upon Christ, for *he* embodies all that is meant by fulfilling the Father's will. He is the book from which one can read this will. Concretely, it is the figure of the Good Shepherd that makes this plain. According to this article, Christ's pastoral love *(caritas pastoralis)* is the fundamental idea that is able to provide the priest's life and work with a unity. In psychological terms we might say: the more the priest assumes and "plays" the role of good shepherd, the more he succeeds in providing his life with a resting point wherein he can gather together all that fills up his day. At the same time, however, the limitations of this idea are also indicated: when the priest consciously puts himself too much into the role of Christ considerable danger arises, that he will arrive at an unhealthy and theologically unjustifiable identification with Christ. In the past many edifying books for priests, even essays from the most eminent sources, have actually conjured up this very danger. Instruction today must include a warning of this danger, and the missionary image of the priest, conceived in terms of the apostolate, provides a good corrective presupposition.

[10] Cf. R. Guardini, *Vorschule des Betens* (2nd ed., 1948), esp. pp. 13–20.

More serious difficulty arises, however, only when, bearing in mind the manifold problems facing pastoral practice today, we begin to ask about the concrete will of God for the pastor here and now. The general notion of pastoral love on the model of Christ is not sufficient to answer this question. A new, concrete criterion of truth has to be added. (The third and last section of the article is devoted to this problem.) Because the priestly ministry is concerned not with a private vocation, but with representing Christ in the Church and hence with representing the Church (the priest is sent by the Church and so shares in the Church's mission), according to the decree the will of God in the concrete case, in respect, for example, of the manner of propounding Christ's teaching, or of new pastoral methods, is always found only in unity with the mission of the Church, in union with the bishops and one's priestly colleagues. And so, "that they may be able to verify the unity of their lives in concrete situations too", priests should remain in constant dialogue with the Church, must never isolate themselves or go their own ways. It is not clear from the text itself what precisely the relationship is between the statement "they should subject all their undertakings to the test of God's will", and its continuation: "which requires that projects should conform to the laws of the Church's evangelical mission". The subject is not discussed until we come to Article 15. This passage merely states the general principle.

Article 15. Articles 15–17 deal with the sphere of the evangelical counsels. The title, meant to set out the leading ideas of these articles, underwent many changes. In both of the drafts of 1964, which devoted only a single article to the subject, the title ran: "On the formation of the priest's life according to the norms of the gospel." In the first draft of 1965 — again containing a single article on the subject — it had been changed to: "Perfect chastity and the other evangelical counsels." This title was arrived at after several interventions which had insisted that celibacy be discussed more explicitly and in greater detail. Even with this, many were still dissatisfied, for now celibacy had all of a sudden received such emphasis — in terms of space alone — that poverty and obedience only appeared on the fringe. It was proposed, therefore, to treat of obedience, celibacy and poverty in three separate articles. The second draft of 1965 followed this pattern. After it had been objected also that by speaking of evangelical counsels one aligned the spirituality of the secular clergy too closely with that of religious, thus taking too little account of its secular character, the word was dropped. In the last drafts the three articles bore the following titles, which were not printed in the final text: 1. "Humility and obedience." 2. "Celibacy highly esteemed as a gift of grace." 3. "The relationship to the world and worldly goods, and voluntary poverty." The title of Part II of Chapter 3 of the decree as it now stands is: "Special Spiritual Needs of the Priestly Life", which says relatively little, showing the perplexity of the authors when faced with the problem of expressing something that is basically concerned with the evangelical counsels. In my opinion the original proposal was the best suited to the material they had in mind: "On the formation of the priestly life according to the evangelical norms."

There is no programmatic significance in the fact that the decree deals first with obedience. Obedience formally corresponds to the theological essence of the ministry in the Church, to mission. Thus, as the introductory section explains, the first thing to be taken into account is obedience to the God who sends. In this context obedience is understood as a listening to the voice of God. As St. Paul could say of himself: "And now, behold, I am going to Jerusalem, bound in the Spirit, not knowing what shall befall me there" (Acts 20:22), so should the priest let himself be led by the Spirit in all his priestly activity, in the execution of his mission. This is possible only if he is a listener. He must be quite clear that "the divine work which the Holy Spirit has raised (him) up to fulfil transcends all human energies and human wisdom", that his talents and capacities are quite inadequate for the task laid upon him. If he wants to do justice to his commission, in all his plans and actions he must allow himself to be led by the redemptive will of God, which desires the redemption of all men, and leave his own will and his own wisdom in the background. He is an obedient listener in the measure in which he places himself as a tool in the hands of God, for the work of man's redemption. In practice this will appear in his accepting anew each day all the circumstances and events of his everyday life as a priest, ever ready to serve men, and always subjecting his actions to the scrutiny of God. It is a good thing — necessary indeed — to set out first of all the deepest and ultimate meaning of Christian obedience; for all obedience to human authority has the sole purpose of leading us to a greater obedience to God by whose commission human authority is set over us, and from whose authority it is derived. Human authority and power to govern, even in the Church, especially in the Church, must therefore be exercised in such a way as to serve God's purposes and open the mind to perceive these purposes.

All of this prepares us for the consideration of ecclesiastical obedience in the second section of the article. At his ordination the priest promised to reverence and obey his bishop. In line with what was said in the first section, the meaning and purpose of this obedience is to enable priests to "dedicate their own wills through obedience to the service of God and their brothers". How is this done? A preliminary answer runs as follows: "Since the priestly ministry is the ministry of the Church,[11] it can be discharged only by hier-

---

[11] If this is to be understood in more than a purely external sense it means that even the priesthood *in* the Church is a priesthood *of* the Church.

277

archical communion with the whole body", i. e. in believing and ready fellowship with "their brothers in the ministry, most of all with those whom the Lord has appointed the visible rulers of his Church".[12] This fellowship must, moreover, be honestly integrated into the order instituted by Christ. Actual obedience emerges for the priest out of this fellowship. According to the decree this obedience is realized in two ways: 1. Priests ought to "accept and carry out in a spirit of faith whatever is commanded or recommended by the Sovereign Pontiff, their own bishop, or other superiors". 2. They should "gladly spend themselves and be spent (cf. 2 Cor 12:15) in any task assigned to them, even the more lowly and poor ones". Under these two headings is summed up the whole field wherein priestly obedience operates. This obedience means *sentire cum Ecclesia* and to hold oneself in ever greater readiness to work for the Church. However, several critical problems remain unsolved, and these form the crux of ecclesiastical obedience today. The decree passes them by. The first thing that comes to mind is that the decree discusses only the obedience of subordinates and has nothing at all to say about the right use of authority. Now this article deals in particular and thematically with obedience — including that of religious —; but one cannot have a balanced discussion of obedience — of all things — without mentioning the reciprocal relation between subordinates and superiors[13] — unless one is content to leave the discussion on the level of edifying generalizations. Nor is it sufficient to say that the relation of the bishop to his diocesan priests will be discussed elsewhere.[14] Authority and obedience form a single complex from which neither component can be removed and viewed in isolation. Unfortunately this has been a favourite practice of those engaged in discussing ecclesiastical authority. Religious obedience as a rule is viewed one-sidedly in terms of asceticism. The moral theological questions about the rights and duties of superiors as well as of subordinates, most of all the question about the limits of authority, and the anthropological questions about the mature obedience of adults, which alone leads to "the freedom of the children of God", are scarcely ever asked. Today this is no longer possible. The Council's Decree on Religious, in its exposition of obedience,[15] contains a special section dealing with the exercise of authority by superiors, and with the duties of superiors. This may well be the first treatment of the

---

[12] On the concept of hierarchical communion *(communio hierarchica)* cf. J. Ratzinger's commentary on the Prefatory Note in vol. I of this series, pp. 297 ff.

[13] "We should not speak exclusively of a 'morality of obedience' but rather of a 'morality of the relationship between command and obedience', and this embraces the duties of both the one who commands and the one who obeys." See Alois Müller, "Authority and Obedience in the Church", *Concilium* 5, no. 2 (1966), p. 42; also the same author's monograph: *Das Problem von Befehl und Gehorsam im Leben der Kirche* (1964).

[14] In this decree, art. 7; in Decree on the Bishops' Pastoral Office, art. 28.

[15] Art. 14.

subject in an official Church document. The most urgent problem of all concerning the relationship between bishops and priests, in this post-conciliar age, is that of collegiality, of fraternal collaboration, the precondition of which is adequate communications and dialogue.[16] Although undoubtedly open to much abuse, it is nonetheless indispensable, not only because it is in harmony with the Spirit of Christ, but because the structure of modern society calls for some such answer. Without the Spirit of love, of readiness to serve, and of obedience to God, to Christ, the one Lord of the Church, and to his Spirit at work in the Church — the Spirit which must fill all who share in the Church's life —, no solution can be found.

The last section of the article discusses this Spirit. It is the Spirit of Jesus Christ, the Spirit of self-emptying and of the ministry of the slave. Christ, by his obedience, has conquered the disobedience that lives in every sin, and so effected redemption: priests, therefore, to whom the work of redemption is specially entrusted, must "make themselves like Christ" in this respect. They do this through "responsible and voluntary humility and obedience". Theologically and ascetically, no more profound statement on Christian obedience can be made than this. But still the problems of concrete obedience, as sketched above, remain unsolved. With all the readiness in the world "to submit to the judgment of those who exercise the chief responsibility for governing the Church of God", the tension still remains between obedience to God and obedience to human agents, no matter how lawful or exalted in the Church; for the will of God is not simply identical with the decisions of official ministers installed by God himself in the Church. Thus there can be a permitted, and on occasion even obligatory, protest against such decisions, for the sake of obedience to God. To sustain this tension truthfully and humbly and without self-deception, but also without surrender of one's own inalienable responsibility, is one of the tasks of the Christian, especially of the Christian priest, today.

Article 16. Although the celibacy of the priesthood was not one of the major themes of the Council, and not much was said officially on the subject, in all phases of the Council it formed a topic for the most heated discussion. In preparation for the Council, votes were supposed to have been sent in from all over the world on the subject of a change in the law concerning clerical celibacy in the Latin Church; but whether or not many votes were cast for change is not known. Soon after the announcement of the Council, however, celibacy became one of the topics on which much was spoken and written. Some suggested a rejection of the general obligation to celibacy,

---

[16] The problem mentioned here is dealt with in the last sentence of the second section of the article on the apostolic initiative of the pastoral clergy and finds an institutional solution in the pastoral council (Decree on the Ministry and Life of Priests, art. 7; Decree on the Bishops' Pastoral Office, art. 27).

which could no longer be maintained as before; some thought it appropriate, in view of the shortage of priests, especially in the tropics, to admit to the priesthood, as assistants to fully authorized celibate priests, married men who had proved themselves in family life, in their profession or trade and in the life of the Church.[17] Pope John played a prominent part in this debate when at the Roman Synod in 1960 he urged his clergy to value their celibacy.[18] In this way he made known his own wish that no deviation be made from the Church's former practice. Like everything else he saw the celibacy of the priest completely in the light of faith, and it hurt him to observe how in this question purely natural considerations were playing an ever increasing part. It was consonant with this view of the Pope, which, however, reflected on the whole only the opinion of the world episcopate and of the Roman Curia, that scarcely anything was said about celibacy in the first schemata on priests.[19] It was assumed as something fixed, not something to call in question: it was not to be debated in the Council.[20] But that was not what happened. As soon as the question was raised, whether young men ought to be admitted to a revived diaconate, without any obligation to celibacy,[21] the question of the celibacy of priests was raised also. Debate was heated and divisions were necessary.[22] The reason for this was not least because of the strong desire to maintain celibacy, and even among bishops who had supported the dropping of celibacy for as yet unmarried candidates for the diaconate, many were pleased that the relevant passage in the draft was rejected by the majority in the Council. As a result of the voices, from the most diverse quarters, that insisted upon the relaxation of the rule of celibacy, and that refused to be silenced, at the same time seventy of the fathers

[17] This sort of view was expressed by P. Raimondo Spiazzi, O.P., of the Angelicum in Rome — and by others — in the periodical, *Monitor Ecclesiasticus* (September 1959). This article created a stir and had an aftermath. On 15 June 1960 Fr. Spiazzi published an article in the *Osservatore Romano* in which he referred to the conclusions drawn in his earlier article and declared himself for the complete retention of celibacy.

[18] Address of 26 January 1960. On the interpretation of the statements regarding celibacy cf. P. Rouquette, S.J., in *Études,* March 1960, pp. 360 f.

[19] The pre-conciliar schema simply said that priests ought to mould their whole lives upon the evangelical counsels of poverty, chastity, and obedience. The schema of 1963 said: "The priest ought to esteem chastity most highly and observe it according to the traditions and precepts of his rite." The short schema of 1964 read: "The priest should account chastity a holy thing and love it honestly."

[20] At a press conference on 17 April 1961, Archbishop Felici said that the question of celibacy would certainly not be dealt with at the Council. He clearly had in mind the Pope's address to the Roman Synod (*Osservatore Romano,* 20 April 1961).

[21] Constitution on the Church, art. 29, second draft 1964.

[22] The result of the voting on the question of admitting married men of riper years to the diaconate was 1598 *for* and 629 *against*. The result of the voting on the proposal to ordain young men without an obligation to celibacy was 839 *for* and 1364 *against*.

demanded a clear exposition and reinforcement in the decree of the Church's traditional teaching. The commission complied with this demand, but in a cautious formulation which left the door open for possible future development. The draft of October 1964 (Article 2) read as follows: "Priests ought to reverence chastity and love it sincerely, and those who, following the counsel or the regulation of the Church, have taken a vow of celibacy, trusting in the grace of God, are to adhere to this with all their heart, rejoicing that in this way they are undividedly united to Christ and freer to serve the family of God."

According to the interpretation added by the commission, the first part of the sentence applied to all priests, the married clergy of the Eastern Church no less than all celibate priests. The second part distinguished once again between those who voluntarily, although primarily because of the Church's rules, had accepted a celibate life, and those who had accepted celibacy as an evangelical counsel in the sense of a "state of perfect chastity" (i. e. in the manner of religious).[23] Many may not have liked this distinction. In view of the continued attacks upon the practice of celibacy in the Latin Church and the increasing change of mood among priests themselves, the significance of celibacy for the priestly ministry would have to be stressed in a quite different way and provided with a deeper theological basis. This was done in the third draft of 1964, composed by the commission immediately after the plenary debate in the Council hall. The very title hinted at the tenor of the article. Without drawing any kind of distinction the decree now begins to speak of perfect chastity and the other evangelical counsels. All priests must look upon celibacy as a gift of grace; only thus can celibacy be practised; the married priest is still the exception. The actual wording of the text was: "Although celibacy may not be an absolute requirement for the priesthood, as is evident from the fact that the presbyterate (even in apostolic times) has always included in its number lawfully married men, yet it is most appropriate to the priesthood." Among other things it can contribute to a "supreme form of human life", through which the priest, "dying to the flesh and awaking to a new life according to the Spirit (cf. 1 Pet 3:18), becomes associated with and configured to Christ, finding that his will is no longer under the yoke of slavery, having received the freedom with which Christ has made him free". This has more than the ring of enthusiasm — like many statements in this draft: it is almost supernaturalistic. What, then, are we to think of marriage! Not a word is devoted to the anthropological preconditions of celibacy. The objection of a non-believing world, that complete continence is an untenable postulate, is countered by our Lord's saying, recorded in St. Luke: "What is impossible with men is possible with God"

---

[23] In the *relatio* on art. 2, notes C and D, printed along with the draft.

(Lk 18:27). This saying is not apposite here and is one that could be used to justify any religious demand with which men do not concur.

The first attempt, therefore, to go into the question of celibacy theologically and ascetically in greater detail, displays considerable weaknesses. Great improvements were made to this draft in the time that passed before the debate in the Council in autumn 1965. As the result of an intervention by Cardinal Bea and a direct instruction from the Pope, greater account was taken of the tradition of the Eastern Church, but even the draft of 1965, presented to the fathers for public discussion, still had its weaknesses. Before this discussion, printed and duplicated memoranda on the question of celibacy, by theologians, doctors and psychologists, were circulated, all aimed at having the article revised along the lines of greater flexibility in the application of the law of celibacy.[24] The discussion was awaited, therefore, with some tension, especially as it was rumoured, that some South American bishops, in view of the scarcity of priests in their countries, would take a definite stand on the issue. But these interventions achieved nothing, although one of them gained considerable publicity and made quite a stir;[25] for, in a letter to Cardinal Tisserant, dean of the praesidium of the Council, the Pope himself had made known his personal view: it was not opportune to discuss this topic in the plenary Council. If any of the fathers wanted to say something on this question, they should set out their views in writing and send their interventions to the praesidium. He himself intended "not only to maintain this ancient, sacred and providential law, in so far as it falls to Us to do so, but to strengthen its observance by reminding the priests of the Latin Church of the reasons and causes — particularly pertinent today — for the supreme suitability of this law, to which priests owe their capacity to direct all of their love to Christ and to devote themselves completely and magnanimously to the service of the Church and of souls."[26]

Most of the bishops applauded these words, some, like the South American episcopal conference, did so publicly and formally.[27] Only a few mentioned celibacy explicitly in their interventions. Chief among these was Cardinal Bea, who expressed the urgent wish that the distinction between celibate and

[24] One of these memoranda contained contributions by S. Lyonnet, S.J., R. Clément, S.J., J.-P. Audet, O.P., A fascicle produced in several languages by eighty doctors and psychologists from a wide variety of countries, bore the title: "De Presbyterorum Coelibatu Libellus"; further documentation in J. C. Hampe, ed., *Die Autorität der Freiheit. Gegenwart des Konzils und Zukunft der Kirche im ökumenischen Disput*, II (1967), p. 236, note 4.

[25] This concerns the intervention of the Dutch bishop Pieter Koop von Lins, Bazil (off-print in Hampe, *op. cit.*, pp. 239 ff.), who on account of the shortage of priests in Latin America, pleaded for the introduction of a supplementary married clergy.

[26] Cf. *DC* 47, no. 1461 (19. Dezember 1965), p. 2183; complete text in Hampe, *op. cit.*, pp. 238 f.

[27] *DC, loc. cit.*, pp. 1384 f.

married clergy be not expressed in a way that suggested that the married were the exceptional cases. But even his intervention remained an exception. The commission's opportunities were limited. The outcome of all sorts of emendations was a text which undoubtedly corresponded to the view of the majority, and considering the situation it can stand up to criticism. It is clearly stated that celibacy is not demanded by the essence of the priesthood; the special regulations of the eastern Church are recognized as legitimate; it is emphasized that priestly celibacy, according to Mt 19:12, is a gift of grace, and at the same time an honest attempt is made to answer the question of how this is consonant with a universal obligation to celibacy; all untenable motives for celibacy — arising from notions of cultic purity or from a subliminal depreciation of the body and of sexuality —, are avoided, motives still commonly mentioned until quite recently in official documents; the chief grounds of expediency of a theological and spiritual kind, which commend celibacy, are expounded, but in all this reasoning the fact shines through that priestly celibacy cannot be fully explained purely theoretically; in the end it is a matter of faith and spiritual experience, otherwise it cannot be fully lived out. One thing more is required for a true assessment of the statements on celibacy contained in this decree: all that is adduced in this article applies only on the presupposition of the full content of the priestly ministry, which lays claim to the whole man, as is the case only in the vocation of the strictly pastoral priesthood. Should other forms of priestly ministry emerge in future, the question of celibacy would have to be raised again.

The article proceeds from the assumption that celibacy is fulfilled not in the realization (however honourable and perfect) of an ecclesiastical precept, but signifies that gift of grace mentioned in Mt 19:11 f. and 1 Cor 7:25 ff. It presumes the knowledge that this "celibacy for the kingdom of heaven's sake" has been most highly esteemed in the Church since the earliest times, and that it has found its deepest basis in spiritual experience, even if, as we must add today, this basis has not always corresponded to the gospel, but has found its origin in non-Christian influences. This is specially true of celibacy in connection with the priestly ministry. On the one hand it must be affirmed that priestly celibacy as such was not primarily dictated from above, but developed spontaneously — at a very early date, and continuously. One may say, therefore, that the New Testament priesthood possesses a spiritual affinity to celibacy as a gift of grace, especially where that priesthood is understood in the full sense as a "priestly service of the gospel" (Rom 15:16), that lays claim to the whole man.[28] Here as there we are dealing with a gracious election (the ministry, too, has its charisma). Both vocations are

[28] Cf. F. Wulf, "Der christologische Aspekt des priesterlichen Zölibats", *GL* 41 (196?

traced back in the same fashion to Christ, and find their centre in him; both involve imitation and service, and are under obligation to serve the Church and mankind. But here more than ever it has to be admitted that, throughout history until very recently, the arguments for the celibacy of the priesthood have not always been genuinely Christian, but have betrayed an intermingling of dualistic and magical-cultic ideas with traditions from the Old Testament. (In this context we are leaving out of consideration the *lex coelibatus,* which brought other material and political motives into play.[29] These are completely absent from the present article, as we have remarked above.) The reason given for the high estimation in which celibacy of the clergy has been held throughout the centuries is this: "It simultaneously signifies and stimulates pastoral charity and is a special fountain of spiritual fruitfulness on earth." So, at all events, is it experienced by those who accept it in faith, and live it out by faith. Their testimony is overcast by no doubt: it cannot be ignored. From a lived-out celibacy, which confers a special union with Christ, with his Church and with men, and which sharpens the clergy's perception of the mystery of grace, the Catholic priesthood has derived a spiritual apostolic fruitfulness, which does not exist in this form outside the Catholic Church. This fact alone allows us to say that celibacy as such (we are not speaking about the law of celibacy) is something quite priceless for the Church, and something that she ought not to relinquish.

A passage follows concerning the practice of the Eastern Churches which have married priests as well.[30] It is introduced by the affirmation: "It is not, indeed, demanded by the very nature of the priesthood", but the way the second section of the article begins by speaking of the appropriateness of priestly celibacy, shows that the sentences about the tradition of the eastern Churches are an interpolation. The article does not treat the two priestly forms of life in exactly the same way, as Cardinal Bea had demanded they ought to be treated, but deals almost exclusively with the celibate clergy. Nonetheless, what is said *de facto* about the married clergy, within the framework of this exposition of celibacy, goes far beyond any previous official statement by the Church on the same theme. The exceedingly cautious and studied phraseology, however, leaves an important issue unresolved. What, for example, is meant by the *nature* of the priesthood? What is its theological essence or ecclesio-sociological status, which the priestly official occupies within the hierarchically structured Church? Strictly speaking, all

---

pp. 118 ff.; likewise: *Seminarium. Rivista di orientamento e di formazione per la Università, per i Seminari, per le vocazioni ecclesiastiche* 19 (1967), pp. 787 ff.

[29] On the origin and history of celibacy cf. the monographs cited in *LTK*, X, col. 1400.

[30] Care must be taken, as the text advises, to note that a married man may indeed be ordained, but an ordained man may not thereafter be married ("who have received the priesthood as married men"). This fact itself suggests a certain order of rank.

that is said is that the priestly ministry is compatible with marriage. Although the married priests of the Eastern rite are praised and encouraged as "optime meriti Presbyteri", nothing is said about their specific way of life — or, should we not say, about their specific vocation? For the sacred vocation, mentioned in the last sentence, and in which married priests are called upon to persevere, is unequivocally that priestly vocation which demands that they "spend their lives fully and generously for the flock committed to them". In this section, too, the accent is placed upon the fact that "this most sacred Synod recommends ecclesiastical celibacy (as an evangelical counsel", in harmony with the Eastern conception, which in no way regards the two priestly ways of life as in every way equal in value, but urges upon priests celibacy for the kingdom of heaven's sake, and chiefly for spiritual and mystical reasons. And so in the commission there was no complaint from the easterns against this interpolation. Obviously they were satisfied that the legitimacy of their practice had been accepted and was not to be called in question.

The second section produces the theological and spiritual reasons for the appropriateness to the priesthood, of celibacy. These are connected both with *mission* and with a special *consecration* of the priest. First in respect of mission: the priest is entrusted with a ministry of supernatural life, of the redemption of men, the originator and mediator of which is Christ, who, through the Spirit, becomes operative in men. Therefore — so runs the unstated conclusion — it is fitting that he should have no family of his own, but live entirely for this ministry. The more total this dedication, and the more he stakes all his own life upon this, the more credible is his work. Without wanting to call in question the convenience of such an arrangement, it might be added that redemption is effected not in a self-contained supernatural sphere, but in the midst of this world and through the agency of this world, in one's profession, in the society of men, and through responsibility for others and for the whole world. Should not the ministry of salvation, therefore, also demand knowledge of this world and of human life, and might not the married priest, who himself has a household to look after (cf. 1 Tim 3:4; Tit 1:6), learn something about pastoral care precisely from this field of experience? To seek the motive for celibacy in consecration likewise poses one or two questions. What is meant here is not the sacramental consecration arising from holy orders, but that connected with the vow of celibacy "for the sake of Jesus[31] and his gospel".[32] Quite apart from the fact

---

[31] The words of our Lord we have cited here (Mk 10:29) suit the context better than Mt 19:11, which are, however, cited in the third section.

[32] On the "consecration" that comes through vowing the evangelical counsels cf. Constitution on the Church, art. 44, and Decree on the Appropriate Renewal of the Religious Life, art. 5.

that it is theologically difficult to explain, and difficult for a normally thinking man to understand, the meaningfulness of a piling up of "consecrations" (for multiplication seems only to bring devaluation), we could easily arrive at quite the opposite conclusion: sacramental union with Christ through the conferring of the priestly ministry leads straight (although not necessarily) to a special devotion to Christ; out of the sacramental grace conferred in ordination to the priesthood there arises an alluring call to accept celibacy, which makes undivided devotion to Christ easier and leaves the priest freer to perform the ministry "to his kingdom and to the work of heavenly regeneration". (There is clearly some doubt whether the intrinsically profound idea of "fatherhood in Christ", referred to in the decree, still has any special appeal to the priests of today. At all events it does not appeal to the younger ones, and it is these very ones who require stronger motives and more authentic experience in order to accept the heart of celibacy, and live it out.) [33] Wherever undivided devotion to the Lord and undivided service of men are lived out (this is the final concept in the second section), priests become a testimony to, and a sign of, the great mysteries of Church and redemption, of the invisible mystery of Christian life in our times, and of eternal life. It is true that all Christians must be a testimony to, and a sign of, these things, but it is those who are celibate for the kingdom of heaven's sake, who fulfil this function in a specially visible and palpable way.

The decisive part of this article is the third and last section. This deals with the *law* of celibacy, and tries, in accord with an intervention of Cardinal Döpfner, [34] to answer the question that was constantly posed and that occupied the centre of the discussion on celibacy: how can a gift of grace, "which the Father gives to some men" (cf. Constitution on the Church, Article 42, following Mt 19:11), be made obligatory for all priests? By way of introduction, there is a short survey of the genesis of the law of celibacy. We must not expect to deduce from a very general statement more than it is capable of yielding. It would be futile, therefore, to search here for details. After an explicit approval and confirmation of the *lex coelibatus* in the Latin Church — and this has special weight as a conciliar statement — there follows the argument explaining why the Council felt itself urged to do this. The Spirit gave them confidence, they said, that the Father would freely give the grace of celibacy if only those, who are called to the priesthood and come to share through the sacrament of orders in Christ's mission, along with the whole Church, humbly and urgently pray for it. At first sight this

---

[33] The whole trend of thought of the second section of this article follows arguments from the exhortation *Menti Nostrae* by Pius XII on the subject of priestly chastity (*AAS* 42 [1950], p. 663).

[34] Intervention on 15 October 1965.

appears to be no answer, but merely an uncontrollable appeal to the Spirit who gives us confidence. But the reason for this appeal is also given. Celibacy is so appropriate to the priesthood of the New Covenant and is so consonant with Christ's priesthood, that God will not deny to those whom he calls to the priesthood, this other grace also. This is a conclusion convincing only to faith, and against which there can be no objection from the court of purely natural reason. (Pope Paul VI's later encyclical *Sacerdotalis Coelibatus* followed the same line of argument.) And so there is no further examination of the psychological and sociological human difficulties that make the fulfilment of celibacy difficult in the present day. These were not ignored, but the Council did not see them as the central issue. To him who truly believes the word of promise that is included in every gracious call, God will not deny the gift of perseverance and fidelity, if only he do all that he can, i. e. accept all the supernatural and natural aids that are at his disposal. In this, too, the accent again is laid upon faith. This argumentation makes sense only to the believing Christian; and it becomes all the easier to understand the more one sees the charisma of celibacy as something not extraordinary, but perfectly normal within the framework of God's gracious guidance. Moreover, one may not think of this charisma, that is so deeply embedded in a man's life, as something self-contained, complete, and given all at once, as something a man either has or has not. It should be conceived, rather, as something put by God into a man's concrete historical anthropological and psychological situation, itself possessing a history and being an adventure — the adventure of faith. In the ups and downs of life, to him who is being freshly called all the time, it brings the experience of God and of Christ, and it also becomes his testing, by placing him in the darkness of loneliness and self-denial. In this way it becomes a help to the priest — as the decree explains — in knowing that celibacy is a gift given to the Church by God, so that its fulfilment is a concern of the intercessory prayer of the whole Church.

This is what the Council has said. The believing Catholic and the priest especially must think it over seriously. One need not keep silent on the problems presented by the law of celibacy, for these problems do exist and in time a better solution may be reached; but one thing, however, is beyond question: despite its awareness of these problems — and during their stay in Rome all of the bishops were able to find out these problems — the Council upheld this law. This means, therefore, that a higher place is accorded in the Church to priestly celibacy than many of the post-conciliar discussions on the topic might lead us to suppose. One may have honest regrets that the encyclical on celibacy, promised by Pope Paul at the Council and published on 24 June 1967, contains many inadequacies[35] and opens few new doors,

---

[35] Cf. *Rundschreiben über den priesterlichen Zölibat*, introd. by F. Wulf (1968), pp. 19 f.

but it, too, is a confirmation of the proposition that celibacy is an inalienable treasure of the Church.

Article 17 continues with the "special spiritual needs of the priestly life" which make up the contents of chapter II. Articles 15 and 16 expounded the dispositions specially characterizing the priest: interior openness to God, willingness to serve, fitting into the community, obedience, complete continence, with special stress upon celibacy. All of these are summed up as a participation in the mind of Christ.

Article 17 speaks of the human values that are commended to the priest's use and of the priest's attitude to the things of this world. It is stressed that mutual intercourse among priests and their meeting with others provide opportunity to cultivate human values and to appreciate earthly goods as gifts of God. No detailed exposition is given in the text of what is meant by human values. In as much as they are cultivated through intercourse we may suggest friendship, brotherliness, helpfulness, courage in all adversity, comradeship, collegiality, respect, consideration for others and, no doubt, the observance of the normal social rules and conventions. These are the virtues we might call natural, for they condition and support social life. These are attitudes which deserve to be adopted simply because they are required by the situation, and are not nourished primarily by the intention to earn merit for eternal life. According to the conciliar text the priest's spiritual life should not be lived apart from his pastoral activity but in and through it. Naturally one must not overlook or underestimate the threats to his interior life which arise precisely out of the priest's pastoral activity. These arise because the priest's pastoral activity in consequence of his vast and varied task can mislead him into over-activity which estranges him from himself. It certainly ought not to be true, and yet it is understandable, when, with Thomas à Kempis we say: "As often as I go among men, I return a worse man."

A help against the danger of externalism is provided by living faith in Jesus Christ, who is operative through his Spirit in every priestly function. The priest, it is true, is appointed to fulfil a special ministry. But he remains a man among men and can perform his redemptive ministry fruitfully only if he meets men as a man and not as some ill-natured, uncultivated obscurantist who constantly offends others. He should manifest the kindness of God to man, which ought to be the creative love within his own person, as it has called all men to salvation.

According to the text this spirit of friendliness should clearly not be confined to priest's confraternals, but should reach out universally to all men. This admonition of the text contains an echo of the words of St. Paul (1 Cor 9:22) who was ready to be all things to all men, not wishing to confine his pastoral care to one particular group, but rather to embrace every economic, social, cultural and racial group in his solicitude. None-theless the Council specially stresses the mission of the priest to the poor.

The above-mentioned natural virtues are not to be employed as clever, tactical, pedagogically effective pastoral instruments. They are, rather, the natural fruit of salvific encounter and salvific intercourse with men. By emphasizing these natural virtues the decree does not mean to deny that the priest must declare the redemption and judgment of God with prophetic voice. His very warning that it is possible to lose one's soul is an expression of human friendliness, for this is no superficial or external thing, but wells up from the depths of a love that cares for men and their destiny. A peculiar dialectic of the priest's existence and function arises from the fact that the priest is orientated towards the redemptive ministry for men, that he is always conscious of his special task at any particular moment, and so cannot ever become completely absorbed in society. This mission carries an irresolv-able conflict into his life. The text before us deals formally only with the dialectic of the priest in respect of things. But this includes the dialectic in respect of people and society. The Council expresses it thus: the priest lives, it is true, in the world, but in respect of his mission is not of the world. He should use the things of this world as though he did not use them. He cannot and may not push them aside. At the same time he must not become enslaved by them. He must tread a path which avoids both contempt of the world and attachment to the world. The world is made for man, as man is for the world. On the one hand he is part of it, while on the other hand it is he who imparts meaning to it. Man cannot live without the world; it gives him food, shelter, clothing, the material for his spiritual activity and the possibility of cultural development. But the world would not be what it is meant to be were it not for man. The motive and aim for the priest's keeping a certain distance from the world is said by the Council to be interior freedom. Even more than other men the priest should refuse to become the slave of avarice, property, love of power, sensuality, because if these took possession of him his freedom would be gone. Only if he possesses interior freedom is he able to fulfil his ministry. Only thus does his heart remain open and ready for God and man, for prayer and love. It is only thus that he learns what is the right attitude towards men. His right attitude to things helps him in his service to men. Neither the gentleman nor the beggar in clerical dress corresponds to the image of the priest depicted in this decree. That is not to say that in special circumstances such forms of priestly life might not legitimately arise and be most fruitful. History shows that they serve a purpose in particular situations.

By refraining from demanding ascetic heights in the priestly renunciation of the world the Council displays a humane countenance. The supernatural ought not to devour the natural in the priest. The text says not only that created goods are necessary for the maturing of the human personality, but that they are indispensable. How could it be otherwise if one sees the world not primarily as a source of temptations but as a gift of God, as Christian faith teaches? Man stands not outside but within the world, belonging to it, obligated to it. But the Council is aware of the dangers, too. They are there in the nature of the case. Precisely because the world, and especially the men whom the priest meets, are gifts and, by analogy, manifestations of God, they are able to attract so much attention to themselves that interest stops there and God is no longer seen in his own creatures. In virtue of their origin in God things and human beings are able to cast a spell upon man's heart and mind and eyes, so that all he sees is the splendour of this world. Here an unavoidable danger looms up out of reality itself, and it cannot be overcome through flight from the world. The priest will survive the danger not by a negative attempt to free his heart from the love of man and of things, but only by a positive practice of the love of God in men and things, never, of course, regarding men and things merely as opportunities for showing love to God, having no intrinsic value.

This will lead to priests taking seriously and obeying the Council's advice to use temporal goods only within the framework supplied by the teaching of the Lord and the regulations of the Church. Without giving chapter and verse the Council refers to the forms laid down in canon law governing the priestly life (*CIC,* can. 124–44, especially can. 137, 139, 141, 142). These prescriptions in canon law, specially prohibit the carrying on of business, even though without formal specification. The rest of the relevant prohibitions in the code are not explicitly mentioned, but this does not alter their legal validity. The fact that the prohibition of commerce is specially singled out may be explained by the tendency of the Council to commend poverty to priests. Priests must not use worldly goods for their own enrichment. They ought, rather, in order to be more like Christ and more mobile in their ministry, to cultivate voluntary poverty. It is worth noting that the Council uttered this admonition emphatically and on several occasions while at the same time and with equal emphasis and frequency advocating that a priest's life should accord with his station.[1]

Again the text busies itself with an inescapable dialectic. On the one hand the priest must dispense the gifts of God with no thought of recompense. These gifts cannot be paid for in worldly coin in any case. To do or attempt to do such a thing would be simony. On the other hand the priest must live and has to be rewarded for his labour. This statement, too, is in harmony with the New Testament. The labourer is worthy of his hire (Mt 10:10). The Council considers him entitled to a life according to his station, without declaring in detail what that means. We can define the notion negatively: his

---

[1] Cf. *CIC,* can. 1473; see K. Mörsdorf, *Lehrbuch des Kirchenrechts,* I (1964), pp. 252–72.

life is not that of the beggar nor is it a life of luxury. Obviously there are many gradations within these extremes. The Council would also agree if we say that in spite of essential equality the variety of priestly tasks makes differentiation in standards of life necessary.

The Council enunciates a general positive norm. Church property is to be used for three purposes only: for the proper celebration of public worship; for the decent support of the clergy; and for apostolic and charitable work, i.e. for the care of the poor. In this precept the Council accepts the current regulations provided in canon law (cf. *CIC*, can. 1473).

The same is true of the Council's precept that Church property must be administered by the clergy (cf. *CIC*, can. 1183, 1476, 1489). A few of the Council fathers wanted the laity to be entrusted with the administration of Church property; at least they wanted a statement to the effect that such property be administered by priests and laymen. This view seemed to be supported by the fact that the complexity of modern economic and monetary affairs demands tremendous expertise, such as cannot be assumed to exist among priests who have had no training in these things. Experience shows also that an unskilled administrator can run into serious difficulties. These considerations are all the more pertinent because the Council explicitly demands that the administration of Church property be carried out "as the nature of the goods requires", that is, in accord with the laws of economic life. Immediately, however, the phrase "as the nature of the goods requires *(secundum rei naturam)*" is qualified by the phrase "as the norms of Church law ... require". Heed was paid to some extent to the desire of a few of the fathers by including the phrase "with all possible help from laymen". In a later passage with an analogous context it is stated that businessmen ought to be called in if it appears advisable to do so.

The passage about the use of Church property finds a parallel in a passage concerning the emoluments priests receive in the course of performing official functions. These, too, must be used in the fulfilment of the duties of their station, for their decent support and not as a means of personal enrichment (cf. *CIC*, can. 122). If something remains after these two charges have been made, this must not be invested as capital, but used, rather, for the good of the Church or for charitable purposes. It counts as the fulfilment of these pursoses if surplus is applied to a fund for aged clergy, as the text explains later on. In this way these contributions return in the end to those who made them. Many of the Council fathers noticed that the draft of the text made it plain that priests and bishops were bound to behave in the same way and they requested that reference to the bishops be deleted. But the text stood, showing that in these matters priests and bishops share the same obligations. However much the Council may have stressed the need to provide priests with a living in harmony with their station — and when we think of the mendicant priests of the Middle Ages and of priests forced to beg after the Second World War, the Council's concern is seen as perfectly justified — their chief interest was in priestly poverty, not as mendicancy, but as liberation from vain luxury. Special mention is made of simplicity of dwelling-place. This must be of such a kind as not to frighten away the poor. The Council might also have spoken about the priest's dress or about the car he needs for his work or about his travel. A special reference is made to the community life of priests (cf. *CIC*, can. 134). What this has in mind is not the custom of curates living in the same house as the parish priest, each having his own stipend and, in some countries, paying the parish priest for his board, but the *vita communis* in which the individual renounces personal income, is responsible to the community for his personal expenditure and submits to the direction of a rector. The exhortation that the priest must resemble Christ the poor man echoes all through the text.

III. THE MEANS OF SUPPORT FOR PRIESTLY LIFE

Articles 18–21 describe "the means of support for priestly life". The distinction between requirements and means is not always clear, for very often the two appear to become interchanged. There are material and spiritual means. First the spiritual means are described.

Article 18. The leitmotif for all the statements made here is union with Christ, which the priest must cultivate in all life's situations. There are many means towards this — old and new. As the text says, the Holy Spirit has not ceased to give ever new impulses. This does not, however, mean that old, long-used means have lost their efficacy. The text expressly indicates those means which the Church has recommended and even prescribed for a very long time. This makes it obvious that the precepts on this subject found in the Code of Canon Law are by no means discounted; they are indeed freshly emphasized. Anyone who expected the text of this decree to loosen the regulations of the Church governing the priestly life would be disappointed by these indications. Although, according to the text, not all of the regulations in the *CIC* are still applicable, the quite specific exceptions only emphasize the continued validity of the rest. At the top of the list of spiritual means in the priestly life are the holy Scriptures and the Eucharist. In this the Council goes a little beyond can. 125 in respect of Scripture. By stressing Scripture it expresses the new theological situation created by the Council. Emphasis on holy Scripture, even before the Eucharist, is in line with the decree *Perfectae Caritatis* (Article 6) and the constitution *Dei Verbum* (Article 21). The new estimation of the Word, frequently expressed in the Council, comes to light when the text says that all of the faithful are nourished at the twofold source of the Scriptures and the Eucharist by the word of God. Hence, in a special measure, priests should gain profit from these two sources of sanctification. If this text may be taken literally the Word is defined as a single redemptive entity embracing Scripture and Eucharist.

The text takes on a fully traditional tone (cf. *CIC*, can. 125) when it proceeds to say that the priest should unite himself to Christ through the worthy reception of the sacraments, above all through frequent use of the sacrament of penance. It is not very clear which sacraments are meant, especially as the Eucharist has already been mentioned. It may be that a traditional phrase of pious exhortation got into the text without anyone noticing its irrelevance. By the sacrament of penance quite obviously the confession of devotion is indicated. In this the results of the historical dogmatic research of recent years have gone unheeded in contrast to the tendency of the Council which elsewhere showed a readiness to pay heed to theological science. In this exhortation the Council held to the interpretation which had developed since the early Middle Ages and became dominant in post-Tridentine theology.

The meaning of "frequent" is defined here as vaguely as it is in canon law (can. 125). It is left to theological speculation or to linguistic appreciation. Does the text have in mind weekly or monthly confession, or would it be satisfied with an even longer interval? In contrast to the concept held by the early Church, the sacrament of penance is understood as a means of turning one's heart to the love of the Father of mercies. The godparent of this notion would seem to be the encyclical *Mediator Dei*. Of special importance is the observation that meditation upon Scripture develops a keen sensitivity towards the action of God in historical events and a readiness to receive the impulses of the Holy Spirit. In fact Scripture study and charismatic action are closely bound up together, for in the Scriptures it is the Holy Spirit himself who speaks to the reader. Thus the priest acquires the capacity for prophetic-critical judgment of the events of his times and of historical movements. Our Lady is taken as the model of the priestly mind. Priests ought to have a very special veneration for the Blessed Virgin Mary and, like her, live by faith in Christ. Some of the Council fathers noticed that at this point there was no emphasis upon the recitation of the rosary as in the Code of Canon Law (can. 125). A proposal to include this was rejected on the grounds that the text was meant to apply to the whole Church, including the Uniat Eastern Churches, and the rosary was not universally in vogue.

This article concludes with three exhortations, which have been partly hinted at already. Paying visits to, and dialogue with, Christ in the Eucharist are stressed. As the Eucharist has been mentioned already we may now ask, in retrospect, what precisely was meant by the earlier text. Presumably it was the total cult of the Eucharist, from which now, following the tradition of the Church, visiting the Blessed Sacrament is being detached and more particularly emphasized. Two things are worth noting at this point. First, a certain independence is given to adoration of the Eucharist apart from the celebration of the eucharistic sacrificial meal; second, there is an implicit statement of unswerving belief in the real presence of Jesus Christ continuing beyond the action of the eucharistic celebration. Both of these elements are in accord with eucharistic faith as it has developed since Trent. In view of the problems emerging in the present discussion, the text must be seen within the framework of the encyclical *Mysterium Fidei.*

The theme of the second exhortation is the need for the priest to withdraw, not just in the sense of making the customary retreat, but in the sense of frequent withdrawal into solitude. Secular priests are obliged by canon law to engage in spiritual exercises in some retreat house at least every third year (*CIC,* can. 126). Obviously the Council had more than this in mind. They were thinking of shorter periods of recollection, but did not go into the question of their frequency.

The third exhortation stresses the much recommended use of spiritual direction by an experienced director. This quite clearly asks priests to take to heart a practice that has existed in monastic life since the days of the early Church.

For the rest, the priest is left free to choose the means which experience has taught him are most conducive to his own salvation. Thus the dangers of routine are avoided.

The text sums up these exhortations by saying that the priest must ask God for the spirit of adoration. The spirit of adoration consists in constant close union with Christ. It comes from a blend of divine grace with human effort. From this the activity of adoration is born as a frequently occurring event. What is meant by the spirit of adoration has been experienced and portrayed by the "French school".[2]

Article 19 designates constant theological education as a further aid to a priestly life. The *CIC* confines itself to the regulation that yearly conferences on moral and liturgical problems shall take place in the episcopal city and in rural deaneries. Other questions may be discussed if the bishop thinks that such discussions will advance the scientific education and the spiritual lives of the clergy. Attendance is compulsory for all secular and regular clergy engaged in pastoral work. Religious who hear confessions must likewise attend if no such conferences take place in their religious houses (can. 591). Practice has long since gone far beyond these regulations. The utterance of

[2] Cf. H. Bremond, *Das wesentliche Gebet* (1954).

the Council is progressive in its re-estimation of the importance of Scripture for theology and spirituality, and in respect of a more universal total orientation. Once again the Scriptures are affirmed to be the first and most important source for theological and pastoral development (cf. the Decree on Priestly Formation, Article 16). The priest must also be familiar with the doctrinal documents of the Church and consult sound, approved theological writers. The text is not discussing theological scholars at this point; but we may conclude that they are included in the term "writers", in view of the esteem shown elsewhere in Council documents for scientific theologians. In the Council's view the priest must be informed about current theological movements. This should be obvious. Were he not so informed, it could happen that interested laymen were more accurately instructed than he on theological questions, and thus he might become excluded from intelligent dialogue with the laity. A few sentences later on it is said that the priest must have a knowledge of theological science.

The text is making an urgent demand when it states that priests must constantly expand and deepen their religious and theological understanding, as well as keep up their standard of general education. In fact the priest must keep up with the level of general education if he is to maintain serious conversation with the men of his time. This makes no small demand upon his time, energy, attention and alertness of mind. The text makes a few suggestions as to how the priest can keep himself up to the mark: congresses, libraries, courses — especially for younger priests — all the methods, indeed, that have for long been used in many countries and are now being introduced in others. The priest must not remain stuck with the knowledge he once possessed, but in thought, action, knowledge and aptitudes must always be dynamic. As theology and pastoral methods advance, so must he. The Council turned its attention specially to newly ordained and young priests. The older and more experienced must come to their aid with advice. At the same time it is presupposed that the younger priests will be prepared to accept such advice. Specially important is the admonition to bishops to see to it that a sufficient number of priests undertake thorough theological studies, so that they may instruct clerics and assist priests to deepen their theological and pastoral knowledge.

Article 20. The text of this decree displays realism by counting the assurance of the material means of life as one of the aids to a priestly life. It is of far-reaching importance that the members of the congregation accept financial responsibility and see that the priest who is their minister of redemption is provided with the means for "a respectable and worthy life". The bishops are admonished to draw the attention of the faithful to this duty. The Council goes into very necessary detail and expresses the desire that the priest's remuneration should enable him to help the poor and also suitably recompense those who work for him. Quite clearly the Council only went into these unexpected details because it was aware of some distressing facts. Here a condemnation is being made of that attitude which repays services rendered with a pious "God will reward you". The Council even mentions vacations — the restoration of the pastor's energies. The duty is squarely laid upon the bishops of ensuring that all priests get a proper holiday. These details are not casuistic; indeed, it is these trivialities that exhibit the modernity of the Council.

Article 21. The Council gives even more detailed instructions concerning the ensuring of a decent livelihood for priests in countries where this is not provided from public resources. In these countries diocesan or inter-diocesan funds must be established into which the offerings of the faithful should be gathered. The bishops are to administer such funds and always take the initiative. In this work the bishops shall delegate functions to priests and, when it is advisable to do so, enlist the help of competent laymen. These funds shall be used for ecclesiastical purposes, to pay those who serve the Church and for the assistance of aged and infirm clergy. Priests themselves should support these arrangements, thus demonstrating their solidarity. Here we find an expression of mutual fraternal responsibility. The Council views these things at the international level when it advocates the joining together of similar agencies in different countries to ensure their more effective operation. Summing up, the text argues: if the priest is relieved by such means from anxiety about sickness and old age, he will be all the better able to live confidently and joyful according to the gospel, to practise poverty and devote his life completely to the care of souls. In principle the Council does not expect priests to accept the type of poverty that involves the danger of starvation.

CONCLUSION AND EXHORTATION

Article 22, in conclusion, comforts priests in the difficulties which they will encounter in their pastoral tasks. Following a list of so many duties, this comfort is most necessary. The Council recognizes that in view of the modern situation in the world, in view of the seeming sterility of much serious effort, priests and faithful together could become oppressed by the feeling that they have no longer any place in this world, that this world no longer takes them seriously, and so become tempted to despair. For the sake of truth and love, these sober observations are most necessary in times when the good and the malicious alike tend to blame the clergy for all the evil that is in the world. We cannot expect large numbers of men to join the ranks of those who enjoy nothing but criticism, coming from within as well as from without. He who looks in faith and not just in resentment at these problems will want neither to keep silent about human failure nor to explain it away, nor will he forget that the deeper roots of the problem go down into the scandal of the Christian faith itself. Seen in any other light, all of these criticisms remain superficial.

The Council offers two motives for continuing to work confidently in all situations. These motives are valid of the priest's activity in all ages, in all epochs of history, and in every culture and civilization, because they are essentially part of the acting out of faith itself. These motives are not, therefore, of special assistance in the present situation. Help comes first from the continuing, effective presence of the Holy Spirit in the Church, and then from the eschatological understanding of all priestly activity. The priest is a member of the pilgrim People of God. As long as these are on the march they will never quite arrive at their destination, which is the perfect kingdom of God. And yet they live in hope of reaching the consummation. God himself will grant this in the future, but the hour has not been revealed to us. If appearances seem to contradict such a hope, we should remember that the gospel of Christ is like seed scattered upon the earth. It germinates and grows without anyone noticing. Our Lord himself said this (Mk 4:17; cf. Col 3:3).

SUBJECT INDEX

Prepared by Lalit Adolphus

Africa 39
Ancient Church 140, 211, 212, 219
Apostles 36, 53, 247, 261
Apostolate of the laity 34, 35, 38, 53, 108, 149, 169, 181, 256
— third world congress of the lay apostolate 259
See also Decree on the Apostolate of the Laity
Apostolic See, see Holy See
Apostolic Succession 173, 216, 221, 235
Art 11
Ascension 124
Asia 39
Authority 244

Baptism 21, 32, 120, 121, 132, 134, 138, 145, 170, 219, 220, 268
— adult baptism 133
— the baptized 21, 22, 24, 237, 255—7
Bible 79, 102, 116, 138, 139, 156, 200, 216, 270, 292, 295; see also New Testament, Old Testament, Scripture and Tradition
— Bible services 134
— biblical theology 22
Bishops 147, 166, 169, 170, 173, 211, 215, 243, 244, 245, 247, 248, 250, 262, 271, 278
— bishops' conferences 7, 107, 159, 165, 167, 169, 171, 174–6, 200
— college, collegiality of 99, 117, 172
— consecration of 234, 238, 247
— relations with priests 196, 238, 241, 254, 278, 279
— synod of 110, 160, 165, 172
See also Decree on the Bishops' Pastoral Office
Breviary 233, 274
Buddhists 128

Canada 39
Canon law 3, 4, 10, 132, 146, 151, 163, 176, 255, 263, 290, 292, 293
Canon of the Mass, see under Mass
Catechetics 12, 24, 71, 130, 139–41, 147, 155, 166, 168, 265
Catechumenate 132, 133, 138

Celibacy 199, 200, 201, 204, 207, 208, 254, 255, 276, 279, 280–3, 285–7
— married priests in the Eastern Churches 200, 204, 207, 281–4
Character formation 33
Charism 153
Chastity 281
Children 17, 20, 22, 23, 32, 71; see also Family, Parents
Christology 113
Christ's threefold office 224
Church
— extra ecclesiam nulla salus 123
— local Churches 106, 107, 243, 260
— membership of the 121
— as mystical body of Christ 11
— particular Churches 145–51, 153, 160, 165, 166, 235
— pilgrim Church 114
— universal Church 145–8, 151, 152, 166
— universality of the 99
See also Dogmatic Constitution on the Church
Civic life 31
Civil law 85
Civilization 36, 86, 197
Clericalism 256
Co-education 33
Collegiality of bishops, see under Bishops
Communications, media of 6, 10, 13, 16, 24, 25, 86, 149, 171; see also Decree on the Instruments of Social Communication, Public opinion
Confirmation 133, 170
Conscience 53, 66, 69, 79
— examination of 274
Consecratio mundi 30
Constitution on the Church, see Dogmatic Constitution on the Church
Constitution on Divine Revelation, see Dogmatic Constitution on Divine Revelation
Constitution on the Sacred Liturgy 11, 24, 136, 140, 151, 231, 233
Conversion 118, 129, 131, 134, 179
Creation 17, 36, 84

Culture 10, 13, 19, 30, 31, 41, 86, 127, 129, 134, 150, 167
Curia 97, 163
— Congregation for the Eastern Church 162
— Congregation of Propaganda 88, 92, 98, 99, 102, 103, 106, 108–11, 132, 140, 155, 159–67, 172, 174
— Congregation for Religious 250
— Congregation of Rites 133
— Congregation for Seminaries and Universities 46

Deacons 135, 138, 140, 247
Declaration on Religious Freedom 11
Declaration on the Relationship of the Church to Non-Christian Religions 122, 127
Decree on the Apostolate of the Laity 12, 31, 149
Decree on the Appropriate Renewal of the Religious Life 13, 111, 141, 143, 144, 158, 177, 179, 292
Decree on the Bishops' Pastoral Office in the Church 107, 110, 111, 133, 136, 147, 165, 167, 173, 176, 228
Decree on the Church's Missionary Activity 11
Decree on Ecumenism 11, 51
Decree on the Instruments of Social Communication 13, 14
Decree on the Ministry and Life of Priests 111, 136, 148, 152, 176, 177, 178, 183
Decree on Priestly Formation 12, 43, 152, 156, 265, 270
Democracy 26
Democratization 16
Dialogue 33, 34, 40, 43, 78, 107, 126, 128, 196, 253
Diocese 30, 169, 171, 172, 174, 249
Divine law 69
Divine Office 233
Divini illius Magistri 13, 14, 19, 20, 21
Dogma 38
Dogmatic Constitution on the Church 49, 113, 116, 122, 123, 132, 135, 136, 141, 151, 152, 154, 159, 170, 173, 181, 187, 191, 199, 214, 218, 227, 228, 231, 234, 238, 240, 242, 261, 265, 271, 286
Dogmatic Constitution on Divine Revelation 136, 270, 292

Easter 124, 133
Eastern Churches 115, 161, 204, 293
— married priests in the, see under Celibacy
Ecclesiae Sanctae 151, 161, 162, 164, 165, 167, 171, 176, 177, 241, 248, 250, 263
Ecclesiam Suam 14, 34, 78, 128
Economics 13, 16, 46, 76, 77, 86
Ecumenism 40, 102, 104, 113, 121, 134, 135, 137, 250; see also Decree on Ecumenism, Secretariat for the Promotion of Christian Unity
Edict of Milan (313) 81, 83
Education 1–48
Episcopal conferences, see under Bishops
Eschatology 22, 123
Ethnology 157, 168
Eucharist 24, 36, 120, 138, 170, 177, 192, 195, 196, 197, 203, 220, 223, 229, 231, 232, 237, 239, 247, 271, 292, 293, 294; see also Holy Communion, Lord's Supper, Mass
Evangelical counsels 188, 201, 203, 232, 276
Evangelii Praecones 136, 157

Faith 24, 28, 34, 41, 65, 66, 69, 80, 117, 121, 125, 126, 132, 134, 155, 181, 205, 230, 260, 273
— and reason 38
— and the sacraments 230
Family 2, 13, 19, 22, 25, 34, 71, 134, 265; see also Children, Parents
Fathers of the Church 113, 114, 216, 243, 248, 262, 265, 268
Fidei Donum 174
France 39

General priesthood of all believers 195, 225, 255
Geography 157
Germany 27, 39
Glorification of God 113, 151
Gospel 10, 35, 80, 84, 85, 106, 119, 120, 127, 136, 157, 166, 180, 231, 235, 236, 256, 271, 276, 296
Grace 18, 138, 179, 196, 213, 220, 230, 276, 281

Hellenistic Judaism 210, 246
Holiness 11, 155, 203, 216, 230, 267, 270, 272, 273
Holland 6
Holy Communion 138, 232, 272; see also Eucharist, Lord's Supper, Mass
Holy See 4, 110, 117, 120, 166, 167, 177, 254
Holy Spirit 21, 33, 113–6, 131, 134, 150, 153, 158, 159, 200, 215, 217, 219, 220, 223, 240, 257, 260, 262, 265, 268, 269, 271, 277, 279, 286, 287, 288, 292, 293, 297
Homilies 265
Hope 22, 155, 230
Human dignity 17, 19, 59, 63, 67, 68, 78, 85
— Convention of the Council of Europe for the Protection of the Rights of Man and Fundamental Liberties 74
— Rights of Man, French Declaration of the (1789) 74
Human nature 17
Humility 132, 158, 201

Immortale Dei 80
Incarnation 18, 68, 78, 115
International organizations 14
Italy 39

Kingdom of God 34, 96, 113, 123, 141, 151, 179, 197, 204, 207, 297

Laity 10, 97, 147, 148, 149, 150, 170, 181, 256; see also Apostolate of the laity
Language 127, 157, 168
Latin America 39, 41, 161
Legislation 26, 27
Leisure 16
Lent 133

Literacy 16

Liturgy 10, 21, 24, 138, 139, 147, 151, 192, 196, 233, 267; see also Constitution on the Sacred Liturgy

Lord's Supper 211, 212; see also Eucharist, Holy Communion, Mass

Love 24, 33, 63, 68, 78, 113, 114, 121, 127, 129, 135, 138, 155, 158, 187, 230, 253, 254, 272, 273, 275

Magisterium 64

Manichaeism 200

Marian devotions 292

Martyrs 83

Mass 232, 272
— Canon of the 239
— daily celebration of 199
See also Eucharist, Holy Communion, Lord's Supper

Mater et Magistra 77

Maximum illud 119, 136, 155

Mediator Dei 293

Medicine 157

Meditation 274, 275

Middle Ages 40, 292, 293

Miracles 78

Missiology 114, 118, 119, 155, 156

Missionary activity 30, 35, 87, 108, 111, 142, 147, 150, 152, 153, 155, 157, 158, 163, 166, 167, 168, 173, 180; see also Decree on the Church's Missionary Activity

Morals 41, 86

Mortification 269, 272, 275

Moslems 128

Music 11

Mysterium Fidei 233, 294

Nature 17, 18

New Testament 210, 211, 212, 213, 217, 222, 229, 244, 246, 253; see also Bible

Non-Christians 43, 114, 118, 122, 129, 131, 133, 137, 153, 165, 167, 169, 177, 179, 181, 203, 222; see also Declaration on the Relationship of the Church to Non-Christian Religions

Obedience 154, 158, 201, 244, 245, 277–9, 288

Old Testament 211, 212, 240; see also Bible

Opus Dei 184

Orders, holy 208, 213, 214, 234, 237, 238, 262, 267, 268

Ordination 177, 213, 215, 216, 217, 230, 234, 235, 240, 247

Pacem in Terris 45, 64, 72, 77

Parents 10, 22, 23, 26, 27, 29, 32, 34, 71; see also Children, Family

Parish 30, 169–72, 178, 250

Parousia 124

Paschal mystery 133

Pastoral Constitution on the Church in the Modern World 13, 14, 17, 30, 31, 129, 151

Pastoral ministry 18, 42, 87, 102, 113, 121, 135, 137, 142, 156, 165, 168, 169, 175, 178, 188, 192, 203, 204, 207, 214, 216, 233, 236, 243, 244, 250, 258, 263, 272, 273, 276, 288, 296; see also Pastoral Constitution on the Church in the Modern World

Peace 75

Peaceful coexistence 13

Penance, sacrament of 293

Pentecost 220; see also Holy Spirit

People of God 14, 114, 116, 118, 122, 132–6, 142, 147, 149, 151, 158–60, 170, 171, 175, 177, 180, 181, 215, 220, 242, 254, 256, 257, 260, 264, 297

Pluralism 65, 147, 150

Politics 28, 86

Pontificale Romanum 240, 265

Popes 64, 114, 117, 160, 166, 221, 239, 241

Population 16, 147

Poverty 158, 201, 276, 290, 296

Prayer 85, 134, 138, 154, 155, 170, 232, 256

Preaching 10, 43, 126, 131, 133, 134, 147, 148, 152, 154, 169, 177, 195, 217, 229–32, 254, 270–2

Press, see Communications, media of

Princeps pastorum 136

Priesthood and ministry of Christ 216

Priests 11, 12, 42, 97, 119, 147, 166, 170, 183
— community life among 253
— Council of 242, 243
— education of 135, 136, 178, 207, 294, 295
— as envoys 258
— life of 259–89
— livelihood of 296
— relations with bishop, see under Bishops
— relations with fellow-priests 245, 252
— relations with laity 255–7
— scarcity of 173
— vocation to priesthood 261–5
See also Decree on the Ministry and Life of Priests, Decree on Priestly Formation

Propaganda Fide, see under Curia

Prophetic office 216

Protestants 43, 51, 70, 118, 119, 135, 170

Psychology 20

Public life 17

Public opinion 24; see also Communications, media of

Race 127, 129

Real Presence 294

Recreation 25

Redemption 23, 155, 179, 230, 272, 279; see also Salvation

Religion, science of 168

Religious 10, 13, 30, 86, 141, 142, 143, 149, 157, 158, 166, 167, 169, 170, 180, 188, 201, 207, 274, 276, 278; see also Decree on the Appropriate Renewal of the Religious Life

Religious freedom 49; see also Declaration on Religious Freedom

Religious indifference 147

Religious institutes 178

Religious instruction, see Catechetics

Repentance 24
Rerum Ecclesiae 136
Research 42, 43, 168
Resurrection 133, 211
Revelation 43, 73, 78, 79, 271; *see also* Dogmatic
   Constitution on Divine Revelation
Roman Empire 81

Sacraments 230, 231
— of initiation 133
   See also individual sacraments
Sacrifice 85, 155, 158, 170, 231
— of Christ 223
Salvation 21, 24, 27, 31, 34, 58, 78, 84, 87, 96,
   113, 115, 118, 119, 121, 124, 134, 149, 169,
   170, 264
— history of 56, 59, 133, 136, 157
   See also Redemption
Sanctification, *see* Holiness
Sapientiae Christianae 80
Scholasticism 25, 268
Schools 1–48
— co-operation between Catholic and non-
   Catholic schools 45
Science 19, 26, 33, 37, 38, 42, 43, 45, 76, 157
Scripture, *see* Bible
Scripture and tradition 216
Secular institutes 169
Secretariat for the Promotion of Christian Unity
   50, 51, 52, 56, 57, 60, 61, 162, 164, 204
Seminaries 137, 189, 190
Sex 19, 20, 33, 129, 200
Sin 115
Social activity 25
Social justice 140
Social life 13
Social progress 16

Social sciences 41
Social system 126
Society 10, 15, 16, 22, 23, 25, 26, 34, 36, 41, 58,
   65
Sociology 168, 249
Spirituality 197, 201, 203, 274, 275
State 2, 10, 13, 22, 23, 26, 27, 31, 32, 35, 50, 53,
   59, 61, 63, 64, 71–76, 83, 86, 135
— totalitarian 71
Stipend 292
Subdeacons 208
Subsidiarity 26
Synod of Bishops, *see under* Bishops

Technology 197
Theology 39, 41–43, 136, 147, 190, 295
Totalitarian States, *see under* State
Tourism 7
Tradition 43, 264
— Scripture and, *see* Scripture and tradition
Trinity 113, 114, 257
Truth 21, 38, 58, 63, 67, 68, 77, 80, 81, 84, 85,
   132, 230

UNESCO 6, 17, 47
Unity of the human race 86
Universities 10, 32, 37, 38, 39, 40, 41, 44–46
UNO 17, 85
Urbanization 147
U.S.A. 6, 39

Vatican Council, First 37

Word of God 21, 33, 43, 85, 138, 173, 229, 270
Worker-priests 251
Worship 36, 138, 139, 200, 203

Youth 6, 20, 21, 25, 33, 47

INDEX OF NAMES

Adjakpley, E. 104
Adler, N. 115
Agagianian, G. P. 87, 89–91, 93, 97, 99–103, 108, 109
Albert the Great 119
Alfrink, B. J. 98, 193, 201, 205, 253, 256
Alvaro del Portillo 207
Amalar 248
Angelli 255
Arneth, M. 253
Arriba y Castro, B. 201
Auda, J. 1
Audet, J.-P. 282
Auf der Maur, I. 136, 144, 152, 155, 157, 173, 180
Augustine, St. 37, 38, 40, 78, 113, 123, 221, 223, 257

Balthasar, H. U. von 123, 223
Baraúna, G. 245
Barbieri, V. 180
Barros Cámara, J. 193
Baudox, M. 254
Bea, A. 50, 98, 172, 201, 204, 282, 284
Beckmann, J. 135, 136, 142
Benedict XV 119, 136, 152, 155, 159, 173
Bernhard of Clairvaux, St. 119
Berutti, P. C. 184
Betz, O. 20, 21
Bierbaum, W. 114
Bluyssen, J. 255
Bornkamm, G. 210, 246
Bosch, D. 124
Bosco, Don 40
Botte, B. 247
Brechter, S. 87, 88, 127, 144
Bremond, H. 294
Bruls, J. 174
Brunot, A. 256
Buber, M. 128
Burridge, W. 152
Buys, L. 104

Campmany, J. 116
Cappello, F. M. 28
Cardijn, J. 256
Caulfield 89
Cauwe 89
Charles, P. 118
Charue, A. M. 205
Chevrier, A. 253
Chiflet, J. 180
Cho 89
Cicognani, A. G. 93, 96, 102, 185
Ciraci, P. 184
Clement of Alexandria, St. 114
Clément, R. 282
Clement, St. 210, 246
Colombo, C. 201
Colson, J. 212, 239
Confalonieri, C. 91
Congar, Y. 100–4, 114, 116, ,117, 119, 180, 207, 240, 255
Cordes, Paul-J. 210
Cornélis, E. 122
Cornelius, St. 247
Courtois, G. 170
Cullmann, O. 124
Cyprian, St. 247

Daem, J. 1, 7, 9, 20
Dammertz, V. 111, 130, 144, 162, 164, 176, 179
Daniel, Y. 250
Daniélou, J. 115, 116, 123, 169, 170
Darmajuwana, J. 258, 263, 265
Darmancier, U. 250
De Barros 263
Degrijse, O. 154, 253
Denis, H. 243
Denzler, G. 98, 161
De Smedt, E. 51–54, 57, 61
Dezza, P. 1, 25, 37, 41
Dibelius, M. 269
Dodd, C. H. 131
Döpfner, J. 97, 201, 203, 205, 226, 248, 253, 258, 263, 286

Doi Tatsuo, P. 98, 201
Dorn, L. 98, 161
Dreissen, J. 1, 30
Dupuy, B. D. 240

Elchinger, A. 254
Eldarov, G. 89, 104, 147
Elders, L. 122
Engel, A. 132
Enrique y Taracón, V. 185
Erlinghagen, K. 20

Falls, T. 201
Feiner, J. 123
Felici, P. 95, 96, 103, 108, 195, 280
Finsterhölzl, I. 122
Fischer, B. 140
Fischer, G. 20
Florit, E. 201, 203–5
Forster, K. 122
Francis of Assisi, St. 244
Francis Xavier, St. 119
Frank, S. 144
Fransen, P. 213, 214
Freitag, A. 118, 156
Fries, H. 122, 180, 213
Frings, J. 98, 99, 175
Fuchs, J. 216
Funk, J. 177

Gaius 248
Gantin, B. 98
Garaygordobil, V. 241
Garonne, G. 172, 199
Gauthier, P. 115, 250
Geise, N. 99
Giblet, J. 261
Glazik, J. 88, 100, 104, 117, 121, 130, 155, 156, 170, 178
Godin, H. 250
Gomes Dos Santos, F. 193, 255
Gorresío, V. 62
Gössmann, E. 156
Gottardi, A. M. 255
Grasso, D. 100, 104, 131, 169
Greco, J. 104, 142, 159, 162
Gregory the Great, St. 50, 266
Greinacher, N. 254
Grentrup, T. 118
Grillmeier, A. 178, 234, 268
Grotti, G. M. 121
Grundmann, W. 217
Guardini, R. 275
Guerra, J. 146
Guerra y Gómez, M. 210
Gufflet, H. 199, 254, 260
Guyot, L. 240

Haas, H. 175
Hakim, G. 250, 251, 256
Hampe, J. C. 96, 282
Hansemann, G. 249
Heckenbach, F. 1

Heenan, J. C. 256
Heislbetz, J. 122
Hengsbach, F. 253
Herranz, G. 207
Herrera y Oria, A. 201
Heuser, A. 30
Hillig, F. 259
Hippolytus, St. 247
Hödl, L. 213
Höffner 242
Hofinger, J. 132, 138, 139
Hofstätter, R. 264
Holzhauser, B. 253
Hornef, J. 138, 140

Ignatius, St. 247

Jaeger, L. 201
Janssen, H. 185
Jeremias, J. 124, 264
John Chrysostom, St. 266
John XXIII 1, 4, 14, 45, 50, 61, 64, 87, 92, 96, 115, 136, 152, 183, 185, 280
Journet, C. 119
Juillard, L. 250
Jungmann, J. A. 231, 239

Kampmann, T. 24
Karrer, O. 265
Kellner, J. 139
Klappert, E. 121
Kleinheyer, B. 247, 265
Klostermann, F. 242, 243
Koenen, G. 180
Köhler, O. 123
Kösters, H. 156
Köstner, J. 193
Koop, P. 200, 282
Kowalsky, N. 88, 159
Kraemer, H. 131
Kruse, H. 122
Küng, H. 122
Kuss, O. 244, 262

Lackmann, M. 96, 98, 99
Lacordaire, H. D. 38
Lamont, D. R. 98
Landázuri, R. J. 201
Larrain, E. E. 200
Laufer, C. 123
Lecuona, L. J. 100, 104, 152
Lécuyer, J. 185, 207, 240, 246, 248
Lefèbvre, J. 194, 201, 256
Leger, P. E. 98, 160, 201, 203
Legrand, F. 122
Le Guillou, M.-J. 121, 135, 170
Leo XIII 61, 64, 80, 119
Lercaro, G. 191, 253
Lercaro, J. 104
Liégé, P.-A. 117, 260
Lissy, R. 170
Loew, J. 250, 259
Loffeld, E. 118, 119, 146

Lokuang, S. 95, 97–100, 104
Lubac, H. de 122
Luneau, A. 114
Luyten, N. A. 38, 40
Lyonnet, S. 282

Maritain, J. 37
Marmy, E. 136, 152, 155, 157, 173, 180
Martin, J. A. 250
Marty, F. 185, 190, 192–5, 200, 201, 205, 209
Massa, P. 98
Masson, J. 118, 136, 159, 174
Mathew, D. 87, 89
Matieu, F. 144
Mayer, A. 1, 2
Mayr, J. 257
Mazerat, H. 185
Menasce, J. de 143
Meouchi, P. 201, 205, 248, 259, 261
Meyer, E. 193
Michaelis, W. 210
Mleinek, E. 1
Mondreganes, P. 115
Moors, P. 99
Moritzen, N. P. 121
Mörsdorf, K. 215, 238, 241–3, 245, 248, 250, 263, 290
Moya, R. 89, 104, 146
Moynagh, J. 98, 99
Mulders, A. 122
Müller, A. 244, 278
Müller, K. 119, 122, 152

Nabaa, Ph. 205
Negri, G. C. 24
Neuhäusler, E. 156
Neuner, J. 100, 104, 150, 265
Neuner, N. 126
Newbigin, L. 116
Nothomb, D. 117

Oberhoffer, M. 180
Ohm, T. 118, 131, 132, 138, 150, 154, 156, 158, 170, 174, 178, 180
Omaechevarria, J. 169
Onclin, G. 185, 207
Otto, J. A. 119, 171, 180

Papali, C. 152, 170
Paul VI 14, 17, 37, 41, 55, 61, 78, 96, 97, 102, 109, 111, 128, 155, 162, 200, 209, 233, 287
Paventi, S. 88, 92, 101, 102, 159, 174, 177
Peeters, Fr. 101, 104, 109
Peireira, P. 263
Pélichy, A. G. de 135
Pellegrino, M. 201
Perbal, A. 118
Pfeil, H. 127
Philips, G. 116
Pironio, E. 236, 253
Pirovano, A. 146
Pius X 269

Pius XI 2, 13, 20, 42, 61, 64, 136, 152, 173, 255, 269
Pius XII 2, 61, 65, 73, 74, 115, 136, 152, 157, 173, 174, 255, 269, 286
Pizzardo, J. 2, 251
Pliny the Younger 81
Pöggeler, F. 1, 30
Pohlschneider, J. 1, 19, 177
Poletti, U. 159
Portillo, A. del 184
Potterie, I. de la 219
Pourchet 248
Promper, W. 139
Provenchères, C. de 205

Quéguiner, M. 142, 169, 178
Quiroga y Palacios 201

Rabanus Maurus 248
Rahner, K. 122, 138, 170, 215, 221, 224, 229–31, 234, 238–40, 243–5, 259, 260, 262
Rathe, G. 143
Ratzinger, J. 100–4, 122, 212, 224, 232–5, 239, 257, 265, 278
Reeper, J. D. 138
Remy, P. 142
Renard, A. 200
Rengstorf, K. H. 261, 264
Rétif, A. 114, 115, 119, 172, 177
Reuter, A. 137
Richaud, P. M. 201
Riobé, G. 99, 100, 104
Rossi, C. 201, 203
Rouquette, P. 280
Roy, M. 201, 249
Rubio, Repullés M. 89
Ruffini, E. 201, 204
Rugambwa, L. 98, 201
Rusch, P. 199
Rusche, H. 262

Sacher, W. 30
Sánchez, Moreno 205
Sansow, H. 273
Sartre, V. 89, 92, 193
Schauf, H. 1
Schelbert, J. 133
Schierse, F. J. 226
Schillebeeckx, E. 38, 39, 213
Schlier, H. 21, 269
Schmauch, J. 180
Schmaus, M. 210, 216
Schmid, J. 212
Schmidlin, J. 118
Schmitt, P. J. 254
Schnackenburg, R. 248
Schneider, T. 223
Schoch, R. 138
Schrenk 257
Schreuder, O. 249
Schulz-Benesch, G. 30
Schürmann, H. 212, 246, 239
Schuster, H. 250

Schütte, J. 88, 89, 91, 100, 101, 103, 104, 109, 114, 119, 121, 131, 147, 150, 152, 159, 169
Seeber, D. A. 96, 98, 99
Seidensticker, P. 223
Selhorst, H. 1
Semmelroth, O. 222, 243
Seumois, A. 89, 149
Seumois, X. 100, 104, 118, 119, 147, 150
Sheen, F. 99
Shehan, L. J. 201, 205
Siefer, G. 249, 250
Sieren, K. 142, 178, 180
Sigmond, S. 185
Six, J.-F. 253
Soiron, T. 30
Spellman, F. 204
Spiazzi, R. 280
Spülbeck, O. 255
Stachel-Zeuner, G. 24
Stangl, J. 254
Straelen, H. van 122
Suenes, L. J. 98, 99, 103, 107, 201, 202, 205, 256
Suhard, E. 250, 251

Tardini, D. 87
Thauren, J. 131
Théas, P. M. 241
Thils, G. 122

Tholans, C. P. 144
Thomas Aquinas, St. 3, 38, 119, 213, 267
Tilmann, K. 24
Tisserant, E. 54, 55, 56, 200, 282
Tomé, L. 205
Trajan 81
Türk, H. J. 126

Urbani, G. 214

Vagaggini, C. 240
Van Valenberg 89
Vidal, P. 27
Vilsmeier 175
Violardo, G. 185
Vorgrimler, H. 138

Wayenbergh, H. M. van 1, 41
Waldenfels, H. 125
Warneck, G. 118
Wernz, F. X. 27
Wiedenmann, L. 124
Wulf, F. 210, 256, 257, 259, 283, 287

Zaffonato, G. 254
Zeller, H. 262, 264
Zizola, G. 194
Zoa, J. 98, 100, 104